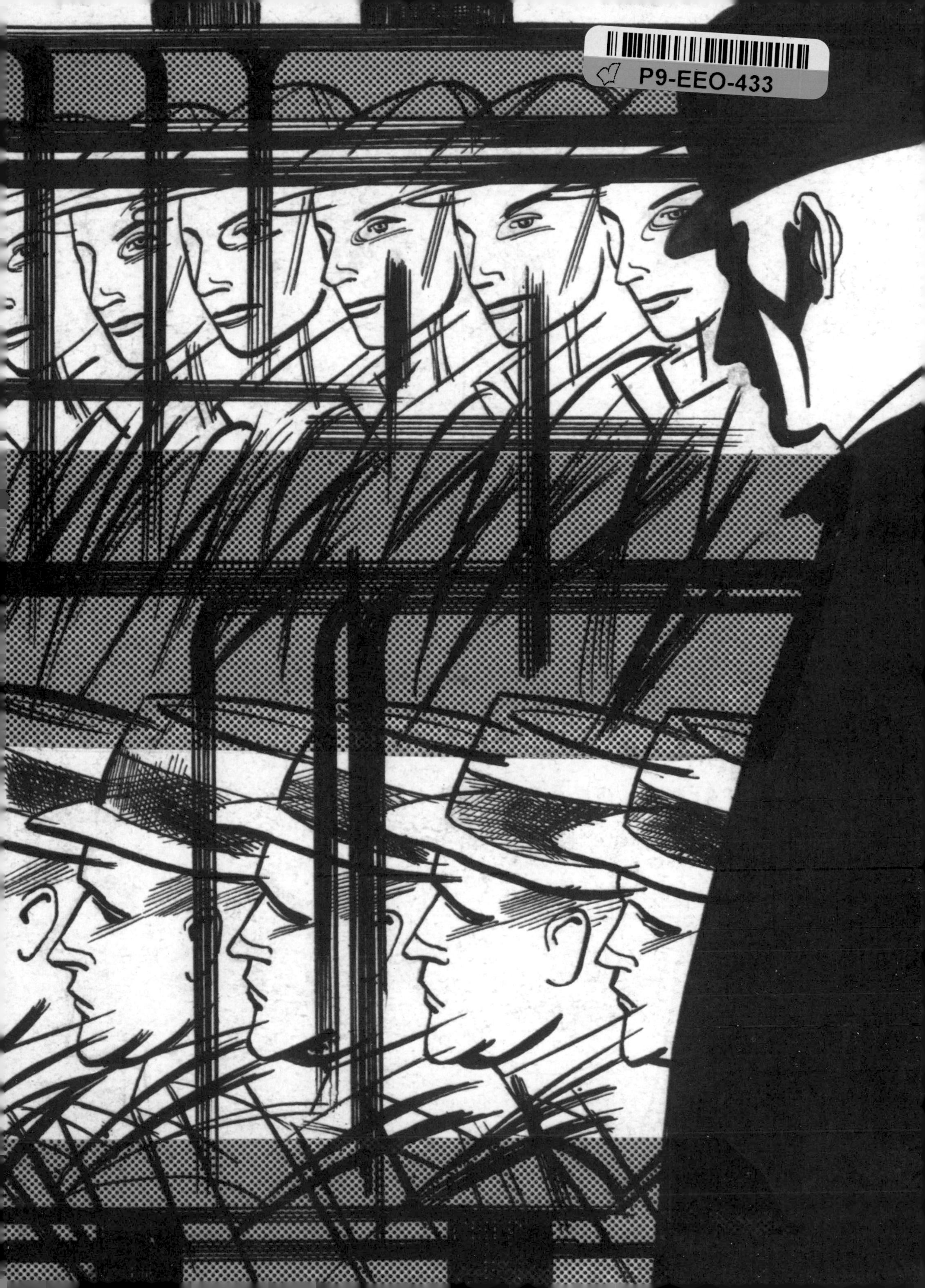

Messages in a Bottle

Comic Book Stories

by B. Krigstein

EDITED AND PRODUCED BY
GREG SADOWSKI

FANTAGRAPHICS BOOKS
SEATTLE, WASHINGTON

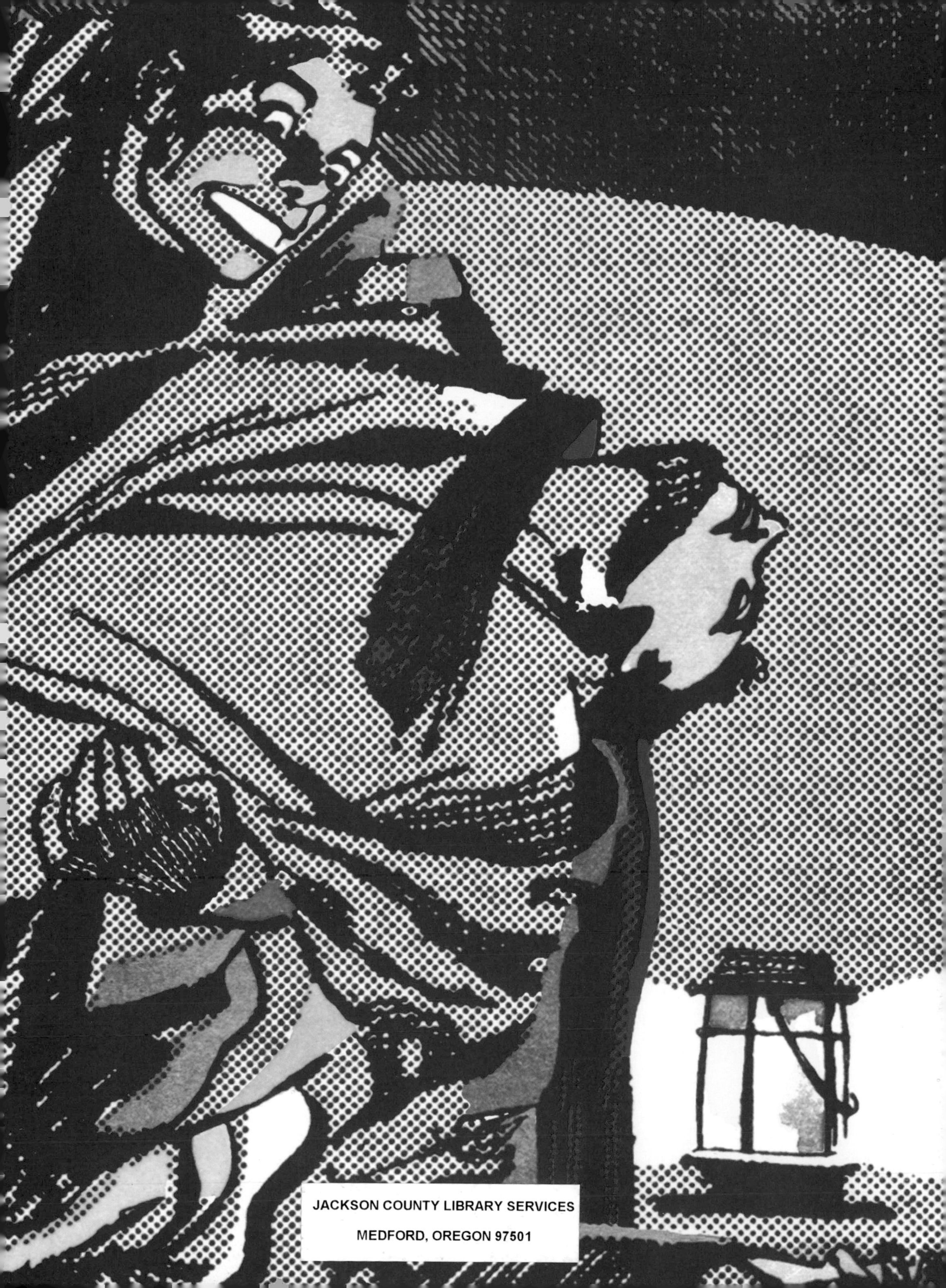

FANTAGRAPHICS BOOKS
7563 Lake City Way NE
Seattle, Washington 98115

Publishers
Gary Groth and Kim Thompson
Associate Publisher
Eric Reynolds
Associate Editor
Jason T. Miles
Editing, Art Direction, Production
Greg Sadowski

Thanks: Jill Armus, Paul Baresh, John Benson, Steven Bialek, Allan Bourne, Ray Bradbury, Sean Burns, Steven Donnelly (www. coollinesartwork.com), Heritage Auctions (www.ha.com), Gavin Lees (cover calligraphy), Marie Severin, Art Spiegelman, Bhob Stewart, Lars Teglbjaerg, and Jim Vadeboncoeur, Jr. Yo, Paige.

To receive a free comics catalog call 1-800-657-1100, write us at the address above, or visit www. fantagraphics.com

Typeset in
Robert Slimbach's *Brioso Pro* and Christian Schwartz's *Neutraface*

First Fantagraphics Books edition April 2013

ISBN 978-1-60699-580-8

Printed in China

To John Benson, Art Spiegelman and Bhob Stewart, who knew all along — and to Marie Severin, a great lady and the first serious colorist in comic books.

Stories in blue recolored for this edition by Marie Severin

BUCK SANDERS

AND HIS PALS!

HERE'S A SURE-FIRE RECIPE FOR TRAGEDY AND TROUBLE... TAKE A CRUSTY OLD MISER AND A HEAP OF HIDDEN TREASURE... ADD A GANGFUL OF GREED AND STIR INTO A SEETHING CAULDRON OF RUTHLESS RAPACITY! SET OVER THE FIRE OF AMBITION AND BOIL RAPIDLY UNTIL READY TO EXPLODE! A *DEADLY* DANGEROUS MIXTURE? YOU BET! BUT FOLLOW *BUCK SANDERS* AND HIS PALS, AND SEE HOW YOUTHFUL AGILITY AND RESOURCEFULNESS UPSET THIS DEVIL'S BREW... RIGHT ONTO THE HEADS OF ITS CHURLISH CHEFS!

ON A SUMMERY DAY IN THE LITTLE TOWN OF OLINVILLE...

SPLENDID IDEA OF YOURS, *BUCK OLD BOY* --- TAKING A RAFT TRIP DOWN THE RIVER!

BUT THESE LUNCHES WERE *MY* IDEA! GOSH, I'M HUNGRY ALREADY!

THIS IS A BUSINESS TRIP, THOUGH! WE'RE GOING TO SELL WAR BONDS TO OLD HERMAN THE HERMIT, WHO LIVES IN THE HOUSEBOAT NEAR THE FALLS!

WE'VE SOLD ABOUT EVERYBODY ELSE IN TOWN!

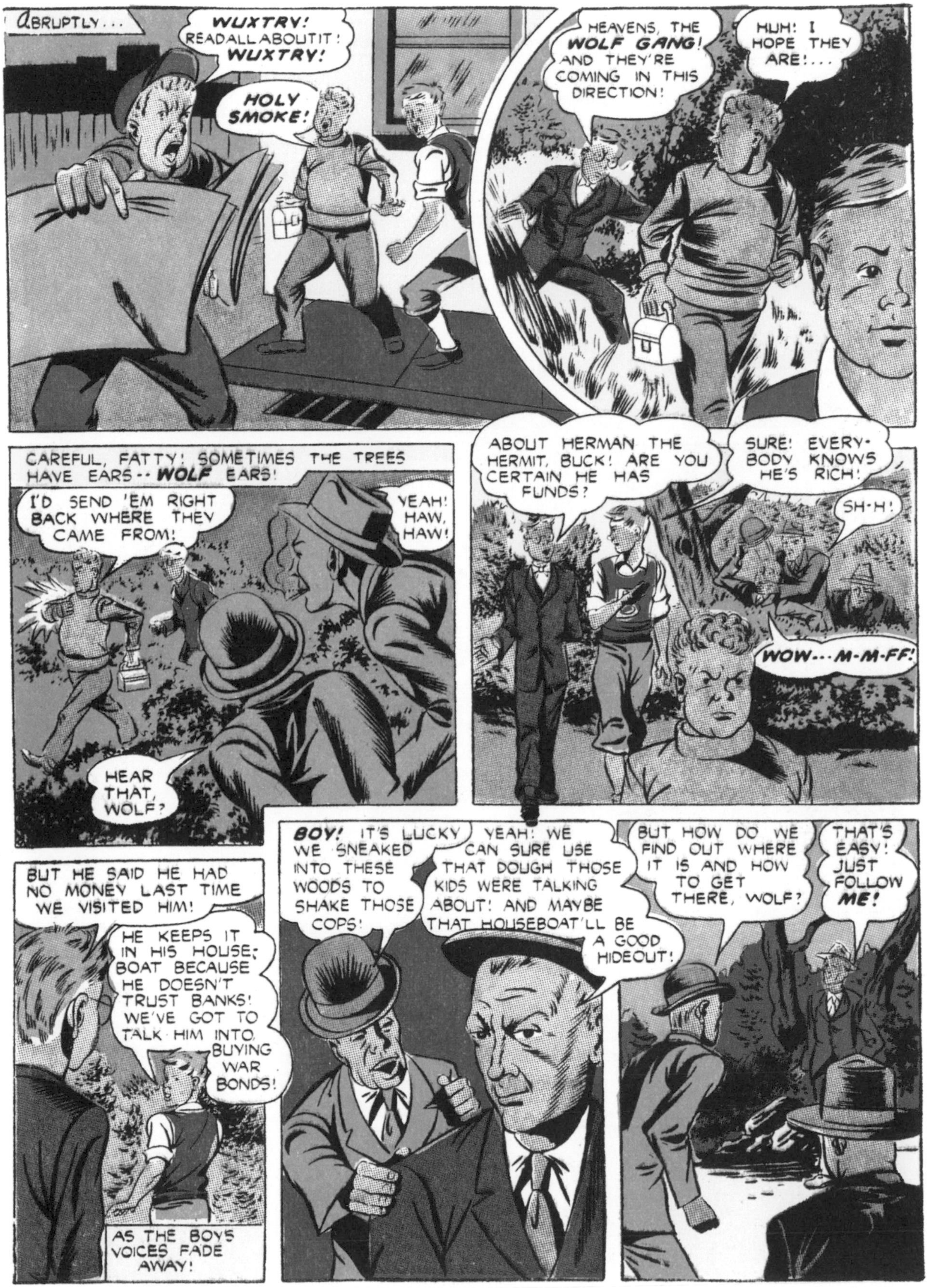
ABRUPTLY...
WUXTRY! READALLABOUTIT! WUXTRY!
HOLY SMOKE!
HEAVENS, THE WOLF GANG! AND THEY'RE COMING IN THIS DIRECTION!
HUH! I HOPE THEY ARE!...
CAREFUL, FATTY! SOMETIMES THE TREES HAVE EARS-- WOLF EARS!
I'D SEND 'EM RIGHT BACK WHERE THEY CAME FROM!
YEAH! HAW, HAW!
HEAR THAT, WOLF?
ABOUT HERMAN THE HERMIT, BUCK! ARE YOU CERTAIN HE HAS FUNDS?
SURE! EVERY-BODY KNOWS HE'S RICH!
SH-H!
WOW---M-M-FF!
BUT HE SAID HE HAD NO MONEY LAST TIME WE VISITED HIM!
HE KEEPS IT IN HIS HOUSE-BOAT BECAUSE HE DOESN'T TRUST BANKS! WE'VE GOT TO TALK HIM INTO BUYING WAR BONDS!
AS THE BOYS VOICES FADE AWAY!
BOY! IT'S LUCKY WE SNEAKED INTO THESE WOODS TO SHAKE THOSE COPS!
YEAH! WE CAN SURE USE THAT DOUGH THOSE KIDS WERE TALKING ABOUT! AND MAYBE THAT HOUSEBOAT'LL BE A GOOD HIDEOUT!
BUT HOW DO WE FIND OUT WHERE IT IS AND HOW TO GET THERE, WOLF?
THAT'S EASY! JUST FOLLOW ME!

PRESENTLY, AT THE TURNPIKE NEARBY...

STOP!

WHAT'S THE MATTER?

HOW DO I GET TO HERMAN THE HERMIT'S HOUSEBOAT?

YOU WALK ABOUT TEN MILES UP THE ROAD, THEN TURN LEFT TILL YOU COME TO THE RIVER!

THANKS, BUD! BUT WE'RE NOT WALKING! WE'RE GONNA BORROW YOUR CAR!

GOOD WORK, WOLF!

WHA---!

MOMENTS LATER...

HAW, HAW! NOW WE GOT NOTHIN' TO WORRY ABOUT, WOLF!

RIGHT! WE'LL BE ROLLING IN DOUGH AND SAFE FROM THE COPPERS!

MEANWHILE, THE PALS POLE SLOWLY TOWARD THEIR OBJECTIVE!

I'M STARVING, BUCK! WHY CAN'T WE EAT BEFORE WE TALK TO OLD HERMAN!

IT'S NOT NOON YET!

BESIDES, THERE'S THE HOUSEBOAT!

NOW COMES THE TOUGH WORK! THE HERMIT'S A REAL MISER!

I WARN YOU, ALL THIS EXERCISE IS ONLY MAKING ME HUNGRIER!

QUIET! I HEAR SOME MEN TALKING---AND HERMAN NEVER HAS VISITORS!

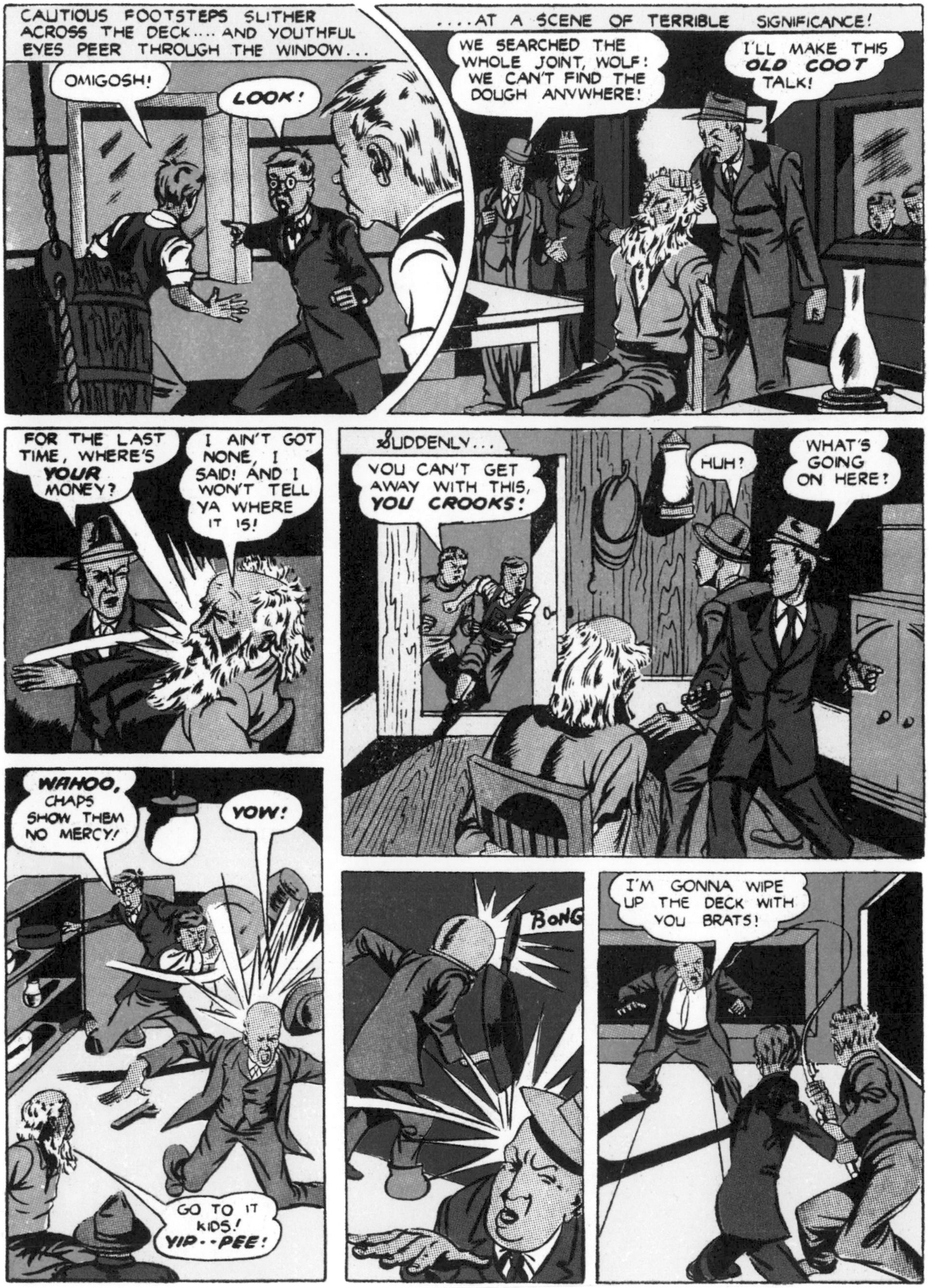
CAUTIOUS FOOTSTEPS SLITHER ACROSS THE DECK.... AND YOUTHFUL EYES PEER THROUGH THE WINDOW...
OMIGOSH!
LOOK!
....AT A SCENE OF TERRIBLE SIGNIFICANCE!
WE SEARCHED THE WHOLE JOINT, WOLF! WE CAN'T FIND THE DOUGH ANYWHERE!
I'LL MAKE THIS OLD COOT TALK!
FOR THE LAST TIME, WHERE'S YOUR MONEY?
I AIN'T GOT NONE, I SAID! AND I WON'T TELL YA WHERE IT IS!
SUDDENLY...
YOU CAN'T GET AWAY WITH THIS, YOU CROOKS!
HUH?
WHAT'S GOING ON HERE?
WAHOO, CHAPS SHOW THEM NO MERCY!
YOW!
GO TO IT KIDS! YIP--PEE!
BONG
I'M GONNA WIPE UP THE DECK WITH YOU BRATS!

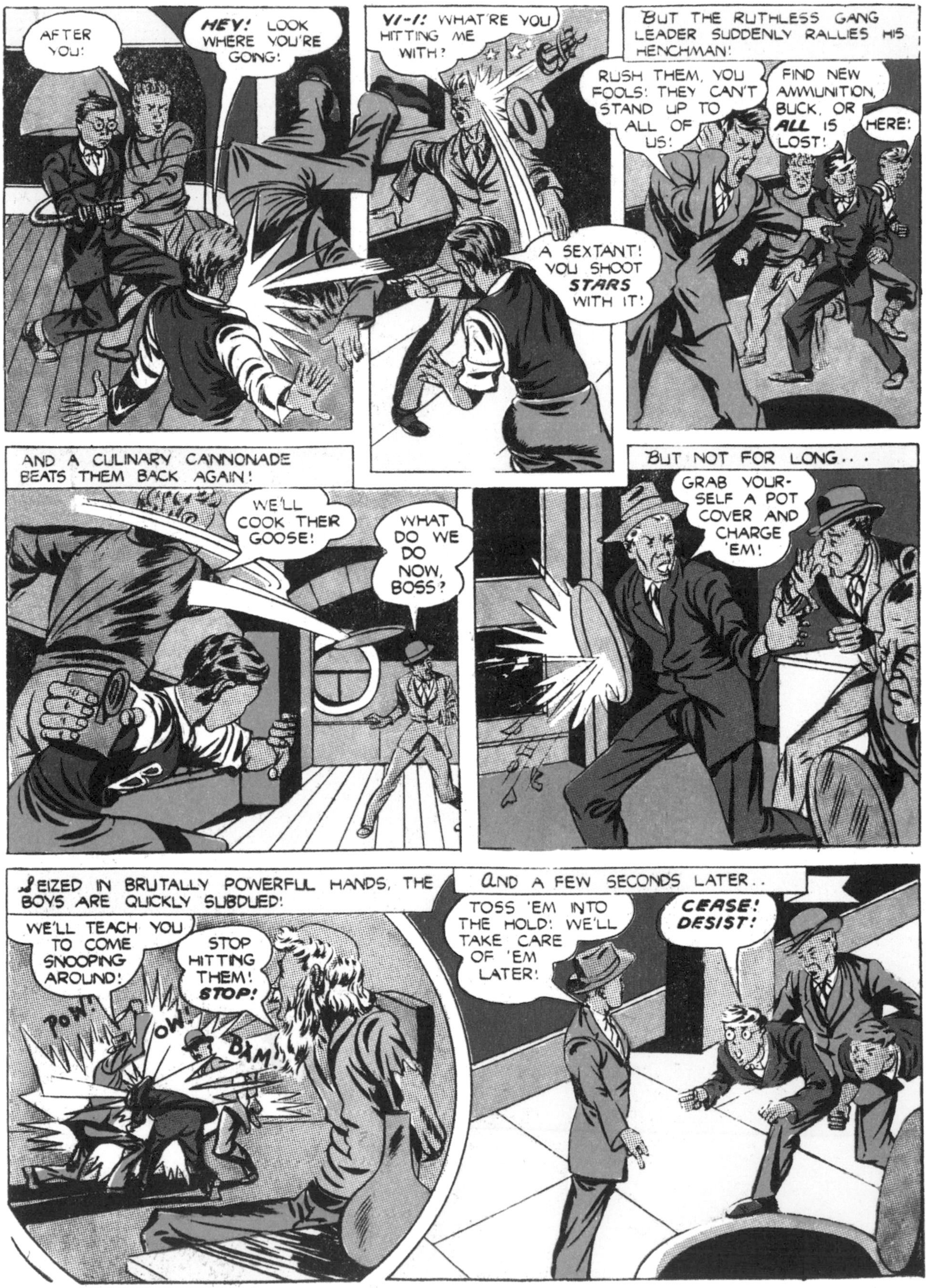
AFTER YOU!
HEY! LOOK WHERE YOU'RE GOING!
YI-I! WHAT'RE YOU HITTING ME WITH?
A SEXTANT! YOU SHOOT STARS WITH IT!
BUT THE RUTHLESS GANG LEADER SUDDENLY RALLIES HIS HENCHMAN!
RUSH THEM, YOU FOOLS! THEY CAN'T STAND UP TO ALL OF US!
FIND NEW AMMUNITION, BUCK, OR ALL IS LOST!
HERE!
AND A CULINARY CANNONADE BEATS THEM BACK AGAIN!
WE'LL COOK THEIR GOOSE!
WHAT DO WE DO NOW, BOSS?
BUT NOT FOR LONG...
GRAB YOURSELF A POT COVER AND CHARGE 'EM!
SEIZED IN BRUTALLY POWERFUL HANDS, THE BOYS ARE QUICKLY SUBDUED!
WE'LL TEACH YOU TO COME SNOOPING AROUND!
STOP HITTING THEM! STOP!
POW!
OW!
BAM!
AND A FEW SECONDS LATER..
TOSS 'EM INTO THE HOLD! WE'LL TAKE CARE OF 'EM LATER!
CEASE! DESIST!

CLICK! OOOFF!

ABRUPTLY, THERE IS THE GRIND OF HIDDEN MACHINERY... STEEL RASPS UPON STEEL... AND...

GOLLY, *LOOK!* HERMAN THE HERMIT'S TREASURE!

I MUST'VE TOUCHED A SECRET BUTTON WHEN I LANDED!

SH-H! TALK LOW!

WHAT ARE WE TO DO? THE GANG'LL TORMENT HERMAN INTO REVEALING THIS HIDING PLACE--AND THEY'LL USE IT FOR FURTHER LAWLESSNESS!

WE'LL HAVE TO SAVE HERMAN AND THE MONEY!

WHAT GOOD WILL THIS DO?

YOU'LL SEE IN A MINUTE! WE'VE GOT TO HURRY BEFORE HERMAN TELLS!

TALK, BLAST YOU! WHERE IS THAT DOUGH?

YOU CERTAINLY HAD BETTER HURRY, FELLOWS! FOR...

HEE! HEE! STOP TICKLING ME! *I'LL TELL!*

BUT WITH THE SPEED OF A STRIKING SNAKE...

WELL?

IT'S DOWN IN THE-- *HUH!*

...A NOOSE SNATCHES THE OLD RECLUSE TO SAFETY!

HEY! COME BACK HERE!

IN A LITTLE WHILE!

SNAP!

GET HIM! HE WAS JUST GOING TO TALK!

MEANWHILE, AS DANGER SWARMS TOWARD THREE OF THE PALS...

THIS REQUIRES SPLIT-SECOND TIMING! HEAVENS, I HOPE IT WORKS AS BUCK SAID IT WOULD! IF NOT--GULP--THE OTHER CHAPS ARE DONE FOR!

READY, BUCK?

YES! CAST OFF!

AND IN A MATTER OF INSTANTS...

LOOK, WOLF! THEM BRATS SET US ADRIFT!

WHEW! MADE IT JUST IN TIME!

THE CURRENT GROWS SWIFTER THE ROAR OF A CATARACT DRAWS NEARER AND NEARER...

WE'RE HEADING FOR THE FALLS!

A-AND I C-CAN'T SWIM!

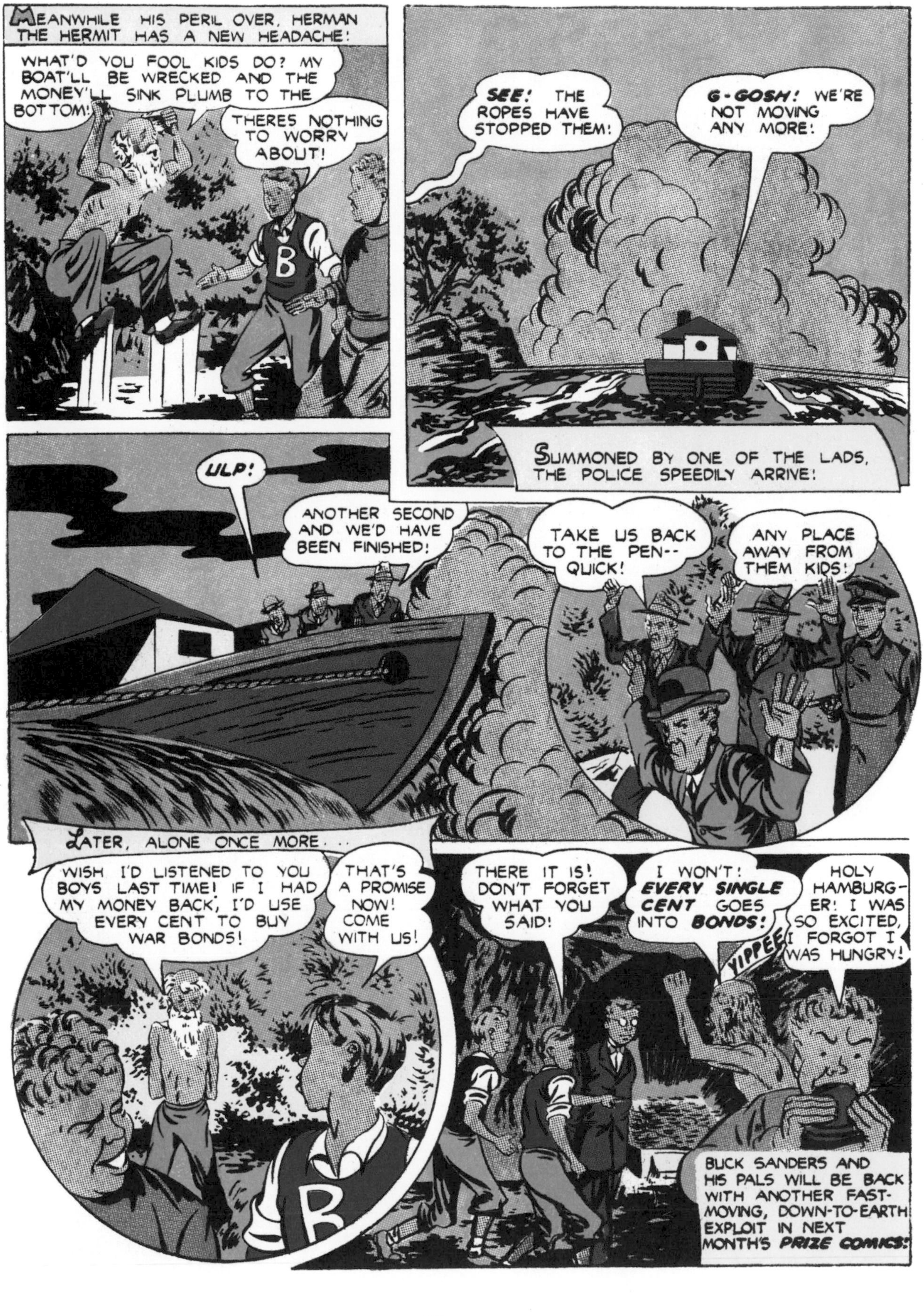
MEANWHILE HIS PERIL OVER, HERMAN THE HERMIT HAS A NEW HEADACHE:
WHAT'D YOU FOOL KIDS DO? MY BOAT'LL BE WRECKED AND THE MONEY'LL SINK PLUMB TO THE BOTTOM!
THERES NOTHING TO WORRY ABOUT!
SEE! THE ROPES HAVE STOPPED THEM!
G-GOSH! WE'RE NOT MOVING ANY MORE!
SUMMONED BY ONE OF THE LADS, THE POLICE SPEEDILY ARRIVE:
ULP!
ANOTHER SECOND AND WE'D HAVE BEEN FINISHED!
TAKE US BACK TO THE PEN--QUICK!
ANY PLACE AWAY FROM THEM KIDS!
LATER, ALONE ONCE MORE...
WISH I'D LISTENED TO YOU BOYS LAST TIME! IF I HAD MY MONEY BACK, I'D USE EVERY CENT TO BUY WAR BONDS!
THAT'S A PROMISE NOW! COME WITH US!
THERE IT IS! DON'T FORGET WHAT YOU SAID!
I WON'T! EVERY SINGLE CENT GOES INTO BONDS!
YIPPEE
HOLY HAMBURGER! I WAS SO EXCITED, I FORGOT I WAS HUNGRY!
BUCK SANDERS AND HIS PALS WILL BE BACK WITH ANOTHER FAST-MOVING, DOWN-TO-EARTH EXPLOIT IN NEXT MONTH'S PRIZE COMICS!

THE TREASURE KEEPER

Do you want to hear another tale of treasure, and DEATH!!? Then LISTEN, and THE TREASURE KEEPER will tell you the story of...

"The Accursed Diamond"

AT A WEST INDIES PORT, EARLY IN THE LAST CENTURY, THE CAPTAIN OF THE "MERRIE MAIDE," A SMUGGLING SHIP, IS ACCOSTED BY A STRANGER...

CAPTAIN... I WANT PASSAGE ON YOUR VESSEL TO ENGLAND!

PASSAGE? DO YE HAVE MONEY, OLD MAN? I TAKE NO DEAD WEIGHT ON MY SHIP! SHE MUST BE LIGHT AND FAST, FOR I'M A SMUGGLER, AS YOU WELL KNOW, YOU OLD RASCAL!

SEE YOU THIS? IT'S A FLAWLESS DIAMOND! IT IS PRICELESS! TAKE ME TO ENGLAND WHERE I CAN DISPOSE OF IT, AND HALF OF THE PROFITS ARE YOURS!

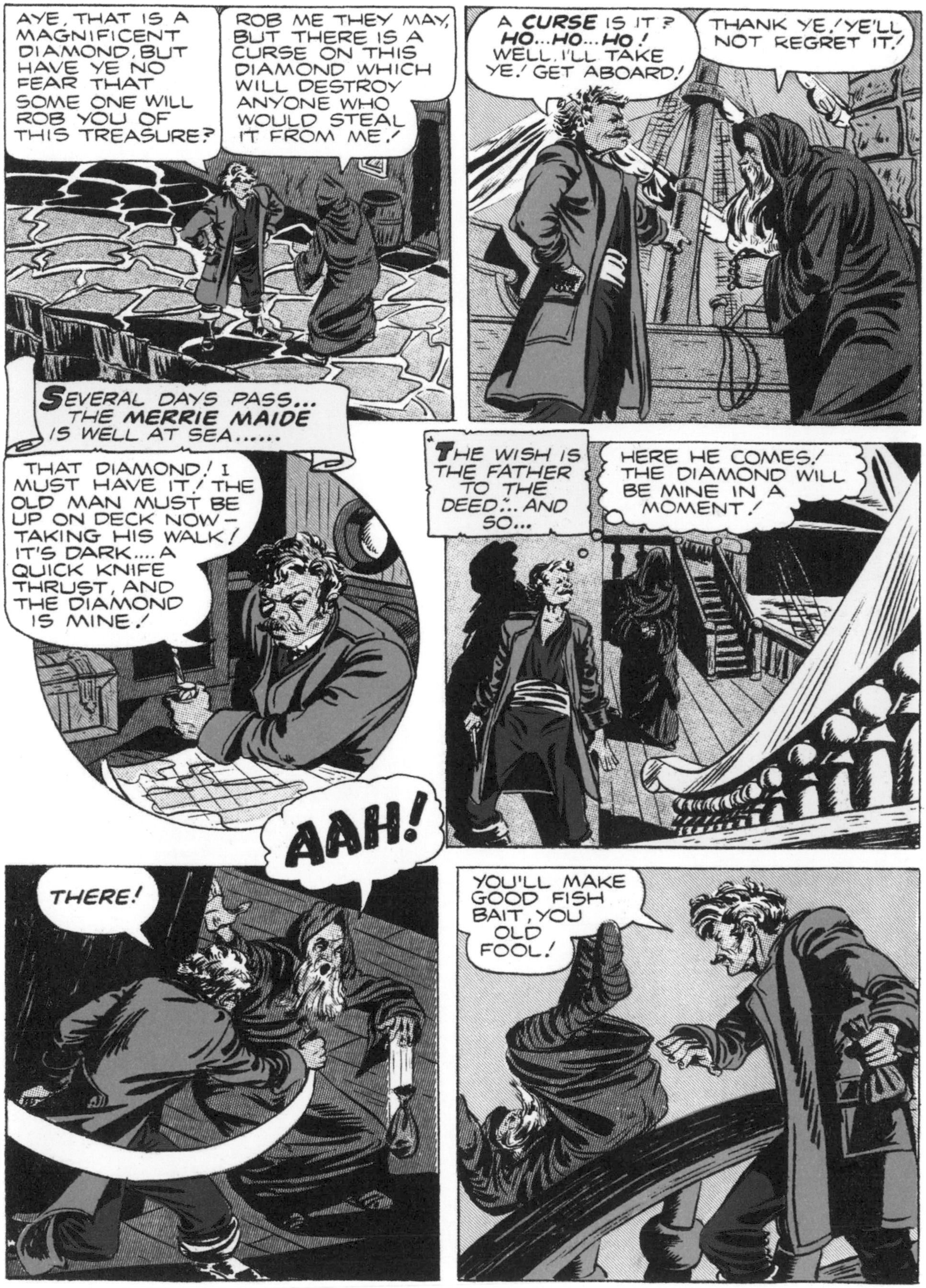
AYE, THAT IS A MAGNIFICENT DIAMOND, BUT HAVE YE NO FEAR THAT SOME ONE WILL ROB YOU OF THIS TREASURE?
ROB ME THEY MAY, BUT THERE IS A CURSE ON THIS DIAMOND WHICH WILL DESTROY ANYONE WHO WOULD STEAL IT FROM ME!
A CURSE IS IT? HO...HO...HO! WELL, I'LL TAKE YE! GET ABOARD!
THANK YE! YE'LL NOT REGRET IT!
SEVERAL DAYS PASS... THE MERRIE MAIDE IS WELL AT SEA......
THAT DIAMOND! I MUST HAVE IT! THE OLD MAN MUST BE UP ON DECK NOW– TAKING HIS WALK! IT'S DARK.... A QUICK KNIFE THRUST, AND THE DIAMOND IS MINE!
"THE WISH IS THE FATHER TO THE DEED"... AND SO...
HERE HE COMES! THE DIAMOND WILL BE MINE IN A MOMENT!
AAH!
THERE!
YOU'LL MAKE GOOD FISH BAIT, YOU OLD FOOL!

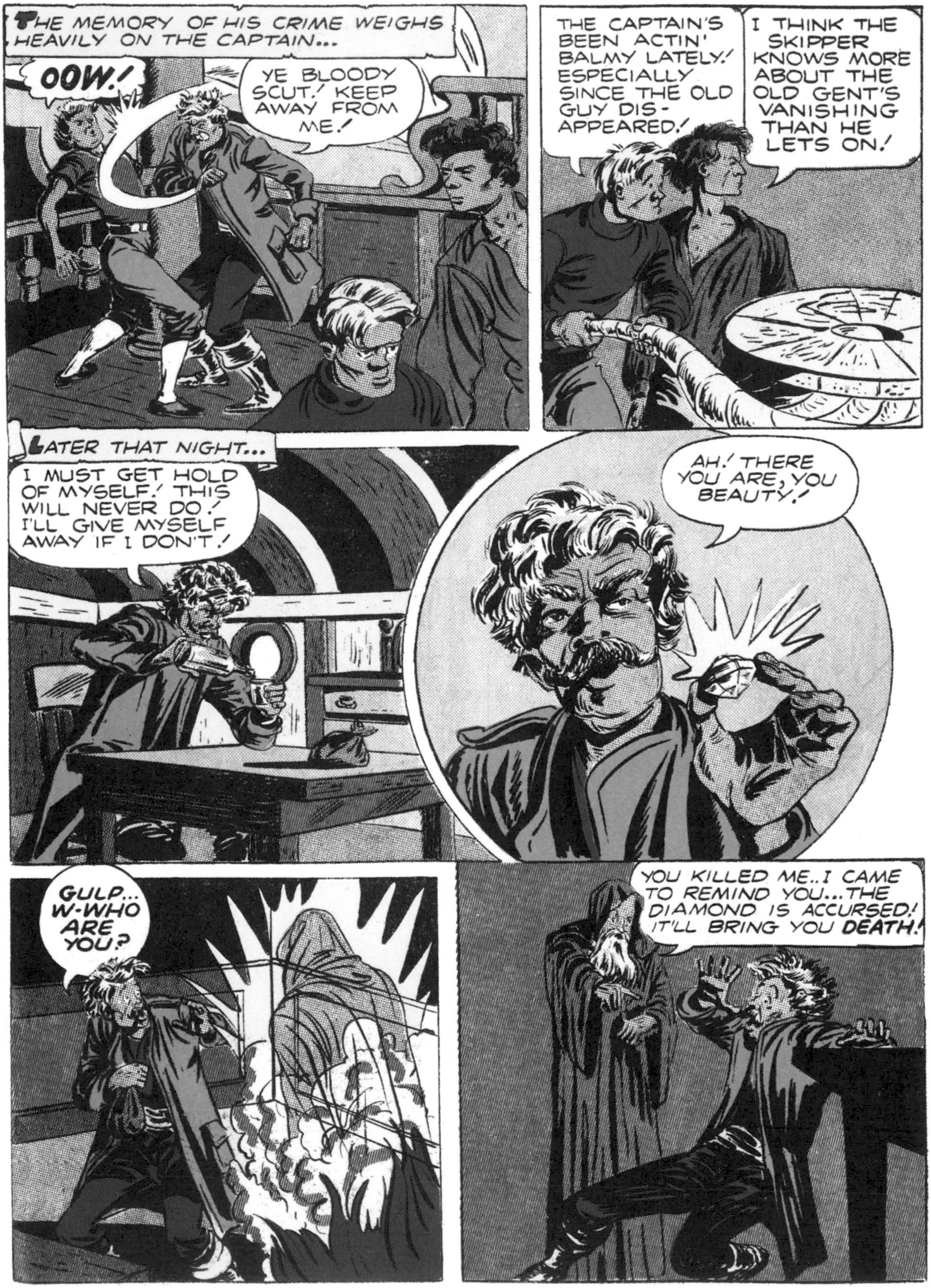
THE MEMORY OF HIS CRIME WEIGHS HEAVILY ON THE CAPTAIN...
OOW!
YE BLOODY SCUT! KEEP AWAY FROM ME!
THE CAPTAIN'S BEEN ACTIN' BALMY LATELY! ESPECIALLY SINCE THE OLD GUY DIS-APPEARED!
I THINK THE SKIPPER KNOWS MORE ABOUT THE OLD GENT'S VANISHING THAN HE LETS ON!
LATER THAT NIGHT...
I MUST GET HOLD OF MYSELF! THIS WILL NEVER DO! I'LL GIVE MYSELF AWAY IF I DON'T!
AH! THERE YOU ARE, YOU BEAUTY!
GULP... W-WHO ARE YOU?
YOU KILLED ME..I CAME TO REMIND YOU...THE DIAMOND IS ACCURSED! IT'LL BRING YOU DEATH!

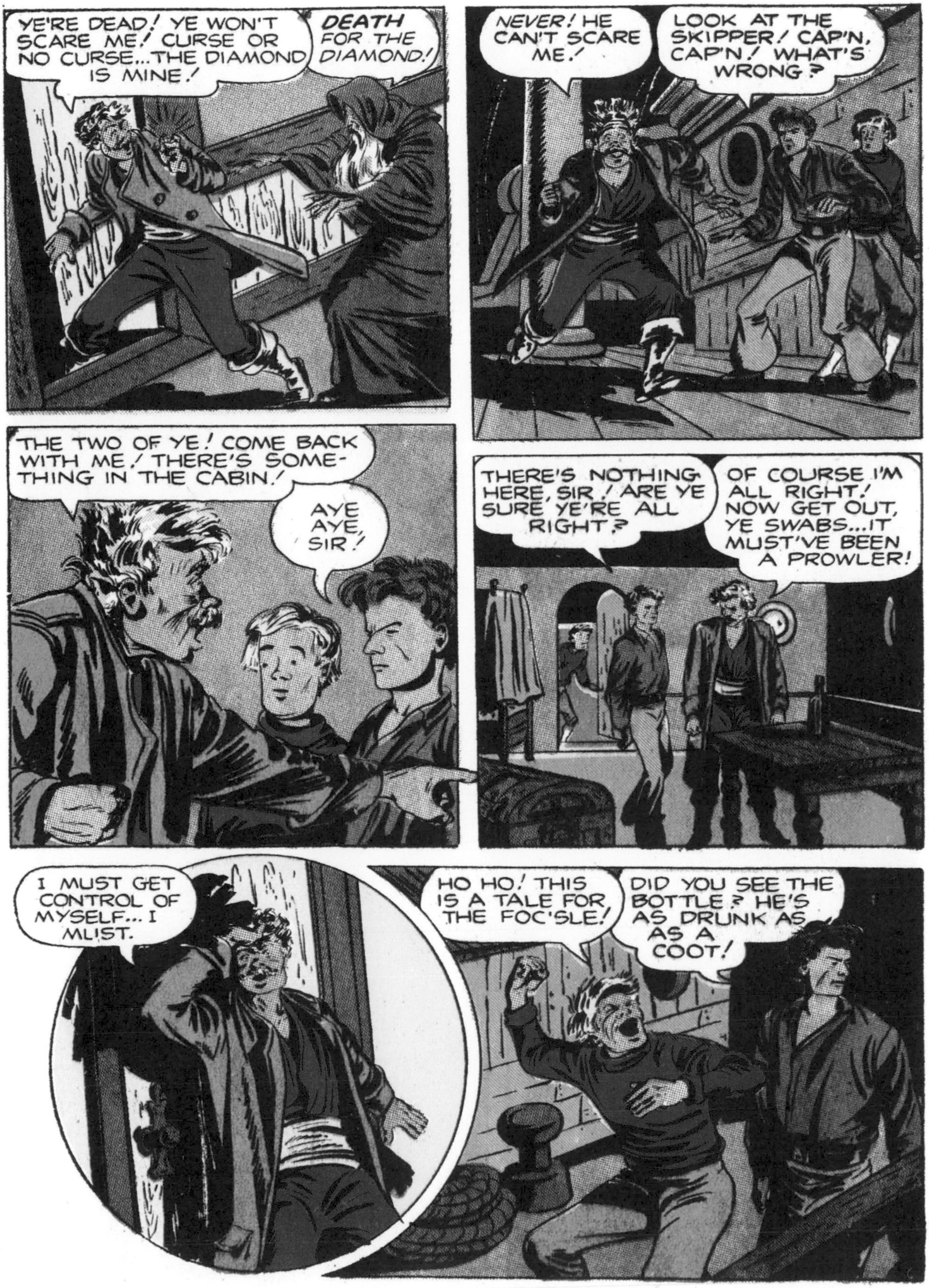
YE'RE DEAD! YE WON'T SCARE ME! CURSE OR NO CURSE...THE DIAMOND IS MINE!
DEATH FOR THE DIAMOND!
NEVER! HE CAN'T SCARE ME!
LOOK AT THE SKIPPER! CAP'N, CAP'N! WHAT'S WRONG?
THE TWO OF YE! COME BACK WITH ME! THERE'S SOME-THING IN THE CABIN!
AYE AYE, SIR!
THERE'S NOTHING HERE, SIR! ARE YE SURE YE'RE ALL RIGHT?
OF COURSE I'M ALL RIGHT! NOW GET OUT, YE SWABS...IT MUST'VE BEEN A PROWLER!
I MUST GET CONTROL OF MYSELF... I MUST.
HO HO! THIS IS A TALE FOR THE FOC'SLE!
DID YOU SEE THE BOTTLE? HE'S AS DRUNK AS AS A COOT!

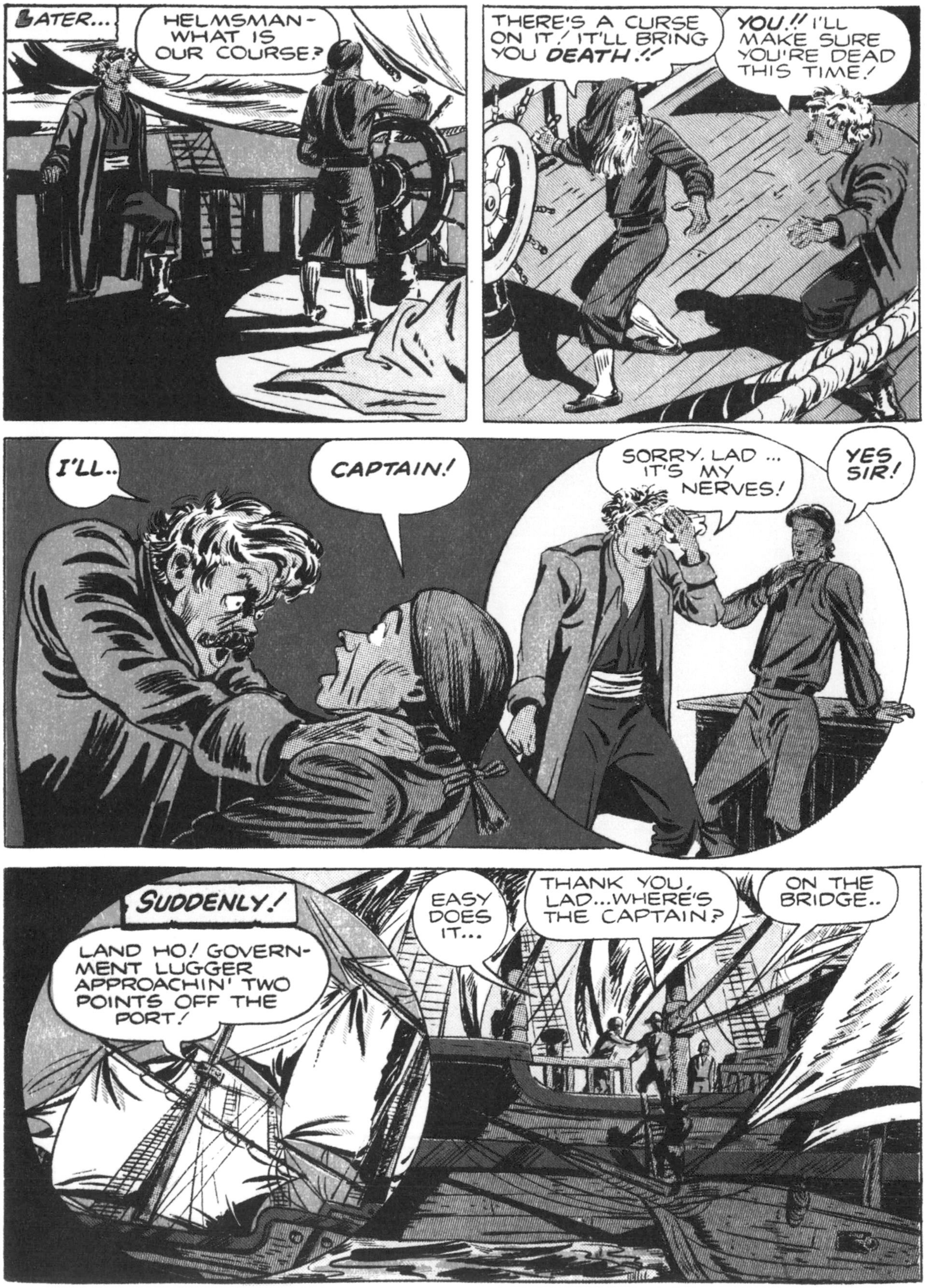
LATER...
HELMSMAN- WHAT IS OUR COURSE?
THERE'S A CURSE ON IT! IT'LL BRING YOU DEATH!!
YOU!! I'LL MAKE SURE YOU'RE DEAD THIS TIME!
I'LL..
CAPTAIN!
SORRY, LAD ... IT'S MY NERVES!
YES SIR!
SUDDENLY!
LAND HO! GOVERNMENT LUGGER APPROACHIN' TWO POINTS OFF THE PORT!
EASY DOES IT...
THANK YOU, LAD...WHERE'S THE CAPTAIN?
ON THE BRIDGE..

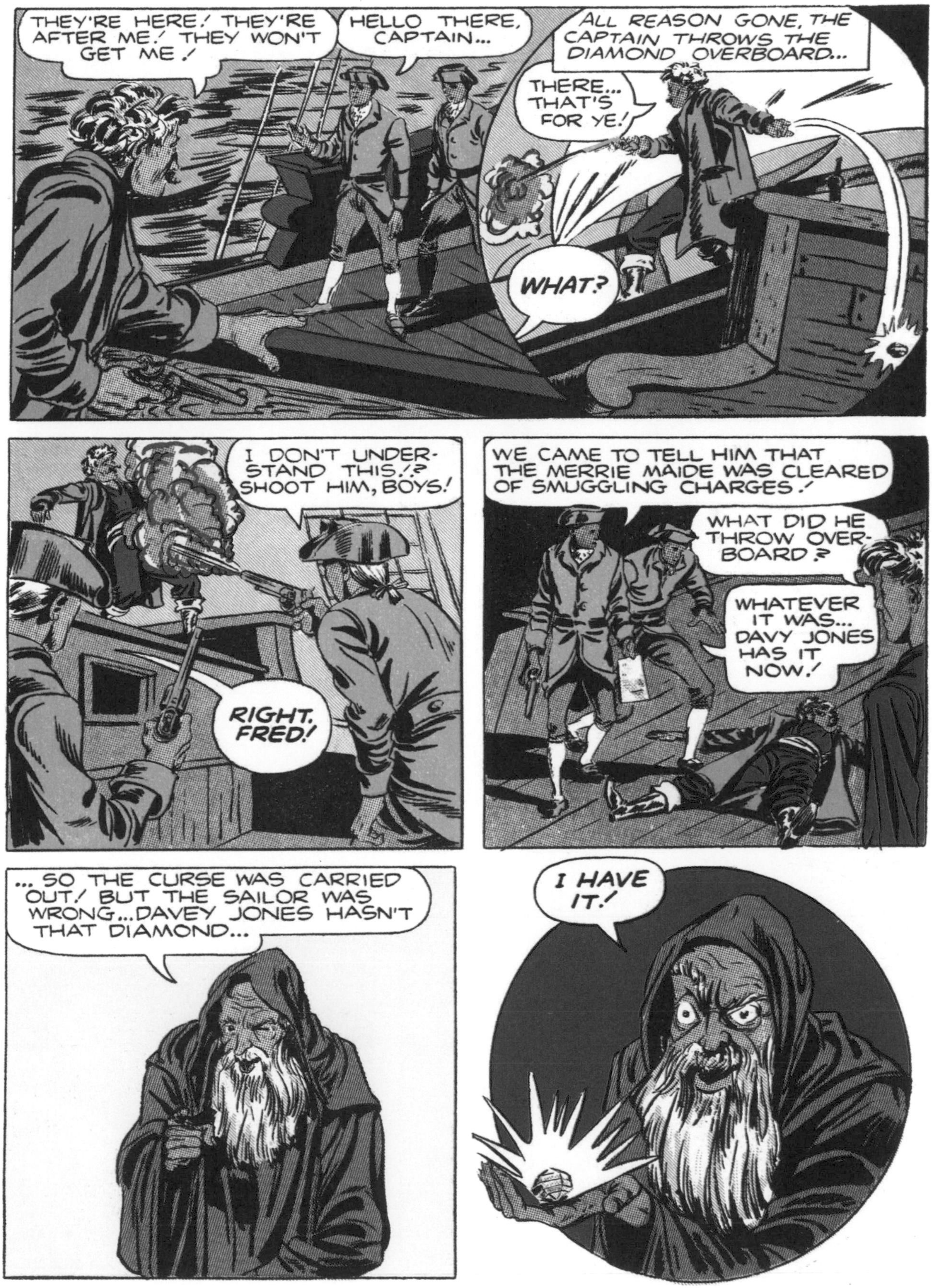
THEY'RE HERE! THEY'RE AFTER ME! THEY WON'T GET ME!
HELLO THERE, CAPTAIN...
ALL REASON GONE, THE CAPTAIN THROWS THE DIAMOND OVERBOARD...
THERE... THAT'S FOR YE!
WHAT?
I DON'T UNDER-STAND THIS!? SHOOT HIM, BOYS!
RIGHT, FRED!
WE CAME TO TELL HIM THAT THE MERRIE MAIDE WAS CLEARED OF SMUGGLING CHARGES!
WHAT DID HE THROW OVER-BOARD?
WHATEVER IT WAS... DAVY JONES HAS IT NOW!
... SO THE CURSE WAS CARRIED OUT! BUT THE SAILOR WAS WRONG...DAVEY JONES HASN'T THAT DIAMOND...
I HAVE IT!

Conning the CONFIDENCE MAN!

HUMAN BEINGS WERE MERE STEPPING STONES TO CUNNING **COUNT RUDOLPH**, **KING** OF THE CONFIDENCE MEN, WHO PARLAYED A COUPLE OF DOLLARS INTO A FORTUNE...BUT HIS WINNING WAYS WERE DUE FOR A RUDE SETBACK WHEN HE INVADED THE PLUSHY NIGHT SPOTS OF NEW YORK ONLY TO BE OUTSMARTED BY A BIG TOWN **BUNCO SQUAD** DETECTIVE ...

I SAY, COUNT RUDOLPH— WHAT MISCHIEF BRINGS YOU TO THE LIMEHOUSE SECTION OF LONDON? WE HAVEN'T SEEN THAT GREEN-EYED, RED MUSTACHED FACE IN SOME TIME NOW!

CURIOSITY, MY DEAR SMITHERS, SHEER CURIOSITY— I JUST WANTED TO SEE IF YOU WERE STILL POUNDING A BEAT AFTER ALL THESE YEARS!

HAD THE BOBBY BEEN ABLE TO FOLLOW THE COUNT'S ROUNDABOUT ROUTE TO THE BACKROOM OF MIKE'S NOVELTY SHOP IN LIMEHOUSE THAT AFTERNOON IN OCTOBER, 1938, HE MIGHT NOT HAVE BEEN SO JOVIAL ...

THERE THEY ARE, COUNT-- THE BEST BEHAVED DICE IN LONDON... I SAVED THEM FOR YOU BECAUSE I HEARD YOU WERE IN A BAD WAY FOR CASH!

I'VE LIVED TOO ROYALLY THESE PAST MONTHS, MIKE-- NOW I MUST GO TO **WORK!** WITH THIS POUND NOTE AND MY PERSONALITY I'LL HAVE ANOTHER FORTUNE WITHIN A FORTNIGHT!

I HEAR BY THE GRAPEVINE, THAT PICKINGS ARE EXTREMELY GOOD AT THE HOTEL METROPOLE WHERE A GROUP OF WEALTHY AMERICAN TOURISTS ARE PLAYING THE RACES HEAVILY!

YOU ALWAYS DID KNOW THE BEST FISHING SPOTS IN LONDON, MIKE-- AND THESE TRAINED DOMINOES OF YOURS NEVER LET ME DOWN YET!

NONE OF THE AMERICAN TOURISTS COULD EXPLAIN HOW THE PERSONABLE STRANGER HAD COAXED THEM INTO THE GAME AT HIS SUITE IN THE HOTEL METROPOLE..BUT BEFORE THEY KNEW IT HE WAS SHOWING THEM DICE TRICKS THEY HAD NEVER SEEN BEFORE...

I SWEAR, GENTLEMEN.. I'VE NEVER HAD SUCH PHENOMENAL LUCK IN MY LIFE!

NOW.. THAT'S THE SEVENTH STRAIGHT TIME HE'S MADE HIS NUMBER!

HEY, WAIT A MINUTE! LET'S SEE THOSE DICE!

I *THOUGHT* THIS REDHEAD WAS TOO LUCKY.. *THESE* DOMINOES ARE LOADED!

WHAT!!

TAKE US FOR A BUNCH OF CHUMPS, DO YOU, RED.. I'LL *FIX* YOU...

I'M SORRY THE GAME HAD TO END ON SUCH AN UN- HAPPY NOTE, GENTLEMEN!

FORGIVE MY RUDENESS.. BUT ALL GOOD THINGS MUST END!

OOOH!

HA..THE COUNT HAS LOST NONE OF HIS TOUCH..THE CUT TELE- PHONE CORD, THE LOCKED DOOR...AND NOW, THE RAPID EXIT TRICK!

ONE QUICK TRANSACTION NOW WITH MY FRIEND INKY WATKINS, IN THE WEST END AND I'LL BE ON MY WAY ACROSS THE CHANNEL FOR BIGGER GAME!

YOU ARE A PUNCTUAL MAN, COUNT... I JUST TOOK THESE BILLS OFF THE MACHINE LESS THAN FIVE MINUTES AGO!

IT MAY PLEASE YOU TO KNOW THAT THEY WILL BE PUT IN CIRCULATION BE- FORE MIDNIGHT TONIGHT...AT NO LESS GLAMOROUS A SPOT THAN THE MONTE CARLO GAMBLING CASINO!

IF COUNT RUDOLPH HAD ANY DOUBT AS TO HIS SWAY OVER THE FAIR SEX, IT WAS QUICKLY DISPELLED, WHEN HIS DANCING GREEN EYES FIRST MET THOSE OF THE GLAMOROUS AMERICAN VISITOR, *VIRGINIA TRAVIS*, OF BOSTON, MASS.

PROMISE YOU WON'T LEAVE MY SIDE WHILE I'M AT THE TABLE, COUNT— I HAVEN'T LOST A SINGLE SPIN SINCE YOU APPEARED.!

YOU ARE VERY FLATTERING, DEAR LADY, BUT YOU HAVE PRESSED YOUR GOOD FORTUNE FAR ENOUGH -- I RECOMMEND YOU JOIN ME FOR SUPPER IN THE GARDEN.!

IT WAS NOT UNTIL THE WAITER PRESENTED THE CHECK THAT COUNT RUDOLPH SUDDENLY MADE AN ALARMING DISCOVERY...

OH MY GOODNESS.. THIS IS DREADFUL..

WHAT IS IT?

I PROMISED MY BROTHER I WOULD MAIL HIM A CHECK TONIGHT FOR FIVE THOUSAND DOLLARS AND I HAVE FORGOTTEN MY CHECK BOOK... PERHAPS YOU COULD DO ME A GREAT FAVOR.!

WHY, CERTAINLY.. IF I CAN..

IT OCCURRED TO ME THAT IF I GAVE YOU THE AMOUNT IN CURRENCY, YOU MIGHT BE KIND ENOUGH TO WRITE OUT A CHECK TO "CASH" FOR THAT AMOUNT.!

IF THAT'S ALL YOU'RE WORRIED. ABOUT, WE CAN TAKE CARE OF THE TROUBLE IN A SECOND -- ALL I NEED IS A PEN!

MY DEAR - YOU WILL NEVER KNOW THE SERVICE YOU HAVE RENDERED ME -- FORGIVE ME IF I RUSH OFF TO DISPATCH THIS CHECK AND GET IT OFF MY CONSCIENCE.

I UNDERSTAND-- TELL YOUR BROTHER I THINK HE HAS A MOST CHARMING BROTHER.!

FIVE MINUTES BEFORE THE BRITTANICA WAS DUE TO SLIP OUT OF HER LIVERPOOL BERTH ENROUTE TO AMERICA THE NEXT MORNING, A SMILING, PANTING FIGURE HUSTLED UP THE GANGWAY...

NOW LET THEM TRY AND KEEP UP WITH COUNT RUDOLPH.. I HAVE A WALLET BULGING WITH MONEY A SHIPLOAD OF WEALTHY SHEEP WAITING TO BE FLEECED AND WE'RE OFF TO CHUMP LAND.. WHAT COULD BE SWEETER?

AT MONTE CARLO, POLICE HEADQUARTERS, MEANWHILE, EXPRESSIONS WERE ANYTHING BUT JOVIAL, AS AUTHORITIES QUESTIONED VIRGINIA TRAVIS...

THE COUNT RUDOLPH YOU DESCRIBE IS AN OLD CUSTOMER ON OUR BOOKS.. BUT I MUST ADMIT HE HAS COME UP WITH A NEW TWIST IN COUNTERFEITING --- OFFERING BAD MONEY IN EXCHANGE FOR A GOOD CHECK!

HE WAS SO CHARMING-- I CAN HARDLY BELIEVE HE WOULD BE CAPABLE OF SUCH A THING!

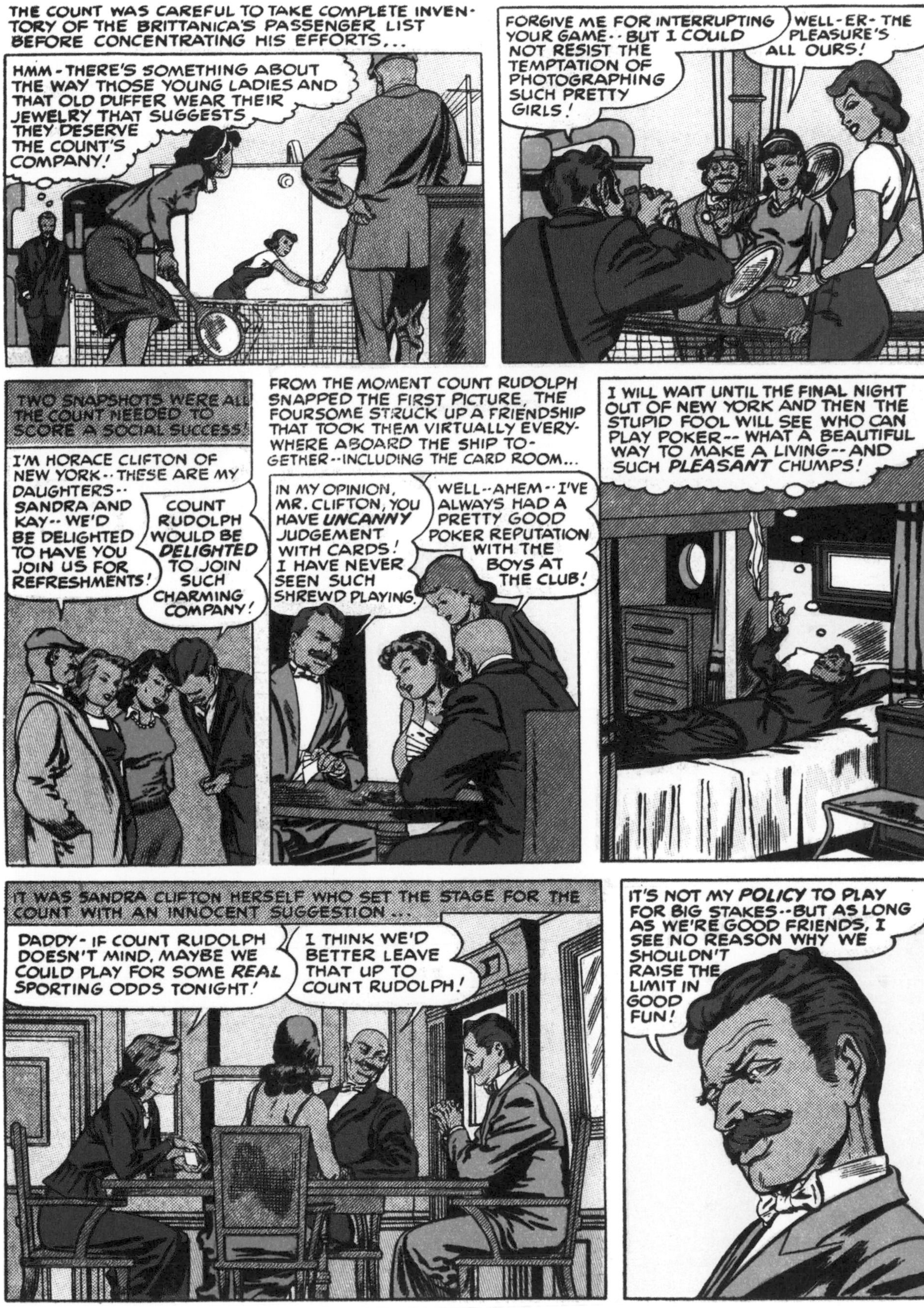
THE COUNT WAS CAREFUL TO TAKE COMPLETE INVENTORY OF THE BRITTANICA'S PASSENGER LIST BEFORE CONCENTRATING HIS EFFORTS...
HMM - THERE'S SOMETHING ABOUT THE WAY THOSE YOUNG LADIES AND THAT OLD DUFFER WEAR THEIR JEWELRY THAT SUGGESTS THEY DESERVE THE COUNT'S COMPANY!
FORGIVE ME FOR INTERRUPTING YOUR GAME.. BUT I COULD NOT RESIST THE TEMPTATION OF PHOTOGRAPHING SUCH PRETTY GIRLS!
WELL-ER- THE PLEASURE'S ALL OURS!
TWO SNAPSHOTS WERE ALL THE COUNT NEEDED TO SCORE A SOCIAL SUCCESS!
I'M HORACE CLIFTON OF NEW YORK.. THESE ARE MY DAUGHTERS.. SANDRA AND KAY.. WE'D BE DELIGHTED TO HAVE YOU JOIN US FOR REFRESHMENTS!
COUNT RUDOLPH WOULD BE DELIGHTED TO JOIN SUCH CHARMING COMPANY!
FROM THE MOMENT COUNT RUDOLPH SNAPPED THE FIRST PICTURE, THE FOURSOME STRUCK UP A FRIENDSHIP THAT TOOK THEM VIRTUALLY EVERYWHERE ABOARD THE SHIP TOGETHER--INCLUDING THE CARD ROOM...
IN MY OPINION, MR. CLIFTON, YOU HAVE UNCANNY JUDGEMENT WITH CARDS! I HAVE NEVER SEEN SUCH SHREWD PLAYING.
WELL--AHEM--I'VE ALWAYS HAD A PRETTY GOOD POKER REPUTATION WITH THE BOYS AT THE CLUB!
I WILL WAIT UNTIL THE FINAL NIGHT OUT OF NEW YORK AND THEN THE STUPID FOOL WILL SEE WHO CAN PLAY POKER-- WHAT A BEAUTIFUL WAY TO MAKE A LIVING--AND SUCH PLEASANT CHUMPS!
IT WAS SANDRA CLIFTON HERSELF WHO SET THE STAGE FOR THE COUNT WITH AN INNOCENT SUGGESTION...
DADDY- IF COUNT RUDOLPH DOESN'T MIND, MAYBE WE COULD PLAY FOR SOME REAL SPORTING ODDS TONIGHT!
I THINK WE'D BETTER LEAVE THAT UP TO COUNT RUDOLPH!
IT'S NOT MY POLICY TO PLAY FOR BIG STAKES--BUT AS LONG AS WE'RE GOOD FRIENDS, I SEE NO REASON WHY WE SHOULDN'T RAISE THE LIMIT IN GOOD FUN!

AN HOUR LATER.

BY JOVE, COUNT... I'VE NEVER SEEN SUCH CARDS AS YOU'VE BEEN DRAWING... IT'S UNBELIEVABLE!

IT'S WORSE THAN THAT--IT'S DOWNRIGHT EMBARRASSING-- HERE, AS A FRIEND I'M TAKING ALL YOUR MONEY! TSK, TSK!

SANDRA AND I HAVE NO MORE READY CASH LEFT, SO WE'RE PUTTING OUR JEWELRY INTO THE POT JUST TO KEEP THE POT GOING!

THIS IS RIDICULOUS--I WON'T HAVE YOU POSTING SUCH VALUABLES IN SUCH A FRIENDLY GAME!

OF COURSE, THE JEWELRY'S WORTH THE POT A HUNDRED TIMES, BUT IF YOU SHOULD WIN IT FOR SECURITY, IT MEANS WE'LL BE SURE TO SEE YOU AGAIN IN NEW YORK--AND YOU CAN'T BLAME US FOR WANTING THAT!

LOOK HERE, I CAN'T TAKE ALL THIS JEWELRY-- YOUR I.O.U. WILL BE ENOUGH!

I'M AFRAID IT'S NO USE ARGUING WITH MY DAUGHTERS, COUNT.. BESIDES WE ALL WANT TO SEE YOU AT OUR APARTMENT AS SOON AS WE'VE UNPACKED!

WHAT FOOLS-- I GAVE THEM A PHONY UPTOWN ADDRESS THAT'LL MEAN NOTHING ... MEANWHILE, I SET UP HEADQUARTERS AT ANOTHER HOTEL UNDER AN ASSUMED NAME AND START WORKING A FRESH FIELD!

AT THEIR SWANK APARTMENT ON PARKSIDE DRIVE 48 HOURS LATER, THE CLIFTON FAMILY MADE A SHOCKING DISCOVERY...

I'VE JUST CALLED THE MAJESTIC HOTEL WHERE THE COUNT SAID HE WOULD BE STAYING--AND THE MANAGEMENT SAID THEY HAD NO SUCH PERSON REGISTERED THERE! SOMETHING MUST BE WRONG!

I HATE TO SUGGEST THIS BUT I'M AFRAID WE'RE FORCED TO CALL THE POLICE-- THAT JEWELRY'S WORTH A FORTUNE!

TWENTY MINUTES LATER, IN THE OFFICE OF LIEUTENANT MARVIN ELDRIDGE, BUNCO SQUAD CHIEF, THE CLIFTON FAMILY FOUND ITSELF DUE FOR ANOTHER SHOCK!

SO YOUR POKER-PLAYING FRIEND HAD RED HAIR AND GREEN EYES, EH? YOU'VE BEEN TRAVELLING IN FAST COMPANY, MR. CLIFTON -- THE MAN WHO TOOK YOUR BANKROLL AND JEWELS IS RUDOLPH DUVALL, THE MOST NOTORIOUS CONFIDENCE MAN IN THE WORLD!

I-I CAN'T BELIEVE IT!

GETTING THE COUNT TO COUGH UP THAT JEWELRY WILL NOT BE EASY..EVEN IF WE'RE LUCKY ENOUGH TO LOCATE HIM..BUT THERE'S NOTHING I'D LIKE BETTER THAN TO TRAP THAT SCOUNDREL WITH THE GOODS ABOARD!

I HAVE A WILD THEORY THAT MIGHT WORK..BUT WE'VE GOT TO PICK UP HIS TRAIL FIRST! WHEN I DO, I'LL LET YOU KNOW HOW YOU CAN HELP US!

I'LL BE AWAITING YOUR CALL, LIEUTENANT!

CHECK EVERY IMPORTANT HOTEL IN TOWN - IF THE COUNT IS OPERATING IN THE CITY, WE'RE BOUND TO SPOT HIM SOONER OR LATER!

WE'VE GOT EVERY IMPORTANT HOTEL IN TOWN COVERED, CHIEF!

TWO HOURS LATER THE BUNCO CHIEF GOT A REPORT FROM DETECTIVE MARSH...

THE COUNT'S REGISTERED AT THE HOTEL AS LORD DUNSMUIR, CHIEF -- THE DESK SAYS HE'S BEEN MEETING A LOT OF HIGH SOCIETY FOLKS IN THE LOBBY AND HUSTLING THEM OUT OF HERE!

THE BUNCO CHIEF'S NEXT MOVE WAS A QUICK CONFERENCE WITH SUSIE CRAWFORD, SWITCHBOARD OPERATOR AT THE MIDWAY HOTEL ...

YOU WANTED TO SEE ME, LIEUTENANT ELDRIDGE ?

THAT'S RIGHT, SUSIE..DETECTIVE MARSH IS TAKING A ROOM AT THE HOTEL..CUT HIM INTO EVERY PHONE CALL INVOLVING LORD DUNSMUIR!

TEN MINUTES AFTER DETECTIVE MARSH CHECKED IN HIS ROOM, A TELEPHONE RING CUT HIM IN ON SOME INTERESTING CONVERSATION ...

I ENJOY YOUR AMERICAN CARD GAMES SO MUCH -- DO YOU SUPPOSE WE COULD PLAY SOME POKER AT THE SKYVIEW CLUB, MISS DESHON ?

SIMPLY SPLENDID, YOUR LORDSHIP! I HAVE TWO WALL STREET FRIENDS WHO WOULD LOVE TO JOIN US!

THERE'S HIS TARGET FOR TONIGHT, CHIEF. APPARENTLY HE'S GOT A CHUMP LIST THAT HE'S FLEECING FROM THE RANKS OF HIGH SOCIETY.' THEY'VE BEEN HYPNOTIZED BY HIS PERSONALITY!

HMMM—I THINK IT'S HIGH TIME I CALLED *MR. CLIFTON!*

WE KNOW *IN ADVANCE* EVERY MOVE THE COUNT IS MAKING.. I WANT YOU TO HAVE FRIENDS OF YOURS PLANTED IN CERTAIN SPOTS, MR. CLIFTON——— I'LL TELL THEM WHAT TO DO!

I'M AFRAID I DON'T UNDERSTAND—BUT YOU CAN COUNT ON MY FULL COOPERATION, LIEUTENANT.

THE NEXT EVENING, THE COUNT SET FORTH ON ANOTHER OF HIS FIXED GAMBLING PARTIES...

YOU MENTIONED LAST NIGHT A DESIRE TO PLAY CARDS FOR INTERESTING STAKES.. I THINK YOU'LL LIKE THE CONTINENTAL CLUB!

THE COUNT AND HIS PARTY COULD SCARCELY HELP BUT OVERHEAR THE WORDS OF THE LOUD VOICED WOMAN AT THE NEXT TABLE....

MY FRIEND, SANDRA JACKSON, HAD ROTTEN LUCK ON HER ATLANTIC CROSSING——SHE LOST HER JEWELRY TO AN INTERNATIONAL CARD SHARP!

YOU DON'T SAY!

EX-EXCUSE ME..I MUST MAKE A TELEPHONE CALL!

SANDRA SAID THIS CROOK HAD RED HAIR AND GREEN EYES!

THAT WAS TOO CLOSE FOR COMFORT—I COULDN'T DARE TAKE THEIR MONEY AFTER THAT—*TAXI!*

YOUR FRIENDS CAME THROUGH IN GREAT STYLE, MR. CLIFTON, BUT WE'VE GOT TO KEEP THE COUNT GROGGY.. I'LL ADVISE YOU WHEN WE NEED THE NEXT PLANT!

I HAVE PEOPLE STANDING BY READY TO HELP US ANY TIME, ANY PLACE, LIEUTENANT.

THE *NEXT* EVENING, A LOUD CONVERSATION AT THE TABLE BEHIND HIM IN THE HOTEL BELAIR DINING ROOM CAUSED THE COUNT TO TURN IN ALARM!

DID YOU HEAR ABOUT THE *CARD SHARP* THAT CAME OVER ON THE LATEST LINER?

I GOT THE STORY FIRST HAND FROM KAY CLIFTON.. SHE AND HER SISTER LOST A BRACELET AND A NECKLACE TO A MAN WITH *RED HAIR* AND *GREEN EYES!*

I-I JUST REMEMBERED A TELEGRAM I WAS SUPPOSED TO SEND -EXCUSE ME!

SHE SAID THIS GUY POSED AS A PHONY ROYALTY!

THAT JEWELRY MUST HAVE A *CURSE* ON IT -- I'VE *NEVER* HAD SUCH BAD LUCK.. IT'S TIME I BLEW TOWN UNTIL THIS JINX WEARS OFF!

I'VE GOT TO CATCH THE MIDNIGHT PLANE FOR BOSTON.. PLEASE HAVE MY BILL READY WHEN I COME DOWNSTAIRS!

VERY WELL, SIR!

MOMENTS LATER..

WE'VE GOT A RUSH JOB, MR. CLIFTON- CAN YOU GET A COUPLE DOWN TO THE AIRPORT IN TWENTY MINUTES?

THEY'RE AS GOOD AS ON THEIR WAY, LIEUTENANT!

SCARCELY HAD THE PLANE LEFT THE GROUND, WHEN THE COUNT WAS HORRIFIED TO HEAR THE CONVERSATION BEHIND HIM...

THIS NEWSPAPER ITEM IS INTERESTING, JOE - THE POLICE ARE LOOKING FOR AN INTERNATIONAL CROOK WITH *RED HAIR* AND *GREEN EYES*..HE'S WANTED FOR SWINDLING THE CLIFTON FAMILY OUT OF SOME EXPENSIVE JEWELRY!

HM! RED HAIR AND GREEN EYES.. SOUNDS LIKE A TRAFFIC LIGHT!

THAT SETTLES IT- I'M TAKING THE NEXT PLANE BACK TO NEW YORK AND GETTING RID OF THAT CURSED JEWELRY BEFORE I LOSE MY MIND!

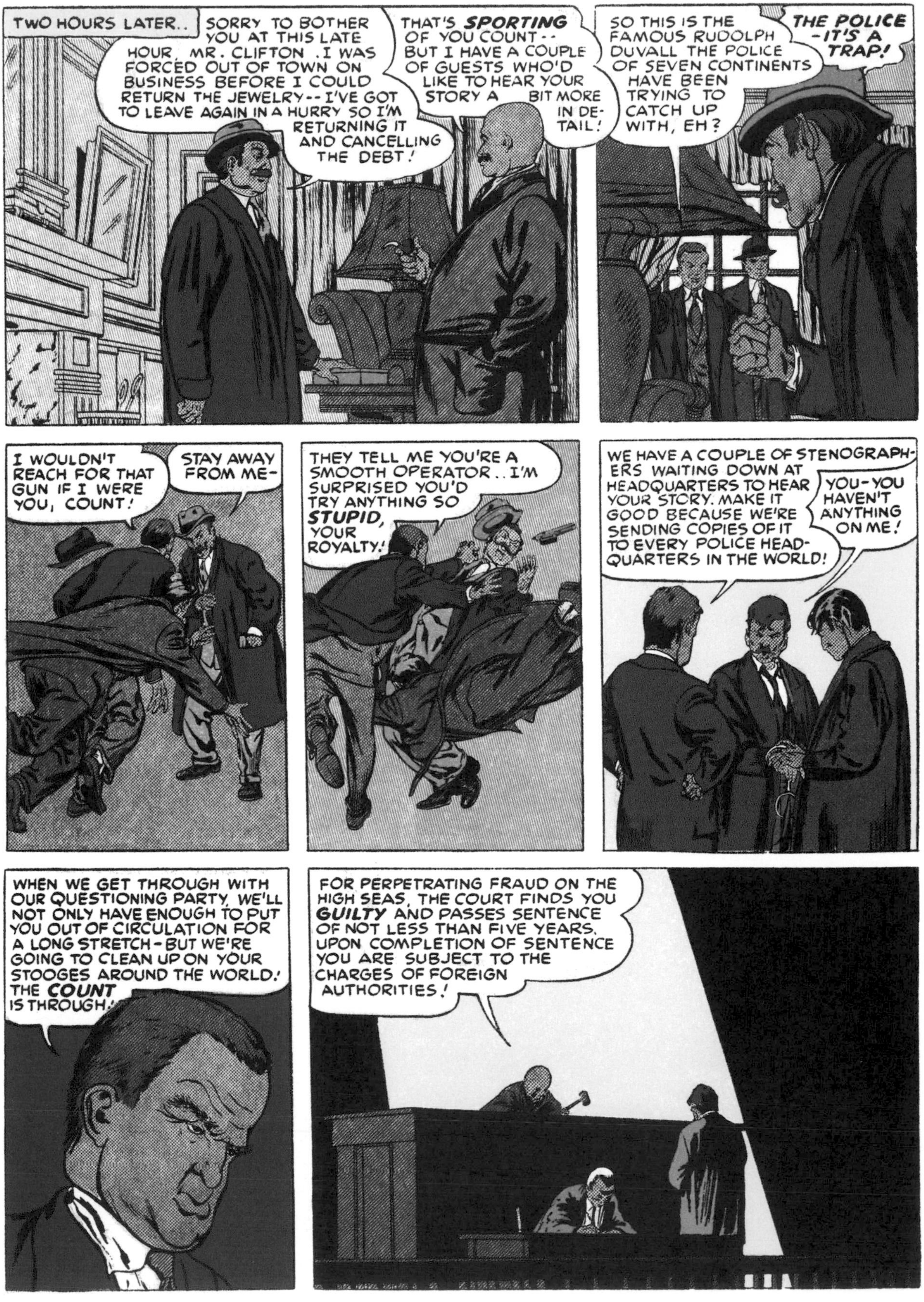
TWO HOURS LATER..
SORRY TO BOTHER YOU AT THIS LATE HOUR, MR. CLIFTON. I WAS FORCED OUT OF TOWN ON BUSINESS BEFORE I COULD RETURN THE JEWELRY-- I'VE GOT TO LEAVE AGAIN IN A HURRY SO I'M RETURNING IT AND CANCELLING THE DEBT!
THAT'S SPORTING OF YOU COUNT-- BUT I HAVE A COUPLE OF GUESTS WHO'D LIKE TO HEAR YOUR STORY A BIT MORE IN DETAIL!
SO THIS IS THE FAMOUS RUDOLPH DUVALL THE POLICE OF SEVEN CONTINENTS HAVE BEEN TRYING TO CATCH UP WITH, EH?
THE POLICE -IT'S A TRAP!
I WOULDN'T REACH FOR THAT GUN IF I WERE YOU, COUNT!
STAY AWAY FROM ME-
THEY TELL ME YOU'RE A SMOOTH OPERATOR.. I'M SURPRISED YOU'D TRY ANYTHING SO STUPID, YOUR ROYALTY!
WE HAVE A COUPLE OF STENOGRAPHERS WAITING DOWN AT HEADQUARTERS TO HEAR YOUR STORY. MAKE IT GOOD BECAUSE WE'RE SENDING COPIES OF IT TO EVERY POLICE HEADQUARTERS IN THE WORLD!
YOU-YOU HAVEN'T ANYTHING ON ME!
WHEN WE GET THROUGH WITH OUR QUESTIONING PARTY, WE'LL NOT ONLY HAVE ENOUGH TO PUT YOU OUT OF CIRCULATION FOR A LONG STRETCH-BUT WE'RE GOING TO CLEAN UP ON YOUR STOOGES AROUND THE WORLD! THE COUNT IS THROUGH!
FOR PERPETRATING FRAUD ON THE HIGH SEAS, THE COURT FINDS YOU GUILTY AND PASSES SENTENCE OF NOT LESS THAN FIVE YEARS. UPON COMPLETION OF SENTENCE YOU ARE SUBJECT TO THE CHARGES OF FOREIGN AUTHORITIES!

THE MISTAKE

THE FINAL PERFORMANCE OF A HIT SHOW STARRING RUPERT AND ETHEL DENNIS....

ALL RIGHT! CURTAIN! BRING UP THE HOUSE LIGHTS! THAT DOES IT!

NO SM

WELL, THIS WINDS UP OUR ACTING CAREERS!

NOW FOR PIPE AND SLIPPERS ...AND PEACE.... SOMETHING WE'VE NOT HAD FOR TWENTY YEARS!

LATER, IN THE DENNIS' DRESSING ROOM....

ETHEL, DARLING! RUPERT! YOU WERE MAGNIFICENT! BUT WAIT UNTIL YOU SEE THE SCRIPT I'VE LINED UP FOR YOU.... WHAT A PLAY!

HOLD IT, MAX! THERE'LL BE NO NEXT SCRIPT!

THAT'S RIGHT, MAX! WE'RE LEAVING THE STAGE, RUPERT AND I, FOR A REST AT MY ESTATE ON LONG ISLAND!

SO TAKE TWO WEEK'S VACATION....THAT'S LONG ENOUGH.... AND WAIT UNTIL YOU SEE THIS SCRIPT!

MAX, YOU DON'T UNDER-STAND....WE'RE RETIRING! I'M GOING TO PLAY MY GREATEST ROLE...GENTLEMAN OF LEISURE!

AND I, LADY IN RETIREMENT!

DISASTER! WHAT A DISASTER! WHY SHOULD YOU DO THIS TO ME? THE MOST MAGNIFICENT ACTING TEAM ON ANY STAGE.... RETIRES! NO! NO!

YES, YES, MAX! CALL IN YOUR PRESS AGENTS....SPREAD THE WORD! NOTHING CAN CHANGE OUR MINDS! TWENTY YEARS OF TROUPING ARE ENOUGH!

VARIETY

RUPERT AND ETHEL TAKE TO THE STICKS!

SHOW BUSI

"WE'RE THROUGH" SAY

DENNIS' RETIRE!

SO THE GREAT TROUPERS RETIRE....TO THE PEACEFUL SURROUNDINGS OF LONG ISLAND

OH, RUPERT, THIS IS MY FONDEST DREAM COME TRUE....NO REHEARSALS, NO EXCITEMENT. JUST THE TWO OF US...WITH NOTHING TO WORRY ABOUT!

AS THE IMMORTAL BARD SAID, "AY THAT'S THE RUB." THERE IS SOME-THING TO WORRY ABOUT!

WHAT, DEAR WHAT?

MONEY!

MONEY? OH, RUPERT, YOU SILLY THING, YOU KNOW HOW MUCH MONEY I INHERITED WHEN UNCLE JOHN DIED!

YES ETHEL.

THAT'S WHAT'S WRONG! IT'S YOUR MONEY!

THE NEXT MONTHS HURRIED BY.... AND THERE WERE MANY GAY PARTIES AT THE DENNIS ESTATE....

ETHEL, YOU ARE MAGNIFICENT! WHEN ARE YOU COMING BACK TO BROADWAY?

NEVER, MAX! I'VE NEVER HAD SO MUCH FUN IN MY LIFE!

BUT RUPERT.... HE DOESN'T LOOK WELL! HE SEEMS ALMOST UNHAPPY!

OH, MAX.... YOU KNOW RUPERT! ACTING, HE'S ALWAYS ACTING! TELL YOU WHAT, MAX, WHY DON'T YOU COME OUT AND SPEND NEXT WEEK-END WITH US? YOU'LL BE ABLE TO CHEER RUPERT, YOU ALWAYS DO!

RUPERT, DEAR, MAX IS COMING TO SPEND NEXT WEEK-END WITH US!

WHY DIDN'T YOU ASK ME? MAYBE I HAD PLANS, OR DON'T I COUNT AROUND HERE ANY MORE?

RUPERT.... OLD MAN....

RUPERT.... WHAT'S WRONG?

PLENTY! EVERYTHING!

I'LL.... CALL.... AGAIN, ...ETHEL....

WHEN WE RETIRED, IT WAS TO BE JUST THE TWO OF US. THAT WAS WHAT I WANTED AND EXPECTED NOT THIS.... THESE PARTIES.... ALWAYS PEOPLE UNDERFOOT!

YES, DEAR, YOU'RE RIGHT! FROM NOW ON, IT WILL BE JUST THE TWO OF US. NO MORE PARTIES!

THREE MONTHS PASS AND THERE ARE NO MORE GAY PARTIES.... THE GREAT HOUSE IS QUIET AND DARK.... THEN, ONE DAY, MAX PAYS A VISIT....

RUPERT! HOW ARE YOU, OLD MAN? AND HOW IS ETHEL?

THEN YOU HAVEN'T HEARD? ETHEL.... SUFFERED A NERVOUS BREAKDOWN THREE MONTHS AGO! AND, MAX THE AWFUL PART IS THAT SHE HAS AGED TERRIBLY.... ALMOST 20 YEARS..... SHE'S AN OLD, BROKEN, WOMAN!

NO! CAN I SEE HER?

SHE WILL SEE NO ONE! THAT IS WHY WE'VE HAD NO PARTIES! SHE IS TOO SHAMED BY THE LOSS OF HER BEAUTY TO FACE PEOPLE! IT'S TRAGIC, MAX, ... TRAGIC!

AND THEN, ONCE IN A WHILE, A BENT OLD CRONE COULD BE SEEN HOBBLING AROUND ON THE ESTATE'S LAWN, NOW ILL KEPT, AND CHOKED WITH WEEDS... NO ONE WOULD HAVE BELIEVED THAT THIS RAVAGED WOMAN WAS THE ONCE BEAUTIFUL ETHEL DENNIS...

MAX, FAITHFUL FRIEND OF THE THEATRICAL COUPLE, TRIED MANY TIMES TO SEE ETHEL, BUT ALL TO NO AVAIL, ALWAYS RUPERT TOLD HIM THAT ETHEL WOULD SEE NO ONE...

ALLAN, YOU'RE HER LAWYER. CAN'T YOU SPEAK TO HER?

SHE WON'T SEE ME. BELIEVE ME, MAX, THE ONLY TIME I SAW HER WAS WHEN I LOOKED THROUGH THE BINOCULARS! IT'S UNBELIEVABLE!

IT'S HEARTBREAKING ALLAN, THE WAY SHE WALKS AROUND IN THE GARDEN, SO OLD, SO WEAK, LIFE IS CRUEL, ALLAN!

AND AT THE ESTATE...

I'VE PARADED AROUND LONG ENOUGH FOR THE FOOLS! LET THEM PITY POOR ETHEL DENNIS! IF THEY ONLY KNEW! IF THEY ONLY KNEW THE TRUTH!

SOME WEEKS PASS, AND ALMOST A YEAR AFTER ETHEL IS STRICKEN, HER LAWYER IS ENGAGED IN A PHONE CONVERSATION WITH RUPERT...

YES RUPERT... I RECEIVED YOUR MESSAGE AS SOON AS I GOT BACK TO THE OFFICE!

ALLAN, ETHEL FEELS SHE CAN NO LONGER MANAGE THE ESTATE SHE INHERITED FROM HER UNCLE JOHN! SHE WANTS YOU TO PREPARE THE NECESSARY PAPERS TO TURN THE ESTATE OVER TO ME! CAN YOU COME ON SATURDAY?

I'LL PREPARE THE PAPERS AND GO OUT WITH MAX! IT'S ALMOST A YEAR SINCE HE'S SEEN HER!

THE FOLLOWING SATURDAY... AT THE ESTATE...

HELLO, ALLAN! AND MAX... HOW ARE YOU, OLD FRIEND?

THE PAPERS ARE READY, RUPERT! I BROUGHT MAX ALONG AS A WITNESS!

ETHEL IS RESTING. PLEASE FORGIVE THE APPEARANCE OF THE HOUSE, WE'VE HAD NO SERVANTS IN A YEAR. THEY DISTURBED ETHEL, SO SHE FIRED THEM!

THAT'S ALL RIGHT, WE UNDERSTAND... NOW, RUPERT, YOU WILL SIGN HERE!

WE'LL NEED ETHEL'S SIGNATURE NOW, RUPERT!

ALL RIGHT, I'LL SEND HER DOWN! PLEASE PREPARE YOURSELVES FOR A SHOCK! YOU'LL FIND ETHEL VERY CHANGED!

HURRYING UPSTAIRS, RUPERT ENTERS A ROOM WHICH CONTAINS THE INGREDIENTS OF A GHASTLY MASQUERADE...

HA, HA! EXIT RUPERT, ENTER ETHEL... ...A BENT, AGED, CRONE! I'M TOO CLEVER FOR THEM! I'M MUCH TOO CLEVER!

WITH NIMBLE, SKILLFUL FINGERS, HE APPLIES THE MAKE-UP WHICH ALTERS HIS FEATURES!

IF THEY ONLY KNEW I KILLED ETHEL! IF THEY ONLY KNEW HOW MUCH I HATED HER... HOW MUCH I ENVIED HER! AND NOW ALL HER VAST FORTUNE WILL BE MINE!

AND IN A MATTER OF MINUTES, HE COMPLETES THE AMAZING DISGUISE...

AND NOW, I'M READY TO CLIMAX THE GREATEST ROLE I EVER PLAYED!

MY FRIENDS... MY DEAR FRIENDS, MAX AND ALLAN... WHAT DO YOU THINK OF YOUR BEAUTY NOW?

ETHEL! OH, ETHEL!

ETHEL I'M... ...SORRY...

DON'T BE SORRY, ALLAN, EACH LIFE MUST PLAY ITS OWN TRAGEDY, THIS IS MINE! GIVE ME THE PEN, ALLAN!

OF COURSE, ETHEL!

OH, HOW CLUMSY OF ME!

I'LL GET IT...

GREAT SCOTT... SHE'S WEARING RUPERT'S SHOES!

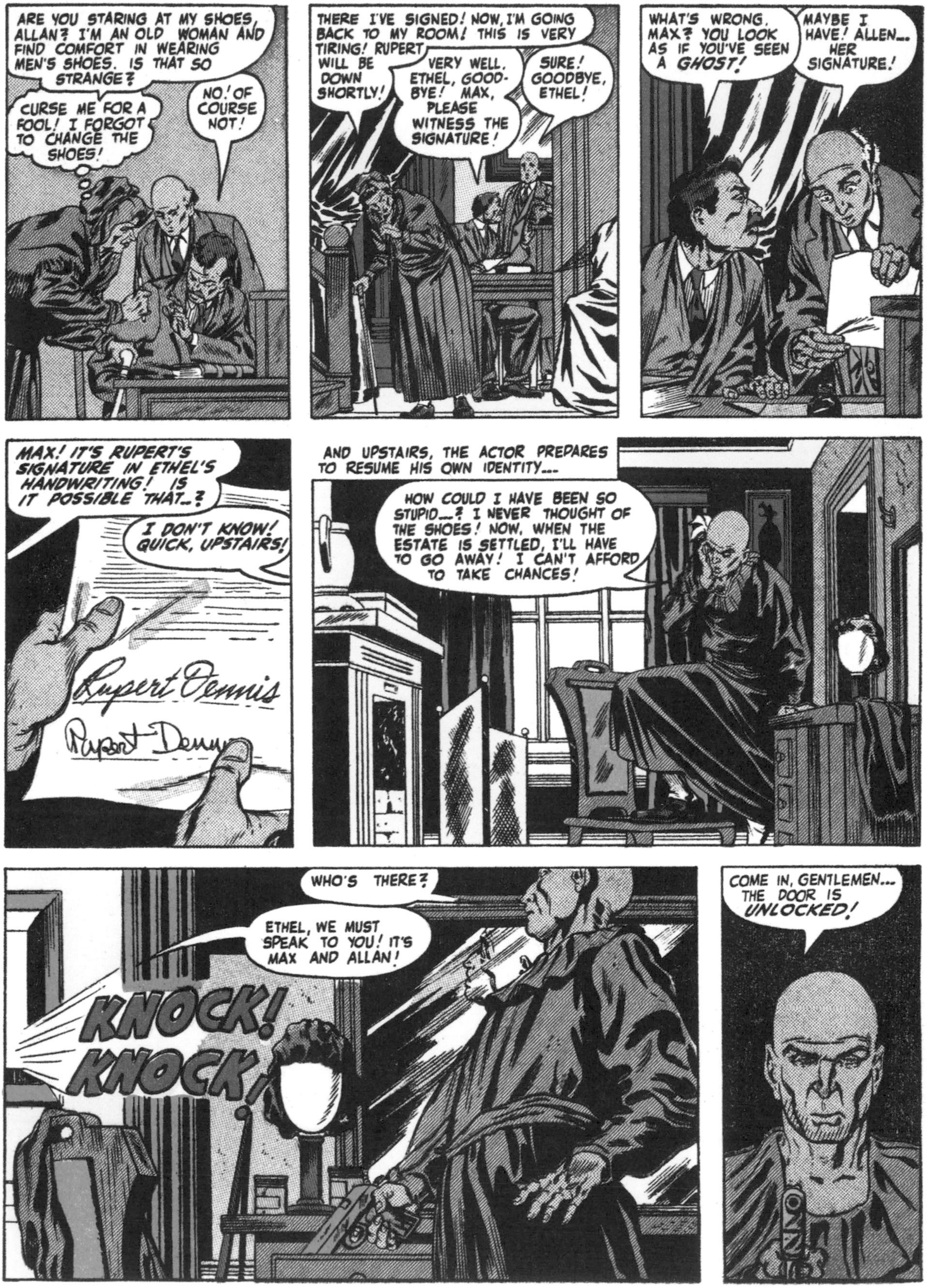
ARE YOU STARING AT MY SHOES, ALLAN? I'M AN OLD WOMAN AND FIND COMFORT IN WEARING MEN'S SHOES. IS THAT SO STRANGE?
CURSE ME FOR A FOOL! I FORGOT TO CHANGE THE SHOES!
NO! OF COURSE NOT!
THERE I'VE SIGNED! NOW, I'M GOING BACK TO MY ROOM! THIS IS VERY TIRING! RUPERT WILL BE DOWN SHORTLY!
VERY WELL, ETHEL, GOOD-BYE! MAX, PLEASE WITNESS THE SIGNATURE!
SURE! GOODBYE, ETHEL!
WHAT'S WRONG, MAX? YOU LOOK AS IF YOU'VE SEEN A GHOST!
MAYBE I HAVE! ALLEN... HER SIGNATURE!
MAX! IT'S RUPERT'S SIGNATURE IN ETHEL'S HANDWRITING! IS IT POSSIBLE THAT...?
I DON'T KNOW! QUICK, UPSTAIRS!
Rupert Dennis
AND UPSTAIRS, THE ACTOR PREPARES TO RESUME HIS OWN IDENTITY...
HOW COULD I HAVE BEEN SO STUPID...? I NEVER THOUGHT OF THE SHOES! NOW, WHEN THE ESTATE IS SETTLED, I'LL HAVE TO GO AWAY! I CAN'T AFFORD TO TAKE CHANCES!
WHO'S THERE?
ETHEL, WE MUST SPEAK TO YOU! IT'S MAX AND ALLAN!
KNOCK! KNOCK!
COME IN, GENTLEMEN... THE DOOR IS UNLOCKED!

RUPERT! YES, MAX, RUPERT... I SEE YOU DISCOVERED MY RUSE... I WILL HAVE TO KILL YOU! BUT I'LL SEE THAT THE PAPERS GO THROUGH!

YOU WON'T GET AWAY WITH THIS, RUPERT!

NO? I'LL...

NO! YOU'VE OVERPLAYED YOUR HAND THIS TIME!

IT WAS THE SHOES! THE ACCURSED SHOES!

NOT THE SHOES, RUPERT, BUT YOUR OWN EGO! YOUR MIND PREYED SO MUCH ON ITSELF THAT YOU SIGNED YOUR OWN NAME IN ETHEL'S HANDWRITING!

SOME MONTHS LATER, IN THE PRESS ROOM OF A NEW YORK CITY COURTHOUSE....

GIMME THE DESK! JOE! THE JURY FOUND DENNIS GUILTY!

YEAH. THE VERDICT WAS MURDER IN THE FIRST DEGREE! IT'S A MANDATORY DEATH SENTENCE!

ON A BLIZZARD-CHOKED STREET IN DECEMBER 1947, THE NEWSPAPERS CARRIED A HEADLINE, AND BUSY TIMES SQUARE LEARNED THAT THE CURTAIN HAD FALLEN ON A DRAMA....

THERE IT IS, ALLAN. DENNIS DIES IN CHAIR!

CURTAIN, MAX. THE LAST CURTAIN FOR RUPERT AND ETHEL!

THERE'S MANY A SLIP 'TWIXT THE CUP AND THE LIP ----BUT HERE, THE SLIP OF A PEN TRAPPED A CRIMINAL... FOR, NO MATTER WHAT HIS DISGUISE, JUSTICE ALWAYS RIPS AWAY THE MASK, AND THE CRIMINAL PAYS THE PRICE FOR HIS CRIMES.

CRIME CANNOT WIN!

NUGGETS NUGENT in DOUBLE TROUBLE

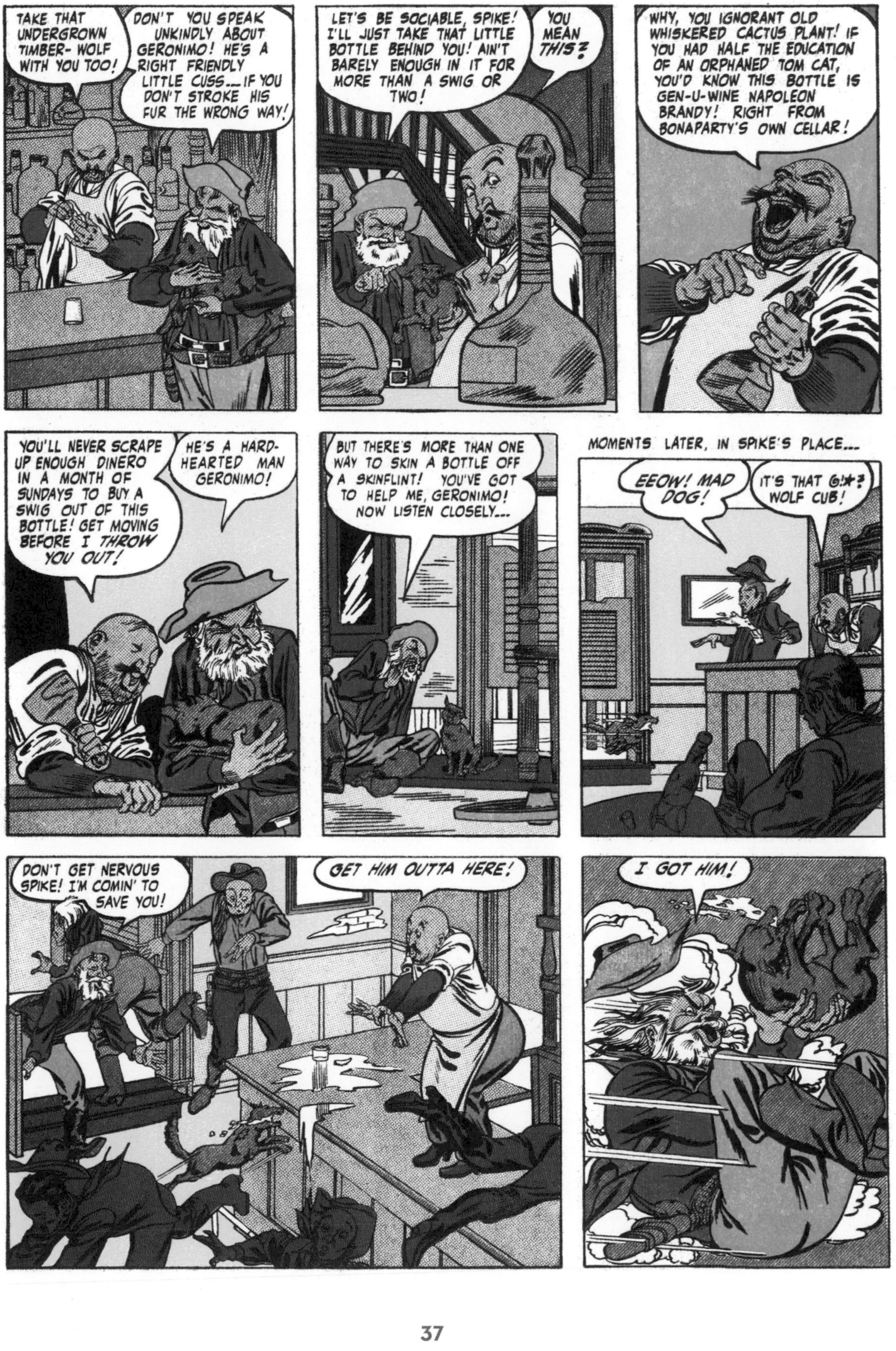
TAKE THAT UNDERGROWN TIMBER-WOLF WITH YOU TOO!
DON'T YOU SPEAK UNKINDLY ABOUT GERONIMO! HE'S A RIGHT FRIENDLY LITTLE CUSS... IF YOU DON'T STROKE HIS FUR THE WRONG WAY!
LET'S BE SOCIABLE, SPIKE! I'LL JUST TAKE THAT LITTLE BOTTLE BEHIND YOU! AIN'T BARELY ENOUGH IN IT FOR MORE THAN A SWIG OR TWO!
YOU MEAN THIS?
WHY, YOU IGNORANT OLD WHISKERED CACTUS PLANT! IF YOU HAD HALF THE EDUCATION OF AN ORPHANED TOM CAT, YOU'D KNOW THIS BOTTLE IS GEN-U-WINE NAPOLEON BRANDY! RIGHT FROM BONAPARTY'S OWN CELLAR!
YOU'LL NEVER SCRAPE UP ENOUGH DINERO IN A MONTH OF SUNDAYS TO BUY A SWIG OUT OF THIS BOTTLE! GET MOVING BEFORE I THROW YOU OUT!
HE'S A HARD-HEARTED MAN GERONIMO!
BUT THERE'S MORE THAN ONE WAY TO SKIN A BOTTLE OFF A SKINFLINT! YOU'VE GOT TO HELP ME, GERONIMO! NOW LISTEN CLOSELY...
MOMENTS LATER, IN SPIKE'S PLACE...
EEOW! MAD DOG!
IT'S THAT G!★? WOLF CUB!
DON'T GET NERVOUS SPIKE! I'M COMIN' TO SAVE YOU!
GET HIM OUTTA HERE!
I GOT HIM!

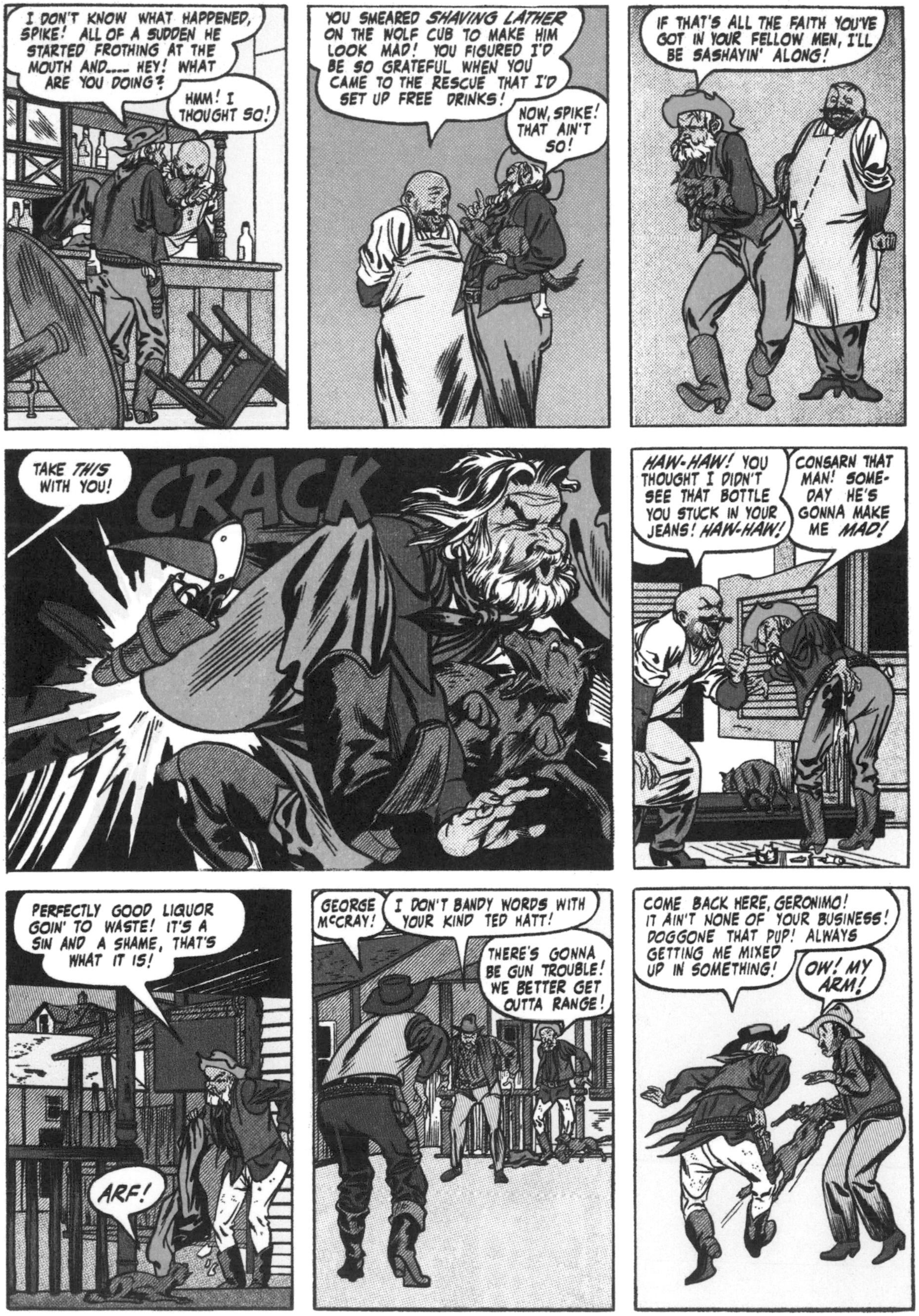
I DON'T KNOW WHAT HAPPENED, SPIKE! ALL OF A SUDDEN HE STARTED FROTHING AT THE MOUTH AND.... HEY! WHAT ARE YOU DOING?
HMM! I THOUGHT SO!
YOU SMEARED SHAVING LATHER ON THE WOLF CUB TO MAKE HIM LOOK MAD! YOU FIGURED I'D BE SO GRATEFUL WHEN YOU CAME TO THE RESCUE THAT I'D SET UP FREE DRINKS!
NOW, SPIKE! THAT AIN'T SO!
IF THAT'S ALL THE FAITH YOU'VE GOT IN YOUR FELLOW MEN, I'LL BE SASHAYIN' ALONG!
TAKE THIS WITH YOU!
CRACK
HAW-HAW! YOU THOUGHT I DIDN'T SEE THAT BOTTLE YOU STUCK IN YOUR JEANS! HAW-HAW!
CONSARN THAT MAN! SOMEDAY HE'S GONNA MAKE ME MAD!
PERFECTLY GOOD LIQUOR GOIN' TO WASTE! IT'S A SIN AND A SHAME, THAT'S WHAT IT IS!
ARF!
GEORGE McCRAY!
I DON'T BANDY WORDS WITH YOUR KIND TED HATT!
THERE'S GONNA BE GUN TROUBLE! WE BETTER GET OUTTA RANGE!
COME BACK HERE, GERONIMO! IT AIN'T NONE OF YOUR BUSINESS! DOGGONE THAT PUP! ALWAYS GETTING ME MIXED UP IN SOMETHING!
OW! MY ARM!

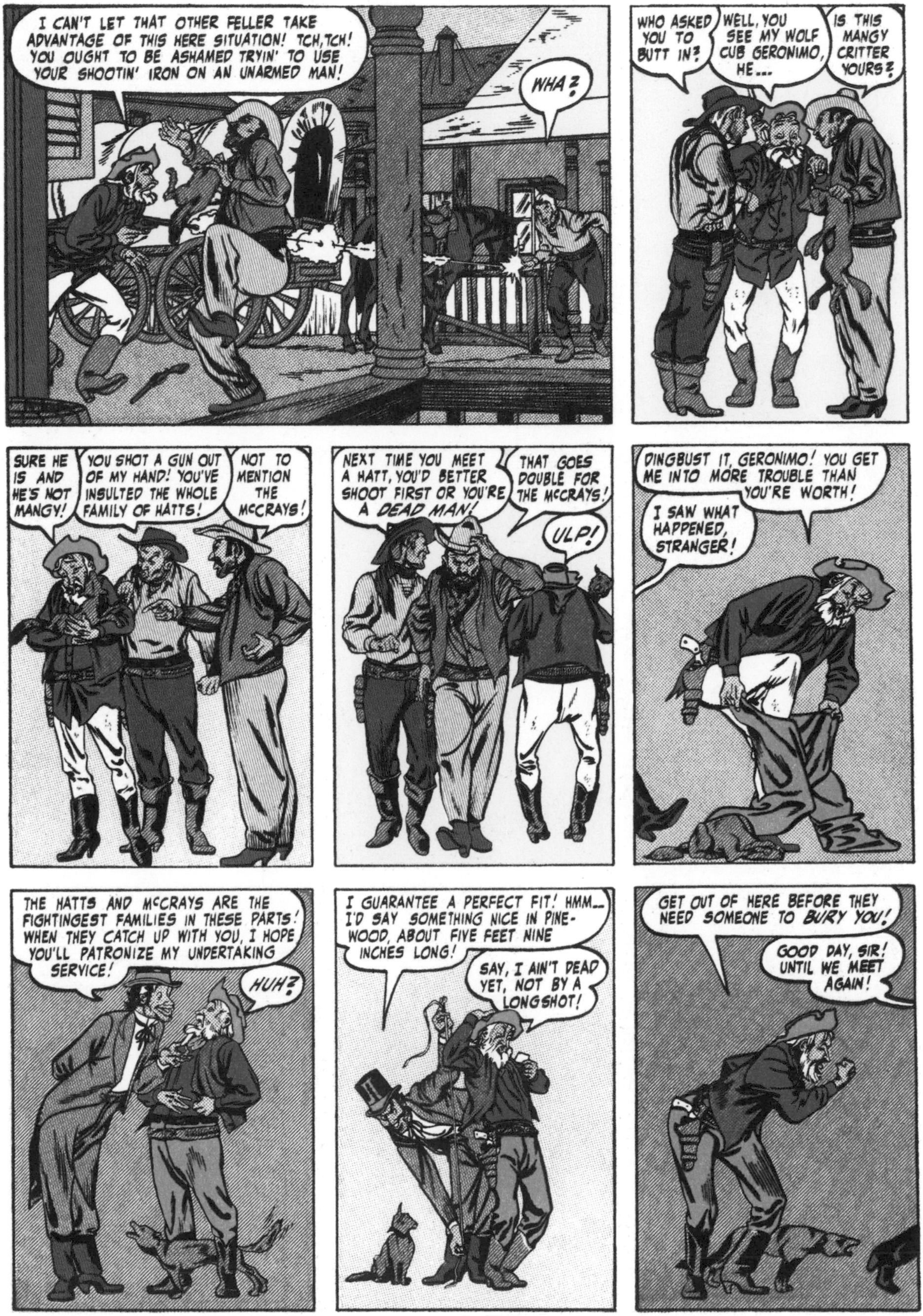

I CAN'T LET THAT OTHER FELLER TAKE ADVANTAGE OF THIS HERE SITUATION! TCH,TCH! YOU OUGHT TO BE ASHAMED TRYIN' TO USE YOUR SHOOTIN' IRON ON AN UNARMED MAN!
WHA?
WHO ASKED YOU TO BUTT IN?
WELL, YOU SEE MY WOLF CUB GERONIMO, HE...
IS THIS MANGY CRITTER YOURS?
SURE HE IS AND HE'S NOT MANGY!
YOU SHOT A GUN OUT OF MY HAND! YOU'VE INSULTED THE WHOLE FAMILY OF HATTS!
NOT TO MENTION THE McCRAYS!
NEXT TIME YOU MEET A HATT, YOU'D BETTER SHOOT FIRST OR YOU'RE A DEAD MAN!
THAT GOES DOUBLE FOR THE McCRAYS!
ULP!
DINGBUST IT, GERONIMO! YOU GET ME INTO MORE TROUBLE THAN YOU'RE WORTH!
I SAW WHAT HAPPENED, STRANGER!
THE HATTS AND McCRAYS ARE THE FIGHTINGEST FAMILIES IN THESE PARTS! WHEN THEY CATCH UP WITH YOU, I HOPE YOU'LL PATRONIZE MY UNDERTAKING SERVICE!
HUH?
I GUARANTEE A PERFECT FIT! HMM... I'D SAY SOMETHING NICE IN PINE-WOOD, ABOUT FIVE FEET NINE INCHES LONG!
SAY, I AIN'T DEAD YET, NOT BY A LONGSHOT!
GET OUT OF HERE BEFORE THEY NEED SOMEONE TO BURY YOU!
GOOD DAY, SIR! UNTIL WE MEET AGAIN!

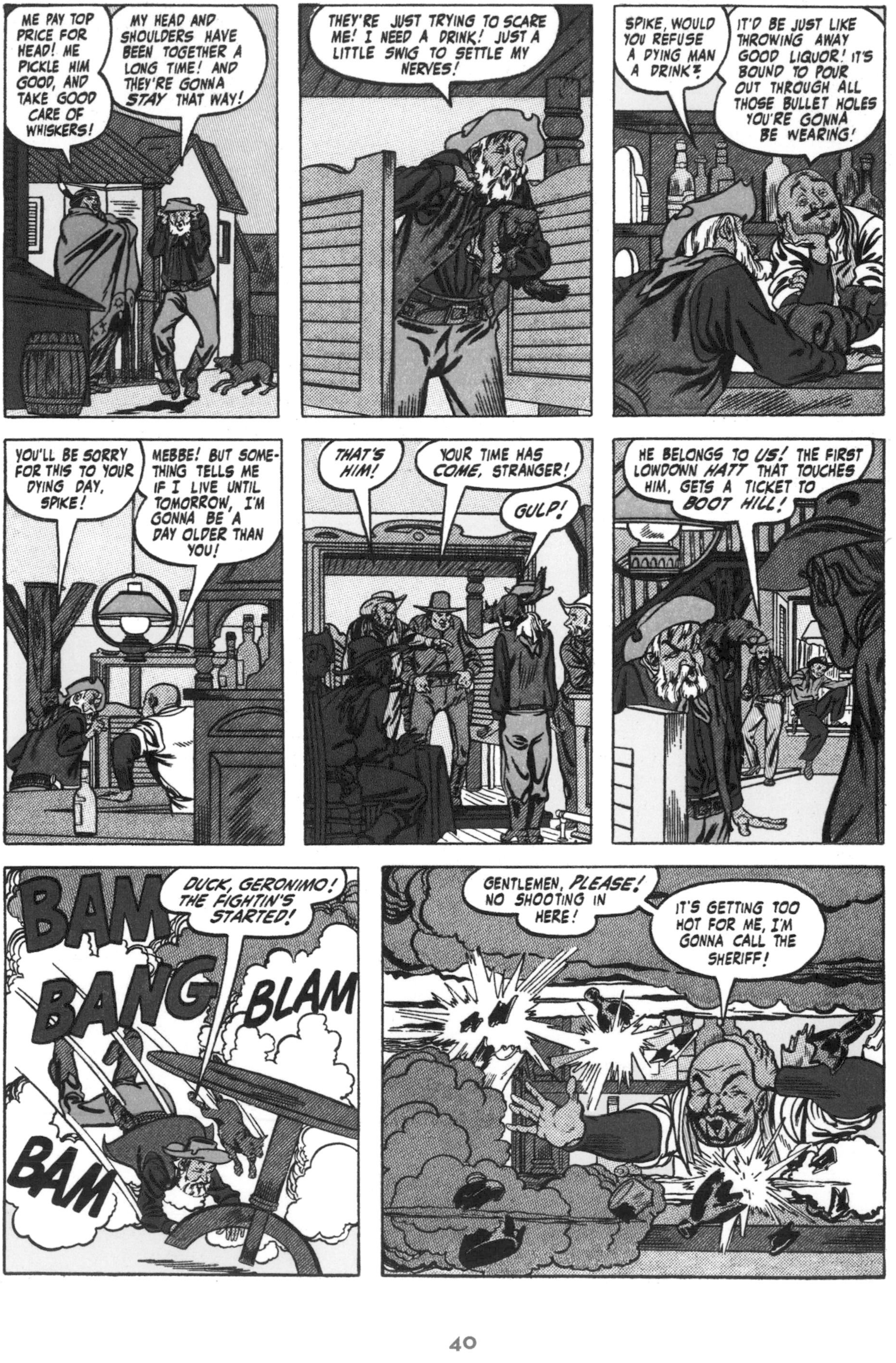

ME PAY TOP PRICE FOR HEAD! ME PICKLE HIM GOOD, AND TAKE GOOD CARE OF WHISKERS!
MY HEAD AND SHOULDERS HAVE BEEN TOGETHER A LONG TIME! AND THEY'RE GONNA STAY THAT WAY!
THEY'RE JUST TRYING TO SCARE ME! I NEED A DRINK! JUST A LITTLE SWIG TO SETTLE MY NERVES!
SPIKE, WOULD YOU REFUSE A DYING MAN A DRINK?
IT'D BE JUST LIKE THROWING AWAY GOOD LIQUOR! IT'S BOUND TO POUR OUT THROUGH ALL THOSE BULLET HOLES YOU'RE GONNA BE WEARING!
YOU'LL BE SORRY FOR THIS TO YOUR DYING DAY, SPIKE!
MEBBE! BUT SOMETHING TELLS ME IF I LIVE UNTIL TOMORROW, I'M GONNA BE A DAY OLDER THAN YOU!
THAT'S HIM!
YOUR TIME HAS COME, STRANGER!
GULP!
HE BELONGS TO US! THE FIRST LOWDOWN HATT THAT TOUCHES HIM, GETS A TICKET TO BOOT HILL!
BAM
DUCK, GERONIMO! THE FIGHTIN'S STARTED!
BANG
BLAM
BAM
GENTLEMEN, PLEASE! NO SHOOTING IN HERE!
IT'S GETTING TOO HOT FOR ME, I'M GONNA CALL THE SHERIFF!

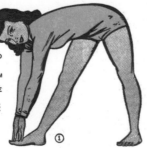

Love Diary no. 2, October 1949. "Tone Up Time," a one-pager (re-formatted here) featuring wife Natalie as model.

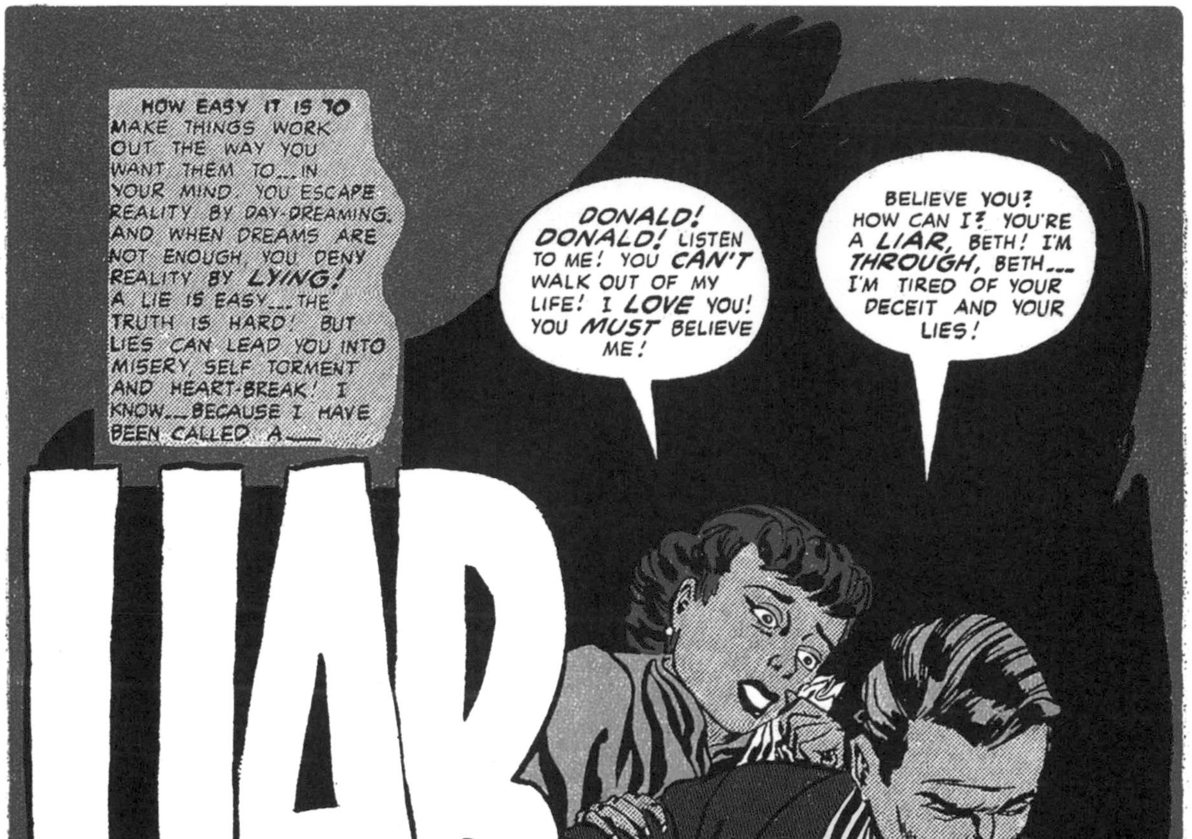
HOW EASY IT IS TO MAKE THINGS WORK OUT THE WAY YOU WANT THEM TO... IN YOUR MIND. YOU ESCAPE REALITY BY DAY-DREAMING. AND WHEN DREAMS ARE NOT ENOUGH, YOU DENY REALITY BY LYING! A LIE IS EASY... THE TRUTH IS HARD! BUT LIES CAN LEAD YOU INTO MISERY, SELF TORMENT AND HEART-BREAK! I KNOW... BECAUSE I HAVE BEEN CALLED A...
LIAR
DONALD! DONALD! LISTEN TO ME! YOU CAN'T WALK OUT OF MY LIFE! I LOVE YOU! YOU MUST BELIEVE ME!
BELIEVE YOU? HOW CAN I? YOU'RE A LIAR, BETH! I'M THROUGH, BETH... I'M TIRED OF YOUR DECEIT AND YOUR LIES!

"I REMEMBER THE FIRST LIE, I REMEMBER IT TOO WELL! IT IS STILL ETCHED IN MY BRAIN... THE FIRST, IN A GOSSAMER WEB OF UNTRUTH, THAT NEARLY MADE A NIGHTMARE OF MY LIFE..."

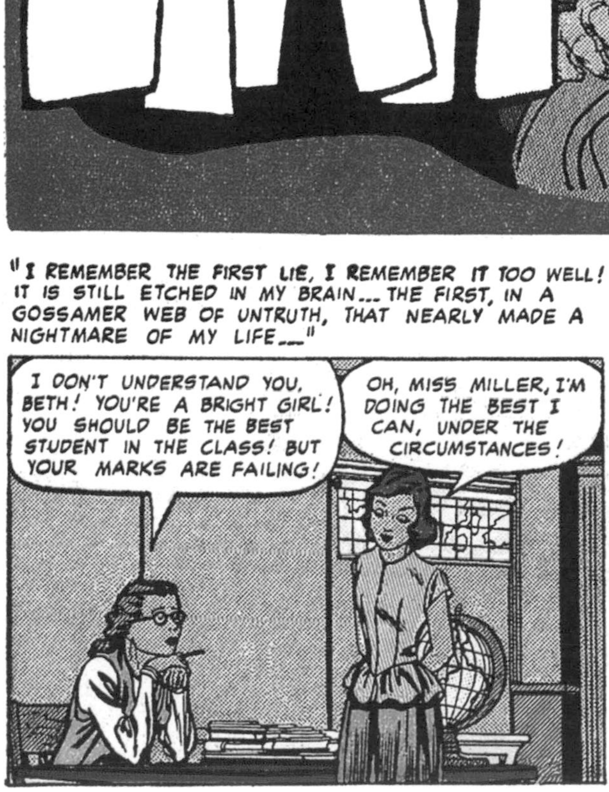
I DON'T UNDERSTAND YOU, BETH! YOU'RE A BRIGHT GIRL! YOU SHOULD BE THE BEST STUDENT IN THE CLASS! BUT YOUR MARKS ARE FAILING!
OH, MISS MILLER, I'M DOING THE BEST I CAN, UNDER THE CIRCUMSTANCES!

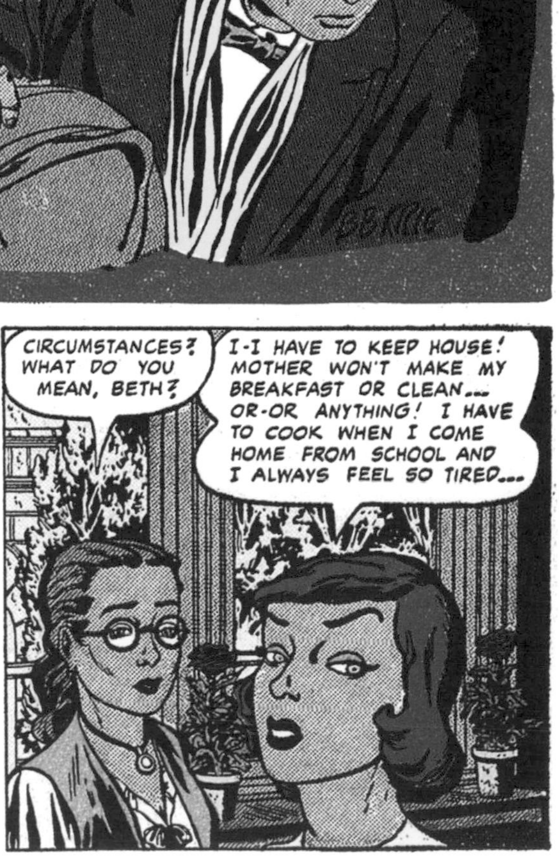
CIRCUMSTANCES? WHAT DO YOU MEAN, BETH?
I-I HAVE TO KEEP HOUSE! MOTHER WON'T MAKE MY BREAKFAST OR CLEAN... OR-OR ANYTHING! I HAVE TO COOK WHEN I COME HOME FROM SCHOOL AND I ALWAYS FEEL SO TIRED...

"IT WAS SO SIMPLE TELLING HER THAT LITTLE LIE! FROM NOW ON I WOULD KNOW HOW TO SETTLE ANY PROBLEM THAT FACED ME!"

WHY, YOU POOR CHILD! I DIDN'T KNOW! I'LL CUT DOWN ON YOUR HOMEWORK ASSIGNMENTS!

TH-THANK YOU, MISS MILLER!

"SEVERAL MONTHS LATER WE MOVED FROM THE LITTLE TOWN WHERE I WAS BORN. PERHAPS, IF WE HAD STAYED, MY LIES WOULD HAVE BEEN DISCOVERED...ONE DAY, WHEN I WAS A SENIOR IN HIGH SCHOOL..."

WHY BETH MORGAN, WHY DON'T YOU REPAIR YOUR COAT, IT'S ALL TORN AND SHABBY! I'D BE ASHAMED TO BE SEEN WEARING IT!

I'M NOT! ONCE THIS COAT WAS A VERY EXPENSIVE ONE! BUT NOW MY FATHER CAN'T AFFORD TO BUY ME ONE ALL THE TIME...

"AGAIN THE LIE SAVED ME. I HAD A BRAND NEW COAT HANGING IN THE CLOSET AT HOME, BUT I DIDN'T WANT TO WEAR IT TO SCHOOL..."

WHEN WE LIVED IN BLAIRTOWN, WE WERE RICH AND LIVED IN LUXURY! BUT DADDY HAS LOST HIS MONEY!

OH, BETH...I'M SORRY! PLEASE FORGIVE ME!

OF COURSE, SHARON, I FORGIVE YOU! HOW WOULD YOU KNOW? BUT... DON'T FEEL SORRY! WE'RE NOT ASHAMED OF BEING POOR!

I KNOW YOU'RE NOT! YOU'RE TOO FINE A PERSON TO LET POVERTY MAKE YOU ASHAMED!

"I HAD PLACED MYSELF IN A FAVORABLE LIGHT, BY USING MY NASTY WEAPON! I COULD HARDLY HIDE MY TRIUMPHANT SMILE, AS THE GIRLS FLOCKED AROUND ME, ASSURING ME OF THEIR UNDYING FRIENDSHIP..."

"WHEN I WAS GRADUATED FROM HIGH SCHOOL, I WENT TO WORK IN THE STENOGRAPHER'S POOL AT A LARGE ELECTRICAL SUPPLY FIRM. IT WAS FUN, WORKING...."

"EVERYDAY I HAD LUNCH IN THE GRILL ROOM OF THE HIGH MOUNT HOTEL! ONE MAGIC LUNCH HOUR, I MET THE MAN I HAD ALWAYS WANTED TO MEET! I DIDN'T SEE HIM UNTIL HE TOOK THE SEAT NEXT TO ME AT THE COUNTER..."

"I HAD TO MEET THIS MAN! THERE WAS SOMETHING ABOUT HIM THAT FASCINATED ME, IN A STRANGE, IRRESISTIBLE MANNER! I HAD TO KNOW HIM....BUT HOW? MY BRAIN WAS RACING AHEAD, AND THEN I KNEW.... ANOTHER LIE!"

"I GASPED AS I FUMBLED IN MY PURSE, AND LOOKED UP WITH PANICKY EYES TO SEE HIS STEADY GRAY EYES TRAINED ON ME! THERE WAS AN EXPRESSION OF CONCERN ON HIS FACE! AND THEN HE SPOKE..."

OH, DEAR... WHAT WILL I DO?

IS THERE SOMETHING WRONG, MISS?

THIS IS SO STUPID! MY COIN PURSE IS MISSING... I-I DON'T KNOW WHAT...

WELL, DON'T WORRY ABOUT IT! THOSE THINGS WILL HAPPEN! I'LL TAKE CARE OF IT!

NO, REALLY, I COULDN'T LET YOU PAY FOR MY LUNCH!

I'M DONALD PETERS, THE NEW MANAGER OF THE HIGH MOUNT! WE'LL CHARGE OFF YOUR LUNCH TO GOODWILL! MISS...

"DONALD PETERS HAD COME INTO MY LIFE, BROUGHT THERE BY A LIE! HE WALKED ME TO THE DOOR, AND I COULD FEEL MY HEART BEAT A HAPPY TATTOO WITH EVERY STEP WE TOOK..."

I'M BETH MORGAN, MR. PETERS! I'M WITH THE MASON ELECTRICAL SUPPLY COMPANY DOWN THE STREET!

SWELL! THEN WE'LL SEE EACH OTHER AGAIN, MISS MORGAN! HOPE YOU ENJOYED YOUR LUNCH!

"I MET DONALD SEVERAL TIMES AFTER THAT, AS IF BY SOME STRANGE COINCIDENCE, WHEN HE WAS ON HIS OWN LUNCH HOUR! ACTUALLY, IT WAS NO COINCIDENCE. I HAD FOUND OUT WHAT TIME HE HAD LUNCH AND HAD RE-ARRANGED MY SCHEDULE TO MEET HIS..."

BETH! OVER HERE! I'VE BEEN WAITING FOR YOU!

HAVE YOU, DONALD? THAT'S NICE! I WAS HOPING TO MEET YOU THIS AFTERNOON!

"HE LED ME TO A SMALL TABLE IN A SECLUDED CORNER OF THE MAIN DINING ROOM! AND IT WAS HERE THAT I TOLD HIM THE SECOND LIE..."

I THOUGHT WE'D LUNCH HERE SO YOU WOULDN'T BE LATE GETTING BACK TO WORK! A HALF-HOUR IS SUCH A SHORT TIME!

OH, BUT I HAVE A FULL HOUR!

YOU SEE, I'M PRIVATE SECRETARY TO MISTER MASON, OWNER OF THE FIRM! THAT'S WHY I HAVE AN HOUR FOR LUNCH!

THAT'S WONDERFUL! SO YOU'RE SMART AND SUCCESSFUL, AS WELL AS PRETTY!

THERE WAS SOMETHING I WANTED TO ASK YOU, BETH, I MAY AS WELL GET IT OFF MY CHEST! ARE YOU FREE SATURDAY NIGHT?

THAT DEPENDS! WHY?

I WONDERED IF YOU WOULD GO OUT WITH ME, BETH? WE CAN DINE AND DANCE RIGHT HERE!

OH, I HAVE A DATE, DON!

"A DATE WITH DONALD! THIS WAS WHAT I HAD BEEN WAITING FOR! OF COURSE I HAD NO OTHER DATE! BUT IF I ADDED THAT LITTLE LIE, IT WOULD MAKE ME ALL THE MORE DESIRABLE TO DON, I REASONED...."

BUT IT'S NOTHING SPECIAL... I'LL BREAK IT, DON! YES, I'LL SEE YOU SATURDAY NIGHT!

"IT SEEMED AN ETERNITY BEFORE SATURDAY... AND EIGHT O'CLOCK SEEMED TO COME ON LEAD-WEIGHTED MINUTES! BUT AT LAST THE DAY AND HOUR ARRIVED! I RUSHED DOWNSTAIRS AS SOON AS I HEARD THE DOORBELL...."

"I HAD TO HURRY DONALD OUT OF THE HOUSE BECAUSE MOTHER AND DAD, BEGAN TALKING AND ASKING QUESTIONS IN THEIR FRIENDLY, NEIGHBORLY WAY! THEY KNEW NO SUBTERFUGES... THEY HAD NOTHING TO HIDE!"

GOSH, I FORGOT ABOUT MOTHER! SHE MIGHT TELL HIM I'M ONLY A TYPIST AND NOT MR MASON'S SECRETARY!

YES! AND THEY'RE JUST AS NICE AS I THOUGHT THEY'D BE!

HELLO, DON! I SEE YOU'VE MET MOTHER AND DAD!

DO YOU WORK WITH BETH, MR. PETERS?

NO, MRS. MORGAN! I MANAGE THE HIGH MOUNT HOTEL! BETH AND I MET WHEN SHE WAS ON HER LUNCH HOUR! SINCE THEN WE'VE SPENT A PLEASANT HOUR EVERY DAY HAVING LUNCH TOGETHER!

A WHOLE HOUR! IS THAT A NEW POLICY AT THE FIRM, BETH?

WHY, NO, DAD! WE'VE ALWAYS HAD AN HOUR!

BUT I REMEMBER YOU AND THE OTHER GIRLS COMPLAINED ABOUT ONLY HAVING HALF AN HOUR!

OH, ROGER! WHAT'S THE DIFFERENCE? CAN'T YOU SEE THEY WANT TO GO?

YOUR FOLKS ARE WONDERFUL, BETH! SO WARM AND FRIENDLY! THEY MAKE A FELLOW FEEL AT HOME!

YES, THEY ARE SWEET-HEARTS, ALL RIGHT! BUT POOR DAD...HE... BUT, OH, WHY TALK ABOUT IT?

"I WAS AFRAID DON WOULD TRAP ME IN THE LIE ABOUT BEING A SECRETARY BECAUSE OF WHAT DAD SAID! TO PROTECT MYSELF, I MADE DON DOUBT DAD'S CREDIBILITY...."

PLEASE, BETH, IS SOMETHING WRONG? I'D LIKE TO HELP IF I CAN!

HELP? THERE'S VERY VERY LITTLE ANYONE CAN DO! DAD DRINKS HEAVILY! HIS MIND WANDERS A LITTLE SOMETIMES! LIKE THE WAY HE ARGUED ABOUT MY LUNCH HOUR!

LUNCH HOUR? I WASN'T EVEN LISTENING! BUT THAT'S TOO BAD ABOUT YOUR FATHER! IT MUST'VE BEEN HARD ON YOUR MOTHER AND YOU!

"I HAD TOLD A USELESS LIE, AND BLACKENED DAD'S NAME! BUT NOW I WAS FORCED TO PLAY IT TO THE HILT...."

IT HASN'T BEEN EASY! AND SINCE I'VE BEEN WORKING, THE ENTIRE BURDEN HAS BEEN MINE! BUT....PLEASE, DON, DON'T LET ON TO DAD THAT YOU KNOW!

TONIGHT YOU'RE GOING TO FORGET YOUR CARES! WE'LL DANCE AND HAVE FUN.... AND YOU CAN TRUST ME, BETH!

THANK YOU, DON! I'M SO GLAD TO BE GOING OUT WITH YOU! I CAN HARDLY EVER GET A CHANCE TO RELAX, DUE TO ALL THIS!

"THAT EVENING DON AND I DANCED, AND THE PRESSURE OF HIS ARMS AROUND ME MADE MY HEART POUND WITH EXCITEMENT. AND THEN, A SINGLE CLOUD IN THE PERSON OF MARGO RAYMOND DARKENED MY SUNSHINE...."

HI, DON....TAKING A BUSMAN'S HOLIDAY?

RIGHT! COME OVER TO OUR TABLE AND BRING YOUR ESCORT!

"I SAW IN MARGO RAYMOND A RIVAL FOR DON....AND ALONG-SIDE HER, I FELT LIKE A WILTED ROSE....HOW COULD I EVER HOPE TO WIN OUT OVER THIS GLAMOROUS CREATURE....?"

BETH MORGAN, MEET MARGO RAYMOND, OUR STAR GUEST, AND HER ESCORT IS MAL HARRIS!

I'M SO GLAD TO MEET YOU BOTH! WON'T YOU SIT DOWN?

NO! I'D RATHER DANCE WITH DON! MAL, YOU TALK TO BETH!

WHAT'S WRONG, BETH? ARE YOU AFRAID MARGO WILL TAKE YOUR BOY FRIEND?

WHY....THE VERY IDEA! I THOUGHT NO SUCH THING!

IF LOOKS COULD KILL, MARGO WOULD BE DEADER THAN A DOOR-NAIL! MARGO'S A MAN-KILLER! AND WHEN SHE GOES AFTER HER MAN, SHE *NEVER* MISSES!

REALLY, MR. HARRIS, YOU HAVE NO RIGHT TO...

MAYBE I SHOULD MIND MY OWN BUSINESS! BUT I KNOW MARGO FOR YEARS! REMEMBER KID, I WARNED YOU! SHE'S AFTER DON PETERS, I KNOW THE SIGNS!

MR HARRIS, YOU'RE VERY CRUDE!

WHAT'S CRUDE ABOUT FACING FACTS, HONEY? I'M A HARD GUY! I SEE THINGS AS THEY ARE! I DON'T DREAM BECAUSE I FACE REALITY! AND *I DON'T LIE* TO MAKE LIFE FIT THE PATTERN I'VE CUT OUT!

I AM NOT INTERESTED IN ANYTHING YOU HAVE TO SAY, MR. HARRIS!

"BUT EVERYTHING MAL HARRIS SAID PENETRATED MY BRAIN! MARGO WAS A THREAT I HAD TO OVERCOME, WITH THE WEAPON I ALWAYS USED...THE LIE!"

DON IS SUCH A WONDERFUL DANCER! DON'T YOU THINK SO, BETH?

YES, YES, HE IS! DON...I·I HAVE A HEADACHE. WILL YOU TAKE ME HOME, PLEASE?

OH, THAT'S TOO BAD! CAN'T I GET YOU SOMETHING FOR IT?

THE HEADACHE CAME ON WHILE I WAS TALKING TO HER! YOU'D BETTER TAKE HER HOME!

WHAT A SHAME! JUST WHEN WE WERE HAVING SO MUCH FUN!

"IN THE CAR... I LOUNGED BACK AGAINST THE CUSHIONS, CONTENT THAT DON WAS ALONE WITH ME..."

HOW ARE YOU FEELING, BETH?

MUCH BETTER! I GUESS I NEEDED SOME FRESH AIR!

MARGO IS A BEAUTY, DON! WHO IS SHE?

THE SISTER OF MY ARMY BUDDY! MAL HARRIS IS IN LOVE WITH HER, BUT SHE'LL HAVE NO PART OF HIM! HE DIGS OIL WELLS ALL OVER THE WORLD!

"THEN, DON STOPPED THE CAR! HE LEANED TOWARDS ME, HIS FACE TENSE... HIS EYES BURNING INTO MINE..."

BETH, THERE'S SOMETHING I'VE WANTED TO TELL YOU SINCE THE FIRST MOMENT I SAW YOU! I LOVE YOU BETH... WILL YOU MARRY ME?

MARRY YOU? OH, DON, YES... I'VE HOPED AND DREAMED FOR THIS MOMENT! OH, MY DARLING!

"HIS ARMS ENCIRCLED ME, AND I COULD FEEL HIS WARM, VIBRANT LIPS PRESSED AGAINST MINE. DON WAS THE MAN I LOVED! THIS WAS THE MOMENT I HAD ALWAYS LIVED FOR..."

"I SNUGGLED DOWN INTO THE SAFETY OF HIS ARMS! BUT THEN HE SAID SOMETHING THAT MADE A WILD SHUDDER OF ALARM RUN THROUGH ME..."

DARLING, THERE'S NO NEED FOR YOU TO WORRY ABOUT YOUR DAD! I'LL HAVE A TALK WITH HIM, AND PERHAPS HE'LL AGREE TO MEDICAL TREATMENT!

NO! Y-YOU MUST NOT, DON! HE'LL RESENT IT!

"AT LAST, THE LIE THAT WAS SUPPOSED TO SMOOTH THINGS OUT, BOOMERANGED...HURTLING STRAIGHT BACK AT ME..."

TAKE IT EASY, HONEY! YOUR DAD ISN'T A BAD SORT! HE'S WEAK! I'LL TALK TO HIM!

OH, DON, YOU MUSN'T! YOU CAN'T! YOU'LL RUIN EVERYTHING!

"NOT KNOWING WHAT ELSE TO DO, I STARTED TO CRY..."

BETH, BETH, IF IT MAKES YOU FEEL THAT BAD, I WON'T MENTION IT TO HIM! NOW DRY YOUR TEARS AND I'LL TAKE YOU HOME!

TH-THANK YOU, DON!

"WHEN WE ARRIVED HOME, I KNEW SOMETHING WAS WRONG! THE LIGHTS WERE ALL ON, AND MOTHER WAS ON THE PORCH."

SOMETHING HAPPENED! MOTHER! *MOTHER!*

BETH! I'M SO GLAD YOU'RE HOME! IT'S YOUR FATHER! HE LEFT THE HOUSE AT NINE FOR A WALK, AND HE ISN'T HOME YET!

WE'LL FIND HIM, MRS. MORGAN, AND DON'T WORRY! THIS WILL BE THE LAST TIME IT WILL EVER HAPPEN!

COME ON, DON! THERE'S NO TIME TO LOSE! WE'LL CALL YOU, MOM!

THE LAST TIME? I DON'T...

WHERE ARE HIS FAVORITE PLACES? WE'LL PROBABLY FIND HIM IN ONE OF THEM!

NO! LET'S GO TO THE POLICE STATION! I KNOW HE'S HAD AN ACCIDENT! HE WOULD NEVER WORRY US!

"WE FOUND DAD AT THE POLICE STATION..."

YEAH, MAYBE THAT'S HIM! WE FOUND HIM IN AN ALLEY SLEEPING OFF A DRUNK!

WE'LL TAKE HIM HOME!

NO! GET A DOCTOR!

"I SUDDENLY REALIZED WHERE THIS WELTER OF LIES HAD BROUGHT ME! DAD, PROBABLY HURT, WAS MISTAKEN FOR A DRUNKARD, WHILE I HID BEHIND A FANTASY TO GET EVERYTHING I WANTED AT THE EXPENSE OF OTHERS!"

DAD NEVER TOUCHED A DROP IN HIS LIFE! PLEASE! PLEASE GET A DOCTOR!

BETH! BUT YOU SAID....

OKAY, LADY! IF YOU WANT AN AMBULANCE, I'LL HAVE TO CALL ONE!

BETH, WHAT IS THE MEANING OF THIS? WHY DID YOU TELL A LIE ABOUT YOUR FATHER?

BECAUSE I'M A.... A LIAR! I WANTED TO WIN YOUR SYMPATHY. I'M NOT A PRIVATE SECRETARY! I'M A TYPIST! AND THAT FIRST DAY I MET YOU I DID HAVE MONEY FOR MY LUNCH!

"I HAD SAID IT! AT LAST I FACED THE FACT THAT I WAS A LIAR!"

BETH! WHY COULDN'T YOU BE HONEST WITH ME?

HOW COULD I BE HONEST WITH ANY-ONE, WHEN I WAS NEVER HONEST WITH MYSELF!

"SOON THE AMBULANCE ARRIVED AND I WAITED BREATHLESSLY FOR THE DOCTOR TO COMPLETE HIS EXAMINATION OF DAD...."

YOUR FATHER IS SUFFERING FROM SHOCK! HE MUST HAVE BEEN STRUCK BY A HIT AND RUN DRIVER! DON'T WORRY, MISS, A FEW DAYS OF REST WILL FIX HIM UP!

OH, THANK YOU, DOCTOR!

"WITHOUT ANOTHER WORD, I TURNED AND WALKED OUT INTO THE STREET! AWAY FROM DON, AND INTO THE MISERY I HAD MADE MORE MYSELF...."

WAIT, BETH! I WANT TO SPEAK TO YOU!

THERE ISN'T MUCH TO SAY, IS THERE?

THERE'S LOTS TO SAY, BETH! YOU'VE LEARNED HOW TERRIBLE A LIE CAN BE! YOU SEE, DARLING, THE TRUTH IS REAL! THIS IS THE TRUTH.... I LOVE YOU BETH!

OH, DON...

"AND FOR THE FIRST TIME IN MY LIFE I FELT STRONG AND SECURE! NOW I WAS READY TO FACE THE BATTLES THAT LAY AHEAD! I WAS ARMED WITH TRUTH AND LOVE, NOT WITH THE PUNY WEAPONS OF DECEIT AND FALSEHOOD! I WAS READY TO LIVE IN THE PRESENT, NOT IN THE FANTASTIC WORLD OF THE LIAR!"

MAGICIAN of MURDER CREEK

IT ALL BEGINS ONE DAY WHEN NUGGETS NUGENT RIDES INTO THE TOWN OF MURDER CREEK!

YIPPEE! I STRUCK IT RICH!

BB KPG

WHAT HAPPENED, NUGGETS? YOU HIT PAY DIRT?

SURE AS SHOOTIN'! JUST STAYED LONG ENOUGH TO DIG ME OUT ENOUGH FOR TWO SACKS FULL AND THEN HIGH-TAILED IT FOR TOWN TO ENJOY MY WEALTH WHILE I'M YOUNG!

PARADISE SALOON

YES, SIREEE! I'M GOLD DUST HAPPY AND GOT A MIND TO SPEND IT!

YOU SURE CAME TO THE RIGHT PLACE, NUGGETS, OLD PAL! COME IN!

I'VE FIXED UP THE PLACE SINCE YOU WERE HERE LAST! A REAL STAGE SHOW, WITH DANCERS AND EVERYTHING! WHAT'LL YOU HAVE TO DRINK?

CAN'T TOUCH THE STUFF, JIM!

DON'T TELL ME YOU'RE ON THE WAGON?

SORROWFUL BUT TRUE, JIM! I HAD A MIGHTY STRANGE EXPERIENCE WITH WILD BILL PECOS DOWN UTAH WAY! I'LL TELL YOU ALL ABOUT IT SOMETIME.

SUDDENLY A LOUD CHORD ON THE PIANO ANNOUNCES---

MARVO! THE GREATEST MAGICIAN IN THE WEST!

BEHOLD! LET ME GIVE PROOF OF MY POWERS!

HAW-HAW! THAT AIN'T NO GREAT SHAKES! I SAW A FELLA PULL A RABBIT OUT OF HIS HEAD ONE TIME IN DODGE CITY! AND HE WASN'T EVEN A MAGICIAN!

YOU ARE SKEPTICAL, SIR? PERHAPS YOU WOULD ENJOY A MORE CONVINCING DEMONSTRATION?

I SURE WOULD! WHAT'RE YOU PLANNING TO DO? PULL OUT AN AMERICAN FLAG? I SAW THE FELLA DO THAT TRICK TOO!

AH! AN EXPERT ON THE SUBJECT! EXACTLY THE TYPE I NEED TO DISPLAY MY PROWESS! LET HIM COME UP!

YOU'LL HAVE TO DO PLENTY TO IMPRESS ME, MISTER! I'VE BEEN AROUND.... AND I'M ONTO YOUR ORNERY TRICKS!

WATCH ME CLOSELY, SIR! THEY SAY THE HAND IS QUICKER THAN THE EYE! IN ONE MOMENT THESE CARDS WILL DISAPPEAR!

IF THEY DO, I CAN TELL YOU WHERE THEY WENT!

VERY WELL, SIR! TELL ME IN WHICH HAND I'VE HIDDEN THE CARDS!

DOGGONE! I MUST'VE TOOK MY EYES OFF YOU FOR A SECOND! I DON'T EXACTLY KNOW AS I COULD TELL YOU!

POP

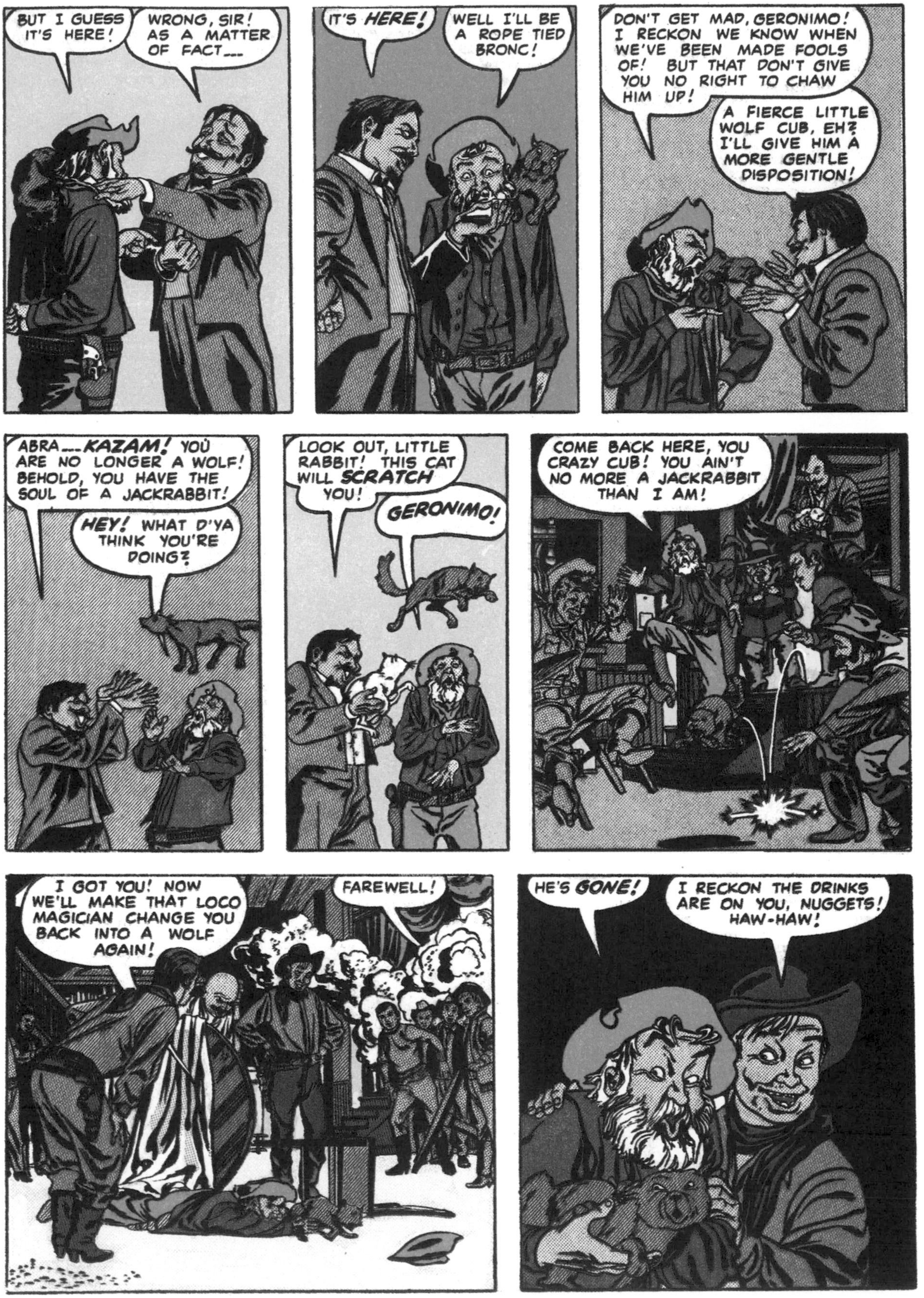
BUT I GUESS IT'S HERE!
WRONG, SIR! AS A MATTER OF FACT...
IT'S HERE!
WELL I'LL BE A ROPE TIED BRONC!
DON'T GET MAD, GERONIMO! I RECKON WE KNOW WHEN WE'VE BEEN MADE FOOLS OF! BUT THAT DON'T GIVE YOU NO RIGHT TO CHAW HIM UP!
A FIERCE LITTLE WOLF CUB, EH? I'LL GIVE HIM A MORE GENTLE DISPOSITION!
ABRA...KAZAM! YOU ARE NO LONGER A WOLF! BEHOLD, YOU HAVE THE SOUL OF A JACKRABBIT!
HEY! WHAT D'YA THINK YOU'RE DOING?
LOOK OUT, LITTLE RABBIT! THIS CAT WILL SCRATCH YOU!
GERONIMO!
COME BACK HERE, YOU CRAZY CUB! YOU AIN'T NO MORE A JACKRABBIT THAN I AM!
I GOT YOU! NOW WE'LL MAKE THAT LOCO MAGICIAN CHANGE YOU BACK INTO A WOLF AGAIN!
FAREWELL!
HE'S GONE!
I RECKON THE DRINKS ARE ON YOU, NUGGETS! HAW-HAW!

DADBLAME IT! I DON'T MIND BUYING THE DRINKS! BUT I SURE WISH THAT MARVO HOMBRE STAYED AROUND LONG ENOUGH TO FIX UP POOR LITTLE GERONIMO HERE!

JUST A MINUTE, YOU OLD SCALAWAG! I THOUGHT THESE SACKS WEIGHED DIFFERENT! THIS IS NOTHING BUT....SAND!

SOME VARMINT SWIPED MY GOLD DUST!

I RECKON I KNOW WHO THE LOW DOWN CROOK IS THAT DID IT! I'M GONNA FIND OUT HOW GOOD MARVO IS AT DUCKIN' LEAD!

WAIT!

THAT GUN CRAZY COOT IS GONNA KILL MARVO! STOP HIM, SOMEBODY! OR HE'LL END UP STRETCHING HIS WHISKERS ON A ROPE!

NOT FAR AWAY, IN MARVO'S HOTEL ROOM....

NOT A BAD HAUL! WE DID PRETTY WELL IN THIS TOWN, EH DWARF?

VERY GOOD, MASTER! BUT WE'D BETTER LEAVE QUICKLY! SOME OF THE MEN WE ROBBED WILL BEGIN TO SUSPECT WHAT HAPPENED!

THESE STUPID COWPOKES HAVEN'T GOT THE BRAINS OF A HALF-WIT MONKEY! THEY WON'T SUSPECT ME UNTIL I'M SAFELY OUT OF TOWN! MEANWHILE I HAPPEN TO KNOW THERE'S A TIDY BUNDLE OF CASH IN THE SAFE AT THE PARADISE SALOON! I'LL PICK THAT UP BEFORE I MAKE TRACKS!

I RECKON YOU'RE WRONG ABOUT THAT, MARVO! YOU'RE MAKIN' TRACKS TO THE NEAREST SHERIFF'S OFFICE!

AH! THEN YOU'VE DISCOVERED MY LITTLE STRATAGEM! IT WAS ALMOST CHILDISHLY SIMPLE TO SUBSTITUTE SAND FOR THOSE GOLD SACKS! YOU WERE SUCH A GULLIBLE VICTIM!

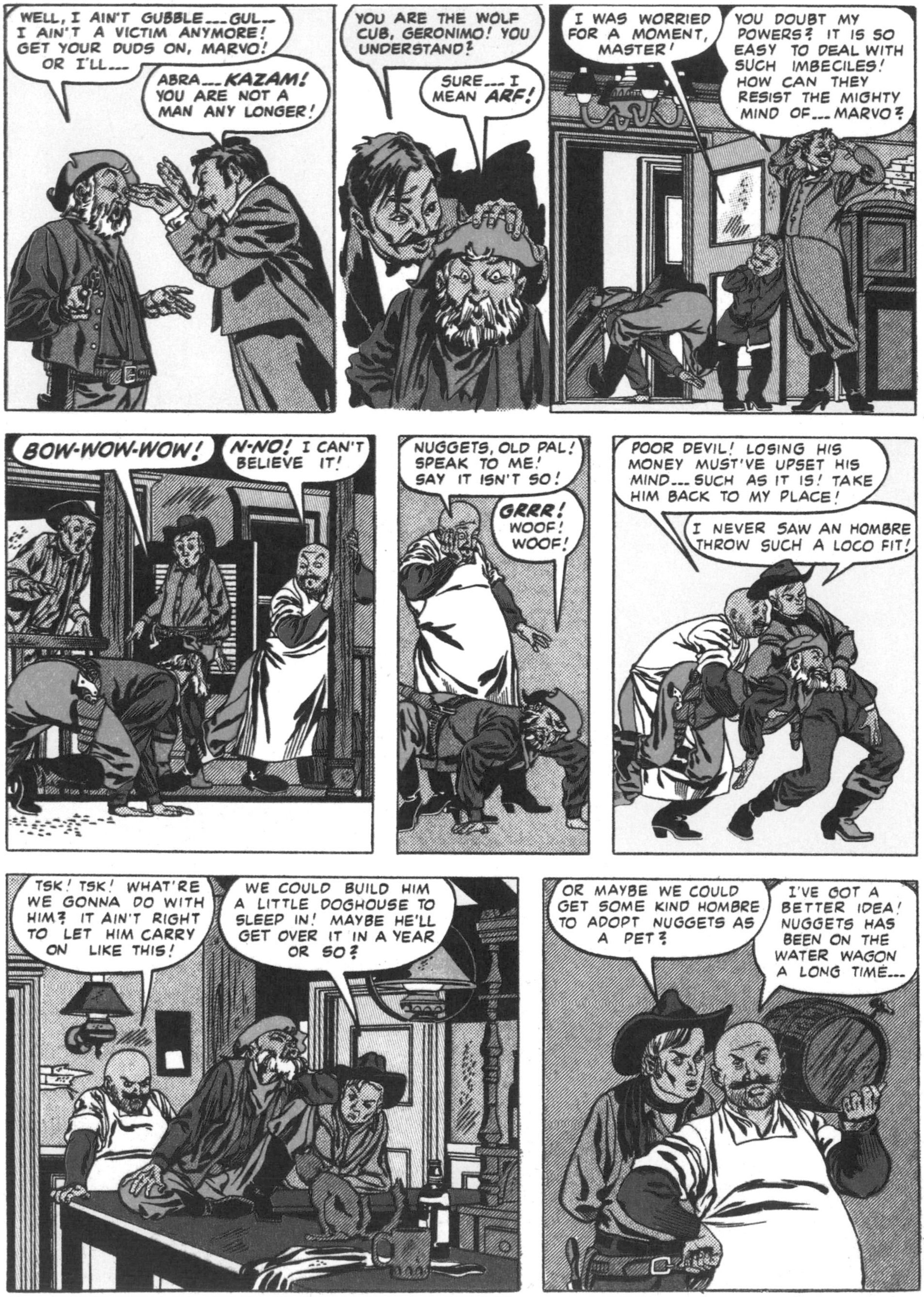

WELL, I AIN'T GUBBLE---GUL-- I AIN'T A VICTIM ANYMORE! GET YOUR DUDS ON, MARVO! OR I'LL---
ABRA---KAZAM! YOU ARE NOT A MAN ANY LONGER!
YOU ARE THE WOLF CUB, GERONIMO! YOU UNDERSTAND?
SURE--- I MEAN ARF!
I WAS WORRIED FOR A MOMENT, MASTER!
YOU DOUBT MY POWERS? IT IS SO EASY TO DEAL WITH SUCH IMBECILES! HOW CAN THEY RESIST THE MIGHTY MIND OF--- MARVO?
BOW-WOW-WOW!
N-NO! I CAN'T BELIEVE IT!
NUGGETS, OLD PAL! SPEAK TO ME! SAY IT ISN'T SO!
GRRR! WOOF! WOOF!
POOR DEVIL! LOSING HIS MONEY MUST'VE UPSET HIS MIND--- SUCH AS IT IS! TAKE HIM BACK TO MY PLACE!
I NEVER SAW AN HOMBRE THROW SUCH A LOCO FIT!
TSK! TSK! WHAT'RE WE GONNA DO WITH HIM? IT AIN'T RIGHT TO LET HIM CARRY ON LIKE THIS!
WE COULD BUILD HIM A LITTLE DOGHOUSE TO SLEEP IN! MAYBE HE'LL GET OVER IT IN A YEAR OR SO?
OR MAYBE WE COULD GET SOME KIND HOMBRE TO ADOPT NUGGETS AS A PET?
I'VE GOT A BETTER IDEA! NUGGETS HAS BEEN ON THE WATER WAGON A LONG TIME---

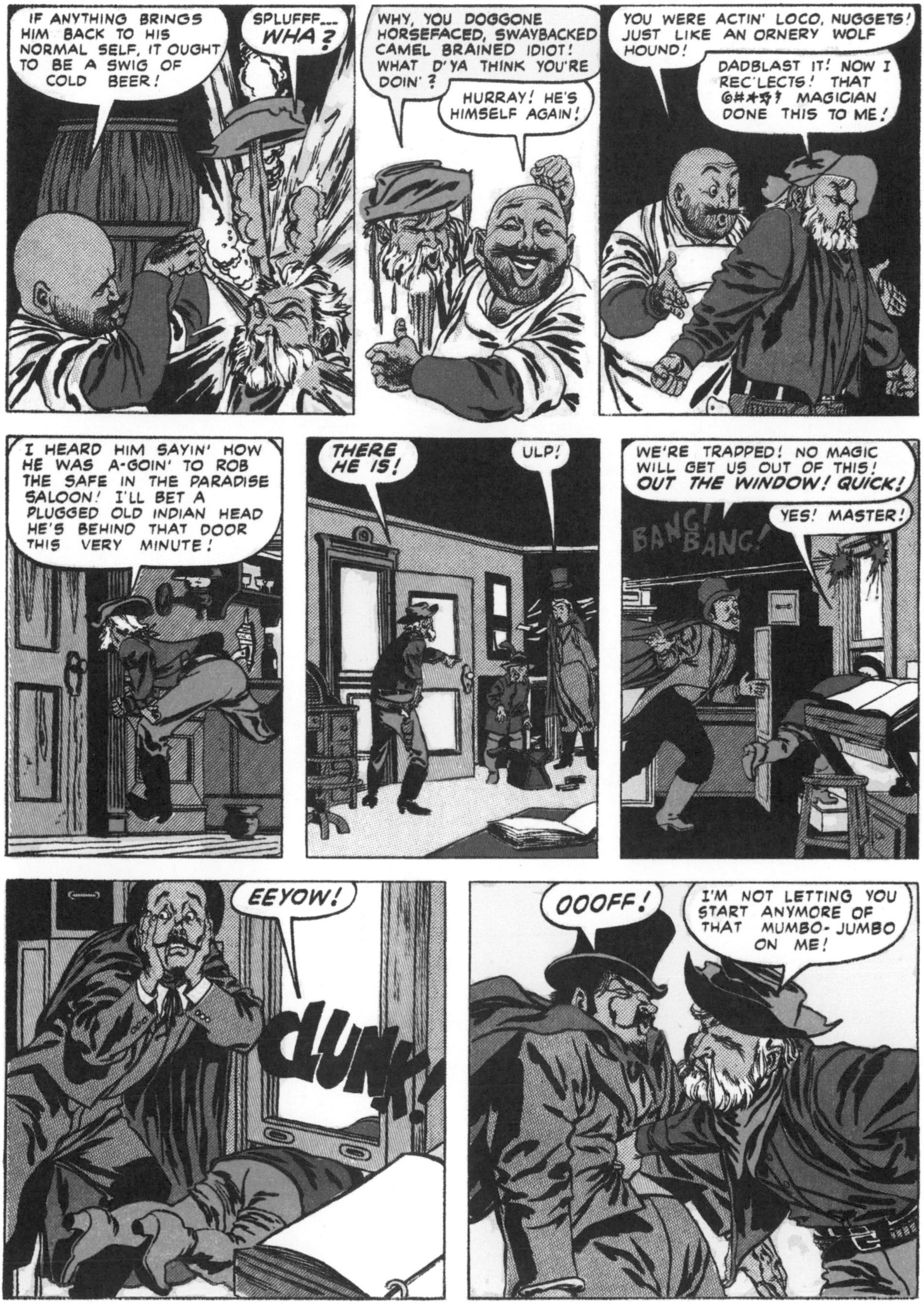
IF ANYTHING BRINGS HIM BACK TO HIS NORMAL SELF, IT OUGHT TO BE A SWIG OF COLD BEER!
SPLUFFF... WHA?
WHY, YOU DOGGONE HORSEFACED, SWAYBACKED CAMEL BRAINED IDIOT! WHAT D'YA THINK YOU'RE DOIN'?
HURRAY! HE'S HIMSELF AGAIN!
YOU WERE ACTIN' LOCO, NUGGETS! JUST LIKE AN ORNERY WOLF HOUND!
DADBLAST IT! NOW I REC'LECTS! THAT @#*%! MAGICIAN DONE THIS TO ME!
I HEARD HIM SAYIN' HOW HE WAS A-GOIN' TO ROB THE SAFE IN THE PARADISE SALOON! I'LL BET A PLUGGED OLD INDIAN HEAD HE'S BEHIND THAT DOOR THIS VERY MINUTE!
THERE HE IS!
ULP!
WE'RE TRAPPED! NO MAGIC WILL GET US OUT OF THIS! OUT THE WINDOW! QUICK!
BANG! BANG!
YES! MASTER!
EEYOW!
CLUNK!
OOOFF!
I'M NOT LETTING YOU START ANYMORE OF THAT MUMBO-JUMBO ON ME!

HOW DO YOU LIKE MY SPECIAL BRAND OF BARE KNUCKLE MAGIC?

OOHHH!

THIS HUMAN COYOTE USED HIS MAGIC JUST TO PULL THE WOOL OVER OUR EYES! HIS REAL TRADE WAS *STEALING...* AND YOU CAN TAKE A LOOK AT HOW GOOD HE WAS!

MY *WATCH!* WHY, THE DIRTY, LOW DOWN SNAKE!

WE OWE YOU A LOT, NUGGETS! THE SHERIFF WILL TAKE CARE OF THOSE TWO VARMINTS!

TELL HIM NOT TO LOOK TOO CLOSE IN THAT MAGICIAN'S EYES! OR THE SHERIFF'LL WIND UP THINKING HE'S A CACTUS PLANT!

LATER... I'M GLAD TO SEE YOU'RE OFF THE WAGON AGAIN, NUGGETS! JUST DIDN'T SEEM NORMAL FOR YOU TO BE DRINKING PLAIN WATER!

I AIN'T GOT NOTHIN' AGAINST WATER, JIM! IT'S FINE STUFF FOR ANY RANNIE WHO'S DIRTY AND NEEDS A *BATH!* BUT AN OLD HELLION LIKE ME NEEDS SOMETHIN' WITH A MITE MORE *KICK* TO IT!

YES, SIREEE! SEEMS TO ME THAT MOST EVERYTHING IS BACK TO NORMAL AGAIN! *GET HIM GERONIMO!*

ONE WAY Street

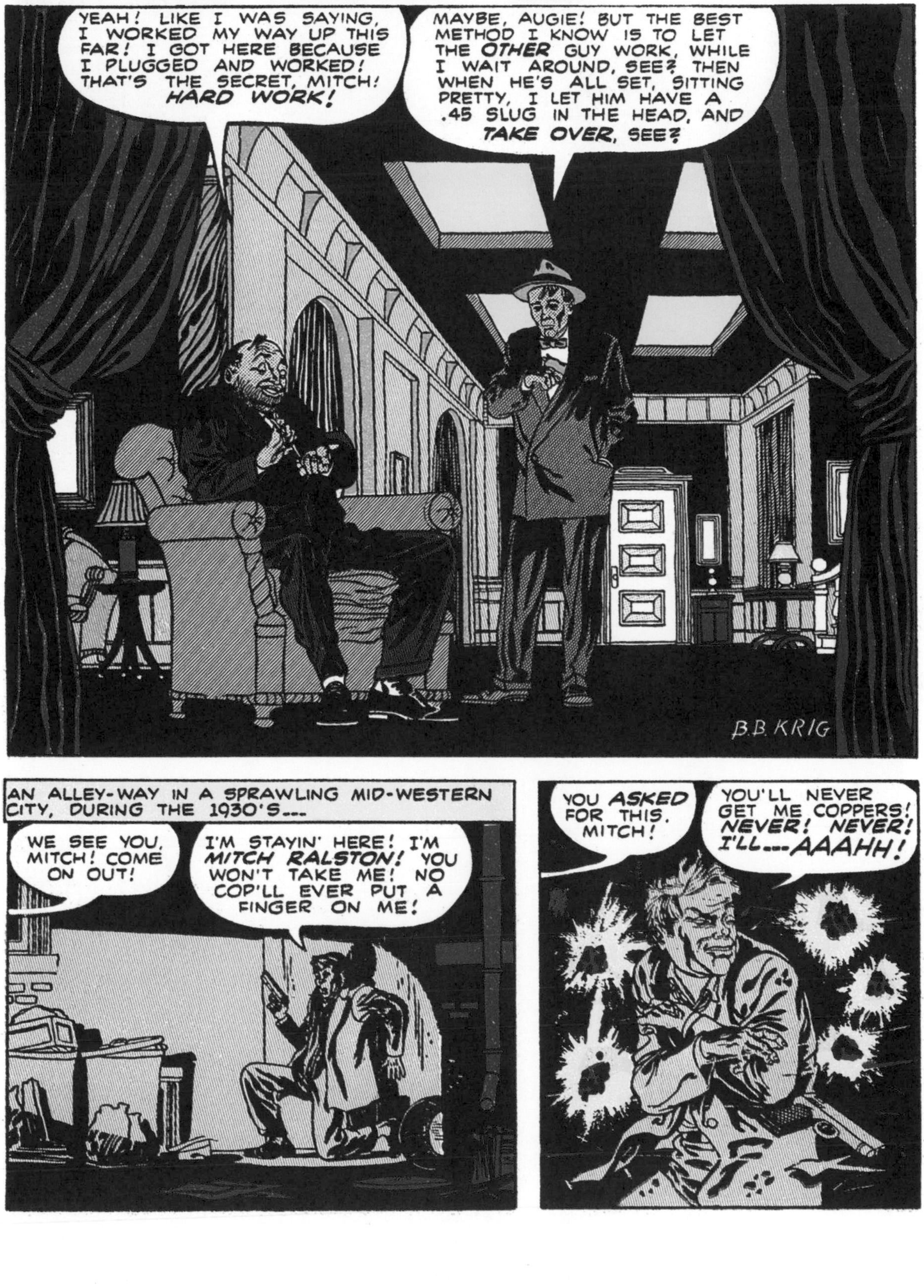

YEAH! LIKE I WAS SAYING, I WORKED MY WAY UP THIS FAR! I GOT HERE BECAUSE I PLUGGED AND WORKED! THAT'S THE SECRET, MITCH! HARD WORK!
MAYBE, AUGIE! BUT THE BEST METHOD I KNOW IS TO LET THE OTHER GUY WORK, WHILE I WAIT AROUND, SEE? THEN WHEN HE'S ALL SET, SITTING PRETTY, I LET HIM HAVE A .45 SLUG IN THE HEAD, AND TAKE OVER, SEE?
B.B. KRIG
AN ALLEY-WAY IN A SPRAWLING MID-WESTERN CITY, DURING THE 1930'S---
WE SEE YOU, MITCH! COME ON OUT!
I'M STAYIN' HERE! I'M MITCH RALSTON! YOU WON'T TAKE ME! NO COP'LL EVER PUT A FINGER ON ME!
YOU ASKED FOR THIS, MITCH!
YOU'LL NEVER GET ME COPPERS! NEVER! NEVER! I'LL---AAAHH!

AND AS MITCH RALSTON'S LIFE EBBS OUT THE FLOOD OF MEMORIES HE HAS LOCKED AWAY, FILE PAST...FOR MITCH, IN THESE FINAL SECONDS, RELIVES THE PAST WHICH HAS BROUGHT HIM TO THIS DISMAL ALLEY...

I'LL MAKE THE SHOT... MITCH... ALWAYS...MAKES...THE SHOT... RACK 'EM UP... I'LL SHOW--- RACK 'EM UP!

"CHARLIE'S PLACE...OVER ON STATE...THE CLICK OF BILLIARD BALLS AND THE TOBACCO SMOKE HUNG LIKE A CURTAIN OVER THE LIGHTS....THIS WAS THE NIGHT I MET AUGIE BERELLI..."

FOURTEEN BALL IN THE SIDE!

THAT'S A TOUGH SHOT, MITCH!

I ALWAYS MAKE THE HARD ONES!

LOOK! IT'S AUGIE BERELLI! I'M GETTING OUT OF HERE! THAT GUY MEANS TROUBLE!

HAW! HAW! THAT'S A GOOD ONE, SPUDS! YOU TELL A MEAN JOKE!

HAW! HAW! HAW!

CUT IT OUT, OVER THERE! HOW DO YOU EXPECT ME TO MAKE THE SHOT? SHUT UP!

SPUDS! DID YOU HEAR WHAT I HEARD? A CERTAIN CHARACTER HERE NEEDS TO BE TAUGHT SOME MANNERS!

YEAH, BOSS! I GET YOU---

P-PLEASE, BOYS! AUGIE, PLEASE... DON'T MAKE TROUBLE HERE!

AHHH! BUTTON YOUR LIP! THERE WON'T BE ANY TROUBLE! YOU'LL HARDLY HEAR A SOUND WHEN I STEP ON THIS PUNK!

COME ON, GORILLA! I'M WAITIN'!

"I WAS HARD AND TOUGH! THE STREET WAS MY TRAINING GROUND! THERE YOU LEARNED HOW TO FIGHT...OR ELSE..."

WHY, I'LL BREAK YOU IN HALF... I'LL ..OHHH!

NOT SO TOUGH NOW, ARE YOU, GORILLA?

TRY TO PULL A ROD ON ME, HUH? WELL, YOU WON'T GET FAR!

MY WRIST! IT'S *BUSTED!*

SWEEP HIM OUT OF HERE, BERELLI! NOT YOU OR YOUR GORILLA, CAN PUSH ME AROUND!

KID! YOU'VE GOT ME WRONG! I DON'T WANT TO PUSH YOU AROUND! I COULD USE A HARD BOY AROUND ME! COME INTO THE BACK ROOM, I WANT TO TALK BUSINESS!

BOSS! WHAT ABOUT ME?

BEAT IT! I DON'T WANT TO SEE YOU AGAIN! IF I CATCH YOU HANGING AROUND, IT'S CURTAINS! YOU UNDERSTAND?

HAW! HAW! GO ON BACK TO THE ZOO, GORILLA!

"SO WE WENT INTO THE BACK ROOM, AND WHAT AUGIE *SAID* WAS LIKE MUSIC IN MY EARS!"

KID, I WANT YOU TO WORK FOR ME! WE'LL GET ALONG FINE! ASK ANYBODY ABOUT AUGIE! THEY'LL TELL YOU I TAKE CARE OF MY BOYS! YOU KNOW MY SET-UP, DON'T YOU?

SURE! YOU'RE KING OF THE WEST SIDE, BERELLI! I'LL WORK FOR YOU! IT'S BETTER THAN MOOCHING A FEW BUCKS, TAKING SAPS OVER AT POOL! WHAT'S THE PITCH?

YOU DO WHAT I SAY, THAT'S ALL!

BUT WHAT ABOUT THE DOUGH? I'M TIRED OF EATIN' IN CHEAP HASH HOUSES, AND SLEEPING IN CRUMMY ROOMS! I DON'T COME CHEAP, BERELLI!

I DON'T BUY ANYTHING CHEAP, MITCH! HERE'S $500! AND THAT'S ONLY THE BEGINNING! THERE'S LOTS MORE WHERE THAT CAME FROM!

FIVE HUNDRED! BUT.... BUT.... *FIVE HUNDRED!* I'LL SAY YOU AIN'T CHEAP!

JUST ONE THING! BEFORE I GIVE YOU THE DOUGH, I WANT TO HEAR YOU CALL ME "BOSS"! IT'S IMPORTANT! SAY IT...

OKAY....BOSS!

"I WORKED WITH BERELLI THREE YEARS TO BE EXACT! A FEW TIMES THE COPS GRILLED ME ABOUT A KILLING... BUT NOBODY COULD PIN ANYTHING ON MITCH...!"

YOU RALSTON?

YEAH! WHO ARE YOU?

THERE'S SOMEBODY OUTSIDE WHO WANTS TO SPEAK TO YOU! LET'S GO, MITCH!

AREN'T YOU STEPPIN' A LITTLE OUT OF LINE, MISTER?

NO, MITCH, NOBODY'S OUT OF LINE WHEN HE'S GOT WHAT'S IN MY POCKET! AND DON'T THINK I WON'T USE IT! NOW LET'S GO!

SURE! THESE MONKEYS WERE ABOUT THROUGH, ANYWAY! I'LL GO!

"I THOUGHT FAST... AND MOVED FASTER... THE SAP DIDN'T KNOW WHAT HAPPENED..."

WHY, YOU CHEAP HOOD.... I OUGHT TO BREAK YOU INTO LITTLE PIECES!

NO! NO... MITCH! HONEST, I WAS CARRYIN' OUT ORDERS!

WHO SENT YOU? TALK, OR I'LL BREAK YOUR ARM!

JOHNNY GORDON, HE WANTS TO SEE YOU! HE'S WAITIN' OUTSIDE, HONEST!

JOHNNY GORDON! HE'S AUGIES WORST ENEMY! HE MUST BE AFTER A DEAL OR ELSE HIS HOOD WOULD'VE BLASTED ME... OKAY, I'LL GO!

"GORDON'S OILY SMILE WAS ENOUGH TO TURN MY STOMACH! I COULD SEE THAT HE NEEDED ME BAD... I SMASHED ENOUGH OF HIS THUGS SO THAT HE HATED ME... THIS WAS BIG, I SENSED!"

GLAD YOU COULD COME, MITCH! HOP IN, I WANT TO TALK!

IT'S STILL A FREE COUNTRY ... I'LL LISTEN! BUT DON'T TRY ANYTHING, JOHNNY! BECAUSE THE FIRST WRONG MOVE AND YOU GET IT, PERMANENT!

"AND THEN JOHNNY DROPPED IT IN MY LAP..."

MITCH HERE'S A PROPOSITION! 15 GRAND IN CASH, AND A FIFTY-FIFTY SPLIT WITH ME ON EVERYTHING, IF YOU GET AUGIE OUT OF THE WAY!

LET ME ROLL IT AROUND IN MY HEAD FOR A WHILE, JOHNNY! I NEED A LITTLE TIME TO GET USED TO THE IDEA!

"I THOUGHT ABOUT IT FOR HALF A MINUTE! JOHNNY KNEW THAT MY ONLY LOYALTY WAS TO THE DOLLAR, SURE...WHAT DID AUGIE MEAN TO ME? ---NOTHING!"

WITH AUGIE OUT OF THE WAY, WE'LL RUN THE TOWN! EVERY DEAL WILL GO THROUGH US! WE'LL RIDE BIG, MITCH! *BIG!*

OKAY! I'LL WORK IT! BUT DON'T TRY NOTHIN' WITH ME, JOHNNY! I'M MEAN WHEN I GET STARTED!

"THE NEXT NIGHT, I HAD MY PLAN ALL WORKED OUT, SO I MADE A PHONE CALL TO AUGIE..."

SURE, BOSS! YOU KNOW I WOULDN'T BOTHER YOU IF IT WASN'T IMPORTANT! MEET ME AT THE POST ROAD AND MORGAN AVENUE!

"I WAITED FOR AUGIE...AND HE CAME! I SAW THE HEAD-LIGHTS OF HIS LIMOUSINE CUTTING THE NIGHT! JOHNNY AND A FEW OF HIS BOYS WERE IN A GET-AWAY CAR NEARBY..."

"IT WAS ALL OVER LIKE THAT...*BANG! BANG! BANG!* THEY NEVER KNEW WHAT HIT THEM..."

WHAT IS IT, MITCH? I...*MITCH! AAHH!*

I JUST WANTED TO TELL YOU I'M IN PARTNERSHIP WITH JOHNNY GORDON NOW, AUGIE! THAT'S ALL!

NICE JOB, MITCH! I'VE NEVER SEEN SUCH NEAT WORK!

I *ALWAYS* WORK NEAT! REMEMBER THAT! NOW LET'S GET OUT OF HERE!

WE WENT TO JOHNNY'S HEADQUARTERS!

BOYS, I WANT YOU TO MEET MY NEW PARTNER, MITCH RALSTON!

HI, MITCH!

YOU SEE, MITCH...I WAS SURE THAT EVERYTHING WOULD WORK OUT RIGHT, SO I ORDERED THE STUFF FOR A PARTY! LET'S HAVE SOME FUN!

YOU'RE A GREAT GUY, JOHNNY!

"WE HAD A GREAT PARTY...IF ONLY WE HAD KNOWN WHAT WE WERE CELEBRATING... WE WOULD'VE BEEN A LOT QUIETER..."

HERE! LET'S TURN ON THE RADIO!

YEAH... TUNE ON THE MIDNIGHT NEWS! THERE OUGHT TO BE BIG NEWS TONIGHT, HUH, MITCH?

THE BIGGEST! I MADE IT!

...AUGIE BERELLI, GANG CHIEF, AND TWO HENCHMEN WERE SHOT TO DEATH! BUT BEFORE HE DIED, BERELLI NAMED MITCH RALSTON AS HIS KILLER! RALSTON HAD GONE OVER TO JOHNNY GORDON, BERELLI'S CHIEF RIVAL AND...

DID YOU HEAR THAT, MITCH? YOU MUFFED THE JOB!

LET'S GET OUT OF HERE!

BOSS! BOSS! THERE'S CARS OUTSIDE, FILLED WITH COPS! THEY'RE CLOSIN' IN! WHAT'LL WE DO, BOSS?

WE'RE TRAPPED! WE'LL BURN! MITCH! MITCH! FIGURE OUT SOMETHING!

SURE! WE'LL SHOOT OUR WAY OUT!

"AND A FEW SECONDS LATER THE POLICE LOUDSPEAKER BLASTED INTO THE ROOM..."

YOU HAVEN'T A CHANCE IN THERE! COME OUT OR WE'LL OPEN FIRE! WHAT'S YOUR ANSWER?

THIS!

"THEY TORE THE PLACE TO PIECES... MACHINE GUN BULLETS RIPPED INTO THE ROOM... AND..."

AAHH! MITCH! MITCH... I'M DONE FOR...

CAN'T STAY HERE! IT'S A DEATH TRAP! MUST GET OUT!

"THEN I REMEMBERED THE ALLEY BESIDE THE HOUSE! MAYBE I COULD GET OUT THE WINDOW, AND HIDE IN THE RUBBISH LITTERED ALLEY... THEN... WELL, THERE'S ALWAYS A CHANCE..."

GET ME OUT OF HERE, MITCH! I....I'M... SUFFERING...DON'T LET ME DIE!

NO, JOHNNY...I WON'T LET YOU SUFFER! I'LL SNUFF YOU OUT MYSELF!

"THE ROOM WAS LIKE A MORGUE. I WAS THE ONLY ONE ALIVE..."

THEY'LL BE HERE IN A MINUTE! NOW'S MY CHANCE!

"AT FIRST I THOUGHT I'D MADE IT... THERE WAS A FENCE AT THE END OF THE ALLEY! IF I COULD GET OVER IT... THERE WAS A GOOD CHANCE... BUT..."

HALT!

IT'S MITCH RALSTON!

WE SEE YOU, MITCH! COME OUT!

I'M STAYIN' HERE! IF YOU WANT ME COME AND GET ME... AAARRGH!

AND SO WE COME TO THE END OF MITCH RALSTON! EVERY ONE WAY STREET CALLED CRIME LEADS TO A DEAD END!

WILD BILL PECOS

THE MOST FEARED GUNMAN IN THE WEST! BUT BROTHERS AND SISTERS YOU'VE NEVER SEEN WILD BILL PECOS IN ACTION UNTIL YOU SEE HIM RIDING THE VENGEANCE TRAIL TO GET THE HOMBRES RESPONSIBLE FOR THE......

Death of Nuggets Nugent

TAKE COVER! QUICK!

EEOWW! WILD BILL PECOS IS HUNTING DOWN THE HOMBRES WHO KILLED HIS PAL, NUGGETS!

B.B. KRIG

WHEN NUGGETS NUGENT REFUSES ANOTHER DRINK, YOU KNOW SOMETHING IS WRONG....

I·I DON'T FEEL SO GOOD! RECKON I'LL GET A BREATH OF FRESH AIR!

DON'T KNOW WHAT'S COME OVER ME! I... ULP!

HAW·HAW!

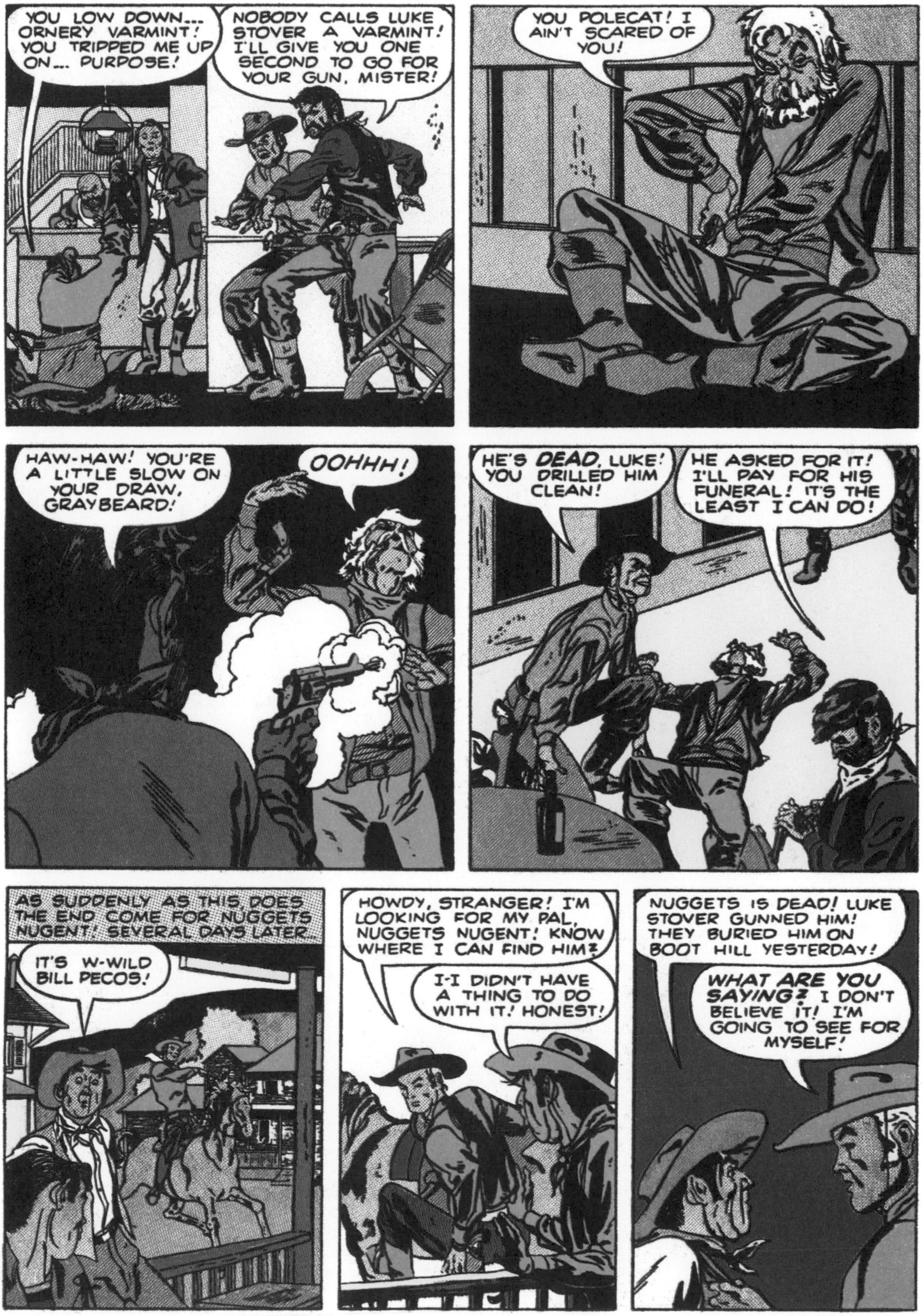
YOU LOW DOWN... ORNERY VARMINT! YOU TRIPPED ME UP ON... PURPOSE!
NOBODY CALLS LUKE STOVER A VARMINT! I'LL GIVE YOU ONE SECOND TO GO FOR YOUR GUN, MISTER!
YOU POLECAT! I AIN'T SCARED OF YOU!
HAW-HAW! YOU'RE A LITTLE SLOW ON YOUR DRAW, GRAYBEARD!
OOHHH!
HE'S DEAD, LUKE! YOU DRILLED HIM CLEAN!
HE ASKED FOR IT! I'LL PAY FOR HIS FUNERAL! IT'S THE LEAST I CAN DO!
AS SUDDENLY AS THIS DOES THE END COME FOR NUGGETS NUGENT! SEVERAL DAYS LATER...
IT'S W-WILD BILL PECOS!
HOWDY, STRANGER! I'M LOOKING FOR MY PAL, NUGGETS NUGENT! KNOW WHERE I CAN FIND HIM?
I-I DIDN'T HAVE A THING TO DO WITH IT! HONEST!
NUGGETS IS DEAD! LUKE STOVER GUNNED HIM! THEY BURIED HIM ON BOOT HILL YESTERDAY!
WHAT ARE YOU SAYING? I DON'T BELIEVE IT! I'M GOING TO SEE FOR MYSELF!

FOR A LONG TIME WILD BILL DOES NOT LEAVE THE CEMETERY! THEN AT LAST, HE TURNS BACK TOWARD THE TOWN.... AND THE GRIM SET OF HIS FEATURES HIDES THE TURMOIL IN HIS HEART....

IT'S TRUE! HERE'S HIS GRAVE! I'LL NEVER SEE NUGGETS AGAIN!

LATER... NUGGETS HAD GONE TO VISIT HIS FRIEND, THE CHIEF OF THE JUJUTE INDIANS! WHEN DID HE GET BACK INTO TOWN?

THE SAME DAY THAT LUKE STOVER PUMPED LEAD INTO HIM, BILL! HE'D BEEN TALKING ALL ABOUT HIS VISIT WITH THE JUJUTE CHIEF!

YOU FELLA THEY CALL WILD BILL?

A JUJUTE INDIAN BOY!

THAT'S ME! WHAT CAN I DO FOR YOU?

ME HEAR MUCH TALK OF YOUR GUN! IT KILL MANY! MAYBE IT KILL COYOTE-MEN WHO TAKE LIFE OF GOOD FRIEND TO MY PEOPLE, NUGGETS NUGENT?

CAN YOU TELL ME WHERE TO FIND THE MEN WHO SHOT NUGGETS?

ME SEE THEM RIDE OFF TO JUJUTE COUNTRY! THREE MEN.... THEY COVER FACES.... SO! BUT ME SEE ENOUGH OF FELLA THEY CALL STOVER! HE ONE WHO KILL NUGGETS!

THANKS!

THERE HE GOES! I'D SURE HATE TO BE STANDIN' IN THE BOOTS OF THE MEN THAT WILD BILL IS AFTER!

ME HOPE HE HAS NO TROUBLE WITH JUJUTES! MY PEOPLE NOT FRIENDLY TO STRANGE WHITE MAN!

DEEP INTO HOSTILE JUJUTE TERRITORY, WILD BILL RIDES ON THE VENGEANCE TRAIL....

WHITE MAN DIE!

THE WARY INSTINCT OF THE BORN PLAINSMAN SAVES WILD BILL'S LIFE....

JUMPIN' GILA MONSTERS! THAT WAS CLOSE!

WHI-IZZZZ

I SPOTTED A MOVEMENT IN THOSE TREES! I DON'T AIM TO SHED ANY RED-SKIN BLOOD! BUT THAT FELLOW'S GOT TO BE DISCOURAGED!

BANG!

EYAAAA!

SPLIT!

THERE YOU ARE!

I FIGURE IT'S TIME WE REACHED AN UNDERSTANDING!

MY SCALP ISN'T GOING TO DECORATE ANY INDIAN TEPEE!

UGHH!

CRA-ACK!

I RECKON WE UNDER-STAND EACH OTHER NOW! YOU'RE GOING TO TAKE ME TO YOUR CHIEF'S WIGWAM....SAVVY?

DON'T GET ANY NOTIONS ABOUT HIGHTAILING IT EITHER! I CAN SHOOT OFF A SQUIRREL'S WHISKER AT A HUNDRED PACES!

A SHORT WHILE LATER, WILD BILL PECOS AND HIS INDIAN GUIDE ARRIVE AT THE CAMP OF THE JUJUTES...

HMMM! THEY SURE DON'T LIKE WHITE MEN! I'M GETTING SOME DOWNRIGHT UNFRIENDLY LOOKS!

SEIZE THE WHITE MAN!

OH-OH! HERE IT COMES!

CAN'T USE MY GUNS! I DON'T WANT TO RILE THESE REDSKINS TOO MUCH!

ON THE OTHER HAND, I DON'T AIM TO BE PUSHED AROUND!

I RECKON THIS OUGHT TO MAKE MY MEANING CLEAR!

EEYAAH!

WHAT'S ALL THE RUCKUS OUTSIDE?

WHITE MAN COMES! HE FIGHT LIKE MANY TIGERS!

SOON HE WILL DIE!

WELL, NOW LET'S NOT BE TOO HASTY! MAYBE HE... JUMPIN' ALLIGATORS! IT'S WILD BILL!

LOOK OUT, BILL!

HUH...? NUGGETS!

I *CAN'T* BELIEVE IT! NUGGETS IS REALLY ALIVE!

UGHH!

YOU CONSARNED OLD MOSSBACKED COYOTE! THEY TOLD ME YOU'D BEEN BUSHWHACKED!

HEE-HEE! I'M AS SKITTERY AS A YOUNG COLT! HOW'D YOU GET AWAY FROM THEM BANDITS?

BANDITS? I DON'T KNOW WHAT YOU'RE TALKING ABOUT!

DOGGONE MY HIDE! I SHOULD'VE KNOWN THEY WERE LYING! LUKE STOVER AND THAT OTHER HOMBRE SWORE THEIR MEN WERE HOLDING YOU PRISONER!

THEY SAID THEY WOULD KILL YOU, IF I DIDN'T HELP THEM MAKE A DEAL WITH MY FRIENDS, THE JUJUTES! THEY'RE AFTER THE FUR PELT CONCESSION....AND THEY KNEW THE JUJUTES WOULDN'T LISTEN TO ANY WHITE MAN BUT ME!

I'M BEGINNING TO UNDERSTAND!

THERE'S LUKE STOVER NOW!

ULP! IT'S WILD BILL PECOS! THE GAME'S UP! WE'VE GOT TO SHOOT OUR WAY OUT OF HERE!

NOT UNTIL THEIR GUNS CLEAR LEATHER, DOES WILD BILL PECOS MAKE HIS MOVE! THEN HIS HANDS SEEM TO COME AWAY FROM HIS HOLSTERS BELCHING FIRE AND SMOKE....

H-HE SHOT THE GUNS RIGHT OUT OF OUR HANDS!

I-I NEVER EVEN SAW WHAT HAPPENED!

BAM!

BANG!

BUT I RECKON YOU CAN *FEEL* WHAT'S HAPPENING NOW!

OOOF!

I RECKON THEY'VE HAD ENOUGH!

TOO BAD! I WAS JUST BEGINNING TO ENJOY MYSELF!

THEY BAD MEN! YOU LEAVE THEM HERE! INJUNS KNOW HOW TO MAKE THEM PAY!

YOU CAN SAY THAT AGAIN! BUT IF IT'S ALL THE SAME TO YOU, CHIEF, WE'LL TAKE 'EM BACK TO FACE THE WHITE MAN'S JUSTICE!

THE GREAT BEARDED ONE SPEAKS WISDOM! HOW!

HOW! NUGGETS SURE HAS THESE REDSKINS EATING OUT OF HIS HAND!

LATER, ON THE HOMEWARD TRAIL...

JUST ONE THING I DON'T SAVVY, NUGGETS! HOW COME EVERYBODY THOUGHT LUKE STOVER GUNNED YOU!

'CAUSE THE VARMINT SPIKED MY DRINK! HE TIMED THE SHOOTIN' SO IT HAPPENED JUST BEFORE I PASSED OUT! THEN HIS PARDNER SWORE I WAS DEAD... AND NOBODY ASKED ANY QUESTIONS!

AND WHEN YOU WOKE UP YOU PLAYED ALONG WITH THEM IN ORDER TO SAVE MY LIFE!

KEE-RECT! I'M PLUMB SORRY I MISSED SEEIN' MY OWN FUNERAL... WHEN THEY BURIED THAT EMPTY COFFIN! YOU KNOW, BILL, I'M GOIN' TO BE THE ONLY HOMBRE WHO EVER CAME BACK TO LOOK AT HIS OWN GRAVE! HEE-HEE!

THE END

THE WORLD'S STRANGEST SHUFFLE

HAROLD LOWE WAS A GAMBLER AND LIAR... HE'D STOOP TO ANYTHING TO GET MONEY FOR HIS GAMBLING... BUT WHEN HE BEGAN PLAYING THE GAME WITH DEATH, THEN HE REALIZED WHAT IT MEANT TO HAVE THE CARDS STACKED AGAINST HIM...
WE BEGIN OUR STORY DURING HAROLD'S MARRIAGE... HE IS WORRIED AS HE APPROACHES HIS WIFE ON THE LAWN BEFORE HER MANSION...

JUST LOOK AT MY "DARLING" WIFE... THE "OLD BAT" HAS EVERYTHING AND I'M BROKE!—I'VE GOT TO GET MORE MONEY FROM HER THIS TIME OR ELSE...

B. Krigstein

DONELLI IS GROWING IMPATIENT... I'D BETTER PAY OFF THE TWO-THOUSAND BUCKS FAST! YOU DON'T LIVE TO WELCH ON SNAP DONELLI A SECOND TIME!

WHAT'S THE MATTER, HAROLD? YOU'RE SO PALE. WHY, YOU'RE TREMBLING!

AHEM--MATILDA...

TREMBLING? YEAH, T-THAT'S RIGHT! I AM... I C-CAN HARDLY HOLD MY HAND STILL!

WHAT IS IT, HAROLD? YOU HAVEN'T LOOKED WELL FOR DAYS. ARE YOU HOLDING ANYTHING BACK FROM ME?

DON'T BE SILLY! BESIDES, A LOT YOU CARE ABOUT WHAT HAPPENS TO ME! I COULD BE DYING -- YOU WOULDN'T SHELL OUT A RED CENT TO SAVE ME!

THAT'S RIDICULOUS! I'VE GIVEN YOU EVERYTHING YOU'VE WANTED AND MORE, HAROLD! I'M NO FOOL! I KNOW WHY YOU MARRIED ME. I'M WEALTHY!

I'M NOT BITTER ABOUT IT, HAROLD IN FACT, I'M GRATEFUL. IF I DIDN'T HAVE THE MONEY, YOU'D NEVER HAVE GIVEN ME A SECOND GLANCE!

YEAH. YOU'RE GRATEFUL. SO GRATEFUL, THE PENNY GETS PINCHED ALL OUT OF SHAPE BY THE TIME IT LEAVES YOUR HAND!

I KNOW YOU'RE A WASTREL AND A GAMBLER. I RESTRAIN YOUR SPENDINGS A LITTLE BECAUSE I REALIZE THAT IF MY MONEY EVER WERE GONE, YOU'D BE GONE WITH IT.

SO! I'M JUST A LAP DOG AROUND HERE? WELL, I'M SICK OF IT--

THERE IS SOMETHING WRONG WITH YOU! YOU'VE NEVER BEEN SO NERVOUS AND UPSET AS THIS. YOU MUST GO TO A DOCTOR, HAROLD. YOU MUST GET YOURSELF EXAMINED. I DON'T CARE WHAT IT COSTS...

YOU D-DON'T? I-- I MEAN -- IT MIGHT COST PLENTY!

WONDERFUL... THE OLD BAT THINKS I'M SICK. I'VE STUMBLED ONTO A NEW PITCH!

YOU WERE RIGHT, MATILDA. I AM HOLDING SOMETHING BACK. IN FACT, THAT'S WHY I'VE BEEN ASKING YOU FOR MORE MONEY. IT'S NOT BEEN FOR GAMBLING, BUT FOR DOCTORS!

HAROLD!

I SAW A BIG DOCTOR YESTERDAY AND HE SAID I MUST TAKE A SERIES OF TREATMENTS, BUT THAT'S OUT OF THE QUESTION. IT'S TOO EXPENSIVE.

BUT WHAT IS IT, HAROLD? WHAT'S WRONG WITH YOU?

IT'S SOMETHING TO DO WITH MY LUNGS. BUT WHAT'S THE DIFFERENCE? I'M JUST NO GOOD. YOU'D BE HAPPIER WITHOUT ME.

YOU FOOLISH BOY! WHY DO YOU SUP- POSE I'VE PUT UP WITH ALL YOUR NEG- LECT AND BRUTALITY? I KNOW THAT DESPITE YOUR FAULTS, I LOVE YOU!

"YOU'LL HAVE ALL THE HELP MEDICAL SCIENCE CAN GIVE YOU! YOU'RE GOING TO START THE TREATMENTS FIRST THING TOMORROW--AND WHAT'S MORE, I'LL GO WITH YOU!"

"I WON'T GO THEN! I WON'T HAVE YOU EXPOSED TO THE MISERY AND GLOOM OF A DOCTOR'S OFFICE!"

"YOU'VE NEVER SHOWN ME ANY CONSIDERATION, HAROLD. PERHAPS IN TIME YOU'LL COME TO LOVE ME--AND NOT BECAUSE OF MY MONEY."

"YOUR MONEY WILL SAVE MY LIFE, MATILDA. I COULDN'T HELP BUT FEEL TENDERLY TOWARD YOU!"

ND SO, THE FOLLOWING MORNING...

"500...1000...1500...2000... THAT SQUARES US, DONELLI. AND NOW-- HERE'S A CENTURY-- RIKERS TO KNOCK OUT WILLEZ TONIGHT!"

"SURE, LOWE!--IN THE CHIPS AGAIN, I SEE. WHAT HAPPENED? YOUR OLD LADY CROAK AND LEAVE YOU A FORTUNE?"

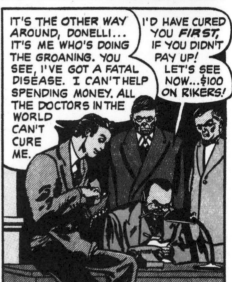

"IT'S THE OTHER WAY AROUND, DONELLI... IT'S ME WHO'S DOING THE GROANING. YOU SEE, I'VE GOT A FATAL DISEASE. I CAN'T HELP SPENDING MONEY. ALL THE DOCTORS IN THE WORLD CAN'T CURE ME."

"I'D HAVE CURED YOU FIRST, IF YOU DIDN'T PAY UP! LET'S SEE NOW...$100 ON RIKERS!"

HE REST OF THE DAY...

"TEN ON BLACK..."

"TWO AND TWO BETTER-- TWO HUNDRED THAT IS!"

"COME ON, YOU EIGHTER FROM DECATUR!"

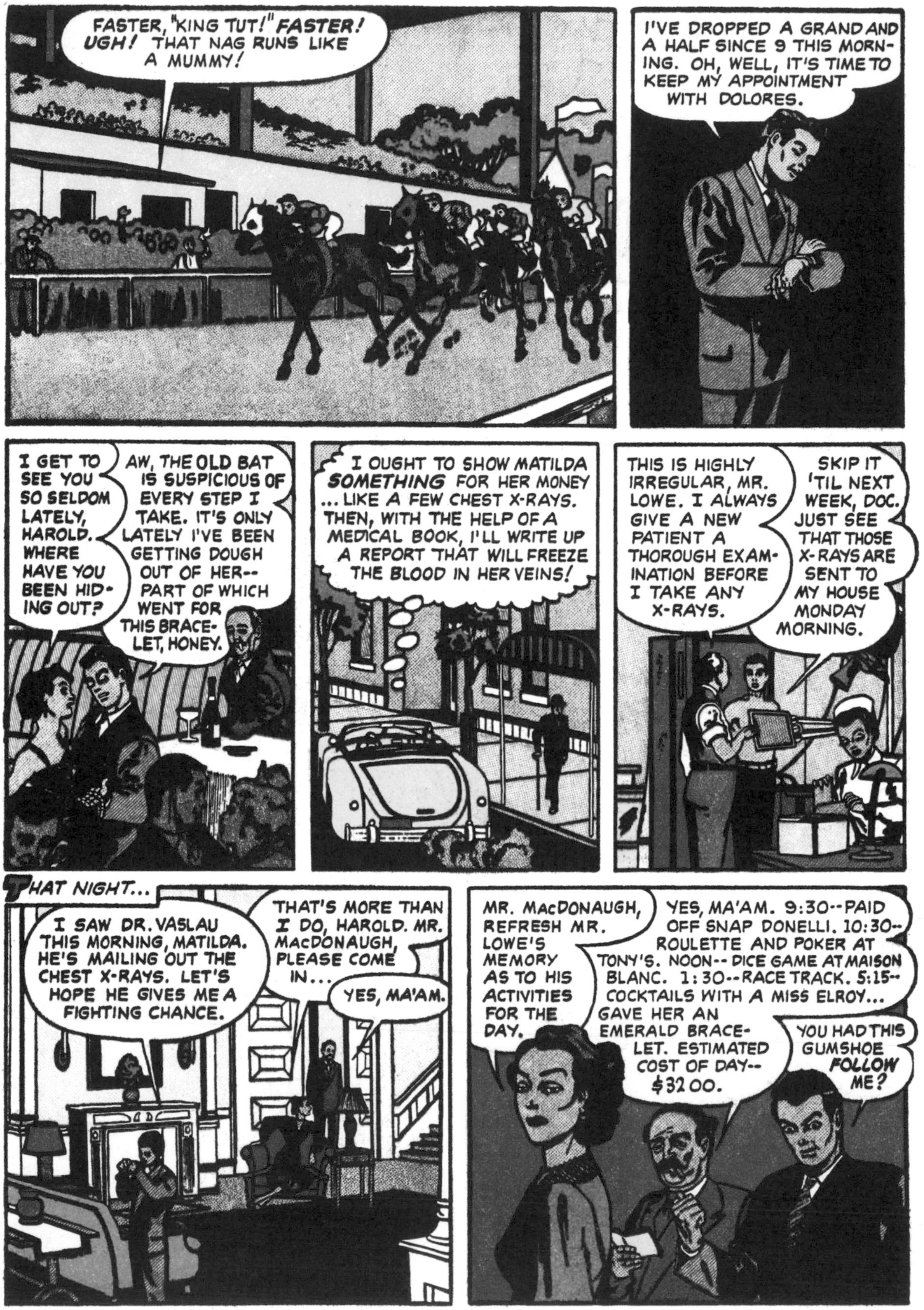

FASTER, "KING TUT!" FASTER! UGH! THAT NAG RUNS LIKE A MUMMY!
I'VE DROPPED A GRAND AND A HALF SINCE 9 THIS MORNING. OH, WELL, IT'S TIME TO KEEP MY APPOINTMENT WITH DOLORES.
I GET TO SEE YOU SO SELDOM LATELY, HAROLD. WHERE HAVE YOU BEEN HIDING OUT?
AW, THE OLD BAT IS SUSPICIOUS OF EVERY STEP I TAKE. IT'S ONLY LATELY I'VE BEEN GETTING DOUGH OUT OF HER-- PART OF WHICH WENT FOR THIS BRACELET, HONEY.
I OUGHT TO SHOW MATILDA SOMETHING FOR HER MONEY ... LIKE A FEW CHEST X-RAYS. THEN, WITH THE HELP OF A MEDICAL BOOK, I'LL WRITE UP A REPORT THAT WILL FREEZE THE BLOOD IN HER VEINS!
THIS IS HIGHLY IRREGULAR, MR. LOWE. I ALWAYS GIVE A NEW PATIENT A THOROUGH EXAMINATION BEFORE I TAKE ANY X-RAYS.
SKIP IT 'TIL NEXT WEEK, DOC. JUST SEE THAT THOSE X-RAYS ARE SENT TO MY HOUSE MONDAY MORNING.
THAT NIGHT...
I SAW DR. VASLAU THIS MORNING, MATILDA. HE'S MAILING OUT THE CHEST X-RAYS. LET'S HOPE HE GIVES ME A FIGHTING CHANCE.
THAT'S MORE THAN I DO, HAROLD. MR. MACDONAUGH, PLEASE COME IN...
YES, MA'AM.
MR. MACDONAUGH, REFRESH MR. LOWE'S MEMORY AS TO HIS ACTIVITIES FOR THE DAY.
YES, MA'AM. 9:30--PAID OFF SNAP DONELLI. 10:30-- ROULETTE AND POKER AT TONY'S. NOON-- DICE GAME AT MAISON BLANC. 1:30--RACE TRACK. 5:15-- COCKTAILS WITH A MISS ELROY... GAVE HER AN EMERALD BRACELET. ESTIMATED COST OF DAY-- $3200.
YOU HAD THIS GUMSHOE FOLLOW ME?

THANK YOU, MR. MacDONAUGH-- THAT WILL BE ALL.

HOW DARE YOU HAVE ME SHADOWED-- AS IF I WERE A CRIMINAL!

YOU *ARE* A CRIMINAL OF A SORT, HAROLD-- A LIAR AND A CHEAT! I'VE FORGIVEN YOU REPEATEDLY, BECAUSE OF MY LOVE FOR YOU. BUT IF THIS SICKNESS STORY TURNS OUT TO BE FALSE, IT'S THE END--THE ABSOLUTE *END!*

BUT *I AM* SICK, MATILDA. THOSE X-RAYS WILL PROVE IT. WHY DO YOU THINK I GAMBLE AND GO TO THE RACES? TO *FORGET!* WHY-- THE SHADOW OF DEATH HANGS OVER MY HEAD!

DON'T MAKE ME LAUGH, HAROLD. I'LL SEE DR. VASLAU MONDAY MORNING. IF YOUR ILLNESS TURNS OUT TO BE ANOTHER LIE, DESIGNED TO SQUEEZE MONEY OUT OF ME, DON'T BOTHER COMING HOME.

I'LL BE ON THE STREET WITHOUT A NICKEL.

YEP! THIS IS MY LAST WEEK-END HERE UNLESS SOMETHING *HAPPENS* BETWEEN NOW AND MONDAY TO KEEP MATILDA FROM SEEING VASLAU...

EVENING, TIM, HOW'S THE BRINEY DEEP?

PRETTY CHOPPY TONIGHT, MR. LOWE. PAPER SAYS SQUALLS TOMORROW. IF YOU'RE THINKIN' ABOUT BOATIN' THIS WEEK-END, *DON'T!* SQUALLS TURN THIS BAY INTO A DANGEROUS PIECE OF WATER. I'VE SEEN WAVES TEN FEET HIGH.

BESIDES, MRS. LOWE AIN'T MUCH OF A SWIMMER!

THAT'S IT! IF AN ACCIDENT HAPPENED... IF THE BOAT OVERTURNED... MATILDA COULD NEVER *SWIM* BACK--NOT AGAINST TEN-FOOT WAVES!

NO, YOU'RE RIGHT, TIM. SHE CAN HARDLY TAKE TEN STROKES WITHOUT TIRING!

*T*HE NEXT DAY, AFTER TIM IS SENT AWAY ON A FOOL'S ERRAND...

HOW ABOUT A SAIL AROUND THE LAKE BEFORE LUNCH, MATILDA? IT'S A BEAUTIFUL DAY AND, AFTER ALL, I'M NOT PROVEN GUILTY AS YET!

I HOPE FOR *BOTH* OUR SAKES, HAROLD, YOU'RE NOT LYING ABOUT DR. VASLAU. ALL RIGHT, I'LL CHANGE AND MEET YOU AT THE BOATHOUSE IN TEN MINUTES.

*S*HORTLY AFTER...

IT'S GETTING DARKER, HAROLD. IT LOOKS LIKE A SQUALL COMING UP! LET'S TURN BACK!

DON'T BE SILLY, MATILDA. IT'LL BLOW OVER. BESIDES, IF ANYTHING DID HAPPEN, YOU COULD COUNT ON ME TO HELP YOU. YOU KNOW THAT.

H-HAROLD! LOOK AT THOSE WAVES! TURN BACK, HAROLD! *TURN BACK!*

TO *WHAT*, MATILDA? TO BEING TURNED OUT ON THE STREET? IN A SECOND, THE BOAT WILL CAPSIZE. SWIM BACK -- IF YOU *CAN!*

A HALF HOUR LATER...

W-WHERE'S MRS. LOWE?

SHE WENT DOWN! SHE NEVER HAD A CHANCE IN THAT CHOPPY WATER. I DIVED FOR HER, BUT I COULDN'T FIND HER... *SOB* IT WAS HORRIBLE... *HORRIBLE!* I WARNED HER ABOUT SQUALLS -- BUT SHE WOULDN'T LISTEN -- SHE INSISTED ON MY TAKING HER OUT! *SOB*

*T*HE NEXT DAY...

MR. MAC-DONAUGH, NOBODY CAN PROVE WHAT YOU'RE THINKING! THERE WERE NO WITNESSES, NO MARKS OF VIOLENCE. WHY NOT FORGET YOUR SUSPICIONS FOR $10,000? YOU SEE, I'M A RICH MAN, NOW.

I SEE MORE THAN THAT, MR. LOWE... BUT AS YOU SAY, I CAN'T PROVE A THING! KEEP YOUR MONEY!

*M*ONDAY AFTERNOON, AFTER THE FUNERAL...

THIS PACKAGE ARRIVED AN HOUR AGO, MR. LOWE!

THANK YOU!

THE X-RAYS. JUST FOR LAUGHS, I'LL SEE WHAT DR. VASLAU'S REPORT SAYS...

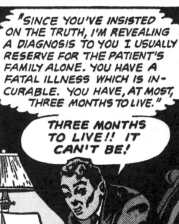

"SINCE YOU'VE INSISTED ON REVEALING A DIAGNOSIS TO YOU I USUALLY RESERVE FOR THE PATIENT'S FAMILY ALONE. YOU HAVE A FATAL ILLNESS WHICH IS IN-CURABLE. YOU HAVE, AT MOST, THREE MONTHS TO LIVE."

THREE MONTHS TO LIVE!! IT CAN'T BE!

SIR -- THE FUNERAL GUESTS ARE WAITING FOR YOU IN THE LIBRARY.

LET 'EM GO TO BLAZES! I'M GOING TO TOWN!

I'VE GOT TO GET OTHER DOCTORS TO DIAGNOSE THESE X-RAYS! I CAN'T ACCEPT A DEATH SENTENCE ON ONE MAN'S OPINION!

*A*N HOUR LATER, IN TOWN...

WELL, I'VE EXAMINED THEM THOROUGHLY, MR. LOWE. ARE YOU *SURE* YOU WANT THE TRUTH?

IS DR. VASLAU RIGHT? HAVE I ONLY T-THREE MONTHS TO LIVE?

DR. VASLAU WAS GENEROUS... I'D GIVE YOU FOUR WEEKS.

N-NO! NO! IT'S A MISTAKE! THIS CAN'T HAPPEN TO ME! NOT WHEN I HAVE MILLIONS IN MY HANDS AND NOBODY TO CONTROL MY SPENDING! I'LL SEE OTHER DOCTORS-- DOZENS OF THEM!

BUT A DOZEN PHYSICIANS HAD ONLY ONE ANSWER.

I'M SORRY, MR. LOWE. I AGREE WITH DR. VASLAU.

IT'S HOPELESS. SURGERY WOULD KILL, NOT CURE.

FATE IS GETTING EVEN WITH ME FOR KILLING MATILDA!

IT'S THE PAYOFF FOR ALL THE CRUELTY I SHOWED HER!

IT'S FATE'S REVENGE... TO BE TORTURED EVERY LAST MINUTE OF MY LIFE! BUT I COULDN'T STAND IT... KNOWING THAT ANY DAY, ANY HOUR, I'LL DIE IN AGONY!

I GOT THE BEST OF EVERY-BODY ALL MY LIFE AND I WON'T LOSE OUT NOW! I'LL CHEAT FATE... EVEN AT LIFE'S END! "TO WHOM IT MAY CONCERN..."

THAT MAN! HE'S--

Y!!! I--I CAN'T LOOK!

HE'S KILLED HIM-SELF! OH, HOW AWFUL, HOW AWFUL!

HE WROTE SOMETHING ON THIS ENVELOPE ...HE SAYS HE MURDERED HIS WIFE... LET HER DROWN IN THE BAY... HIS FATAL LUNG DISEASE IS PUNISHMENT FOR WHAT HE DID, BUT HE'S PROUD TO HAVE CHEATED FATE TO THE END!

BUT AT THE LOWE HOME, A SHORT WHILE LATER...

MR. LOWE ISN'T HERE. I'M THE FAMILY LAWYER. THE BUTLER SAID YOUR MESSAGE WAS VERY IMPORTANT.

IT IS! I'M FROM DR. VASLAU'S OFFICE. MR. LOWE RUSHED EVERYBODY SO MUCH THE DAY HE TOOK HIS X-RAYS, I'M AFRAID WE MISSPELL-ED HIS NAME. WE HAVE ANOTHER PATIENT NAMED "LOEW." I SENT MR. LOWE THE WRONG SET OF PICTURES!!

MR. LOWE IS IN PERFECT HEALTH. BUT IT WAS MR LOEW'S REPORT HE RECEIVED BY MISTAKE! AND MR. LOEW IS DYING OF AN INCUR-ABLE DISEASE. I HOPE I HAVEN'T COME TOO LATE!

READ THIS. IT'S A MESSAGE WE JUST RECEIVED FROM THE POLICE DEPARTMENT.

"HAROLD LOWE COMMITTED SUICIDE THIS EVENING AFTER CON-FESSING THE MURDER OF HIS WIFE. IT SEEMS HE KNEW HE WOULD SOON DIE OF NATURAL CAUSES, SO HE KILLED HIMSELF IN AN EFFORT TO CHEAT DESTINY!"

YES, HAROLD LOWE WAS A CHEAT. BUT THE ONLY MAN HE CHEATED IN THE END WAS HIMSELF

NOW I CAN DIE EASY...

IN A SPEEDING GETAWAY CAR ARE FOUR BANK BANDITS, FLEEING A JOB WHERE ONE OF THEM HAS BEEN SHOT. IN THE TRADE THEY ARE KNOWN AS LOUIE, SLUG, BENNY AND JOE... AND NOW IN HIS LAST PITIFUL MOMENTS THE DYING JOE THINKS ONLY OF HIS BABY SON... A SON WHOSE LIFE IS GOING TO FOLLOW A STRANGE PATTERN...

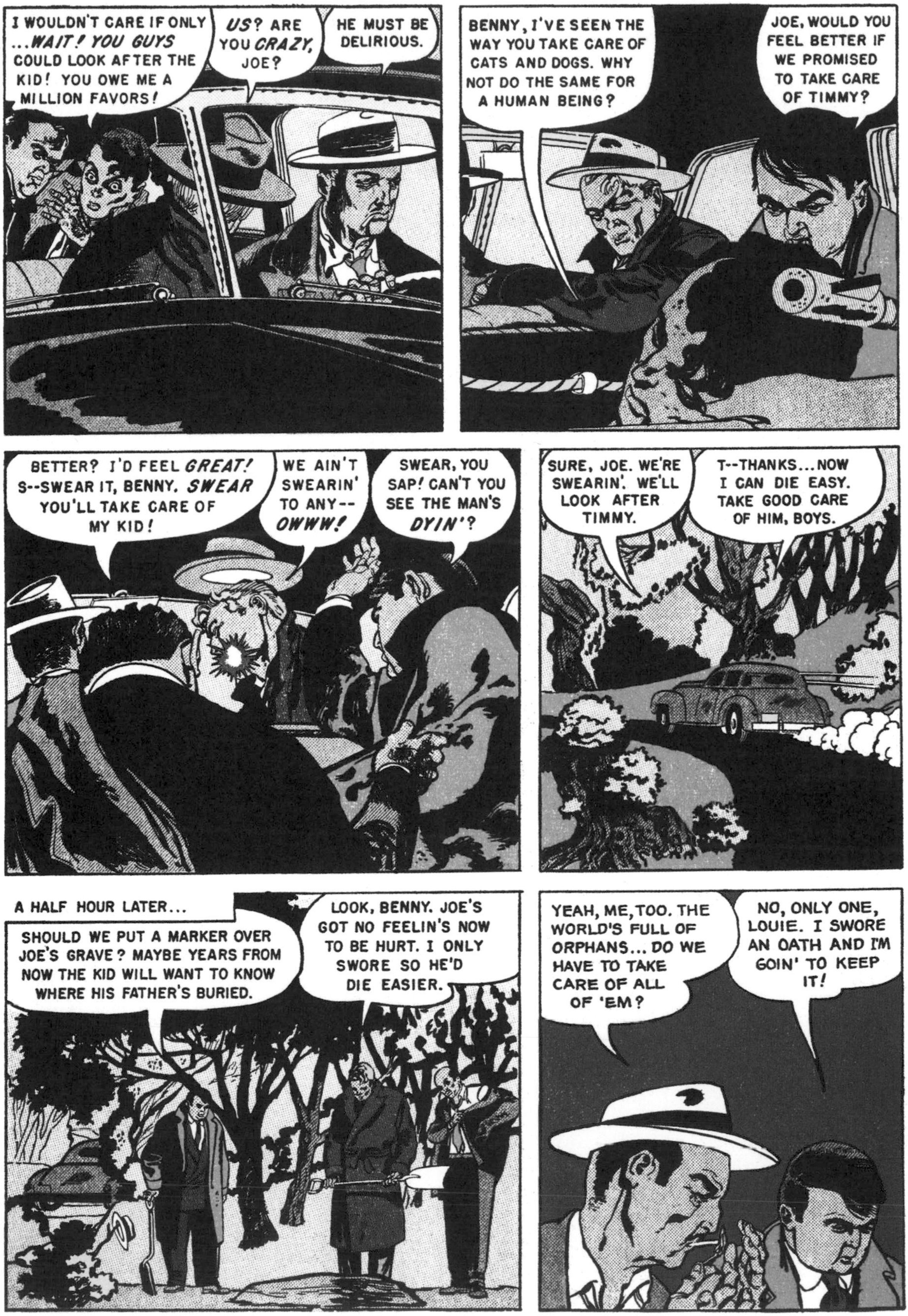
I WOULDN'T CARE IF ONLY ...WAIT! YOU GUYS COULD LOOK AFTER THE KID! YOU OWE ME A MILLION FAVORS!
US? ARE YOU CRAZY, JOE?
HE MUST BE DELIRIOUS.
BENNY, I'VE SEEN THE WAY YOU TAKE CARE OF CATS AND DOGS. WHY NOT DO THE SAME FOR A HUMAN BEING?
JOE, WOULD YOU FEEL BETTER IF WE PROMISED TO TAKE CARE OF TIMMY?
BETTER? I'D FEEL GREAT! S--SWEAR IT, BENNY. SWEAR YOU'LL TAKE CARE OF MY KID!
WE AIN'T SWEARIN' TO ANY-- OWWW!
SWEAR, YOU SAP! CAN'T YOU SEE THE MAN'S DYIN'?
SURE, JOE. WE'RE SWEARIN'. WE'LL LOOK AFTER TIMMY.
T--THANKS... NOW I CAN DIE EASY. TAKE GOOD CARE OF HIM, BOYS.
A HALF HOUR LATER...
SHOULD WE PUT A MARKER OVER JOE'S GRAVE? MAYBE YEARS FROM NOW THE KID WILL WANT TO KNOW WHERE HIS FATHER'S BURIED.
LOOK, BENNY. JOE'S GOT NO FEELIN'S NOW TO BE HURT. I ONLY SWORE SO HE'D DIE EASIER.
YEAH, ME, TOO. THE WORLD'S FULL OF ORPHANS... DO WE HAVE TO TAKE CARE OF ALL OF 'EM?
NO, ONLY ONE, LOUIE. I SWORE AN OATH AND I'M GOIN' TO KEEP IT!

TWO HOURS LATER... AFTER THE CAR IS DITCHED...

IT'S ABOUT TIME YOU GUYS SHOWED UP! THIS KID AIN'T STOPPED CRYIN' FOR A MINUTE! YOU CAN TELL JOE IT'S THE LAST TIME I MIND HIS BABY. HEY!... WHERE *IS* JOE?

HE'S DEAD, MIN. A COP'S BULLET.

AND REMEMBER MIN...YOU DON'T KNOW *WHAT* HAPPENED TO JOE *OR* HIS KID.

JUST GIMME MY THREE BUCKS FOR MINDIN' HIM. I AIN'T SEEN NOTHIN'.

NOW WHAT? YOU GOIN' TO SEND THE KID TO COLLEGE?

HEY, THAT'S AN IDEA. MAYBE THEY'LL TAKE HIM NOW!

BEAT YOUR GUMS ALL YOU LIKE. THE KID'S STAYIN' WITH US... AN' WE'RE BRINGIN' HIM UP!

A WEEK LATER...

KEEP HIM QUIET, WILL YA? I AIN'T SLEPT IN A WEEK!

WE'RE BROKE, BENNY. A KID NEEDS MEDICINE AND MILK. LET'S LEAVE HIM IN THE STREET SOMEWHERE. SOMEBODY'LL PICK HIM UP!

IF I HEAR ANY MORE TALK ABOUT KILLIN' THIS KID, THERE'LL BE KILLIN' APLENTY AROUND HERE. IF YOU GUYS NEED DOUGH, GO OUT AN' GET SOME!

NOT WITHOUT *YOU*, LITTLE MOTHER. YOU NEED DOUGH AS BAD AS US. PARK THE KID AND LET'S GO!

SO, AN HOUR LATER...

THIS IS A STICK-UP, BUD. TURN YOUR BACK TO THE WALL AN' DON'T GIVE US ANY BACKTALK!

TAKE ANYTHING YOU WANT... ONLY DON'T SHOOT P--PLEASE...

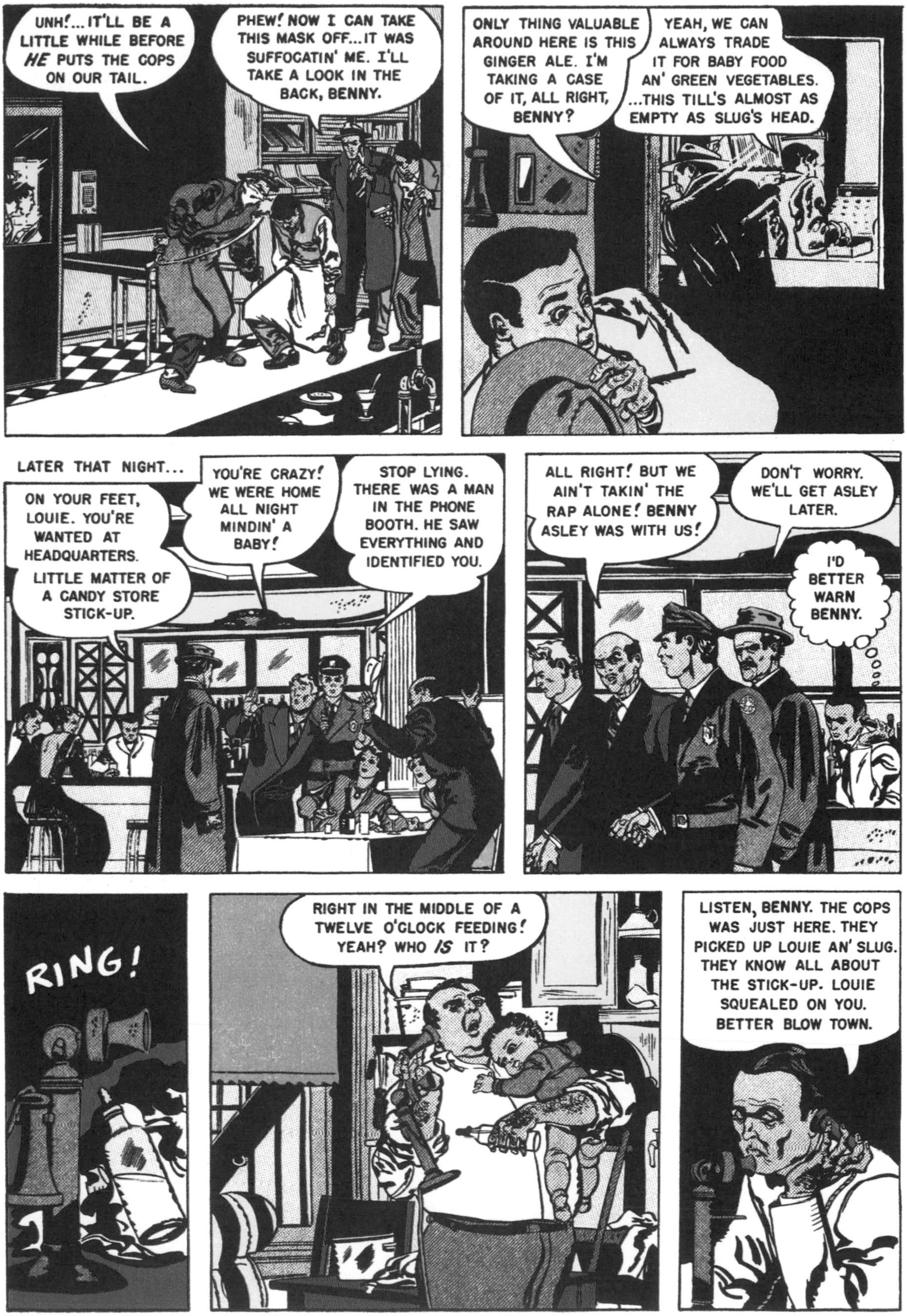

UNH!... IT'LL BE A LITTLE WHILE BEFORE HE PUTS THE COPS ON OUR TAIL.
PHEW! NOW I CAN TAKE THIS MASK OFF... IT WAS SUFFOCATIN' ME. I'LL TAKE A LOOK IN THE BACK, BENNY.
ONLY THING VALUABLE AROUND HERE IS THIS GINGER ALE. I'M TAKING A CASE OF IT, ALL RIGHT, BENNY?
YEAH, WE CAN ALWAYS TRADE IT FOR BABY FOOD AN' GREEN VEGETABLES. ...THIS TILL'S ALMOST AS EMPTY AS SLUG'S HEAD.
LATER THAT NIGHT...
ON YOUR FEET, LOUIE. YOU'RE WANTED AT HEADQUARTERS. LITTLE MATTER OF A CANDY STORE STICK-UP.
YOU'RE CRAZY! WE WERE HOME ALL NIGHT MINDIN' A BABY!
STOP LYING. THERE WAS A MAN IN THE PHONE BOOTH. HE SAW EVERYTHING AND IDENTIFIED YOU.
ALL RIGHT! BUT WE AIN'T TAKIN' THE RAP ALONE! BENNY ASLEY WAS WITH US!
DON'T WORRY. WE'LL GET ASLEY LATER.
I'D BETTER WARN BENNY.
RING!
RIGHT IN THE MIDDLE OF A TWELVE O'CLOCK FEEDING! YEAH? WHO IS IT?
LISTEN, BENNY. THE COPS WAS JUST HERE. THEY PICKED UP LOUIE AN' SLUG. THEY KNOW ALL ABOUT THE STICK-UP. LOUIE SQUEALED ON YOU. BETTER BLOW TOWN.

LATER THAT NIGHT...

AND SO THE YEARS PASSED... FOR SLUG AND LOUIE, THEY PASSED BEHIND BARS...

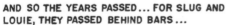

FOUR MONTHS LATER, OUTSIDE THE JUDSON COUNTY PEN...

WHAT ARE YOU LICE THINKIN' OF? IF YOU MESS UP THAT KID'S LIFE...IF YOU TRY *KIDNAPPIN'* HIM... I'LL *KILL* YOU!

KIDNAP HIM? TAKE IT EASY, PAPA! NOTHIN' WAS FURTHER FROM MY THOUGHTS!

YOU GET THE SCREWIEST IDEAS, BENNY. WHY, YOU CAN GET THE *HOT SEAT* FOR KIDNAPPIN'!

THAT NIGHT... AN' WHO TAKES CARE OF THE KID? *OUTSIDE* THE HOUSE, I MEAN.

A NURSE, AN OLD LADY. THEY GO OUT FOR A WALK ABOUT TWO. ...THEN ABOUT 3:30, THE CHAUFFEUR PICKS THEM UP ON THE SOUTH DRIVE ... WHICH, INCIDENTALLY, GOES UP PAST OUR OLD HIDEOUT IN THE HILLS!

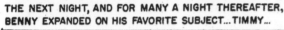

THE NEXT NIGHT, AND FOR MANY A NIGHT THEREAFTER, BENNY EXPANDED ON HIS FAVORITE SUBJECT...TIMMY...

DOES VAN CLEEF KEEP A LOT OF CASH HE CAN LAY HIS HANDS ON OVERNIGHT?

THE GUY'S *LOADED!* WHY DON'T YOU GUYS GO OVER THE GROUNDS SOMEDAY? YOU'LL SEE WHAT A SOFT SPOT I GAVE THAT KID!

YEAH, MAYBE WE WILL. MAYBE TOMORROW, EH, LOUIE?

THE FOLLOWING AFTERNOON...

TOO BAD YOU DON'T FEEL WELL ENOUGH TO GO WITH US, BENNY.

YEAH, BUT MAYBE I'LL SEE THE KID NEXT WEEK...WHEN I FEEL BETTER. DID YOU RENT THAT CAR, SLUG?

YEAH. SURE RUNS SMOOTH.

SEVERAL HOURS LATER...ON THE VAN CLEEF ESTATE...

WHAT A SUCKER! HE ANSWERED EVERY QUESTION! WE CAN SNATCH THAT KID EASIER THAN PICKIN' A POSY OFF A PARK LAWN!

PIPE DOWN! THEY'RE COMIN' NOW. TWO O'CLOCK ON THE BUTTON! COME ON!

LATER THAT AFTERNOON...

I CONTACTED VAN CLEEF AND IT'S IN THE BAG. HE'LL HAVE THE DOUGH FOR ME AT SIX TONIGHT! *200 GRAND!*

GOOD! IT WAS AWFUL NICE OF BENNY TO PICK THE KID A RICH FAMILY...

FIVE P.M....

WISH ME LUCK, LOUIE. IF EVERYTHING GOES RIGHT, I'LL BE BACK IN A COUPLE OF HOURS WITH A FORTUNE!

DON'T WORRY, SLUG. I WON'T GO AWAY!

YOU BET YOU WON'T GO AWAY, LOUIE. KEEP 'EM UP HIGH! THERE WAS NEVER ANYTHIN' WRONG WITH MY AIM -- NOR MY BRAINS, EITHER. GET INSIDE!

BENNY! WHAT ARE YOU DOIN' HERE? I--I THOUGHT YOU WERE SICK!

I AM. *VERY* SICK. SICK OF BEIN' A POOR BUM. BUT I THINK MY LUCK'S READY TO CHANGE NOW!

WAIT A MINUTE! Y--YOU KNEW *ALL THE TIME* WE WERE PLANNIN' TO KIDNAP THE KID! WHY, *YOU* SUGGESTED IT TO US -- PRETENDIN' YOU COULDN'T STOP TALKIN' ABOUT TIMMY BECAUSE YOU WERE SO CRAZY ABOUT HIM!

CORRECT. YOU AND SLUG DO THE DIRTY WORK WHILE I REAP THE PROFITS. YOU SEE, I WOULDN'T HAVE HAD SO TOUGH A TIME THESE FIVE YEARS IF YOU AN' SLUG HADN'T SENT THE COPS AFTER ME. BUT I FIGURE 200 GRAND SHOULD EVEN THE SCORE...

BUT WE WERE KIDNAPPIN' THE KID! I THOUGHT YOU *LIKED* HIM!

WHEN HE WAS AN INFANT, MAYBE. BUT I LIKE *DOUGH* BEST OF ALL. BESIDES, I KEPT MY OATH TO JOE. I SAW THAT THE KID GOT A GOOD UPBRINGIN', DIDN'T I? WHY SHOULDN'T *I* GET PAID FOR BEIN' SO NICE?

I--I CAN'T GET OVER IT. DOUBLE-CROSSED, LIKE I WAS A CHUMP BEGINNER...

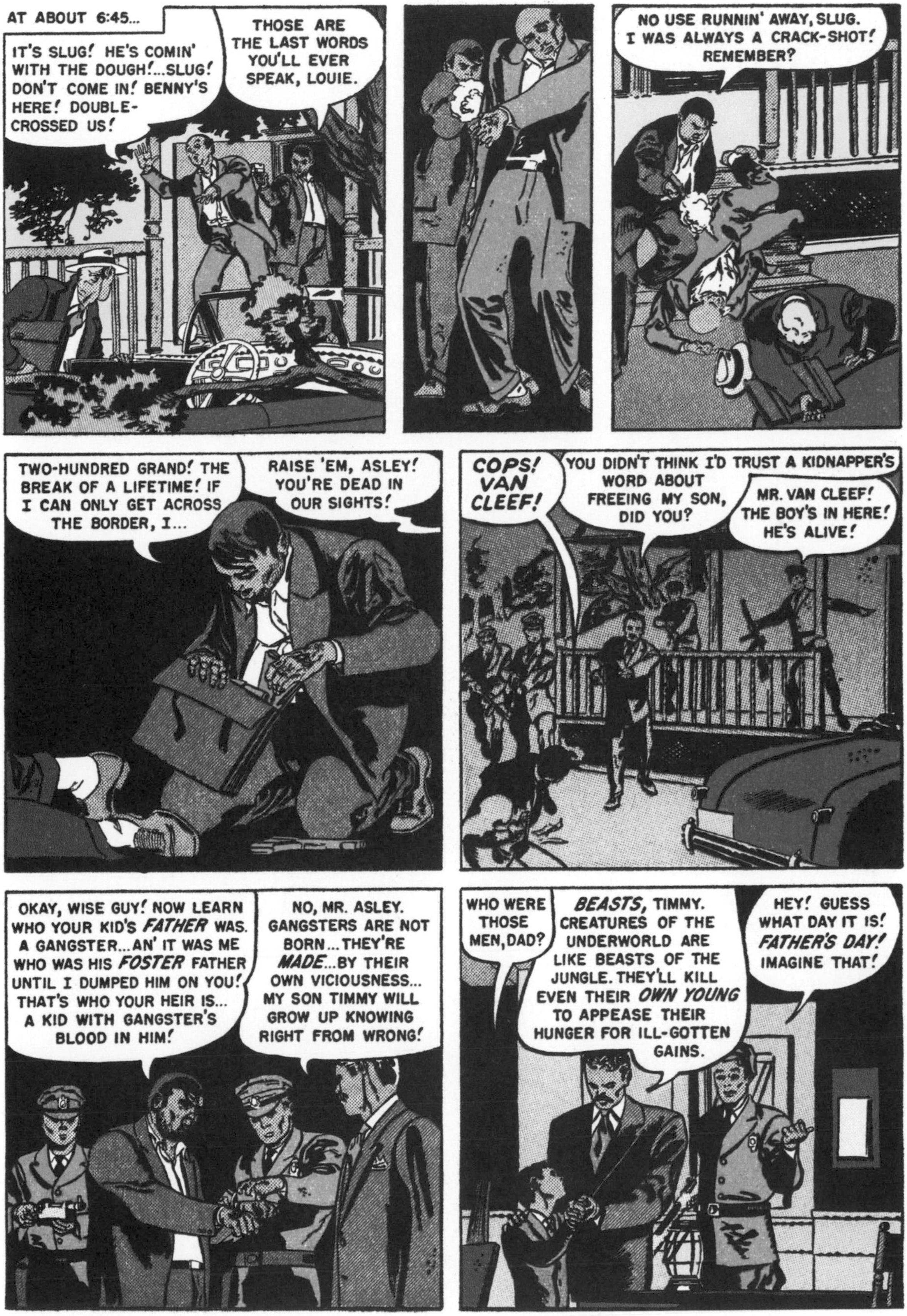
AT ABOUT 6:45...
IT'S SLUG! HE'S COMIN' WITH THE DOUGH!...SLUG! DON'T COME IN! BENNY'S HERE! DOUBLE-CROSSED US!
THOSE ARE THE LAST WORDS YOU'LL EVER SPEAK, LOUIE.
NO USE RUNNIN' AWAY, SLUG. I WAS ALWAYS A CRACK-SHOT! REMEMBER?
TWO-HUNDRED GRAND! THE BREAK OF A LIFETIME! IF I CAN ONLY GET ACROSS THE BORDER, I...
RAISE 'EM, ASLEY! YOU'RE DEAD IN OUR SIGHTS!
COPS! VAN CLEEF!
YOU DIDN'T THINK I'D TRUST A KIDNAPPER'S WORD ABOUT FREEING MY SON, DID YOU?
MR. VAN CLEEF! THE BOY'S IN HERE! HE'S ALIVE!
OKAY, WISE GUY! NOW LEARN WHO YOUR KID'S FATHER WAS. A GANGSTER...AN' IT WAS ME WHO WAS HIS FOSTER FATHER UNTIL I DUMPED HIM ON YOU! THAT'S WHO YOUR HEIR IS... A KID WITH GANGSTER'S BLOOD IN HIM!
NO, MR. ASLEY. GANGSTERS ARE NOT BORN...THEY'RE MADE...BY THEIR OWN VICIOUSNESS... MY SON TIMMY WILL GROW UP KNOWING RIGHT FROM WRONG!
WHO WERE THOSE MEN, DAD?
BEASTS, TIMMY. CREATURES OF THE UNDERWORLD ARE LIKE BEASTS OF THE JUNGLE. THEY'LL KILL EVEN THEIR OWN YOUNG TO APPEASE THEIR HUNGER FOR ILL-GOTTEN GAINS.
HEY! GUESS WHAT DAY IT IS! FATHER'S DAY! IMAGINE THAT!

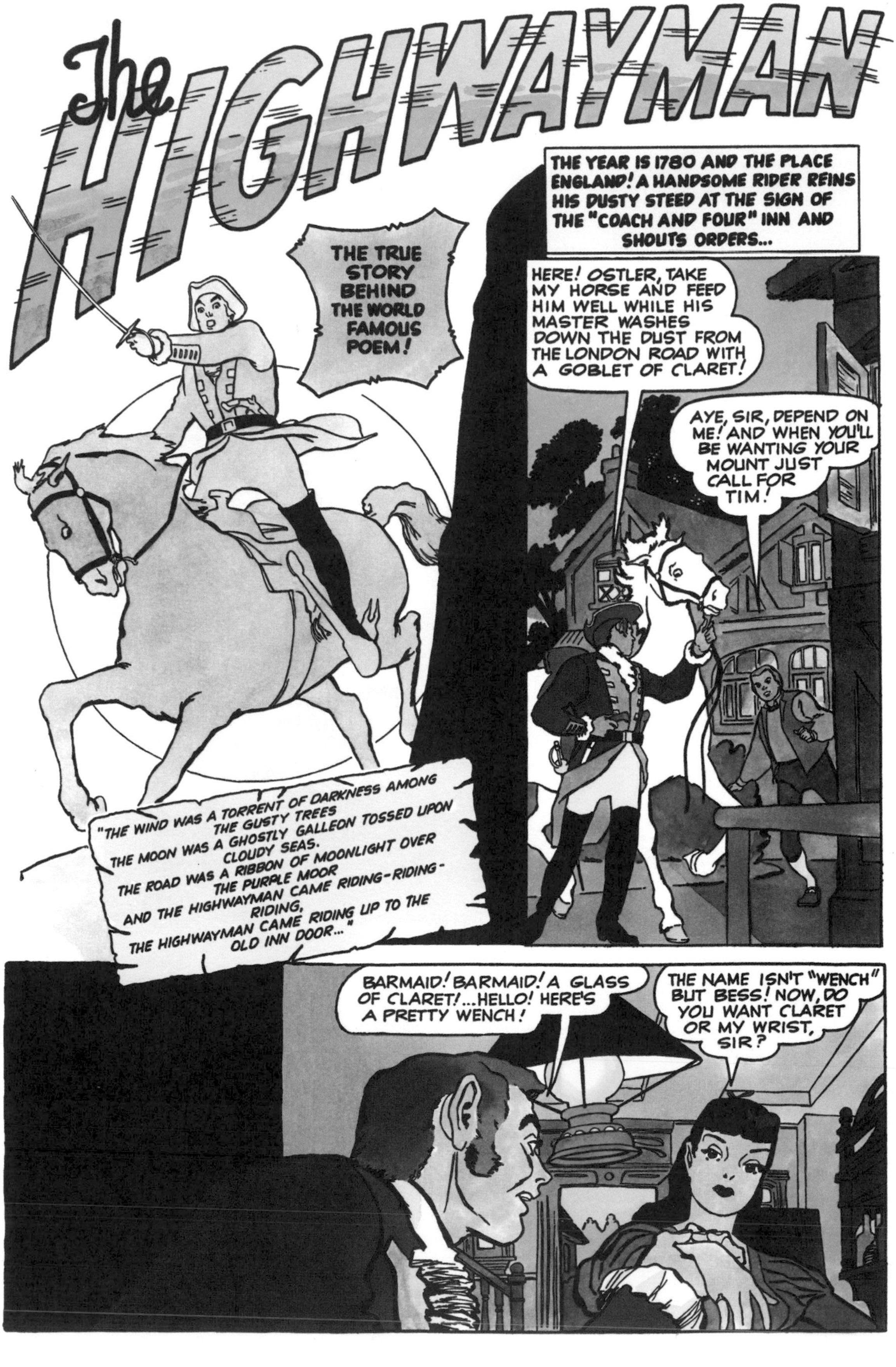
The HIGHWAYMAN
THE TRUE STORY BEHIND THE WORLD FAMOUS POEM!
THE YEAR IS 1780 AND THE PLACE ENGLAND! A HANDSOME RIDER REINS HIS DUSTY STEED AT THE SIGN OF THE "COACH AND FOUR" INN AND SHOUTS ORDERS...
HERE! OSTLER, TAKE MY HORSE AND FEED HIM WELL WHILE HIS MASTER WASHES DOWN THE DUST FROM THE LONDON ROAD WITH A GOBLET OF CLARET!
AYE, SIR, DEPEND ON ME! AND WHEN YOU'LL BE WANTING YOUR MOUNT JUST CALL FOR TIM!
"THE WIND WAS A TORRENT OF DARKNESS AMONG THE GUSTY TREES
THE MOON WAS A GHOSTLY GALLEON TOSSED UPON CLOUDY SEAS.
THE ROAD WAS A RIBBON OF MOONLIGHT OVER THE PURPLE MOOR
AND THE HIGHWAYMAN CAME RIDING-RIDING-RIDING,
THE HIGHWAYMAN CAME RIDING UP TO THE OLD INN DOOR..."
BARMAID! BARMAID! A GLASS OF CLARET!...HELLO! HERE'S A PRETTY WENCH!
THE NAME ISN'T "WENCH" BUT BESS! NOW, DO YOU WANT CLARET OR MY WRIST, SIR?

THE PRETTY DARK HAIRED DAUGHTER OF THE LANDLORD RETURNS WITH THE DRINK...

TO YOU, MY BONNY LASS, A SIGHT WELL WORTH RIDING THE LONG HIGHWAY FOR!

WATCH HOW YOU TALK TO HER, SIR! SHE'S, BESS, THE LANDLORD'S DAUGHTER, *MY GIRL!*

FORGIVE ME IF I DAMPEN YOUR SPIRITS AND CLAIM THE MAIDEN *MINE!*

'ELP!

THERE'S A ROGUE'S TRICK! YOU'VE SPOILED A GOOD BARREL OF MY BEST WINE! CAN YOU PAY FOR IT?

PAY FOR IT! ZOUNDS, MAN, YOU SHOULD PAY *ME* FOR FLAVORING IT! YOUR OSTLER'S GOT A SHARP TONGUE THAT SHOULD SPICE YOUR WINE NICELY!

FIRST YOU FLIRT WITH MY DAUGHTER, THEN RUIN MY PORT!

HOLD YOUR TONGUE, HOST! IF IT'S *GOLD* YOU WANT -- HERE!

THE OVERWHELMED LANDLORD SWEEPS UP THE GOLDEN GUINEAS AS THE LAUGHING RIDER STARTS FOR THE DOOR...

FAREWELL, *MY BESS!* THE MOON'S PEEPING OVER THE TREETOPS, THE HIGHWAY CALLS AND I HAVE A NIGHT'S WORK TO DO, BUT I'LL BE BACK FOR YOU!

YES, DO COME BACK! COME BACK OFTEN, YOUR LORDSHIP -- AS SOON AS YOU'VE FINISHED YOUR NIGHT'S WORK, *YOUR GRACE!*

BUT "HIS LORDSHIP'S" AND "HIS GRACE'S" WORK IS HARDLY THE *OCCUPATION* OF A NOBLEMAN! THOUGH ON HIS NIGHTLY ROUNDS HE OFTEN MEETS NOBLEMEN WHOSE UNFORTUNATE COACHES HE STOPS TO ROB! FIVE HOURS LATER, AS DISTANT LONDON SLEEPS, THE HIGHWAYMAN *COMES RIDING*...

WHOAA!

HALT! HALT! A BRACE OF PISTOLS ARE POINTING AT YOUR HEAD! STOP YOUR COACH OR YOU'LL TEMPT ME TO TRY THEIR ACCURACY!

THE COACH GRINDS TO A HALT AND THE FRIGHTENED PASSENGERS DISMOUNT FEEBLY TRYING TO HIDE THEIR VALUABLES! BUT AS THE LAST PASSENGER STEPS FROM THE KINGSBRIDGE COACH...

AND ME TRYING TO PAY A PEACEFUL VISIT TO MY OLD AUNT DOWN KINGSBRIDGE ROAD... *YOU!*

WE MEET AGAIN!

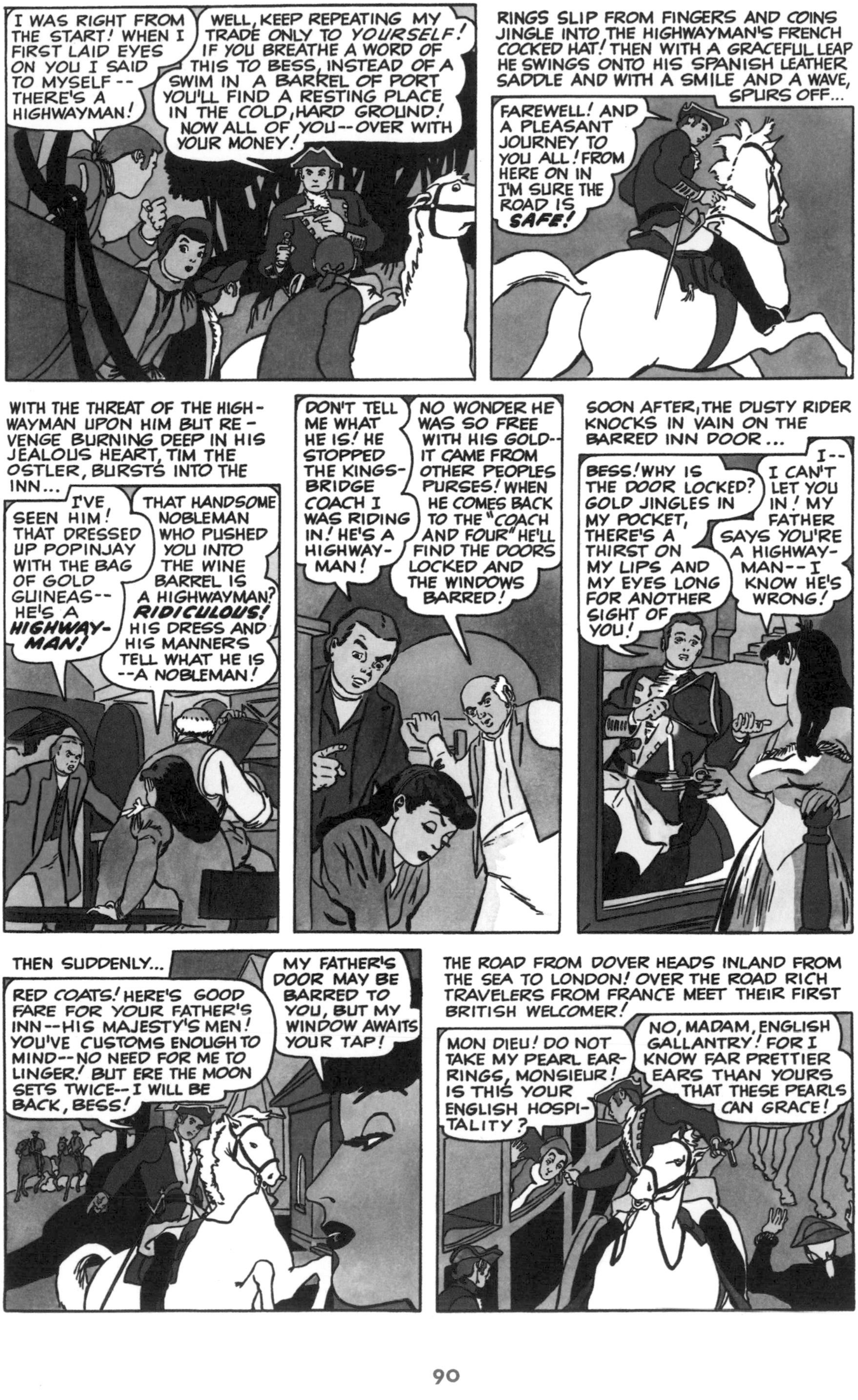
I WAS RIGHT FROM THE START! WHEN I FIRST LAID EYES ON YOU I SAID TO MYSELF -- THERE'S A HIGHWAYMAN!
WELL, KEEP REPEATING MY TRADE ONLY TO YOURSELF! IF YOU BREATHE A WORD OF THIS TO BESS, INSTEAD OF A SWIM IN A BARREL OF PORT YOU'LL FIND A RESTING PLACE IN THE COLD, HARD GROUND! NOW ALL OF YOU--OVER WITH YOUR MONEY!
RINGS SLIP FROM FINGERS AND COINS JINGLE INTO THE HIGHWAYMAN'S FRENCH COCKED HAT! THEN WITH A GRACEFUL LEAP HE SWINGS ONTO HIS SPANISH LEATHER SADDLE AND WITH A SMILE AND A WAVE, SPURS OFF...
FAREWELL! AND A PLEASANT JOURNEY TO YOU ALL! FROM HERE ON IN I'M SURE THE ROAD IS SAFE!
WITH THE THREAT OF THE HIGHWAYMAN UPON HIM BUT REVENGE BURNING DEEP IN HIS JEALOUS HEART, TIM THE OSTLER, BURSTS INTO THE INN...
I'VE SEEN HIM! THAT DRESSED UP POPINJAY WITH THE BAG OF GOLD GUINEAS--HE'S A HIGHWAYMAN!
THAT HANDSOME NOBLEMAN WHO PUSHED YOU INTO THE WINE BARREL IS A HIGHWAYMAN? RIDICULOUS! HIS DRESS AND HIS MANNERS TELL WHAT HE IS --A NOBLEMAN!
DON'T TELL ME WHAT HE IS! HE STOPPED THE KINGSBRIDGE COACH I WAS RIDING IN! HE'S A HIGHWAYMAN!
NO WONDER HE WAS SO FREE WITH HIS GOLD--IT CAME FROM OTHER PEOPLES PURSES! WHEN HE COMES BACK TO THE "COACH AND FOUR" HE'LL FIND THE DOORS LOCKED AND THE WINDOWS BARRED!
SOON AFTER, THE DUSTY RIDER KNOCKS IN VAIN ON THE BARRED INN DOOR...
BESS! WHY IS THE DOOR LOCKED? GOLD JINGLES IN MY POCKET, THERE'S A THIRST ON MY LIPS AND MY EYES LONG FOR ANOTHER SIGHT OF YOU!
I--I CAN'T LET YOU IN! MY FATHER SAYS YOU'RE A HIGHWAYMAN--I KNOW HE'S WRONG!
THEN SUDDENLY...
RED COATS! HERE'S GOOD FARE FOR YOUR FATHER'S INN--HIS MAJESTY'S MEN! YOU'VE CUSTOMS ENOUGH TO MIND--NO NEED FOR ME TO LINGER! BUT ERE THE MOON SETS TWICE--I WILL BE BACK, BESS!
MY FATHER'S DOOR MAY BE BARRED TO YOU, BUT MY WINDOW AWAITS YOUR TAP!
THE ROAD FROM DOVER HEADS INLAND FROM THE SEA TO LONDON! OVER THE ROAD RICH TRAVELERS FROM FRANCE MEET THEIR FIRST BRITISH WELCOMER!
MON DIEU! DO NOT TAKE MY PEARL EARRINGS, MONSIEUR! IS THIS YOUR ENGLISH HOSPITALITY?
NO, MADAM, ENGLISH GALLANTRY! FOR I KNOW FAR PRETTIER EARS THAN YOURS THAT THESE PEARLS CAN GRACE!

I WILL HAVE THEM BACK! MY HUSBAND SPENT A FORTUNE FOR THEM!

AND MONEY WELL SPENT! BUT I AM SURE IF HE SAW ME TAKING THEM TO A FAR YOUNGER WOMAN HE WOULD APPLAUD MY NOBLE ACT! *AWAY!*

THE MOON RIDES HIGH AND THE TWO PEARLS SPARKLE IN THE HIGHWAYMAN'S HAND AS HE STARTS FOR THE "COACH AND FOUR," BUT THE JEALOUS OSTLER WALKS OUTSIDE THE INN AS IF ON GUARD...

NOW TO GET RID OF HIM! I'LL RELEASE THE HORSES AND SEE WHICH IS GREATER-- HIS LOVE FOR BESS OR HIS DUTY TO THE HORSES!

OFF WITH YOU!

AS THE HORSES RACE FROM THE STABLE THE WATCHFUL OSTLER TURNS...

HEY! WHOA! WHAT MISCHIEVOUS WITCH OR GOBLIN SET YOU FREE? WHOA! HALT, I PRAY YOU, *HALT!*

BESS! BESS!

YOU HAVE COME BACK!

I'LL ALWAYS COME BY MOONLIGHT, AT THE SILVER HOUR! I RODE HARD THROUGH THE NIGHT TO BRING A RICH PRESENT FOR ONE SO FAIR AS YOU -- HERE!

PEARL EARRINGS! THEY'RE BEAUTIFUL! WHERE DID YOU GET THEM?

SAY I FETCHED THEM FROM THE INDIES! RIDING MY VALIANT WINGED STEED ACROSS THE OCEAN I SAW THEM IN THE WATERY DEPTH BELOW AND FOR MY LOVE I DOVE AND BROUGHT THEM UP! THEN I RACED HERE WITH THEM UP THE DOVER ROAD!

THAT'S A PRETTY STORY! AND IF YOU SAY THAT'S HOW THEY CAME TO ME -- WHY THEN I STILL FEEL THE WATER OF THE INDIAN SEAS CLINGING TO THEM AND THEY'RE COOLING TO MY EARS!

THEN TILL TOMORROW NIGHT, AND WHO KNOWS WHAT PRIZES THE STARRY NIGHT MAY BRING?

LATE THE NEXT AFTERNOON A FASHIONABLE COACH STOPS AT THE "COACH AND FOUR" AS ITS FOREIGN PASSENGERS SEEK REFRESHMENT ON THEIR WAY FROM LONDON TO CAMBRIDGE...

WHAT CAN I GET FOR YOUR LADYSHIP?

MADEMOISELLE, YOU MAY BRING ME -- THOSE EARRINGS, *THEY ARE MINE!*

THEY CAN'T BE YOURS! MY LOVER GAVE THEM TO ME LAST NIGHT!

IF YOUR GENTLE-MAN IS A HAND-SOME ROGUE WITH A CLARET DOUBLET AND SHINY PISTOLS --IT IS HE WHO TOOK THEM FROM ME LAST NIGHT ON THE ROAD FROM DOVER!

I TOLD YOU HE WAS A COMMON *HIGHWAY-MAN!*

H-HERE-- TAKE THEM IF THEY'RE YOURS...

THE HAPPY OSTLER FOLLOWS BESS UP TO HER ROOM BUT HIS MOMENT OF JEALOUS TRIUMPH IS CUT SHORT AS SHE SLAMS THE HEAVY OAK DOOR SHUT IN HIS FACE...

NO! (SOB!) IT CAN'T BE...HIS WORDS ARE POETRY, HIS MANNERS MAJESTIC...BUT HE'S JUST A HIGHWAYMAN (SOB!)...BUT I DON'T CARE WHAT HE IS SO LONG AS HE COMES BACK TO ME AGAIN TONIGHT-- *I LOVE HIM!*

NIGHT DRAWS HER DARK CLOAK ACROSS THE COUNTRY ROAD AND THE HIGHWAYMAN STARTS BACK ON HIS PERILOUS ROUTE...

YE WON'T BE STEALING MY PURSE, CUTTHROAT! BY MY RIGHT ARM, I'LL RUN YE THROUGH!

SO BE IT! YOUR RIGHT ARM AGAINST MINE-- TO THE WINNER THE PURSE!

AIEE!

NEXT TIME-- IF THERE IS A NEXT TIME FOR YOU, SIR--PARRY WHEN YOUR OPPONENT THRUSTS!

I'LL TAKE THE DUEL'S PRIZE --YOUR PURSE--AND BE OFF! THERE'S A BONNY LASS WHO WAITS FOR ME, AND IF YOUR PURSE BE FULL ENOUGH, THEN MY WORK'S DONE FOR THIS NIGHT!

"OVER THE COBBLES HE CLATTERED AND CLASHED IN THE DARK INN-YARD, AND HE TAPPED WITH HIS WHIP ON THE SHUTTERS...AND WHO SHOULD BE WAITING THERE..."

BESS, YOUR PRETTY EYES ARE RED FROM TEARS... AND WHERE ARE THE PEARL EARRINGS I FETCHED YOU FROM THE FAR OFF INDIES?

THE FRENCH WOMAN WHO WAS ROBBED OF THEM ALONG THE DOVER ROAD HAS THEM AGAIN!

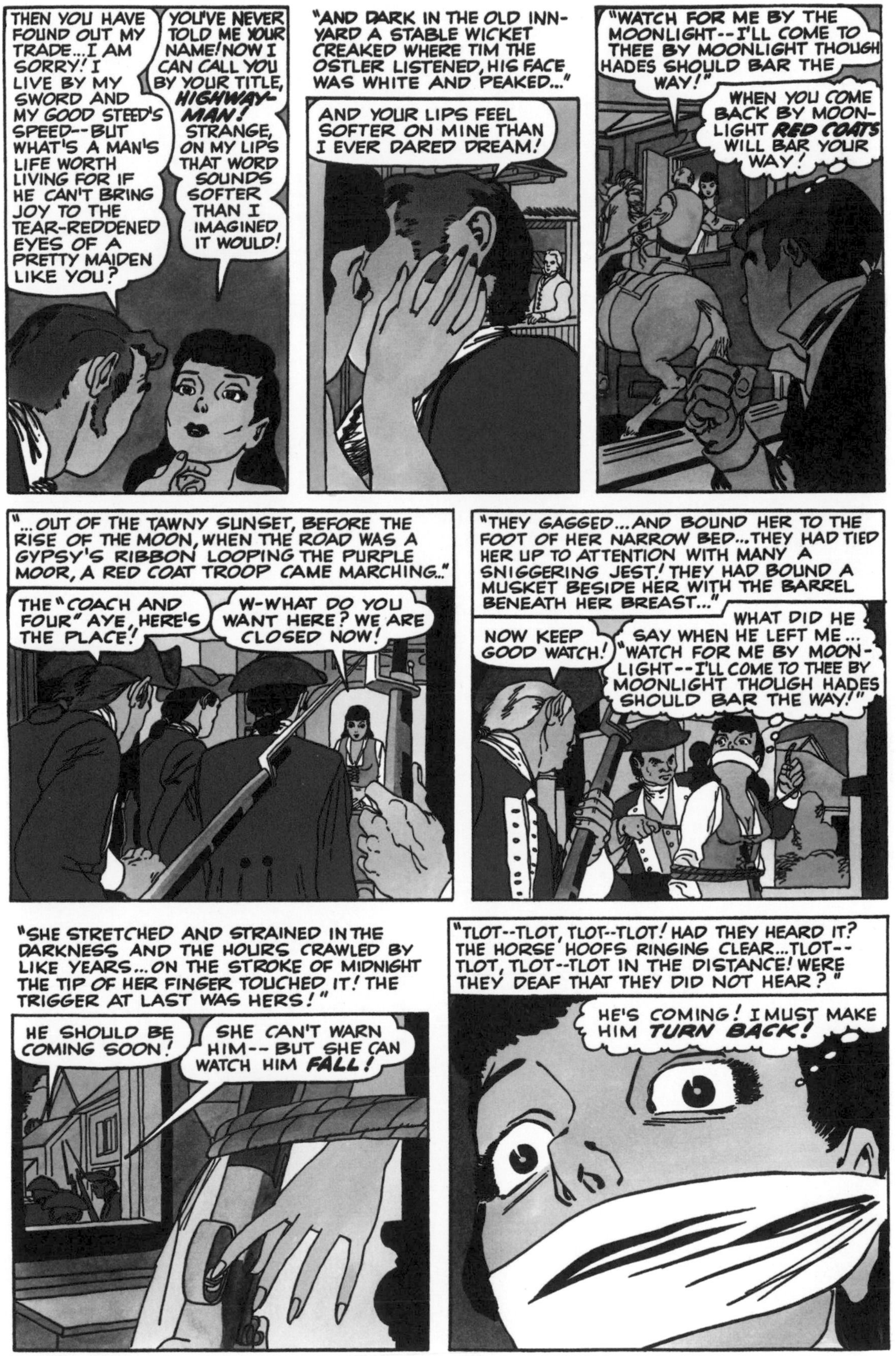
THEN YOU HAVE FOUND OUT MY TRADE...I AM SORRY! I LIVE BY MY SWORD AND MY GOOD STEED'S SPEED--BUT WHAT'S A MAN'S LIFE WORTH LIVING FOR IF HE CAN'T BRING JOY TO THE TEAR-REDDENED EYES OF A PRETTY MAIDEN LIKE YOU?
YOU'VE NEVER TOLD ME YOUR NAME! NOW I CAN CALL YOU BY YOUR TITLE, HIGHWAY-MAN! STRANGE, ON MY LIPS THAT WORD SOUNDS SOFTER THAN I IMAGINED IT WOULD!
"AND DARK IN THE OLD INN-YARD A STABLE WICKET CREAKED WHERE TIM THE OSTLER LISTENED, HIS FACE WAS WHITE AND PEAKED..."
AND YOUR LIPS FEEL SOFTER ON MINE THAN I EVER DARED DREAM!
"WATCH FOR ME BY THE MOONLIGHT--I'LL COME TO THEE BY MOONLIGHT THOUGH HADES SHOULD BAR THE WAY!"
WHEN YOU COME BACK BY MOON-LIGHT RED COATS WILL BAR YOUR WAY!
"...OUT OF THE TAWNY SUNSET, BEFORE THE RISE OF THE MOON, WHEN THE ROAD WAS A GYPSY'S RIBBON LOOPING THE PURPLE MOOR, A RED COAT TROOP CAME MARCHING..."
THE "COACH AND FOUR" AYE, HERE'S THE PLACE!
W-WHAT DO YOU WANT HERE? WE ARE CLOSED NOW!
"THEY GAGGED...AND BOUND HER TO THE FOOT OF HER NARROW BED...THEY HAD TIED HER UP TO ATTENTION WITH MANY A SNIGGERING JEST! THEY HAD BOUND A MUSKET BESIDE HER WITH THE BARREL BENEATH HER BREAST..."
NOW KEEP GOOD WATCH!
WHAT DID HE SAY WHEN HE LEFT ME... "WATCH FOR ME BY MOON-LIGHT--I'LL COME TO THEE BY MOONLIGHT THOUGH HADES SHOULD BAR THE WAY!"
"SHE STRETCHED AND STRAINED IN THE DARKNESS AND THE HOURS CRAWLED BY LIKE YEARS...ON THE STROKE OF MIDNIGHT THE TIP OF HER FINGER TOUCHED IT! THE TRIGGER AT LAST WAS HERS!"
HE SHOULD BE COMING SOON!
SHE CAN'T WARN HIM--BUT SHE CAN WATCH HIM FALL!
"TLOT--TLOT, TLOT--TLOT! HAD THEY HEARD IT? THE HORSE HOOFS RINGING CLEAR...TLOT--TLOT, TLOT--TLOT IN THE DISTANCE! WERE THEY DEAF THAT THEY DID NOT HEAR?"
HE'S COMING! I MUST MAKE HIM TURN BACK!

"DOWN THE RIBBON OF MOON-LIGHT, OVER THE BROW OF THE HILL THE HIGHWAYMAN CAME RIDING--RIDING..."

HERE HE COMES! READY...AIM...

"THEN HER FINGER MOVED IN THE MOONLIGHT, HER MUSKET SHATTERED THE MOONLIGHT...SHATTERED HER BREAST IN THE MOONLIGHT AND WARNED HIM --WITH HER DEATH..."

BOOM!

"HE TURNED AND SPURRED TO THE WEST..."

AWAY! SOMEONE FIRED A WARNING SHOT! I SHAN'T WAIT TO FIND OUT WHO!

"...HE DID NOT KNOW WHO STOOD...BOWED WITH HER HEAD OVER THE MUSKET, DRENCHED WITH HER OWN RED BLOOD...NOT TILL THE DAWN HE HEARD IT...BACK HE SPURRED LIKE A MADMAN, SHRIEKING A CURSE TO THE SKY..."

I'LL KILL EVERY RED COAT WHO BARS MY WAY! I'LL SEE MY FALLEN BONNY BESS AGAIN! I'LL SEE HER OR DIE!

"WITH THE WHITE ROAD SMOKING BEHIND HIM AND HIS RAPIER BRANDISHED HIGH..."

BESS! BESS! I MUST GET THROUGH TO HER!

FIRE!

"BLOOD RED WERE HIS SPURS IN THE GOLDEN NOON, WINE RED WAS HIS VELVET COAT WHEN THEY SHOT HIM DOWN IN THE HIGHWAY, DOWN LIKE A DOG IN THE HIGHWAY..."

BESS! BESS!

BOOM!

"AND STILL OF A WINTER'S NIGHT THEY SAY WHEN THE WIND IS IN THE TREES,...WHEN THE MOON IS A GHOSTLY GALLEON TOSSED UPON CLOUDY SEAS...WHEN THE ROAD IS A RIBBON OF MOONLIGHT OVER THE PURPLE MOOR...A HIGHWAYMAN COMES RIDING, RIDING, RIDING...A HIGHWAY-MAN COMES RIDING UP TO THE OLD INN DOOR!"

BLACKSMITH BELLE MALONE

"JIM MALONE WAS A MIGHTY GOOD BLACKSMITH — BUT HIS MIND WASN'T ON HIS WORK... BECUZ HE HAD THE GOLD ITCH — THAT GNAWING POISON OF THE YELLOW STUFF THAT MAKES PRINCES AND PAUPERS OVERNIGHT. NOW JIM'S WIFE BELLE WAS AS FINE A WOMAN AS YOU'D MEET IN A DAY'S WALK, AND SHE WORRIED AWFUL ABOUT JIM... JUST LIKE SHE'S DOING NOW — AS A TRAVELER GETS JIM EXCITED ABOUT A NEW STRIKE "...

YOU SAY THERE'S A NEW GOLD STRIKE AT YOSEMITE? MAN!—THAT'S WHERE I'D LIKE TO BE, DIGGIN' UP A FORTUNE!

MIND WHAT YOU'RE DOIN' TO THAT WAGON RIM, JIM MALONE, AND LEAVE OFF WITH THOSE WILD THOUGHTS OF GOLD PROSPECTIN'!

JIM MALONE
BLACKSMITH

IT'S ALL RIGHT, BELLE... JUST SOME IDLE TALK WHILE I FINISH UP THIS JOB...NOW WHAT WERE YA SAYIN' ABOUT THEM NUGGETS?

LOOK, MR. MALONE, I'VE GOT TO MAKE CAMP AT DAGGET CREEK ...THAT'S TWENTY MILES AWAY. WOULD YOU PLEASE HURRY UP?

JIM, STOP THE PALAVER AND FINISH THE JOB!

"THAT EVENING..."

BELLE... WHY ARE YOU SO AGAINST MY GOIN PROSPECTIN' AN' BRINGIN' HOME A KABOODLE FULL O' GOLD?

WE'VE HAD THIS OUT BEFORE, JIM. THERE'S A BIG FUTURE FOR US RIGHT HERE IN STOCKTON CITY AND I MEAN TO STAY PUT!

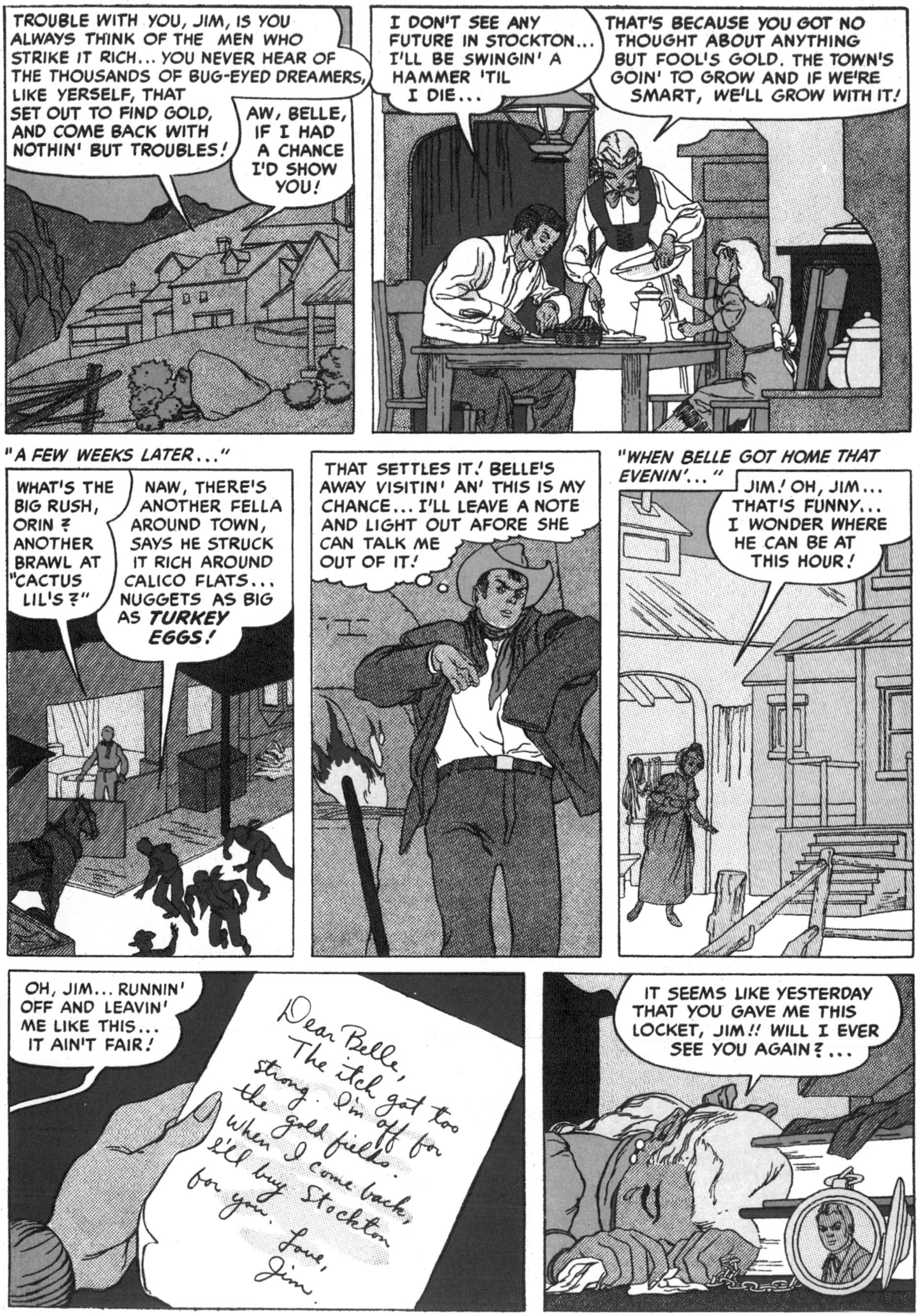
TROUBLE WITH YOU, JIM, IS YOU ALWAYS THINK OF THE MEN WHO STRIKE IT RICH... YOU NEVER HEAR OF THE THOUSANDS OF BUG-EYED DREAMERS, LIKE YERSELF, THAT SET OUT TO FIND GOLD, AND COME BACK WITH NOTHIN' BUT TROUBLES!
AW, BELLE, IF I HAD A CHANCE I'D SHOW YOU!
I DON'T SEE ANY FUTURE IN STOCKTON... I'LL BE SWINGIN' A HAMMER 'TIL I DIE...
THAT'S BECAUSE YOU GOT NO THOUGHT ABOUT ANYTHING BUT FOOL'S GOLD. THE TOWN'S GOIN' TO GROW AND IF WE'RE SMART, WE'LL GROW WITH IT!
"A FEW WEEKS LATER..."
WHAT'S THE BIG RUSH, ORIN? ANOTHER BRAWL AT "CACTUS LIL'S?"
NAW, THERE'S ANOTHER FELLA AROUND TOWN, SAYS HE STRUCK IT RICH AROUND CALICO FLATS... NUGGETS AS BIG AS TURKEY EGGS!
THAT SETTLES IT! BELLE'S AWAY VISITIN' AN' THIS IS MY CHANCE... I'LL LEAVE A NOTE AND LIGHT OUT AFORE SHE CAN TALK ME OUT OF IT!
"WHEN BELLE GOT HOME THAT EVENIN'..."
JIM! OH, JIM... THAT'S FUNNY... I WONDER WHERE HE CAN BE AT THIS HOUR!
OH, JIM... RUNNIN' OFF AND LEAVIN' ME LIKE THIS... IT AIN'T FAIR!
Dear Belle, The itch got too strong. I'm off for the gold fields. When I come back I'll buy Stockton for you. Love, Jim
IT SEEMS LIKE YESTERDAY THAT YOU GAVE ME THIS LOCKET, JIM!! WILL I EVER SEE YOU AGAIN?...

"THE NEXT DAY..." SHOP'S CLOSED! MY MAN'S GONE TO THE CUSSED GOLD FIELDS. THERE'S NO MORE BLACKSMITH IN STOCKTON!

BUT WHAT ARE WE GOIN' TO DO, BELLE? HORSES NEED SHOEIN', WAGONS NEED MENDIN'...WE NEED A BLACKSMITH!

WHAT'S IT TO ME, HARRY? AIN'T IT ENOUGH MY JIM'S GONE?

I DON'T WANT TO BOTHER YOU, BELLE—I KNOW IT'S TOUGH...BUT MY KID'S SICK AN' I GOTTA FETCH THE DOCTOR IN HEMLOCK!

"WELL, SIR, BELLE JEST ROLLED UP HER SLEEVES AN' WENT TO WORK..."

STOP GAWKIN' AN' GRINNIN'! BRING ON THAT PLUG O' YOURS, HARRY!

SURE ENOUGH, BELLE! YOU SWING A BETTER HAMMER THAN JIM EVER DID!

DON'T SAY NOTHIN' AGAINST MY MAN! HE'S A GOOD BLACKSMITH WHEN HE'S GOT A MIND TO BE ONE!

I STILL SAY YOU'RE A BLAMED LOT HANDIER THAN JIM EVER WAS!

WHEN A WOMAN TAKES IT INTO HER HEAD, THERE AIN'T HARDLY ANYTHING SHE CAN'T DO BETTER'N A MAN!

THANKS A MILLION, BELLE! SAY, LOOKEE, HALF THE TOWN'S WATCHIN' YOU!

THIS AIN'T NO SHOW! SHOO!! NOW, SCAT! IF YOU WANT ANY WORK DONE, MALONE IS STILL IN BUSINESS!!

HURRAY FOR BELLE! OUR LADY BLACKSMITH!

WHAT A WOMAN!

"BUT BELLE MISSED JIM...AN' SO DID LITTLE NANCY..."

WHEN IS DADDY COMING BACK, MUMMY?

I DECLARE...I DON'T KNOW, NANCY HONEY... BUT WHEN HE DOES, HE'LL HAVE SOMETHIN' MIGHTY PURTY FOR YA!

HI, BELLE! SORRY, NO LETTERS. I GUESS JIM AIN'T THE WRITIN' KIND.

GUESS YOU'RE RIGHT ...HE'LL JUST BARGE IN WHENEVER HE FINDS HIS OLD GOLD MINE.

"BUT JIM WASN'T FINDIN' ANY GOLD MINES...INSTEAD, ONLY BAD LUCK SEEMED TO FOLLOW THE FORMER BLACKSMITH OF STOCKTON CITY..."

C'MON, DAISY. THERE AIN'T ENOUGH GOLD TO FILL A TOOTH HERE. LET'S TRY DOWN THE RIVER!

HAW-HAW! THERE GOES "GOLD-NUGGETS" MALONE! SAY, MALONE, HAVE YOU STRUCK IT RICH YET?

AW, SHUT UP!

THAT MAN CAN'T STICK! HE'S LEFT PLACES WHERE OTHER PROSPECTORS HAVE GONE IN AND DUG OUT A FORTUNE!

JUST A MONTH'S GRUBSTAKE, MR. BREWSTER! I'LL PAY YOU BACK DOUBLE WHEN I STRIKE IT!

HOW ABOUT LAST MONTH'S GRUBSTAKE, MALONE? GO ON BACK HOME! YOU'VE GOT AS MUCH CHANCE OF STRIKIN' IT AS A GRASSHOPPER! NO MORE CREDIT FOR YOU! BEAT IT!

"WELL, THE YEARS PASSED, FIFTEEN TO BE EXACT, AN' STOCKTON CITY GREW...AN' JEST LIKE SHE SAID...BELLE GREW WITH IT..."

HOW'S THAT LOOK, BELLE?

THAT'S FINE, BOYS! I WONDER HOW JIM'LL FEEL WHEN HE SEES THAT, NANCY...

OH, MOM, IT WOULD BE PERFECT IF HE CAME HOME NOW.

MALONE BLACKSMITH

MORNIN', MRS. MALONE! HEAR THEY'RE DEDICATIN' THE NEW POST OFFICE BUILDING ON MAIN STREET.

YES, THEY'VE INVITED ME TO SAY A FEW WORDS...WAIT A MINUTE, FRANK, THAT'S NO WAY TO SHOE A HORSE!

YOU'RE HURTIN' THE POOR BEAST THE OTHER WAY! YOU GOTTA TAKE THE WEIGHT ON YOURSELF!

I RECKON BELLE'S THE FINEST BLACKSMITH IN THE WEST. MEN USED TO COME FIFTY MILES TO GET THEIR HORSES SHOED.

JUST GOT THESE GOVERNMENT PAPERS, AND AS MAYOR OF STOCKTON CITY I'M RIGHT PROUD TO ANNOUNCE OUR POST MISTRESS WILL BE-- *BELLE MALONE.*

THANK YOU, MAYOR HADLEY! I AM VERY HAPPY ABOUT THE APPOINTMENT, BUT MORE SO BECAUSE I'M A CITIZEN OF STOCKTON CITY!

"THERE WAS A BIG CELEBRATION IN HONOR OF BELLE, THE POST OFFICE AN' STOCKTON... AN' WHEN IT WAS ALL OVER, MAYOR TOM HADLEY WALKED BELLE HOME..."

BELLE... THIS AIN'T THE FIRST TIME I'VE ASKED YOU TO MARRY ME... I'VE KNOWN YOU TWELVE YEARS AN'...

BELLE... LET'S NOT START THAT OVER AGAIN, TOM...

DON'T YOU THINK YOU'VE WAITED LONG ENOUGH? JIM'S LEGALLY DEAD!

HUSH UP, TOM! JIM'S BEEN GONE ALMOST FIFTEEN YEARS, BUT TO ME IT SEEMS LIKE ONLY YESTERDAY. IT WON'T BE ANY GOOD. I'D ALWAYS THINK OF HIM!

AHH, NANCY, YER DAD WAS A GOOD MAN, BUT HE COULDN'T SIT STILL...HE HAD TO GO OUT...

HE'S PROBABLY A MILLIONAIRE NOW, AND HAS FORGOTTEN ABOUT US! HOW I WISH HE COULD ATTEND MY WEDDING NEXT WEEK!

"YEP, THAT'S RIGHT...LITTLE NANCY WAS GETTIN' HITCHED, BUT JIM MALONE PLUMB FERGOT ABOUT HIS WIFE AN' DAUGHTER...HE JEST KEPT PLUGGIN'..."

LISSEN, STRANGER, ALL I NEED'S A HUNDRED DOLLARS ...THERE'S ENOUGH GOLD IN THAT MINE TO LOAD A WAGON... AN'...

LOOK, MALONE, TAKE YORE PAWS OFFEN ME, I HEARD ABOUT YOU AND YORE MINE A HUNDRED TIMES...NOW GIT OUTA M'WAY!

"EVERYONE THOUGHT JIM WAS LOCO...HE SOON BECAME THE TOWN FOOL AN' PEOPLE GAVE HIM DRINK AN' FOOD JEST TO HEAR HIS WILD STORIES.."

...THANKS, STRANGER! NOW LEMME TELL YA ABOUT...

I ALREADY HEERED THAT ONE, "GOLD NUGGETS!" TELL ME 'NOTHER...

NEVER MIND "GOLD NUGGETS," HANK... I GOT NEWS... I JEST COME BACK FROM STOCKTON CITY AN' SHE'S A-GROWIN' FAST... THEY GOT A POST OFFICE, AN'...

STOCKTON CITY! THAT'S MY HOME TOWN!

...AN' THEY GOT A LADY POSTMASTER ...USED TO BE A BLACKSMITH, I HEAR TELL, AN' THAT SHE OWNS A LOT OF PROPERTY THERE!

THAT MUST BE BELLE MALONE— FINEST BLACKSMITH IN THE WEST! WHAT A WOMAN! SHE'S STOCKTON CITY'S PRIDE AND JOY.

BELLE MALONE? ...W-WHY THAT'S MY WIFE!

HAW-HAW! YOUR WIFE? HAW!

HA-HA! BELLE MALONE MARRIED TO YOU? WHY SHE WON'T BE SEEN ON THE SAME STREET WITH YOU-- HA, HA!

BELLE MALONE'S MY WIFE, AN' I CAN PROVE IT!

HAW-HAW! THAT KILLS ME, BELLE MALONE'S HUSBAND!

HERE COMES "GOLD NUGGETS!"

WATCH YOUR POCKETS! WATCH YOUR HORSES!

JIM MALONE'LL HAVE THE LAST LAUGH ON YOU COYOTES!

I'LL BORROW THIS NAG... WHOA...EASY NOW!

"AN' BACK IN STOCKTON CITY, NANCY WAS PREPARIN' FOR HER WEDDIN'..."

GIVE MY REGARDS TO BOB GREY. HE'S MARRYIN' THE FINEST GAL IN STOCKTON CITY.

THAT'S SWEET OF YOU, TOM! GOOD-BYE!

GOOD-BYE, BELLE. BEST OF LUCK, NANCY!

BYE, TOM! BYE, ALL.

"YEP, NANCY WAS GETTIN' MARRIED, AN' AS THE STAGE PLOWED THROUGH THE ROCKY COUNTRYSIDE, OL' JIM MALONE SAT ATOP HIS 'BORRERED' HORSE LOOKIN' AT THE STAGE AN' NOT KNOWIN' WHO WAS INSIDE..."

I CAN'T GO BACK EMPTY-HANDED ...NOT SINCE BELLE IS SUCH A BIG SHOT...*THAT STAGE!!* THAT'S IT!!

"AN' ON ANOTHER SIDE O' THE ROAD..."

LOOK, SAM, SOME OTHER ROAD AGENT IS STOPPIN' THE STAGE! HE'S HOLDIN' IT UP!

HEY! HE CAN'T DO THAT TO US! WE HAD THIS JOB LINED UP! LET'S GO, RINK!

NOW G-GET DOWN OFF THAT STAGE AND BRING THE STRONGBOX WITH YOU. YOU WOMEN! OUTSIDE, PRONTO!

MOTHER... HE'LL KILL US! WHAT'LL WE DO?

HE DON'T LOOK LIKE A KILLER TO ME!

HAW-HAW! SAM, LOOKIT THE *ROBBER!* IT'S THAT BUSHWHACKER, "GOLD NUGGETS!"

ALL RIGHT, "GOLD NUGGETS," PUT THAT GUN AWAY AN' KEEP THE LADIES COMPANY! ALL RIGHT...PILE OUT, LADIES!

IT'S...IT'S BELLE...AN JUST AS PRETTY AS EVER... AN' THAT MUST BE MY LITTLE NANCY...

HE'S A COWARD, MOTHER! HE'S SHAKING ALL OVER....!

THIEVES ARE REALLY ALL COWARDS AT HEART, NANCY! IT TAKES NERVE TO FACE LIFE HONESTLY.

OUTA THE WAY, "GOLD NUGGETS!" I'M EXPERIENCED AT THESE THINGS...NOW GIMME THAT THERE LOCKET, MA'AM... LOOKS LIKE IT MAY BE WORTH A FEW DOLLARS...

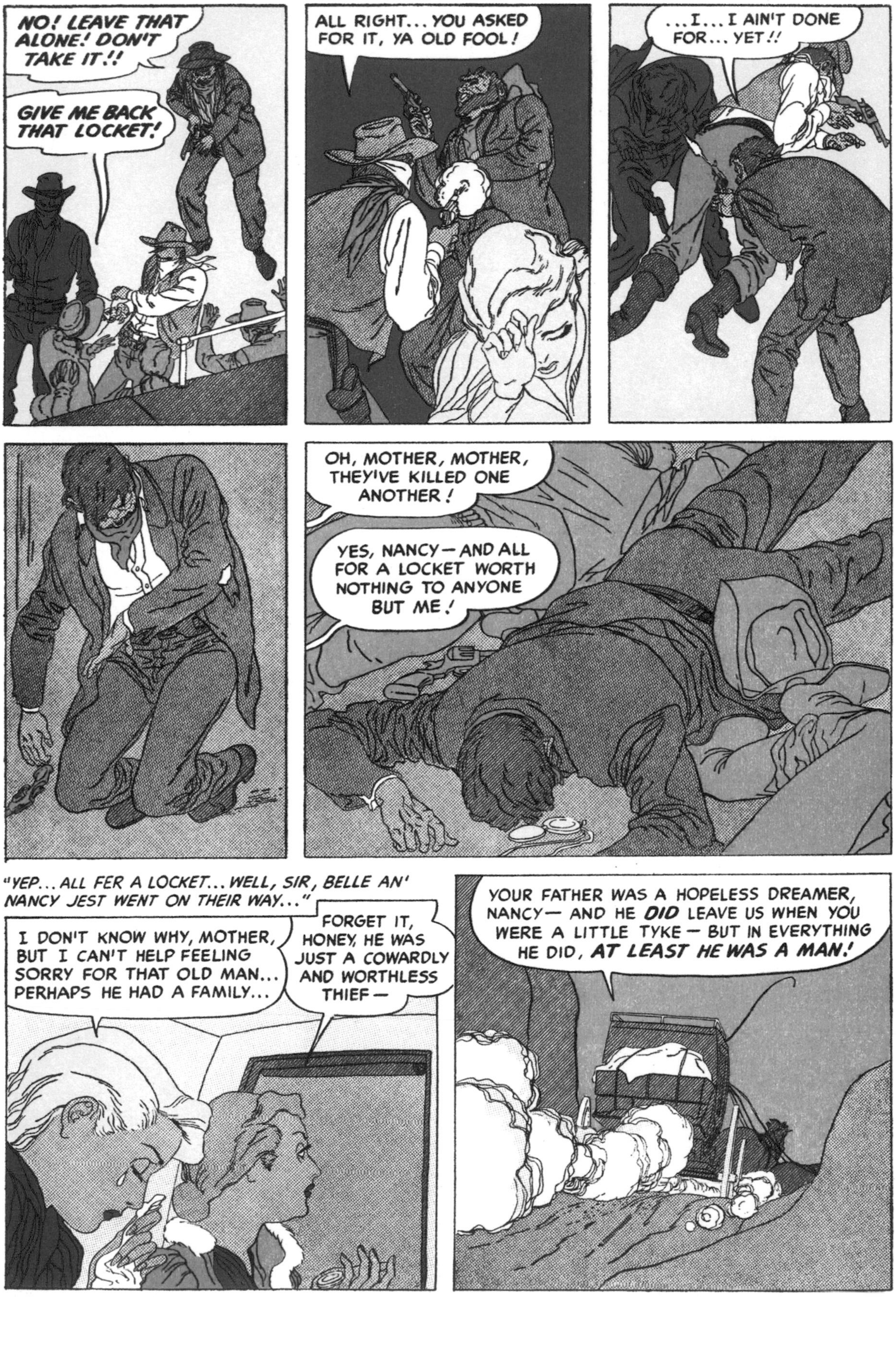
NO! LEAVE THAT ALONE! DON'T TAKE IT!!
GIVE ME BACK THAT LOCKET!
ALL RIGHT... YOU ASKED FOR IT, YA OLD FOOL!
...I... I AIN'T DONE FOR... YET!!
OH, MOTHER, MOTHER, THEY'VE KILLED ONE ANOTHER!
YES, NANCY— AND ALL FOR A LOCKET WORTH NOTHING TO ANYONE BUT ME!
"YEP... ALL FER A LOCKET... WELL, SIR, BELLE AN' NANCY JEST WENT ON THEIR WAY..."
I DON'T KNOW WHY, MOTHER, BUT I CAN'T HELP FEELING SORRY FOR THAT OLD MAN... PERHAPS HE HAD A FAMILY...
FORGET IT, HONEY, HE WAS JUST A COWARDLY AND WORTHLESS THIEF—
YOUR FATHER WAS A HOPELESS DREAMER, NANCY— AND HE DID LEAVE US WHEN YOU WERE A LITTLE TYKE— BUT IN EVERYTHING HE DID, AT LEAST HE WAS A MAN!

MONSTER OF THE SEAS

IN THE DAYS OF PIRACY THERE WAS ONE BUCCANEER WHO CAUSED MORE CHILLS THAN ALL THE REST OF THEM PUT TOGETHER...BECAUSE CAPTAIN SPLINT HAD A PARTNER "GORO" WHO WAS AN INTELLIGENT GORILLA. HERE WE SEE A DUTCH MERCHANT SHIP AS IT RUNS AFOUL OF SPLINT'S BLACK CREW—AND SPLINT SHOUTS ORDERS TO THE APE...

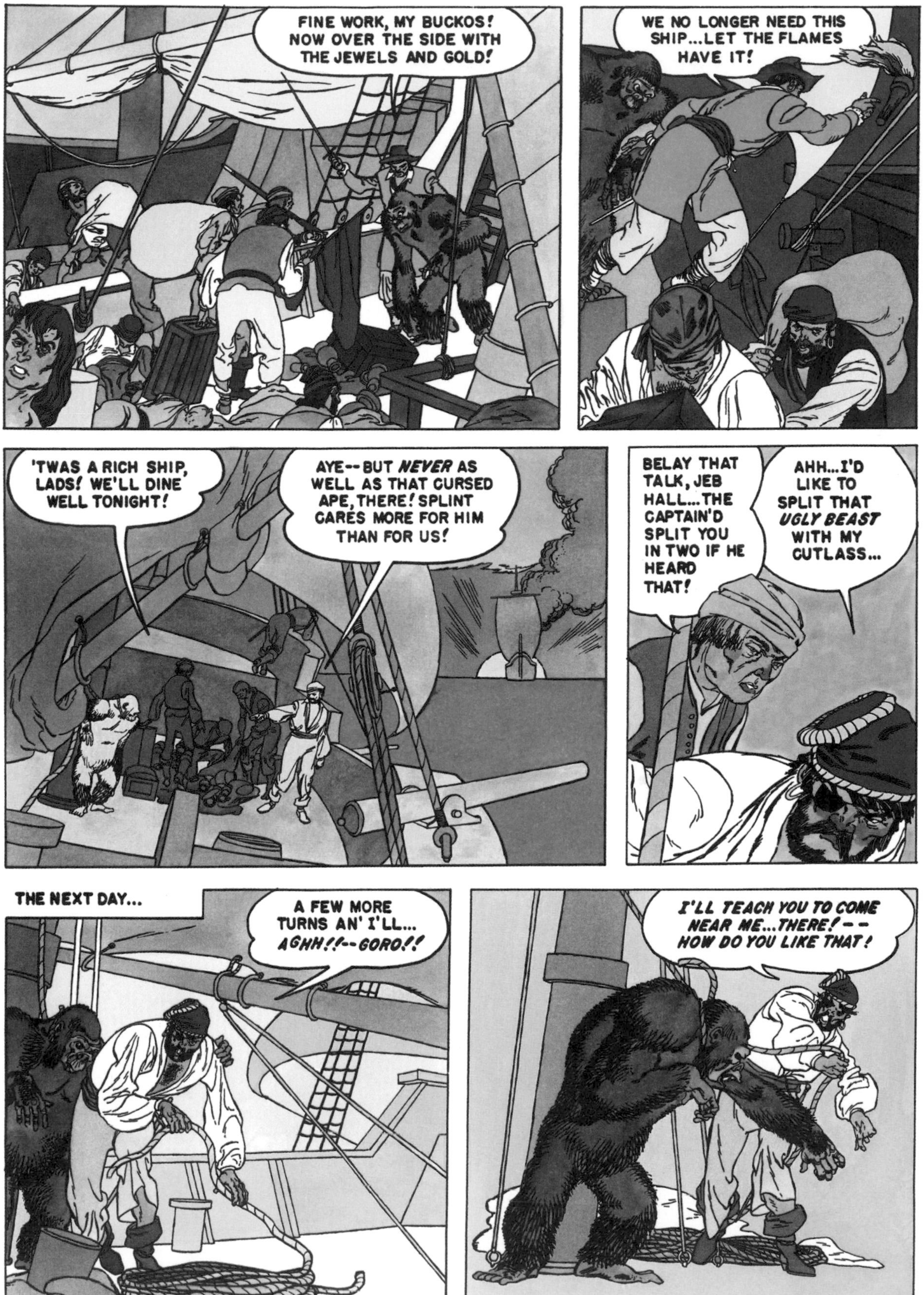
FINE WORK, MY BUCKOS! NOW OVER THE SIDE WITH THE JEWELS AND GOLD!
WE NO LONGER NEED THIS SHIP...LET THE FLAMES HAVE IT!
'TWAS A RICH SHIP, LADS! WE'LL DINE WELL TONIGHT!
AYE--BUT *NEVER* AS WELL AS THAT CURSED APE, THERE! SPLINT CARES MORE FOR HIM THAN FOR US!
BELAY THAT TALK, JEB HALL...THE CAPTAIN'D SPLIT YOU IN TWO IF HE HEARD THAT!
AHH...I'D LIKE TO SPLIT THAT *UGLY BEAST* WITH MY CUTLASS...
THE NEXT DAY...
A FEW MORE TURNS AN' I'LL... *AGHH!!--GORO!!*
I'LL TEACH YOU TO COME NEAR ME...THERE!-- HOW DO YOU LIKE THAT!

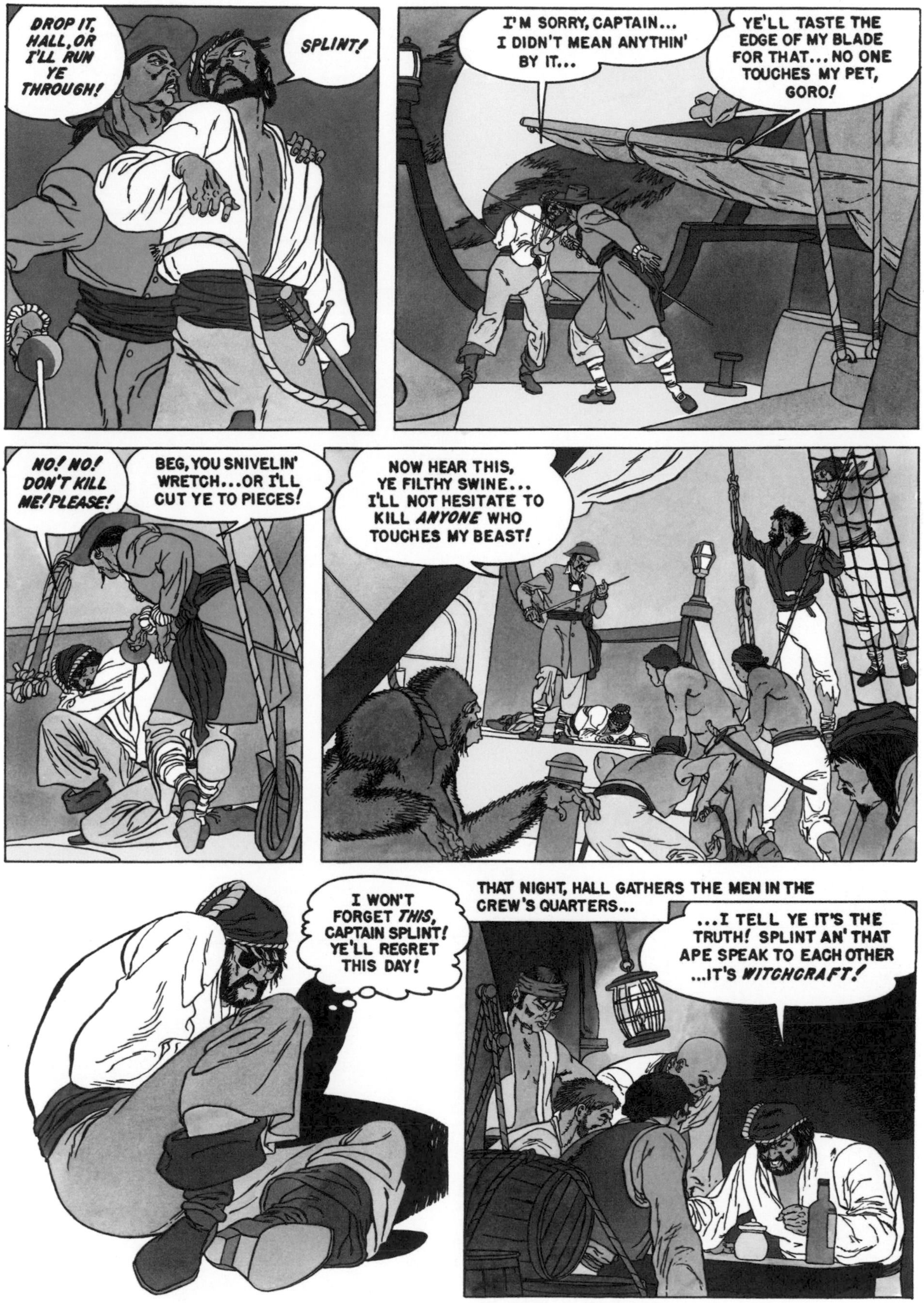
DROP IT, HALL, OR I'LL RUN YE THROUGH!
SPLINT!
I'M SORRY, CAPTAIN... I DIDN'T MEAN ANYTHIN' BY IT...
YE'LL TASTE THE EDGE OF MY BLADE FOR THAT... NO ONE TOUCHES MY PET, GORO!
NO! NO! DON'T KILL ME! PLEASE!
BEG, YOU SNIVELIN' WRETCH... OR I'LL CUT YE TO PIECES!
NOW HEAR THIS, YE FILTHY SWINE... I'LL NOT HESITATE TO KILL ANYONE WHO TOUCHES MY BEAST!
I WON'T FORGET THIS, CAPTAIN SPLINT! YE'LL REGRET THIS DAY!
THAT NIGHT, HALL GATHERS THE MEN IN THE CREW'S QUARTERS...
...I TELL YE IT'S THE TRUTH! SPLINT AN' THAT APE SPEAK TO EACH OTHER ...IT'S WITCHCRAFT!

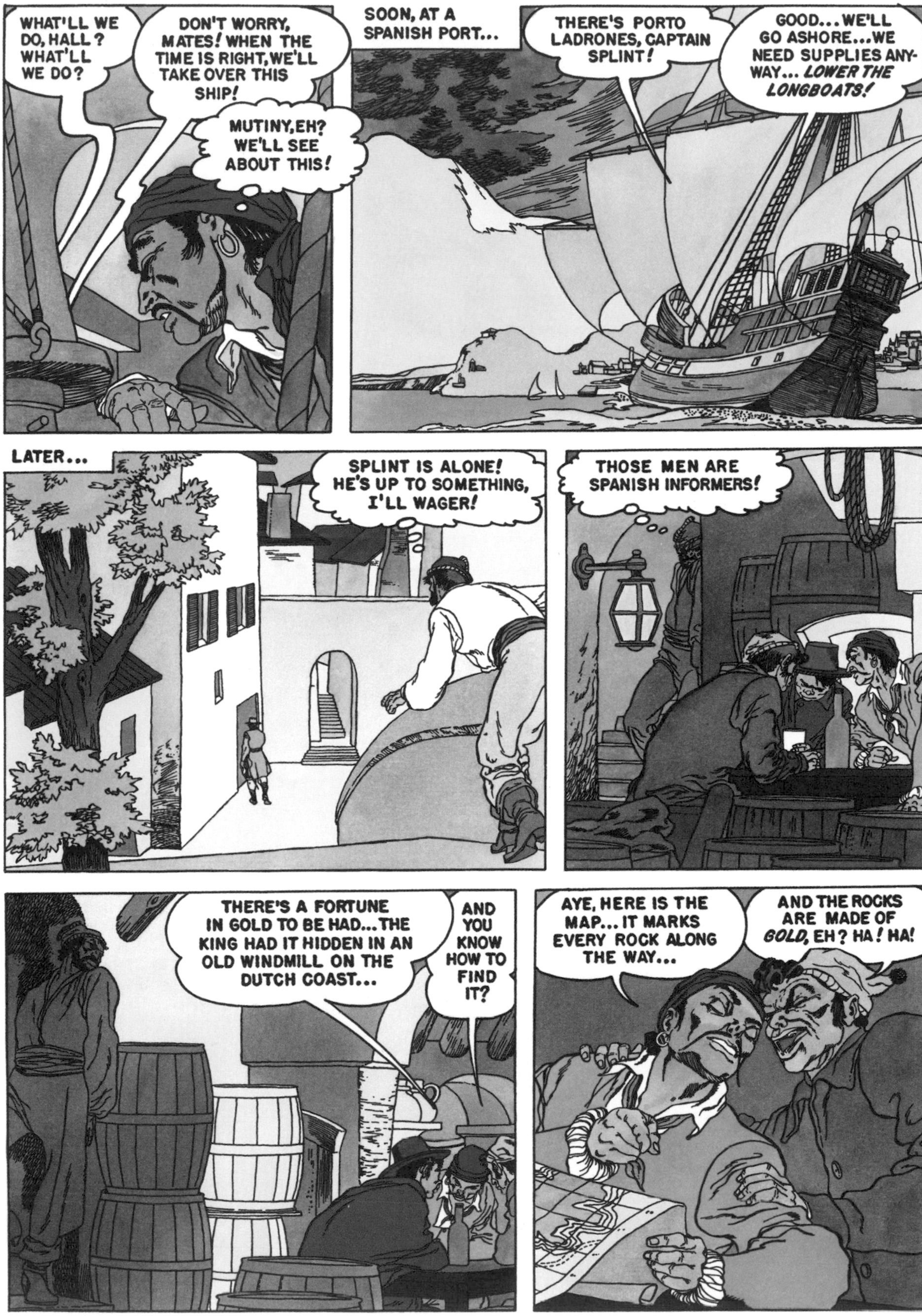
WHAT'LL WE DO, HALL? WHAT'LL WE DO?
DON'T WORRY, MATES! WHEN THE TIME IS RIGHT, WE'LL TAKE OVER THIS SHIP!
MUTINY, EH? WE'LL SEE ABOUT THIS!
SOON, AT A SPANISH PORT...
THERE'S PORTO LADRONES, CAPTAIN SPLINT!
GOOD... WE'LL GO ASHORE... WE NEED SUPPLIES ANYWAY... *LOWER THE LONGBOATS!*
LATER...
SPLINT IS ALONE! HE'S UP TO SOMETHING, I'LL WAGER!
THOSE MEN ARE SPANISH INFORMERS!
THERE'S A FORTUNE IN GOLD TO BE HAD... THE KING HAD IT HIDDEN IN AN OLD WINDMILL ON THE DUTCH COAST...
AND YOU KNOW HOW TO FIND IT?
AYE, HERE IS THE MAP... IT MARKS EVERY ROCK ALONG THE WAY...
AND THE ROCKS ARE MADE OF *GOLD*, EH? HA! HA!

HALL WASTES NO TIME AND RUSHES TO THE DUTCH CONSULATE...

THIS RAGGED PIG WISHES AN AUDIENCE WITH YOU, YOUR EXCELLENCY!

PLEASE! I HAVE VALUABLE INFORMATION FOR THE DUTCH AMBASSADOR!

SPEAK UP, MAN! I AM THE AMBASSADOR!

YES, YOUR EXCELLENCY! IT IS ABOUT THE PIRATE, SPLINT!

SPLINT! HE WITH THE MAD GORILLA?

AYE! HE PLANS TO ATTACK A WINDMILL NEAR THE DUTCH COAST WHERE YOUR KING HAS STORED GOLD!

THE SURPRISED AMBASSADOR IMMEDIATELY SCRAWLS A MESSAGE, AND...

SEE THAT THIS IS DELIVERED WITHOUT DELAY!

YES, EXCELLENCY!

AND THAT NIGHT, AS SPLINT'S SHIP SETS SAIL FOR THE DUTCH COAST, A MESSENGER STREAKS NORTHWARD...

MEANWHILE, ABOARD SPLINT'S SHIP OFF THE COAST OF HOLLAND, JEB HALL IS SET TO STRIKE...

AH!--WHEN HE TURNS HIS BACK I'LL KILL HIM!

NOW!

YOU SWINE!

YOU MISSED, HALL...THAT WAS YOUR LAST FOUL DEED... GET HIM, GORO!

HELP! STAY AWAY! HELP!

GRRRRRRRRR!

NO!!-- DON'T!! NO!! GAAAAAAA...

MEANWHILE, A SMALL ARMY OF DUTCH SOLDIERS AWAIT SPLINT'S ARRIVAL...

HERE THEY COME! GET TO YOUR POSTS!

SPLINT'S CRUEL CAREER OF PIRACY WAS OVER! TWO MONTHS LATER HE MET HIS END ON A DUTCH SCAFFOLD!

BLACK SILVER HEART

IT COULD ONLY HAPPEN ONCE IN A LIFETIME—AND IT HAPPENED TO STRIKE TAYLOR—BECAUSE STRIKE WAS A PROSPECTOR WHO FOUND A MAN WHO TOOK HIS HAND AND LED HIM TO THE TREASURE AT THE RAINBOW'S END. BUT STRIKE HAD A BLACK DOUBLE-CROSSING HEART—AND NOW OUR STORY BEGINS AS STRIKE TRUDGES INTO A SLAM-BANG TOWN—A TOWN THAT STILL DOESN'T HAVE ENOUGH ACTION TO SUIT HIM....

WHY DO I WASTE MY TIME COMIN' TO *THIS* TOWN... IT'S AS QUIET AS A SUNDAY SCHOOL PICNIC... THERE AIN'T NO *REAL* EXCITEMENT HERE... NO SIR, NOT FOR "STRIKE" TAYLOR!! ... NOTHIN' LIKE A *GOOD* BRAWL TO...

B. KRIGSTEIN

HELP! HELP! OWWW!!

HEY!! THAT SOUNDS MIGHTY INTERESTIN'!

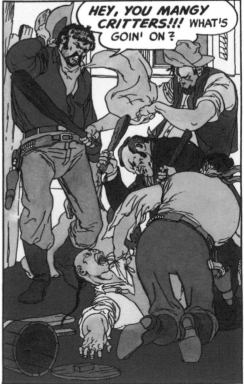

HEY, YOU MANGY CRITTERS!!! WHAT'S GOIN' ON?

WHAT'S IT TO **YOU**? GIT OUT AND MIND YER OWN BUSINESS!

YEAH? WELL, I DON'T LIKE THE ODDS THIS GUY IS UP AGAINST... RECKON I'LL GIVE HIM A HAND!

NOT THAT I'M ANY GREAT HAND AT FAIR FIGHTIN' MYSELF...BUT IT GIVES ME A GOOD EXCUSE TO GET INTO THIS BRAWL...

...RECKON THIS AIN'T GONNA BE MUCH OF A BRAWL, THOUGH!

IN FACT IT'S ALL OVER! **COME BACK AN' FIGHT,** YA LILY-LIVERED MUD-GRUBBERS!

THE BLESSINGS OF MY ANCESTORS ON YOU! YOU HAVE SAVED WO SUNG'S LIFE!

IS THAT A FACT? TELL ME, MISTER, WHY WAS THEM BOYS PLAYING SO ROUGH WITH YOU?

THEY WERE TRYING TO FORCE LOCATION OF BIG SILVER STRIKE I MAKE...

WELL, WELL! SO YOU HIT THE JACKPOT, HUH? COME ON OVER TO MY CAMP AN' LET'S TALK THIS OVER!

VERY GOOD! YOU SAVE WO SUNG'S LIFE! IT IS WRITTEN, WISE MAN SHARES WEALTH WITH BENEFACTOR! I SHARE MINE WITH YOU!

LATER AT STRIKE'S CAMP...

IT IS IN THE VALLEY OF THE WINDS THAT I FIND THIS VEIN OF SILVER! IT IS ALMOST PURE... THERE ARE CHUNKS AS BIG AS A MAN'S HEAD!

GO ON...GO ON... I CAN ALREADY SEE US LIGHTING DOLLAR CIGARS WITH THOUSAND-DOLLAR BILLS!

FOR TWENTY YEARS I'VE STARVED AN' FROZE TRYIN' TO MAKE MY BIG STRIKE! *TWENTY YEARS!* I'D MURDER OR STEAL FOR MONEY...AN' NOW IT'S HANDED TO ME...I CAN HAVE EVERYTHIN' I WANT AN' *STILL* BE HONEST!

SHAKE, WO SUNG! WE'RE PARTNERS FROM HERE ON IN!

YES, WE PARTNERS! TOMORROW I TAKE YOU TO VALLEY OF WINDS... SHOW YOU!

EARLY THE NEXT DAY AT WO SUNG'S SILVER STRIKE...

WO SUNG... *IT'S TRUE!* THIS VEIN RUNS PURE SILVER... AND IT'S *ALL OURS!* IT'S TRUE...IT AIN'T NO NIGHTMARE!

C'MON, GRAB YOUR SHOVEL... THE MORE WE DIG THE RICHER WE'LL BE...

AS YOU SAY, STRIKE!

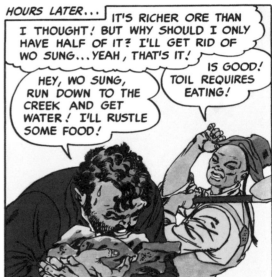

HOURS LATER...

IT'S RICHER ORE THAN I THOUGHT! BUT WHY SHOULD I ONLY HAVE HALF OF IT? I'LL GET RID OF WO SUNG...YEAH, THAT'S IT!

HEY, WO SUNG, RUN DOWN TO THE CREEK AND GET WATER! I'LL RUSTLE SOME FOOD!

IS GOOD! TOIL REQUIRES EATING!

STRIKE FOLLOWED WO SUNG TO THE CREEK, AND...

THERE...THAT'S DONE! GUESS THAT ENDS OUR PARTNERSHIP!

NOW I'LL JUST DUMP HIM IN THE CREEK...AN' THE MINE'LL BE ALL STRIKE TAYLOR'S...I'LL BE RICH ...I WON'T HAVE TO SHARE IT WITH NO ONE!

LATER, AFTER STRIKE HAD LEFT...

UGGHHH! WHERE AM I? WATER... WATER... YES, STRIKE... SHOT ME! THREW ME IN THE CREEK! WATER REVIVED ME! I SHALL LIVE...TO CLAIM WHAT IS MINE!

I AM WOUNDED...IN BACK... BUT I WILL NOT DIE... NO, NOT UNTIL I HAVE GOTTEN EVEN WITH STRIKE! IT MAY TAKE YEARS...BUT SOMEDAY...

AND AS WO SUNG LAID HIS PLANS, STRIKE WORKED FEVERISHLY AT DEVELOPING HIS STOLEN MINE...

YES SIR... MY MINE DOES TEN THOUSAND DOLLARS A DAY... IT'S ONE OF THE BEST IN THE WEST... WITH ALL THAT DOUGH, I'LL SHOW PEOPLE REAL STYLE...

AND STRIKE **DID** SHOW PEOPLE STYLE...

WOW, STRIKE... I BET YOU EVEN GOT RUNNIN' WATER IN THAT NEW HOUSE OF YOURS...

RUNNIN' WATER? WHY I'M EVEN PUTTIN' IN BATHTUBS! GENUINE *IMPORTED* BATHTUBS... JUST IN CASE I GET SOME EASTERN DUDE VISITORS!

STRIKE THOUGHT OF EVERYTHING...

WOW! THIS IS A REAL HIGH-CLASS TOUCH! A SPITTOON BESIDE EVERY CHAIR!

YES SIR! — AN' EVERY ONE IS SOLID SILVER ...DIRECT FROM THE MINE...

AND THEN ONE DAY, AT THE TOWN OPERA HOUSE...

SAY, THAT IRENE DAME IS NICE...I GOTTA MEET HER... SHE'S *JUST* WHAT I BEEN LOOKIN' FOR!

MME IRENE DIRECT FROM PARIS in ARIAS from the OPERA

AND SO...BACKSTAGE AFTER THE OPERA...

MA'AM, I GOT TO CONFESS I FELL IN LOVE WITH YOU AT FIRST SIGHT... I GOT NOTHIN' TO OFFER EXCEPT SILVER AN' MY LOVE!

I'M VERY HONORED MR. TAYLOR! I MUST CONFESS, I FEEL THE THE SAME WAY ABOUT YOU!!

AND SOON AFTER...

BOY! — THIS WALRUS IS LOADED...

YIPPEE! LONG LIVE STRIKE AND IRENE! YAHOO!

HOW'D YA LIKE IT, HONEY! AND REMEMBER, THAT STUFF THEY'RE THROWING IS **POWDERED SILVER!** NO CRUMMY OLD RICE FOR US!

OHHH, STRIKE! I THINK WE'RE GOING TO HAVE A WONDERFUL LIFE TOGETHER!

AS LONG AS YOUR MINE HOLDS OUT!

THE ONLY HONEYMOON THAT WOULD DO WAS A WORLD CRUISE! BUT BEFORE STRIKE LEFT...

WATKINS, HIRE ME A GOOD MAN TO LOOK AFTER MY HOUSE! IT'LL BE AT LEAST A YEAR BEFORE WE GET BACK!

I THINK I KNOW JUST THE MAN, MR. TAYLOR!

THE YEAR PASSED QUICKLY... AND ON STRIKE'S RETURN HOME...

WELCOME BACK, BOSS! YOUR HOUSE IS ALL READY! GOT A WONDERFUL FELLOW TAKING CARE OF IT!

WELL, NOW, THAT'S RIGHT FINE! IF HE'S DONE A REAL GOOD JOB I'LL SEE HE'S REWARDED!

AND THE HOUSEMAN WATKINS HAD HIRED HAD DONE A REAL FINE JOB... SO...

HERE, HERE'S A THOUSAND DOLLARS FOR YOUR GOOD WORK! BY THE WAY WHAT'S YOUR NAME?

JUST CALL ME CHI, MISTER TAYLOR!

AS THE HOUSEMAN LEFT...

YES SIR, A CHINESE BROUGHT ME ALL MY MONEY... SO IT'S ONLY FAIR, I GIVE ANOTHER ONE A LITTLE OF IT...

AT THE SAME TIME...

IT IS GOOD! STRIKE TAYLOR DOES NOT RECOGNIZE ME AS THE MAN HE TRIED TO KILL! THE MAN HE **STOLE** THE MINE FROM! I HAVE WAITED **YEARS... NOW** I SHALL HAVE MY REVENGE!

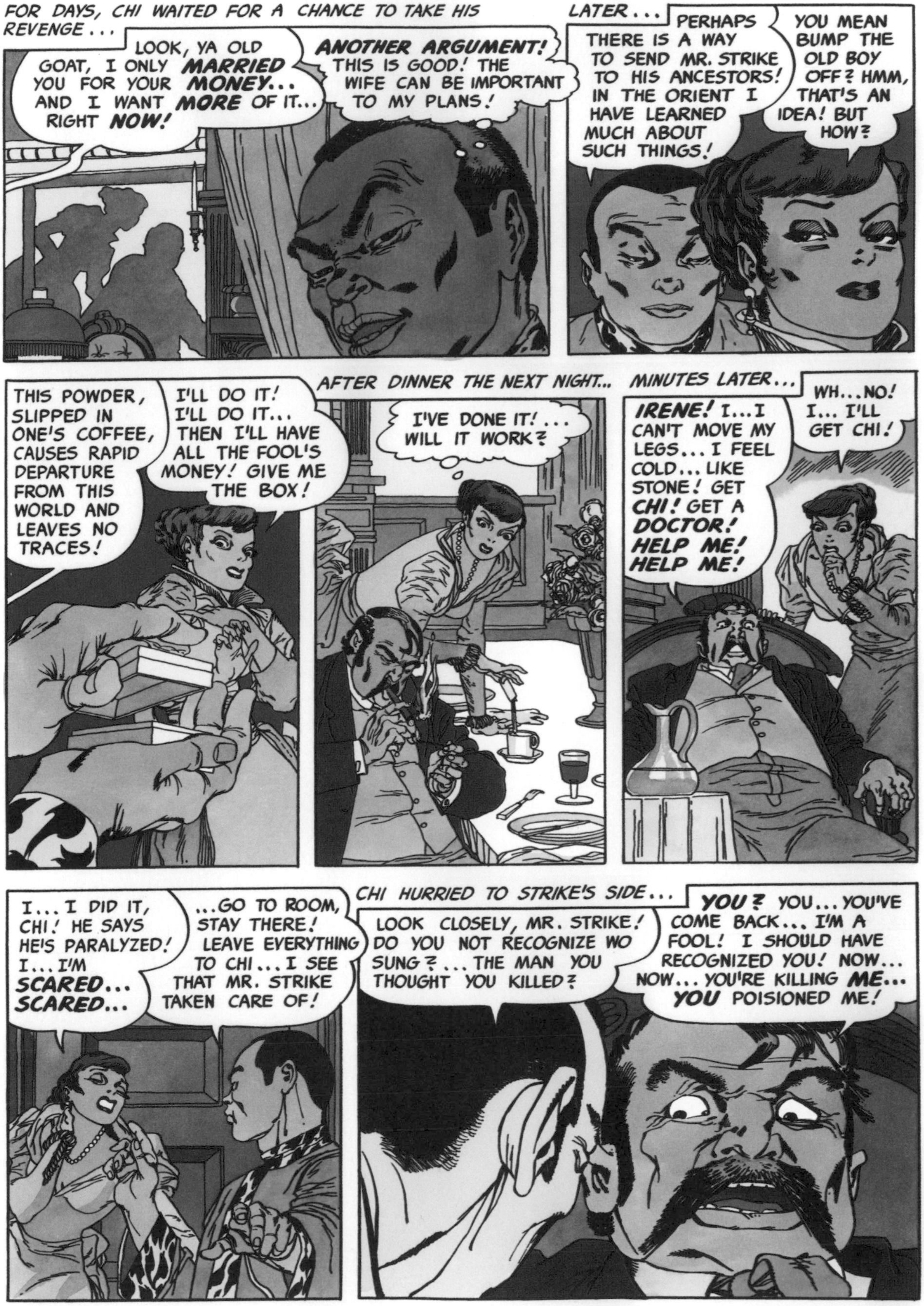
FOR DAYS, CHI WAITED FOR A CHANCE TO TAKE HIS REVENGE...
LOOK, YA OLD GOAT, I ONLY MARRIED YOU FOR YOUR MONEY... AND I WANT MORE OF IT... RIGHT NOW!
ANOTHER ARGUMENT! THIS IS GOOD! THE WIFE CAN BE IMPORTANT TO MY PLANS!
LATER...
PERHAPS THERE IS A WAY TO SEND MR. STRIKE TO HIS ANCESTORS! IN THE ORIENT I HAVE LEARNED MUCH ABOUT SUCH THINGS!
YOU MEAN BUMP THE OLD BOY OFF? HMM, THAT'S AN IDEA! BUT HOW?
THIS POWDER, SLIPPED IN ONE'S COFFEE, CAUSES RAPID DEPARTURE FROM THIS WORLD AND LEAVES NO TRACES!
I'LL DO IT! I'LL DO IT... THEN I'LL HAVE ALL THE FOOL'S MONEY! GIVE ME THE BOX!
AFTER DINNER THE NEXT NIGHT...
I'VE DONE IT!... WILL IT WORK?
MINUTES LATER...
IRENE! I...I CAN'T MOVE MY LEGS... I FEEL COLD... LIKE STONE! GET CHI! GET A DOCTOR! HELP ME! HELP ME!
WH...NO! I... I'LL GET CHI!
I... I DID IT, CHI! HE SAYS HE'S PARALYZED! I...I'M SCARED... SCARED...
...GO TO ROOM, STAY THERE! LEAVE EVERYTHING TO CHI... I SEE THAT MR. STRIKE TAKEN CARE OF!
CHI HURRIED TO STRIKE'S SIDE...
LOOK CLOSELY, MR. STRIKE! DO YOU NOT RECOGNIZE WO SUNG? ... THE MAN YOU THOUGHT YOU KILLED?
YOU? YOU... YOU'VE COME BACK... I'M A FOOL! I SHOULD HAVE RECOGNIZED YOU! NOW... NOW... YOU'RE KILLING ME... YOU POISIONED ME!

DURING THE NEXT FOUR HOURS...

The KID TALKS TOUGH

NO DOUBT ABOUT IT, YOUNG BUD KINCAID WAS A TOUGH HOMBRE... HE LIKED TO BRAG THAT HE'D CUT HIS TEETH ON A SIX-GUN. RIGHT NOW BUD IS IN A TOWN HE'S NEVER SEEN BEFORE, AND HE'S GOT SOMETHING MIGHTY IMPORTANT ON HIS MIND -- HE WANTS TO TALK TO THE SHERIFF ABOUT A LITTLE MATTER OF A KILLING...

WAITIN' FOR ME, STRANGER? WHAT CAN I DO FOR YOU?

I CAME HERE *LOOKIN'* FOR A MAN, SHERIFF—NOW IT SEEMS LIKE I'VE GOT TO STAY TO *KILL* A MAN! I FIGURED YOU MIGHT HELP ME LOCATE THE GENT!

WANTED
INFORMATION ABOUT THE DIRTY COYOTE THAT DRY-GULCHED SAM KINCAID
REWARD!

B. KRIGSTEIN

MAYBE YOU'D BETTER START EXPLAININ'! THIS MAY BE A PRETTY WILD TOWN, BUT WE DON'T WELCOME KILLERS!

I'M BUD KINCAID! SAM KINCAID WAS MY PA—AN' SOMEBODY KILLED HIM!

SO NOW I'VE GOT TO FIND THE HOMBRE THAT DID IT AN' PAY HIM OFF!

YOU TALK MIGHTY BIG FOR A KID! BETTER WATCH YOUR STEP!

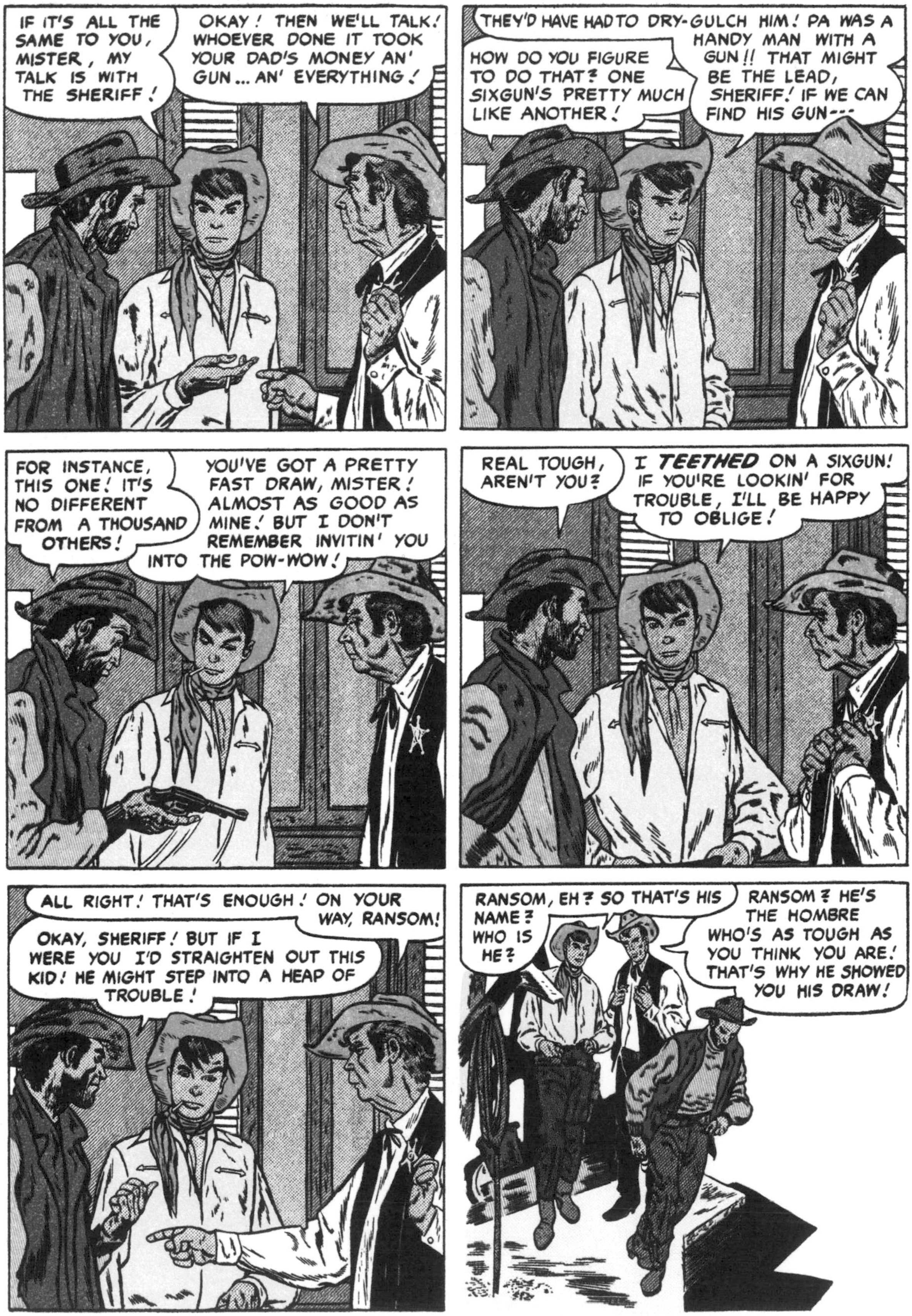
IF IT'S ALL THE SAME TO YOU, MISTER, MY TALK IS WITH THE SHERIFF!
OKAY! THEN WE'LL TALK! WHOEVER DONE IT TOOK YOUR DAD'S MONEY AN' GUN... AN' EVERYTHING!
THEY'D HAVE HAD TO DRY-GULCH HIM! PA WAS A HANDY MAN WITH A GUN!! THAT MIGHT BE THE LEAD, SHERIFF! IF WE CAN FIND HIS GUN---
HOW DO YOU FIGURE TO DO THAT? ONE SIXGUN'S PRETTY MUCH LIKE ANOTHER!
FOR INSTANCE, THIS ONE! IT'S NO DIFFERENT FROM A THOUSAND OTHERS!
YOU'VE GOT A PRETTY FAST DRAW, MISTER! ALMOST AS GOOD AS MINE! BUT I DON'T REMEMBER INVITIN' YOU INTO THE POW-WOW!
REAL TOUGH, AREN'T YOU?
I TEETHED ON A SIXGUN! IF YOU'RE LOOKIN' FOR TROUBLE, I'LL BE HAPPY TO OBLIGE!
ALL RIGHT! THAT'S ENOUGH! ON YOUR WAY, RANSOM!
OKAY, SHERIFF! BUT IF I WERE YOU I'D STRAIGHTEN OUT THIS KID! HE MIGHT STEP INTO A HEAP OF TROUBLE!
RANSOM, EH? SO THAT'S HIS NAME? WHO IS HE?
RANSOM? HE'S THE HOMBRE WHO'S AS TOUGH AS YOU THINK YOU ARE! THAT'S WHY HE SHOWED YOU HIS DRAW!

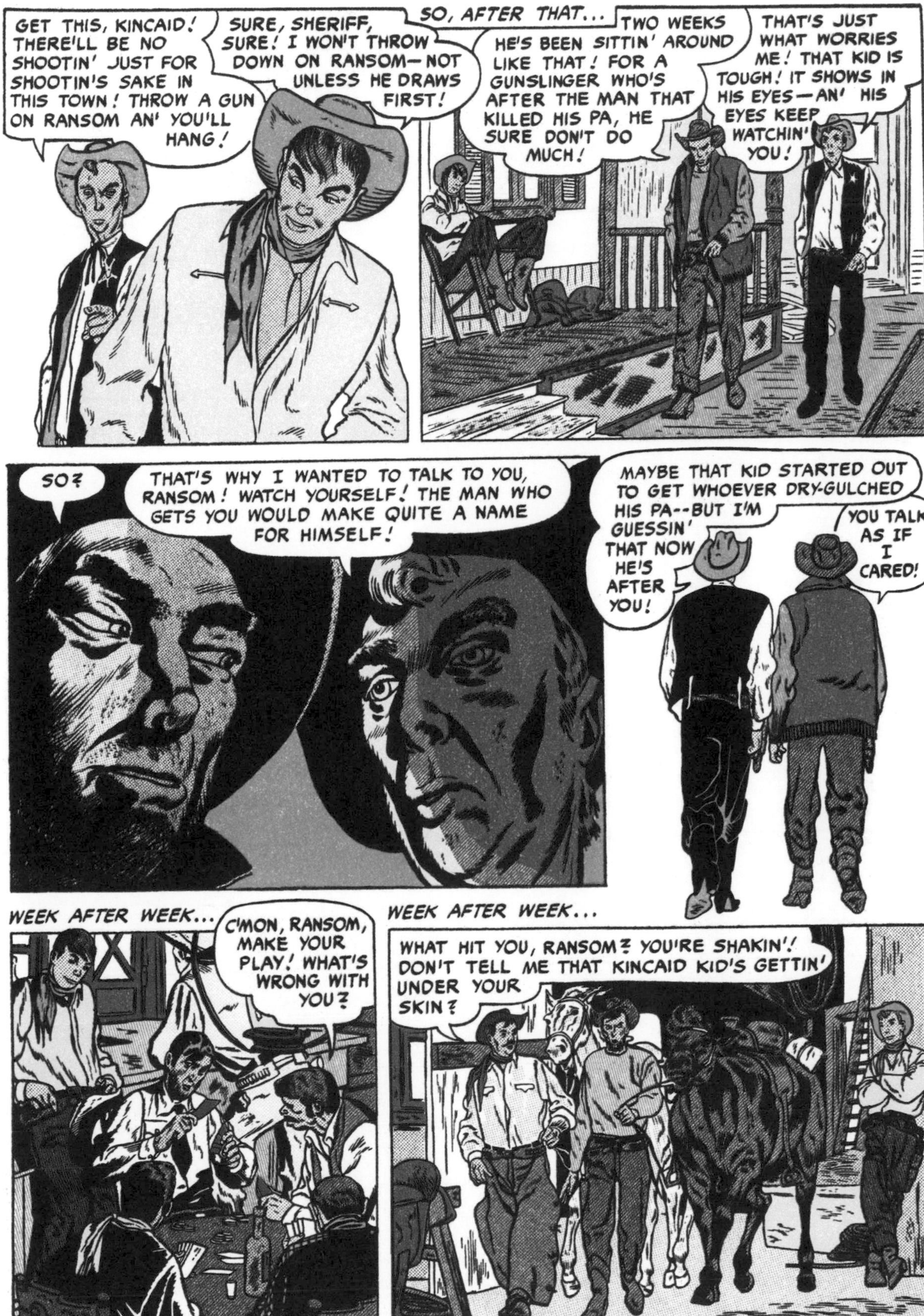
GET THIS, KINCAID! THERE'LL BE NO SHOOTIN' JUST FOR SHOOTIN'S SAKE IN THIS TOWN! THROW A GUN ON RANSOM AN' YOU'LL HANG!
SURE, SHERIFF, SURE! I WON'T THROW DOWN ON RANSOM—NOT UNLESS HE DRAWS FIRST!
SO, AFTER THAT... TWO WEEKS
HE'S BEEN SITTIN' AROUND LIKE THAT! FOR A GUNSLINGER WHO'S AFTER THE MAN THAT KILLED HIS PA, HE SURE DON'T DO MUCH!
THAT'S JUST WHAT WORRIES ME! THAT KID IS TOUGH! IT SHOWS IN HIS EYES—AN' HIS EYES KEEP WATCHIN' YOU!
SO?
THAT'S WHY I WANTED TO TALK TO YOU, RANSOM! WATCH YOURSELF! THE MAN WHO GETS YOU WOULD MAKE QUITE A NAME FOR HIMSELF!
MAYBE THAT KID STARTED OUT TO GET WHOEVER DRY-GULCHED HIS PA--BUT I'M GUESSIN' THAT NOW HE'S AFTER YOU!
YOU TALK AS IF I CARED!
WEEK AFTER WEEK...
C'MON, RANSOM, MAKE YOUR PLAY! WHAT'S WRONG WITH YOU?
WEEK AFTER WEEK...
WHAT HIT YOU, RANSOM? YOU'RE SHAKIN'! DON'T TELL ME THAT KINCAID KID'S GETTIN' UNDER YOUR SKIN?

MAYBE THIS'LL TEACH YOU I DON'T WORRY ABOUT *ANY* MAN!

PRETTY TOUGH, AREN'T YOU? IT MUST TAKE A HEAP OF NERVE TO HIT A MAN WHO AIN'T EXPECTIN' IT!

KEEP YOUR NOSE OUT, KINCAID— THIS AIN'T YOUR DEAL!

SEEMS TO ME I REMEMBER *YOU* BUTTIN' IN NOT LONG AGO, RANSOM!

HE *WANTS* ME TO DRAW... AN' HE SAID ONCE— HIS DRAW WAS FASTER'N MINE!

RANSOM! HOLD IT!

GET YOUR HAND OFF THAT GUN-BUTT, RANSOM! AN' YOU, KINCAID! I TOLD YOU WHAT WOULD HAPPEN IF YOU EVER THREW DOWN ON RANSOM!

I DIDN'T DRAW, SHERIFF! BUT IF HE DREW FIRST —I'D HAVE TO TAKE CARE OF MYSELF!

SO THAT'S THE IDEA! YOU FIGURE TO GET RANSOM TO GO FOR HIS IRON FIRST!

YOU CAN'T STOP ME IF THAT'S WHAT I'M TRYIN' TO DO, SHERIFF! BUT I DON'T THINK RANSOM'S GOT *NERVE* ENOUGH TO DRAW!

SO...

THEY'RE LAUGHIN' AT ME! THEY THINK THE KID'S GOT ME BUFFALOED!

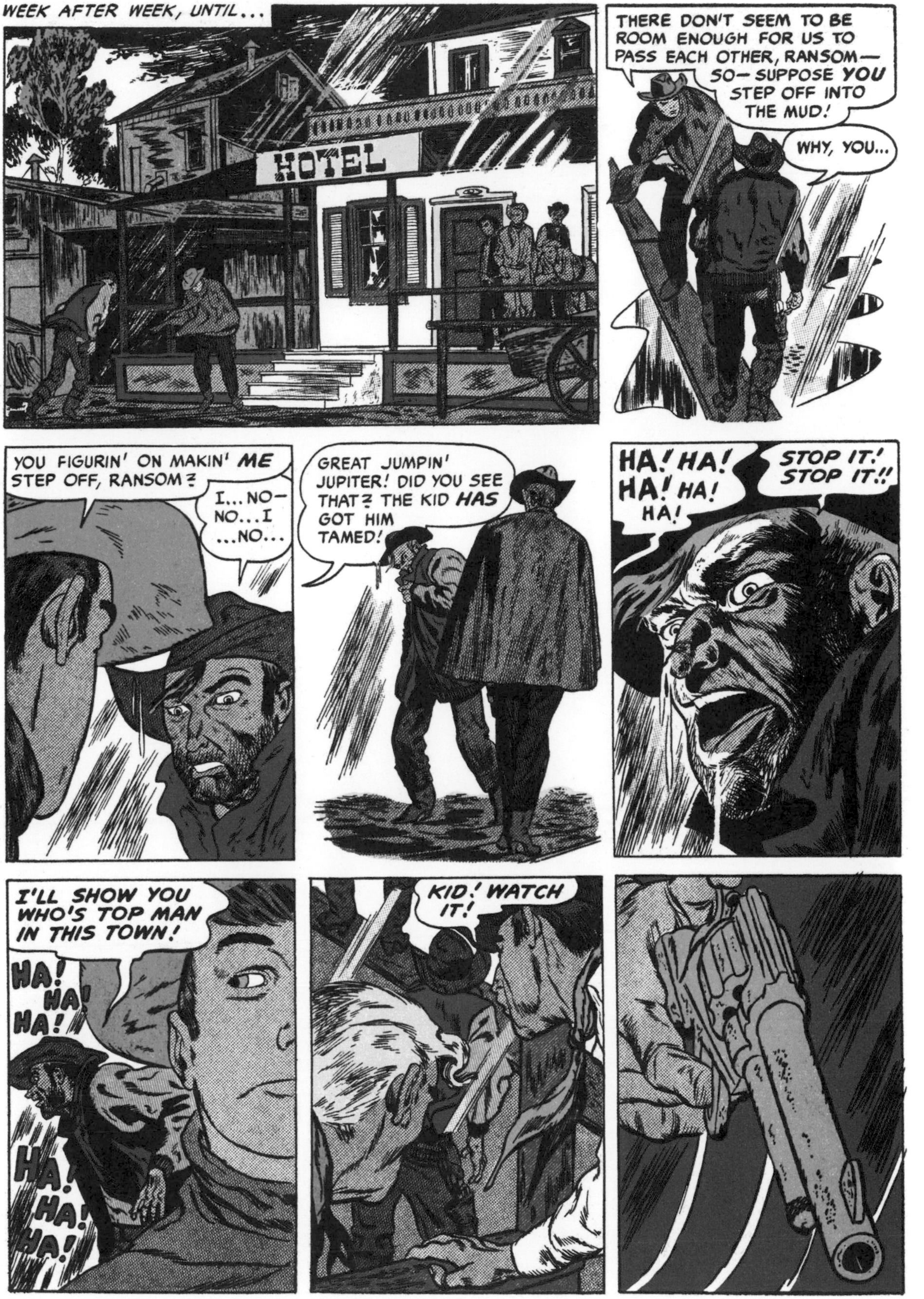

WEEK AFTER WEEK, UNTIL...
HOTEL
THERE DON'T SEEM TO BE ROOM ENOUGH FOR US TO PASS EACH OTHER, RANSOM— SO— SUPPOSE YOU STEP OFF INTO THE MUD!
WHY, YOU...
YOU FIGURIN' ON MAKIN' ME STEP OFF, RANSOM?
I...NO— NO...I ...NO...
GREAT JUMPIN' JUPITER! DID YOU SEE THAT? THE KID HAS GOT HIM TAMED!
HA! HA! HA! HA! HA!
STOP IT! STOP IT!!
I'LL SHOW YOU WHO'S TOP MAN IN THIS TOWN!
HA! HA! HA!
HA! HA! HA!
KID! WATCH IT!

YOU *KILLED* HIM! JUST FOR A REPUTATION! YOU HAD TO BE TOUGH!

I—I AIN'T TOUGH, SHERIFF! IT JUST *HAD* TO BE THIS WAY!

ALL THAT TALK ABOUT TEETHIN' ON A SIXGUN— THAT WASN'T JUST TALK!

NO, IT WASN'T JUST TALK, SHERIFF! BUT LIKE I SAID... IT *HAD* TO BE THIS WAY! THIS GUN— IT WAS MY PA'S!

THERE'S ONLY *ONE WAY* THAT RANSOM COULD HAVE GOT IT! BY BEIN' THE MAN THAT GOT PA! THAT FIRST DAY HE WAVED IT UNDER MY NOSE I RECOGNIZED IT!

YOU'RE LOCO! ONE SIXGUN'S LIKE ANOTHER!

EXCEPT FOR ONE THING! I *WASN'T* JUST TALKIN', SHERIFF! I *DID* TEETHE ON A SIXGUN! THIS *ONE*! THOSE NICKS WERE MADE BY MY FIRST TEETH!

GOING MY WAY?

IT ALL STARTED SIMPLY ENOUGH...AS THESE TRIPS OF MINE HAD ALWAYS STARTED! I WAS ON MY WAY TO MAKE ANOTHER SWING BY AUTO THROUGH MY TERRITORY IN NEW YORK STATE AS SALESMAN FOR LABRUCE FARM SUPPLY CO.! I SAID GOODBYE TO MY WIFE ELLEN...

GOODBYE, DARLING, AND BE VERY CAREFUL IN THIS STORM!

DON'T WORRY, ELLEN! YOU KNOW I'M A GOOD DRIVER! I'VE BEEN THROUGH THESE THINGS HUNDREDS OF TIMES! SEE YOU IN TWO WEEKS!

I DROVE UP THE WEST SIDE DRIVE IN THE RAIN AND THRU THE TACONIC STATE PARKWAY! SURE IT WAS ROUGH GOING, BUT I TOOK MY TIME AND WAS CAREFUL...

WHEW! IT IS ROUGH...AND I'M THE ONLY CAR ON THE ROAD! RAIN MUST'VE SCARED THE OTHERS OFF, I GUESS! WELL, WITH MY EXPERIENCE, I WON'T HAVE TOO MUCH TROUBLE!

IT WAS AT HAWTHORNE CIRCLE THAT IT HAPPENED! I HAD JUST DECIDED THAT IT WAS TOO AWFUL TO CONTINUE DRIVING AND THAT IT WOULD BE WISE TO STOP FOR THE NIGHT! SUDDENLY I SAW THE FIGURE OF A HITCHHIKER STANDING BESIDE THE ROAD...

FOR PETE'S SAKE! AND IN ALL THIS RAIN, TOO! I'LL PICK THE POOR GUY UP!

I GOT CLOSE TO HIM AND STOPPED! JUST THEN A FLASH OF LIGHTNING LIT UP HIS FEATURES... AND I SCREAMED AND SCREAMED!

GOING MY WAY?

AAAAEEEEHH!

MY BLOOD RAN COLD AS I SAW THAT HORRIBLE FACE GLEAMING AT ME IN THE DARK! AUTOMATICALLY, I SHIFTED GEARS AND STEPPED ON THE GAS TO GET AWAY AS FAST AS I COULD FROM THAT FIGURE OF DEATH ON THE ROAD!

WHAT'S THE MATTER WITH ME, ANYWAY? IT WAS PROBABLY JUST A GAG... A GUY WEARING A MASK... BUT WHAT AN AWFUL IDEA OF A GAG! LET HIM CATCH PNEUMONIA FOR ALL I CARE!

I SWUNG OFF THE PARKWAY AT SHRUB OAK TO LOOK FOR A PLACE TO SLEEP AND SPOTTED A LITTLE HOTEL...

AH! THERE'S A PLACE! IT'S ALL DARK BUT SOMEBODY'S ON THE FRONT PORCH!

HOTEL

BUT WHEN I DREW CLOSE, I SAW IT WAS...

GOING MY WAY?

THIS WAS MORE THAN JUST A HORRIBLE JOKE NOW! NOT TWICE! I HAD LEFT HIM MILES BEHIND... AND NO CAR HAD PASSED ME ALL THE WAY... AND HERE HE WAS AGAIN... WAITING FOR ME! AGAIN I RACED AWAY FROM THAT STILL, TALL FORM WITH A FACE OF DEATH!

I DON'T KNOW HOW I MANAGED TO CONTROL THE CAR, BUT I DID, SPEEDING OVER THE NARROW ROAD AS FAST AS I COULD GO!

WHAT THE HECK IS THE MATTER WITH ME? AM I IMAGINING ALL THIS? I MUST BE AWFULLY TIRED... OR THAT RAIN IS PLAYING TRICKS ON ME... AND LOOK AT THAT! I'M ALMOST OUT OF GAS! HOPE I FIND A GAS STATION OPEN AT THIS HOUR!

I FOUND ONE...NEAR MAHOPAC! IT WAS CLOSED BUT I HONKED MY HORN! I DIDN'T CARE ABOUT ANYTHING BUT GETTING ENOUGH GAS TO GET FAR AWAY FROM THERE!

WAKE UP THERE! I'M OUT OF GAS!

BEEP! BEEEP!

HE CAME OUT OF THE SHADOWS, STRAIGHT INTO THE BEAM OF MY LIGHTS... *THE SAME ONE!*

NO! NO! NOT AGAIN! NO!

I DON'T KNOW WHAT MADE ME DO IT, BUT I CHARGED STRAIGHT AT HIM, WANTING TO GRIND HIS BODY UNDER THE WHEELS!

I'LL KILL YOU! I'LL KILL YOU! LEAVE ME ALONE! STOP FOLLOWING ME! STOP FOLLOWING ME!

I SHOULD HAVE HEARD A THUD AS I HIT HIM BUT I DIDN'T! INSTEAD, HE SEEMED TO GET MIXED UP IN THE HAZE OF THE DOWNPOUR! ANYWAY, I KEPT GOING, PRAYING I'D RUN INTO AN OPEN GAS STATION A LITTLE FURTHER ON!

I MUST BE SICK OR SOMETHING! I GOTTA GET SOMEPLACE WHERE I CAN GET SOME REST BEFORE I COLLAPSE! GOSH, I HOPE I DON'T SEE *HIM* AGAIN!

JUST OUTSIDE OF CARMEL, I SAW A PARKED CAR! I WAS DESPERATE, SO I STOLE SOME GAS FROM IT...

HEY, YOU! WHATCHA DOIN' OUT THERE?

HUH? OH... I'LL... I'LL PAY YOU FOR IT!

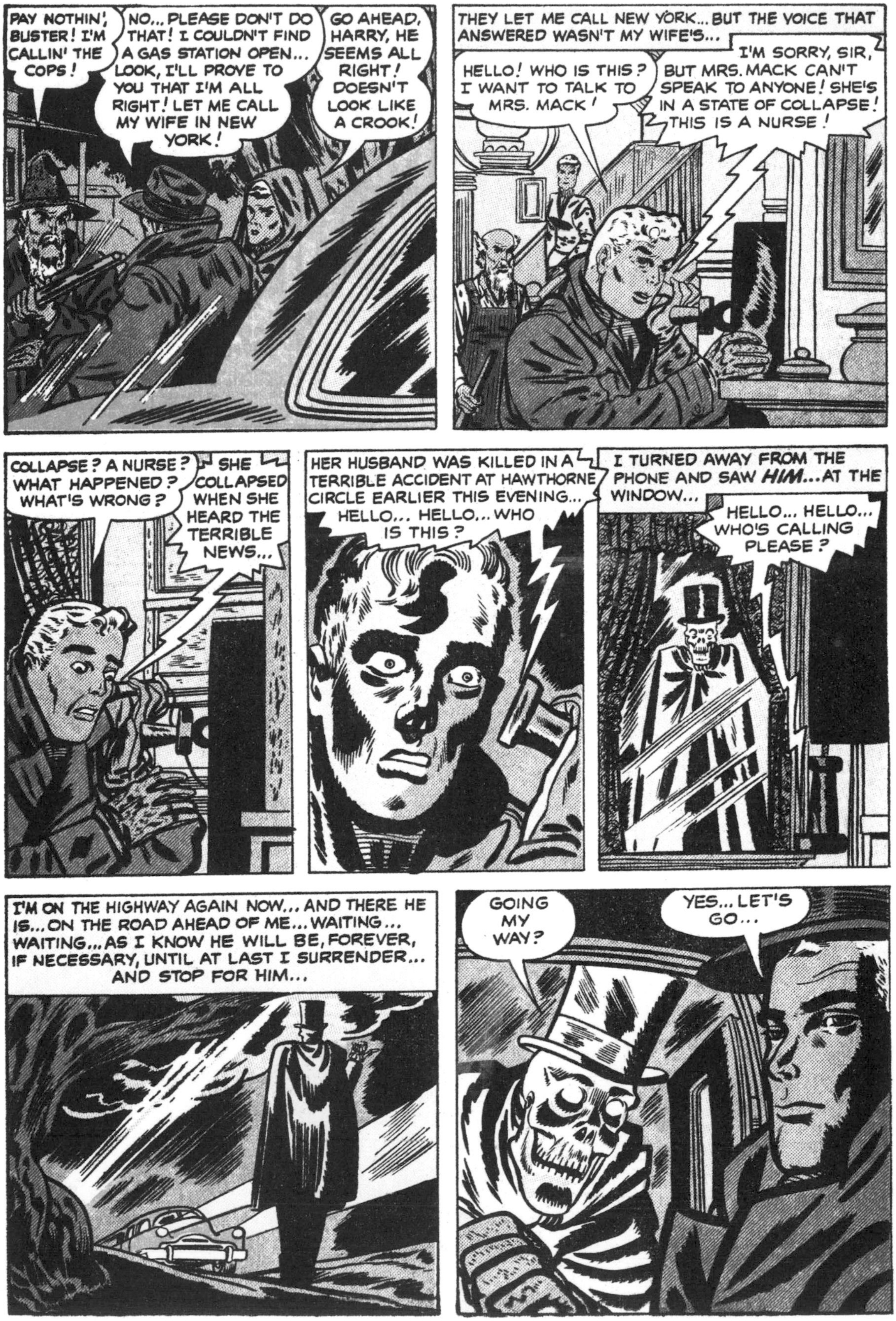

PAY NOTHIN'! BUSTER! I'M CALLIN' THE COPS!
NO... PLEASE DON'T DO THAT! I COULDN'T FIND A GAS STATION OPEN... LOOK, I'LL PROVE TO YOU THAT I'M ALL RIGHT! LET ME CALL MY WIFE IN NEW YORK!
GO AHEAD, HARRY, HE SEEMS ALL RIGHT! DOESN'T LOOK LIKE A CROOK!
THEY LET ME CALL NEW YORK... BUT THE VOICE THAT ANSWERED WASN'T MY WIFE'S...
HELLO! WHO IS THIS? I WANT TO TALK TO MRS. MACK!
I'M SORRY, SIR, BUT MRS. MACK CAN'T SPEAK TO ANYONE! SHE'S IN A STATE OF COLLAPSE! THIS IS A NURSE!
COLLAPSE? A NURSE? WHAT HAPPENED? WHAT'S WRONG?
SHE COLLAPSED WHEN SHE HEARD THE TERRIBLE NEWS...
HER HUSBAND WAS KILLED IN A TERRIBLE ACCIDENT AT HAWTHORNE CIRCLE EARLIER THIS EVENING... HELLO... HELLO... WHO IS THIS?
I TURNED AWAY FROM THE PHONE AND SAW HIM... AT THE WINDOW...
HELLO... HELLO... WHO'S CALLING PLEASE?
I'M ON THE HIGHWAY AGAIN NOW... AND THERE HE IS... ON THE ROAD AHEAD OF ME... WAITING... WAITING... AS I KNOW HE WILL BE, FOREVER, IF NECESSARY, UNTIL AT LAST I SURRENDER... AND STOP FOR HIM...
GOING MY WAY?
YES... LET'S GO...

GHOUL'S GOLD

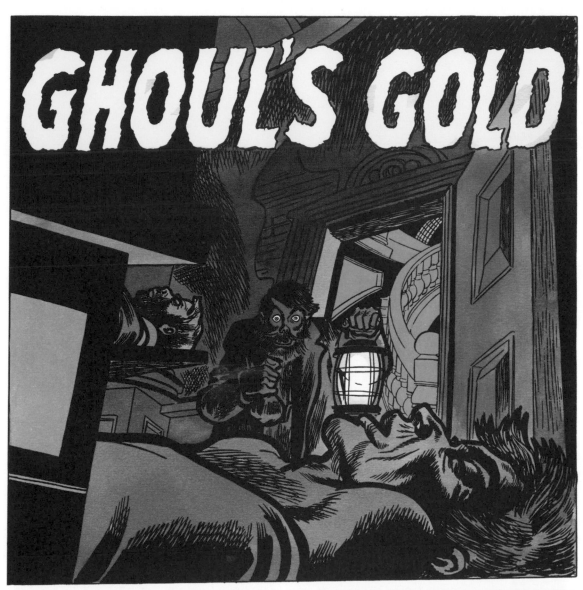

HE CLOSES THE DOOR TO THE COLD ROOM WHERE THE CORPSES LAY! THE DOOR CREAKS...IT'S OLD... THE BUILDING'S OLD...A WOODEN BUILDING WITH ROTTEN TIMBERS...GOOD ENOUGH FOR THE DEAD!

HE HURRIES DOWN THE CORRIDOR TO HIS DIRTY LITTLE ROOM, CLUTCHING A SMALL BAG AND CHUCKLING...A STRANGE SOUND IN THIS HOUSE OF DEATH!

GRIMM'S ROOM IS ALMOST BARE...BUT THE TABLE IN THE MIDDLE OF THE ROOM HOLDS STRANGE EQUIPMENT FOR A MORGUE ATTENDANT...

HE LIGHTS THE BURNER AND THEN OPENS UP THE LITTLE BLACK BAG...

NO ONE SEES, AND NO ONE KNOWS WHAT GRIMM WORKS ON ALL NIGHT...

AND EARLY THE NEXT MORNING, GRIMM ENTERS THE GOLD-BUYING ESTABLISHMENT HE'S BEEN TO SO OFTEN DURING THE PAST YEAR...

AH, MASTER GRIMM...BACK AGAIN!

YES! BUSINESS HAS BEEN GOOD! I HAVE MORE GOLD TO SELL!

MR. COWDRY, THE MAN WHO OWNS THE GOLD-BUYING ESTABLISHMENT, IS SUSPICIOUS! AFTER GRIMM LEAVES, HE SITS LOOKING AT THE SMALL GOLD BRICK!

I'VE PAID HIM A SMALL FORTUNE FOR THE GOLD HE'S BROUGHT IN DURING THE PAST YEAR! I WONDER WHERE HE GETS IT? WHERE CAN A MORGUE ATTENDANT GET SO MUCH GOLD?

I DON'T KNOW, BUT THERE'S SOMETHING FISHY ABOUT IT-- AN' I'M GOIN' TO THE POLICE!

MR. COWDRY TELLS HIS STORY TO THE POLICE -- AND THEY'RE INTERESTED...VERY INTERESTED...

YOU WERE ABSOLUTELY RIGHT IN COMING TO US, MR. COWDRY! WE'LL TAKE IT FROM HERE! THANK YOU, AND GOOD DAY!

IF THERE'S ANYTHING FURTHER I CAN DO TO HELP, YOU KNOW WHERE YOU CAN REACH ME!

I'M THROWING THIS IN YOUR LAP, JIM! HOW DO YOU SUPPOSE A MORGUE ATTENDANT GOT HIS HANDS ON SO MUCH GOLD...? AND IN SMALL BRICKS, TOO?

I DON'T KNOW... BUT I'M GOING TO FIND OUT!

DETECTIVE JIM BELLIN SHADOWS GRIMM--FOLLOWS HIS EVERY MOVE...BUT FINDS OUT NOTHING!

ALL HE DOES IS GO TO THE STORE FOR GROCERIES, AND BACK TO THE MORGUE! THE GUY GIVES ME THE CREEPS...MAYBE BECAUSE I ASSOCIATE HIM WITH HIS JOB... AND THE DEAD!

IF HE'S FOUND A HIDDEN CACHE OF GOLD SOMEWHERE -- IT ISN'T OUTSIDE...IT MUST BE IN THE MORGUE! I'LL GO AROUND BACK AND SEE IF I CAN FIND WHAT HE'S UP TO!

DETECTIVE BELLIN LOCATES GRIMM'S WINDOW AND PEERS IN THROUGH A TINY HOLE IN THE SHADE...

THIS MORGUE BUILDING SHOULD'VE BEEN CONDEMNED LONG AGO! IT'S A FIRE TRAP!

INSIDE THE ROOM GRIMM USES THE BUNSEN BURNER... USES IT TO MELT TINY PIECES OF GOLD...FORMING THEM INTO SMALL BRICKS... WEIGHING THEM ON THE SCALE!

GRIMM LIGHTS HIS LANTERN AND LEAVES THE ROOM--HE GOES DOWN THE CORRIDOR TOWARD THE CORPSE ROOM!

NO ADMITTAN

SO HE MAKES HIS OWN GOLD BRICKS! MAYBE IF I FOLLOW HIM NOW I'LL FIND OUT WHERE HE GETS THE GOLD!

QUIETLY, BELLIN WALKS DOWN IN THE CORRIDOR! THE DOOR AT THE END IS AJAR...LIGHT SEEPS THROUGH THE CRACKS IN THE WOODEN FRAME!

THREE NEW BODIES CAME IN TODAY! MAYBE HE'S JUST LOOKING AT THEM! THAT FOOL OUGHT TO KNOW BETTER THAN TO USE A KEROSENE LAMP IN THIS FIRE TRAP!

DETECTIVE BELLIN PEERS INTO THE ROOM AND SEES GRIMM BENT OVER ONE OF THE DEAD BODIES...

HOLY SMOKES! SO THAT'S WHERE THE DIRTY LEECH GETS HIS GOLD!

HAH! THIS IS THE BEST ONE YET! GOLD CAPS ON MOST OF THE TEETH, THE REST FILLED WITH GOLD!

GRIMM, YOU DIRTY GHOUL... YOU'RE UNDER ARREST! HEY-- LOOK OUT FOR THAT LAMP!

HUH? WHO ARE... OH--H!

GRIMM! COME OUT OF THERE! THIS PLACE WILL GO UP LIKE MATCHWOOD!

YES, YES...IN A MINUTE! IT'S ALMOST LOOSE... SOLID GOLD...

GRIMM, YOU FOOL... COME OUT...

HELP! I'M CAUGHT ...I'M TRAPPED... HELP!

BELLIN REACHES THE STREET! HE HEARS THE ROAR OF THE BUILDING COLLAPSING BEHIND HIM! HE TURNS! GRIMM HASN'T COME OUT...

WHY DIDN'T HE COME OUT? HE COULD HAVE MADE IT DOWN THAT CORRIDOR SAME AS I DID! WHAT DID HE MEAN, HE WAS CAUGHT...TRAPPED?

WHEN THE ASHES COOL, DETECTIVE BELLIN GETS HIS ANSWER...

HOLY SMOKES...NO WONDER HE COULDN'T GET OUT! THAT CORPSE...

130

CHECK BACK THRU HISTORY AND YOU'LL ALWAYS FIND THAT IT WAS A MAN ON A HORSE WHO WON A BATTLE OR LOST AN EMPIRE! THAT'S WHAT WAS HAPPENING IN 1862 AT THE BATTLE OF SEVEN PINES NEAR RICHMOND, VIRGINIA! THE MAN ON THE HORSE WAS GENERAL ROBERT E. LEE!

WAR HORSE!

B. KRIGSTEIN

I WASN'T THERE, BUT I HEARD ABOUT IT LATER! THE PEACEFUL COUNTRYSIDE HAD BECOME A ROARING BEDLAM OF VIOLENCE AND DESTRUCTION...

GEN'RAL LEE, SUH! THE YANKEES HAVE TURNED OUR LEFT FLANK! GEN'RAL JOHNSTON'S BEEN WOUNDED AND OUR RANKS ARE ABOUT TO COLLAPSE!

JOHNSTON WOUNDED? TAKE COMMAND HERE, CAPTAIN! I'LL TRY TO REACH THAT SECTOR!

HOLD, BOYS! WE'LL TURN THAT YANKEE TIDE BACK!

HE WAS A BIG MAN TO CARRY EVEN FOR A BIG HORSE, THAT FELLOW LEE! BUT HE RODE LIKE A FEATHER, AND BROUGHT THE BEST OUT OF ANY HORSE UNDER HIM!

GET BETWEEN US, SUH! WE CAN'T AFFORD TO LOSE YOU NOW!

THESE YANKEE BULLETS WILL HAVE TO FLY FASTER TO TAKE ME!

GENERAL LEE! LOOK OUT, SUH!

ARE YOU HURT, SUH?

NO! IT'S A PITY ABOUT THE HORSE, THOUGH! I'LL HAVE TO TAKE YOURS, CAPTAIN!

HE'S MADE OF IRON! HEAVEN HELP THE SOUTH IF WE LOSE HIM!

SO McCLELLAN TURNED OUR FLANK, EH? I KNOW HIS TACTICS! HE'LL TRY TO PRESS THE ADVANTAGE WITHOUT PROTECTING HIS OWN FLANKS! THAT'S HIS WEAKNESS, AND I INTEND TO EXPLOIT IT!

I KNOW, SUH! YOU DON'T HAVE TO ASK ME! HE'S YOURS, SUH!

THANKS, LIEUTENANT! I DON'T SUPPOSE I'M VERY POPULAR WITH HORSES! CAN'T SAY I BLAME THEM!

HE REACHED GENERAL JOHNSTON'S POSITION AND TOOK OVER! THAT BATTLE RAGED FOR SEVEN DAYS, AND WHEN IT ENDED THE TIDE HAD BEEN STEMMED...

GENTLEMEN, McCLELLAN IS FINISHED AS FAR AS SEVEN PINES IS CONCERNED! THE UNION ARMY IS IN RETREAT!

IT WAS WEEKS LATER, ON HIS WAY TO MARYLAND, THAT I MET GENERAL LEE! I WAS ROMPING ACROSS THE MEADOWS IN GREENBRIAR COUNTY WHEN I SAW HIM...

I GUESS WE SAW EACH OTHER AT THE SAME TIME! SOMETHING CLICKED INSIDE ME AND SOMEHOW I KNEW I WAS LOOKING AT THE ONE MAN WHO COULD BE MY MASTER!

CAPTAIN, THAT'S THE MOST MAGNIFICENT HORSE I'VE EVER SEEN! DO YOU KNOW WHOM HE BELONGS TO?

EVERYBODY IN VIRGINIA KNOWS THAT HORSE, SUH! HIS NAME IS JEFF DAVIS! MAJOR THOMAS BROUN OWNS HIM, BUT HE'S NEVER BEEN ABLE TO RIDE HIM!

THAT HORSE WAS BORN FOR ME AND I FOR HIM! BY GEORGE, I'LL MOVE HEAVEN AND EARTH TO OWN HIM! LET'S GET IN TOUCH WITH MAJOR BROUN AT ONCE!

I KNEW I WAS HIS WHEN HE RAN HIS HAND DOWN MY FLANKS! I KNEW THAT HERE WAS A MAN I'D CARRY PROUDLY, COME WHAT MAY...

HOW MUCH, SUH? MONEY COULDN'T BUY JEFF DAVIS, BUT HE'S YOURS AS A GIFT! I'D BE A SORRY PATRIOT IF I REFUSED HIM TO THE GREATEST MAN IN THE CONFEDERACY! RIDE HIM, AND MAY GOD BE WITH YOU BOTH!

I'M DEEPLY TOUCHED AND GRATEFUL, SUH! BE ASSURED THAT ONLY DEATH WILL EVER SEPARATE US!

HE WAS ON MY BACK AND HIS GREAT STRENGTH IMBUED ME WITH A SENSE OF POWER AND EXHILARATION I HAD NEVER KNOWN BEFORE!

YOU SUIT EACH OTHER, SUH! I'M PROUD TO HAVE BROUGHT YOU TWO REBELS TOGETHER!

'TRAVELLER', I'LL CALL HIM! TRAVELLER, BECAUSE WE'LL TRAVEL THE YEARS AHEAD TOGETHER, TILL DEATH DO US PART! GOOD-BYE, MAJOR!

I STOOD SIXTEEN HANDS HIGH, BUT MY HEAD TOUCHED THE CLOUDS WITH MY NEW MASTER ON MY BACK! NO OTHER HORSE COULD BEAR HIS WEIGHT LONG, BUT I BORE IT LIGHTLY, FOR I LOVED HIM DEARLY!

IT WAS IN SEPTEMBER OF 1862 AND BIG THINGS WERE IN THE AIR! I COULD SENSE IT BY THE HUSTLE OF TROOPS, THE TENSION, THE NERVOUSNESS AND THE RESTLESS SPIRIT AROUND ME...

WOULD THAT WE HUMANS HAD THE NOBILITY OF YOUR THOUGHTS, TRAVELLER! YOU ARE INNOCENT, AND YET BY DAWN TOMORROW YOU'LL BE PLUNGED INTO THE CHAOS OF WAR... HUMAN WAR! THIS IS THE EVE OF BATTLE!

THOSE ARE THE FIRES OF OUR ENEMY, TRAVELLER! AND WE ARE THEIR ENEMY AS WELL, EVEN THOUGH WE ARE BROTHERS... COUNTRYMEN! THUS HAVE WE HUMANS COME TO FIGHT LIKE JUNGLE BEASTS FOR THINGS WE CALL PRINCIPLES!

TOMORROW IS THE BATTLE, BOY! TAKE CARE OF ME WELL, TRAVELLER, AND IF WE FALL, LET US FALL TOGETHER!

I REMEMBER WELL THAT DAWN... THE CLASH OF SOUND, THE SCREAMS OF DYING AND WOUNDED, THE STENCH OF DEATH...

ATTACK!! PRESS THEM HARD, BOYS! HE WHO FALTERS... LOSES! HIT THEM HARD!

IT CAME WITH SICKENING FORCE... THE CLASH OF HORSE AGAINST HORSE, MAN AGAINST MAN...

I FELT MY FLANKS TREMBLING! I WANTED TO RUN, TO REAR AND TO PLUNGE, BUT THE GREAT MAN ON MY BACK DROVE ME FURTHER AND I RESPONDED...

WE FORCED A BREECH IN THEIR RANKS THROUGH WHICH OUR SOLDIERS RUSHED!

LOOK TO THE RIGHT, YONDER! THEY'RE BRINGING UP REINFORCEMENTS! CONSOLIDATE OUR LINES! KNIT THEM CLOSE, BOYS! WE'VE GOT TO HOLD!

BUT WE DIDN'T HOLD! THAT WAS AT ANTIETAM, AND IN VICTORY I SMELLED THE BITTER STENCH OF DEFEAT...

LOST...BUT NOT BEATEN! SEND ORDERS FOR OUR TROOPS TO DISENGAGE! WE'LL HAVE TO FALL BACK TO VIRGINIA AGAIN!

IF I MAY SAY SO, SUH, AH BELIEVE YOU OUGHT TO CHANGE HOSSES! TRAVELLER HASN'T HAD A REST SINCE WE LEFT ANTIETAM!

YES, ANY OTHER HORSE WOULD HAVE DROPPED BY NOW! BETTER FETCH UP A FRESH MOUNT, CAPTAIN! TRAVELLER DESERVES A REST!

ME REST? ME, STRIKE MY COLORS AND LET ANOTHER BEAR THE PRECIOUS BURDEN? NOT ME!

WH..??! WHOA, BOY! EASY... EASY!

LOOK OUT! REIN HIM, SUH, BEFORE HE CHEWS THIS HOSS TO BITS!

BY THE LORD HARRY! I BELIEVE TRAVELLER'S GOT SOMETHING TO SAY ABOUT CHANGING HORSES! ALL RIGHT, BOY! IF YOU CAN STAND IT, SO CAN I!

NO, WE WEREN'T LICKED YET! WE ROARED INTO BATTLE AT FREDERICKSBURG AND SMASHED GENERAL BURNSIDE'S ARMY THERE IN DECEMBER 1862...

AND IN MAY OF 1863, WE DID IT AGAIN TO HOOKER'S FORCES IN CHANCELLORVILLE! OH, HOW PROUDLY I CARRIED MY MASTER THEN!

VICTORY WAS SWEET, BUT IT WAS SHORT! MY HEART ALMOST BURST AT GETTYSBURG BECAUSE THE HEART OF THE MAN I CARRIED BEGAN TO CRACK...

WE'RE FALLING BACK ACROSS THE ENTIRE FRONT, SUH! ARE THERE ANY ORDERS, SUH?

YES! GIVE THEM COLD STEEL AND ADVANCE!

THREE DAYS THE BATTLE RAGED AND THE STENCH OF DEATH FILLED MY NOSTRILS! SOMEHOW I SENSED THIS WAS THE BEGINNING OF THE END...

IF THIS BE YOUR DIVINE WILL, SO BE IT! I AM SOLDIER ENOUGH TO KNOW THAT GETTYSBURG IS THE DECISIVE BATTLE OF THE WAR! LORD HELP THE SOUTH, AND MAY ORDER COME FROM THIS CHAOS!

YES, THAT WAS THE FIRST GREAT DEFEAT... AND THEN, IN SHORT ORDER, CAME THE BATTLES OF WILDERNESS, SPOTTSYLVANIA AND COLD HARBOR...

THE CONFEDERACY IS FINISHED! THE DREAM OF THE SOUTH IS ENDED! IT IS ONLY A QUESTION OF TIME NOW!

AND THAT TIME CAME AT THE COURTHOUSE OF APPOMATTOX IN 1865, WHEN TWO GREAT GENERALS MET... ONE IN DEFEAT, THE OTHER IN VICTORY...

I TRUST SIR, THAT YOU ARE PREPARED TO SIGN THE ORDERS OF SURRENDER!

I AM, SUH!

THE WAR ENDED, AND HAPPIER DAYS BEGAN FOR US AS MY MASTER BECAME THE HEAD OF WASHINGTON AND LEE UNIVERSITY...

WE'RE GETTING FAT AND LAZY, EH TRAVELLER? I GUESS THIS ISN'T THE LIFE FOR A PAIR OF OLD WAR HORSES LIKE US, EH?

MY BELOVED MASTER DIED IN 1870... FOR THE FIRST TIME IN MY LIFE, I BOWED MY HEAD IN GRIEF...

BUT IT WASN'T LONG AFTER THAT I JOINED HIM! AND NOW WE GALLOP THROUGH THE SOUTHERN HEAVENS EVERY NIGHT!

THE RED SQUAD WAS OUT HUNTING FOR HIM... THEY WERE CLOSING IN! AND ALL HE HAD LEFT TO KEEP THEM OFF WAS HIS...

LAST BULLET

FUNNY, WHEN WE STARTED OUT, IT SEEMED LIKE ANOTHER ROUTINE RECONNAISSANCE PATROL!... "TRAVEL LIGHT," THE C.O. SAID! "JUST TAKE YOUR .45! THAT'S ALL YOU'LL NEED..."

CLACK!

YEAH, WE TRAVELED LIGHT AND FAST! IT WASN'T EVEN DAWN WHEN WE CRAWLED UNDER THE BARBED WIRE AND WORKED OUR WAY DEEP INTO NO MAN'S LAND...

ONE LOUSY SLUG!... BETTER LOAD IT INTO THE PISTOL FAST! I'LL BE NEEDING IT SOON! THE REDS ARE BOUND TO FIND ME IN A FEW MINUTES, BUT THEY WON'T TAKE ME BEFORE I PLUG ONE MORE COMMIE!

DOWN!... COMMIE PATROL NOSING AROUND UP AHEAD!

THEY'RE JUST RECLAIMING WEAPONS FROM THE DEAD REDS WE CUT DOWN LAST NIGHT!

WHAT A SET-UP, HARRY! I COULD UNLOAD MY .45 BEFORE THEY KNEW WHAT HIT 'EM!

EASE OFF THE TRIGGER! OUR JOB'S TO LOCATE AND STUDY THE REDS' POSITION, NOT TO TRY WINNING THE WAR OURSELVES!

ALRIGHT, HARRY! ...BUT WE WON'T GET A SWEET TARGET LIKE THAT VERY OFTEN!

IT WASN'T EASY RESISTING THE TEMPTATION TO SHOOT UP THOSE REDS, BUT WE HAD A MISSION... AND AS THE COMMIES PULLED BACK, WE INCHED FORWARD...

OVER HERE! I'VE GOT A VIEW TO MAKE YOUR EYES POP!

WHAT'S UP? DID A COUPLE OF U.S.O. GIRLS GET LOST OUT THERE?

BROTHER! A WHOLE COMMIE BATTALION!

SEE IF YOU CAN MAKE OUT HOW THEY'RE ARMED OR WHAT UNIT THEY ARE!

BILL CHECKED 'EM WITH THE BINOCULARS AND ED NOTED DOWN THE STUFF...IT DIDN'T ADD UP PRETTY FOR OUR SIDE...

LET'S SCRAM! IF WE CAN GET THIS INFORMATION BACK TO OUR ARTILLERY, THEY MAY BE ABLE TO CHOP UP THAT BATTALION BEFORE THEY MOVE OUT!

HARRY! THEY'VE GOT PATROLS OUT UP AHEAD! WE'D BETTER KEEP LOW AND QUIET!

THUP!

We ran like blazes across no man's land, a commie squad on our heels and slugs screaming around us...

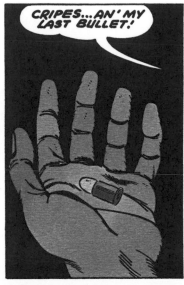

I SAW THEM RAKE AWAY...DASHING FROM COVER TO COVER EVERY FEW YARDS! I KEPT PEPPERING AWAY AT THE COMMIES WITH MY .45, AND THE REDS NEVER GOT OFF A SHOT AT MY BUDDIES! THEN I LOOKED DOWN AT THE EMPTY CLIPS IN THE SHELL HOLE AROUND ME...

I'D BETTER CHECK MY AMMO... THIS IS MY *LAST* CLIP!

CRIPES...AN' MY *LAST BULLET!*

YEAH, THAT'S HOW I GOT HERE STUCK WITH ONE LAST BULLET! I MUST'VE DROPPED SIX REDS WITH THE OTHER SHOTS! THEIR COMRADES WON'T BE TOO POLITE WHEN THEY GRAB ME... BUT THEY *WON'T* TAKE ME WITHOUT A FIGHT!

CLICK-CLICK

I'VE GOT ONE LAST HOPE... THE GUYS MUST'VE MADE IT BACK! MAYBE THEY'LL SEND OUT HELP TO... OH...OH... *TOO LATE!*...HERE COME COMMIES AND I'VE GOT NOTHING TO STOP 'EM WITH!

NOTHING BUT ONE BULLET...AN' I'M NOT GONNA WASTE IT! IF I'M GOING TO GO, I MIGHT AS WELL LET THE LAST BULLET TAKE ONE OF THOSE RED RATS WITH ME!

OR MAYBE I CAN BLUFF 'EM...YEAH... EITHER I GET THE ACADEMY AWARD AND TWO REDS FOR THIS ACTING JOB, OR I'LL GET HISSED OFF THE STAGE WITH COMMIE SLUGS!

SURRENDER, COMRADES!...SURRENDER OR DIE!

AS THE REDS RAISED THEIR RIFLES TO FIRE, HIS .45 BARKED FIRST...

ALRIGHT, COMRADES! WHO'S NEXT?... STEP UP AND DIE, OR *SURRENDER!*

CRACK!

AS THE DEAD COMMIE FELL AGAINST HIS COMRADES, THEY TURNED FOR A SECOND FROM THE LONE G.I., WHO RACED UP WITH DEFIANT CALM...

THROW DOWN YOUR GUNS! *SURRENDER!*

DROP YOUR WEAPONS! DROP 'EM OR I'LL *SHOOT!*

WITH THE SICKENING PRESENCE OF DEATH ALL AROUND THEM, AND THE SMOKING .45 THAT CAUSED IT WAVING FROM ONE TO THE OTHER AT POINT-BLANK RANGE, THE REDS LET THEIR WEAPONS FALL...

THAT'S BEING GOOD BOYS! NOW START MOVING TO OUR LINES! *ON THE DOUBLE!*

THE REDS MOVED LIKE SILENT PUPPETS, AS HARRY PRODDED THEM ON, HIS .45 JABBING THEM IN THE BACK...

HEY, LOOK...IT'S HARRY! HE MADE IT...AN' HE'S GOT A COUPLE OF PRISONERS!

GEE, HARRY, THEY'LL MAKE YA AN' INSTRUCTOR WHEN THEY HEAR OF THIS!

WELL, IF THEY DO I'M GONNA GIVE EVERY ROOKIE A SHORT COURSE IN *ACTING*...

IS HE KIDDIN'?

SURE, JUST PUTTIN' ON AN *ACT!*

ON JUNE 18, 1815, NAPOLEON BONAPARTE'S ARMY ADVANCED UPON A SMALL TOWN IN BELGIUM, ABOUT TWELVE MILES SOUTH OF BRUSSELS! NAPOLEON EXPECTED TO DESTROY THE ENGLISH ARMY UNDER THE COMMAND OF THE DUKE OF WELLINGTON! BUT THE NAME OF THE LITTLE TOWN TOWARD WHICH NAPOLEON MARCHED ON THAT SUMMER DAY WAS WATERLOO! AND THIS IS THE STORY OF THAT FATEFUL DAY AS SEEN BY RAOUL, THE...

DRUMMER OF WATERLOO

NOW THE THUNDER OF THE GUNS IS SILENT--THE BATTLE IS OVER! PROUD AND VICTORIOUS, THE ENGLISH TROOPS FORM RANKS TO HEAR THEIR COMMANDER SPEAK--BUT SUDDENLY, ANOTHER SOUND IS HEARD...

A FRENCH DRUM SIGNALING FOR AN *ATTACK!*

IMPOSSIBLE! NAPOLEON'S ARMY HAS BEEN DESTROYED!

TA-ROOM-POOM-POOM!

B. KRIGSTEIN

TAROOM-POOM-POOM!
TA-ROOM-POOM-POOM!
TA-ROOM-POOM-POOM!

STAND READY! AIM! F—!

NO! DON'T FIRE!

TA-ROOM-POOM-POOM!

CEASE SOUNDING THE ATTACK, MY SON! THERE ARE NO SOLDIERS FOLLOWING YOU!

I CANNOT STOP, M'SIEU! THE ORDER WAS GIVEN TO ME BY NAPOLEON HIMSELF!

TA-ROOM-POOM-POOM!

HE SPOKE TO ME, M'SIEU! THE ORDER WAS GIVEN TO ME BY MON EMPEREUR!

TA-ROOM-POOM-POOM!

ARE YOU SURE YOU SPOKE WITH *NAPOLEON,* MY SON?

I REMEMBER QUITE CLEARLY, M'SIEU! INDEED, I SHALL NEVER FORGET! I WAS STANDING NEAR THE LITTLE HILL ON WHICH MON EMPEREUR WAS WATCHING THE BATTLE!

TA-ROOM POOM! POOM!

"IT WAS THEN HE CALLED TO ME..."

DRUMMER BOY!

TA-ROOM-POOM-POOM!

TA-ROOM-POOM!

I WAS SOUNDING THE ATTACK, M'SIEU, EVEN AS I AM DOING NOW...

I-I-SIRE?

OUI! YOU THERE! COME HERE!

YOUR DRUMS BEAT THE ATTACK BRAVELY, MON ENFANT! NEVER CEASE SOUNDING IT...UNTIL WE HAVE GAINED THE VICTORY! OUI! DO NOT STOP, UNTIL A MARSHAL OF THE ARMY GIVES YOU THE ORDER! UNDERSTAND? OBEY NO ONE LESS THAN A MARSHAL!

I--I UNDERSTAND, MON EMPEREUR! AND I SHALL OBEY!

"AFTER NAPOLEON SPOKE TO ME..."

THE ATTACK IS ABOUT TO BEGIN! FIRST THE ARTILLERY WILL LAY DOWN A BARRAGE...

LIGHT UP THE CANNON! WE WILL GIVE THE ENGLISH GOOD REASON TO REMEMBER THIS DAY!

BAROOOM

"AND BEHIND A CURTAIN OF CANNON FIRE, I ADVANCED WITH THE FOOT SOLDIERS..."

SOUND THE ATTACK, MON EMPEREUR TOLD ME! OUI! THIS WILL BE A DAY OF GREAT VICTORY!

TA-ROOM-POOM!

"AT ONE O'CLOCK, WE STRUCK AT THE CENTER OF THE BRITISH LINE..."

TA-ROOM-POOM-POOM!

"BUT THE BRITISH HELD FIRM! AND SHORTLY AFTERWARD, I SAW ONE OF OUR OFFICERS GALLOP TOWARD THE SCENE..."

MARSHAL NEY NEEDS REINFORCEMENTS! IF WE DO NOT GET HELP AT ONCE, THE ATTACK WILL FAIL!

WE MUST BREAK THROUGH THE BRITISH BEFORE THE PRUSSIANS ARRIVE TO HELP THEM OR WE ARE LOST!

IF THE PRUSSIANS GET HERE-- NOT EVEN BONAPARTE WILL BE ABLE TO SAVE US!

SEND IN THE CAVALRY! THE OLD GUARD HAS WON THE DAY FOR US BEFORE!

"THE OLD GUARD! THE FLOWER OF THE FRENCH CAVALRY... VETERANS WHO HAD FOLLOWED NAPOLEON TO VICTORY IN MANY CAMPAIGNS.."

OUR HOUR OF GLORY IS AT HAND, MES COMPATRIOTS! ONCE AGAIN OUR EMPEROR GIVES US THE HONOR OF LEADING THE FINAL ATTACK! FOLLOW YOUR STANDARD INTO BATTLE... IT SHALL NOT FAIL YOU!

 "MY HEART LEAPED AS THE CAVALRY LEADER SINGLED ME OUT..."

DRUMMER! FILL OUR SOULS WITH THE MUSIC OF THE CHARGE!

THERE THEY GO... THE CAVALRY! SOON THE BATTLE WILL BE OVER!

TA-ROOM-POOM-POOM!

I HAVE HEARD THE SOLDIERS TELL OF THE OLD GUARD! THEY WILL FRIGHTEN THE BRITISH OUT OF THEIR WITS! LOOK AT HOW FIERCELY THEY RIDE!

 "BUT, SHORTLY, AS THE CAVALRY RODE HEADLONG TOWARD THE CENTER OF THE ENEMY LINE, THE BRITISH COUNTERATTACKED ON OUR FLANK..."

THE BRITISH ARE ATTACKING ON THIS FLANK! DRUMMER! TAKE COVER!

NEVER!

WHERE ARE YOU RUNNING? SOLDIERS OF FRANCE, IT IS NOT RETREAT I AM SOUNDING!

ZIIIP!

ZINNNG!

TA-ROOM!

ATTACK! NAPOLEON HIMSELF GAVE THE COMMAND! ATTACK! ATT--

BRAMM!

MY DRUM! I... MUST... KEEP... SOUNDING... THE... ATTACK! MON EMPEREUR... TOLD ME... ONLY A MARSHAL... COULD MAKE ME STOP...

"FROM THE HILL... THROUGH DAZED EYES...I SAW THE FINAL STAGE OF THE BATTLE OF WATERLOO... OUR CAVALRY SWOOPING DOWN ON THE BRITISH.."

STAND FAST! HERE'S THE FRENCH CAVALRY... IF WE HOLD HERE IN THE CENTER, WE CAN ROLL THEM UP ON BOTH FLANKS!

"DOWN THEY SWEPT...THEIR GLEAMING SABRES BRANDISHED IN THE AIR...THE FAMED OLD GUARD OF NAPOLEON..."

HOLD RANKS! FIRE ON ORDER!

FIRE!

KPOW!

"AGAIN AND AGAIN THEY CAME ON-- THE VALIANT OLD GUARD! AND IN THIS HOUR WAS HEARD A CRY THAT SHALL NEVER BE FORGOTTEN... "

THE OLD GUARD DIES -- BUT NEVER SURRENDERS!

"AND THEN THERE CAME THE DREAD NEWS THAT TOLLED DOOM FOR NAPOLEON BONAPARTE AND HIS GLORIOUS ARMY... "

THE PRUSSIANS ARE COMING! WE ARE HOPELESSLY OUTNUMBERED! RETREAT!

"IT WAS THEN, THAT I LOST CONSCIOUSNESS! AND WHEN I RECOVERED.."

W-WHAT HAPPENED? WHERE IS EVERYBODY? I-I DO NOT HEAR SOUNDS OF FIRING! BUT OUR SOLDIERS MUST BE SOMEWHERE NEAR! THEY WOULD NOT HAVE DESERTED MON EMPEREUR ...

I WILL ROUSE THEM AGAIN!... LET THEM HEAR THE DRUMS... AND THEY WILL COME FORTH-- THEY WILL ATTACK!... WE WILL GAIN THE VICTORY-- JUST AS NAPOLEON SAID ...

TA-ROOM-POOM! TAROOM-POOM-POOM!

"ALL NIGHT LONG, I WANDERED THE FIELD OF THE SLAIN ..."

"AND WHEN MORNING CAME, I MOUNTED A SMALL HILL, AND SAW THE ENGLISH IN THEIR VICTORY ARRAY ..."

BUT I MUST STILL SOUND THE ATTACK, M'SIEU! ONLY A MAR-SHAL OF THE ARMY CAN ORDER ME TO STOP!

A MARSHAL--? THEN YOU MAY STOP NOW, MY SON!

TA-ROOM-POOM!
TA-ROOM-POOM!
TA-ROOM-POOM-
TA-ROOM-POOM!

BUT M'SIEU, MY EMPEROR'S ORDER... ONLY A MARSHAL OF THE ARMY...

I AM A MAR-SHAL, MY SON! MY NAME IS ARTHUR WELLSLY--DUKE OF WELLINGTON! HERE--YOU HAVE EARNED THIS MEDAL MANY TIMES OVER...

GENTLEMEN-- SALUTE A HERO!

SO RAOUL, THE FRENCH DRUMMER BOY, WON A MEDAL FOR VALOR FROM A FORMER ENEMY! AND THEN, AT LAST, THE DRUMS WERE SILENT ON THE FIELD AT WATERLOO ...

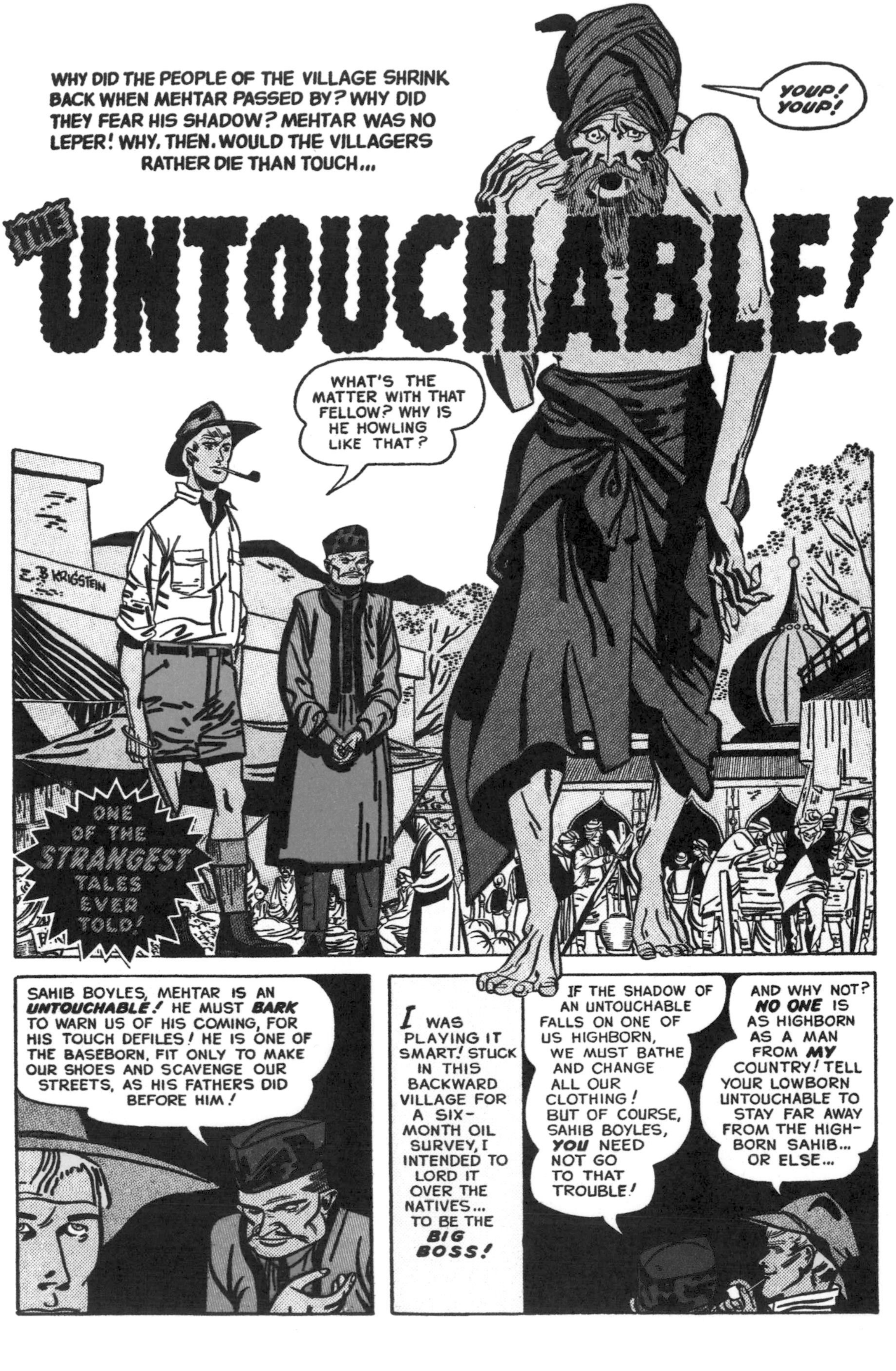
WHY DID THE PEOPLE OF THE VILLAGE SHRINK BACK WHEN MEHTAR PASSED BY? WHY DID THEY FEAR HIS SHADOW? MEHTAR WAS NO LEPER! WHY, THEN, WOULD THE VILLAGERS RATHER DIE THAN TOUCH...
YOUP! YOUP!
THE UNTOUCHABLE!
WHAT'S THE MATTER WITH THAT FELLOW? WHY IS HE HOWLING LIKE THAT?
B. KRIGSTEIN
ONE OF THE STRANGEST TALES EVER TOLD!
SAHIB BOYLES, MEHTAR IS AN UNTOUCHABLE! HE MUST BARK TO WARN US OF HIS COMING, FOR HIS TOUCH DEFILES! HE IS ONE OF THE BASEBORN, FIT ONLY TO MAKE OUR SHOES AND SCAVENGE OUR STREETS, AS HIS FATHERS DID BEFORE HIM!
I WAS PLAYING IT SMART! STUCK IN THIS BACKWARD VILLAGE FOR A SIX-MONTH OIL SURVEY, I INTENDED TO LORD IT OVER THE NATIVES... TO BE THE BIG BOSS!
IF THE SHADOW OF AN UNTOUCHABLE FALLS ON ONE OF US HIGHBORN, WE MUST BATHE AND CHANGE ALL OUR CLOTHING! BUT OF COURSE, SAHIB BOYLES, YOU NEED NOT GO TO THAT TROUBLE!
AND WHY NOT? NO ONE IS AS HIGHBORN AS A MAN FROM MY COUNTRY! TELL YOUR LOWBORN UNTOUCHABLE TO STAY FAR AWAY FROM THE HIGH-BORN SAHIB... OR ELSE...

I LIVED LIKE A KING FOR A MONTH OR TWO!

THIS HEAT! IT'S LIKE AN OVEN! WHY DOESN'T IT RAIN?

IT WILL NOT RAIN, SAHIB! THE TIME FOR THE RAINS IS LONG PAST! IT WILL BE A FAMINE YEAR... MANY WILL DIE!

WELL, I WON'T DIE, AND THAT'S ALL I CARE ABOUT! I BROUGHT SIX MONTHS' SUPPLIES WITH ME, AND WHEN THEY RUN SHORT, I'LL RIDE MY CAMELS OUT OF THIS DEVILISH PLACE!

NO, SAHIB! THAT WILL NOT BE POSSIBLE! EVEN *NOW* THE CAMELS ARE TOO WEAK TO TRAVEL FROM LACK OF FOOD!

WHAT THE BLAZES! YOU WERE SUPPOSED TO BUY FODDER FOR THEM! THOSE CAMELS HAVE *GOT TO LIVE* NO MATTER HOW MANY *NATIVES* HAVE TO *DIE!*

SAHIB BOYLE, YOU DO NOT UNDERSTAND... WHEN THERE IS NO RAIN THERE IS *NOTHING*... NO GRASS, NO MILLET... NOT EVEN A WEED!

SO THAT'S THE WAY IT WAS! THE SELFISH NATIVES WERE EATING THE GRAIN AND FODDER THAT I NEEDED FOR MY CAMELS! THEY WOULDN'T SELL IT AT *ANY* PRICE... SO MY CAMELS DIED!

I'VE GOT NOTHING TO WORRY ABOUT! WHEN I DON'T COME OUT ON SCHEDULE MY COMPANY WILL SEND A CARAVAN IN TO RESCUE ME... OR PERHAPS A PLANE!

THE NATIVES WERE DYING LIKE FLIES, STARVING TO DEATH! BUT *I* HAD PLENTY OF FOOD, SO I COULD STILL GET A LAUGH ONCE IN A WHILE!

THEY SAY A HINDU WON'T EAT FOREIGN FOOD, BUT I WAS CERTAIN A STARVING MAN WOULD EAT *ANYTHING!* I WASN'T TAKING ANY CHANCES!

FROM NOW ON WE'LL TAKE TURNS GUARDING THIS FOOD AT NIGHT, RANGH! I'LL SHOW YOU HOW TO USE THE GUN! AND IF ANYONE COMES SNEAKING AROUND HERE... *SHOOT TO KILL!*

OWW! *HELP!* THEY PUNISH ME!

HOW *DARE* YOU TRY TO DRAW WATER FROM THE VILLAGE WELL! GO TO YOUR OWN FILTHY WELL! AND IF IT IS DRY, THEN DRINK FROM THE MUDDY RIVER! IT IS TOO GOOD FOR SUCH AS YOU!

HA! HA!

I WAS RIGHT! A STARVING MAN WILL EAT ANYTHING... A HANDFUL OF PARCHED CORN FROM LAST YEAR'S HARVEST...A SPOONFUL OF RICE! BUT WHEN THAT IS GONE...

SAHIB! I HAVE NOT EATEN FOR MANY DAYS!

DO YOU EXPECT *ME* TO FEED THE WHOLE VILLAGE?

UNSANITARY! LEAVING THEIR DEAD LYING AROUND LIKE THIS!

SAHIB! MY CHILD! ONE LITTLE CAN OF MILK... A BOWL OF MEAL OR HE DIES!

THERE'D BE ONE LESS MOUTH TO FEED THEN!

MEHTAR, THE UNTOUCHABLE, WAS IN A BAD WAY... FOR WHEN THERE *WAS* FOOD TO SHARE, HIS SHARE CAME LAST... AND LEAST...

THEY'VE HAD FAMINES BEFORE... THEY'RE USED TO IT! A MAN HAS TO LOOK OUT FOR HIMSELF IN THIS WORLD!

SAHIB... A SCRAP ...FROM YOUR TABLE?

BUT HOW DARE HE APPROACH ME! *ME!*

GET OUT OF HERE, *YOU FILTHY UNTOUCHABLE!*

SAHIB! NO, NO! THIS MEANS DEATH FOR YOU!

NATURALLY, I PAID NO ATTENTION TO RANGH AND HIS PRIMITIVE SUPERSTITIONS! IT WAS HIS TURN THAT NIGHT TO GUARD THE STORAGE HUT... I SLEPT SOUNDLY... VERY SOUNDLY!

RANGH! WHAT IS THIS MESS ON MY PLATE? AREN'T THESE THE SCRAPS I LEFT FOR YOU LAST NIGHT? WHERE ARE MY POWDERED EGGS AND MY CANNED BACON?

THERE IS NO MORE FOOD, SAHIB! WHEN *THIS* IS GONE ...*NO MORE!*

WHAT? WHAT ARE YOU TALKING ABOUT?

SAHIB, YOU HAVE SAID MANY TIMES YOU ARE OF THE *HIGHBORN!* LAST NIGHT, WHEN YOU WHIPPED MEHTAR FROM THE YARD, THE SUN WAS LOW AND THE SHADOWS WERE LONG! *THE SHADOW OF THE FILTHY UNTOUCHABLE FELL ON THE CASES OF FOOD!* IT WAS MY DUTY TO DISPOSE OF THEM FOR YOU!

ALL NIGHT I WORKED WHILE YOU SLEPT! CASE BY CASE I DRAGGED TO THE RIVER AND ROWED THEM FAR AWAY! IT IS DEEP BENEATH THE WATER WHERE IT CAN NEVER BE FOUND! BETTER TO STARVE, SAHIB, THAN TO EAT FOOD CONTAMINATED BY THE *SHADOW* OF THE *UNTOUCHABLE!*

I RUSHED MADLY TO THE STORAGE HUT!

*I*T WAS EMPTY...

RANGH HAD DROPPED THE *GUN* IN THE WATER TOO!

YOU IDIOTIC FOOL!

I TRIED TO BUY FOOD FROM THE VILLAGE... I OFFERED EVERY CENT I HAD, BUT *NO ONE* WOULD SELL ME *FOOD!*

I PAWED THROUGH THE DUST FOR A GRAIN OF CORN! I LOST TEN POUNDS.. TWENTY POUNDS! I TRADED MY CLOTHES FOR A BITE TO EAT HERE AND THERE...

I MUST KEEP ACTIVE UNTIL THEY COME IN TO RESCUE ME! BUT THEY THINK I *HAVE* FOOD! IT MAY BE MONTHS ...*MONTHS!*

THEN, ONE DAY, I SAW MEHTAR WITH A SCRAP OF NATIVE BREAD! AND I WAS STILL STRONGER THAN HE WAS!

I CREPT UP ON HIM...

I GRABBED THE BREAD...

I STUFFED IT INTO MY MOUTH...

ANYTHING TO KEEP ALIVE A LITTLE LONGER!

THEN I REALIZED WHAT I HAD DONE!

HE TOOK FOOD FROM MEHTAR THE *UNTOUCHABLE* AND *ATE IT!*

I *TOO* SAW IT!

AND *I!*

I HAD EATEN FOOD TAKEN FROM THE HANDS OF ONE "UNCLEAN"... AND I KNEW I WOULD BE *THE NEXT TO DIE!* FOR NOW I TOO AM...*AN UNTOUCHABLE!*

JOSEPH AND HIS BRETHREN

JOSEPH WAS THE MOST BELOVED OF THE SONS OF JACOB, FOR HE WAS THE CHILD OF JACOB'S OLD AGE.

BECAUSE JACOB LOVED HIS SON SO, HE MADE HIM A BEAUTIFUL GARMENT... A COAT OF MANY COLORS. WHEN HIS BROTHERS SAW THIS, THEY HATED JOSEPH AND WERE ENVIOUS.

BUT JOSEPH KEPT ON TENDING THE FLOCKS WITH HIS BROTHERS AND WALKED IN THE WAYS OF THE LORD.

ONE DAY HE TOLD THEM OF WHAT HE HAD DREAMED. "I DREAMED," HE SAID, "WE ALL BOUND SHEAVES OF WHEAT, AND LO, MY SHEAF STOOD UPRIGHT, AND YOURS BOWED TO MY SHEAF."

HIS BROTHERS SNEERED AND SAID: "WHAT IS THIS, YOU DREAMER? DO YOU REALLY THINK YOU SHALL BE OUR KING AND RULE OVER US, YOUR BROTHERS?" AND THEY HATED HIM THE MORE.

THEN HE DREAMED AGAIN... AND HE DREAMED THAT THE SUN AND THE MOON AND THE ELEVEN STARS BOWED DOWN TO HIM.

"WHAT IS THIS YOU HAVE DREAMED?" SAID HIS FATHER. "SHALL I AND YOUR MOTHER AND YOUR BROTHERS REALLY COME TO BOW OURSELVES BEFORE YOU?" JOSEPH SAID: "THIS I HAVE DREAMED, MY FATHER."

AND HIS BROTHERS HATED HIM THE MORE. THEY DECIDED TO KILL JOSEPH, AND ONE DAY, THEIR CHANCE CAME IN THE DESERT.

THEY SEIZED HIM, AND STRIPPED AWAY HIS COAT OF MANY COLORS.

THEN THEY THREW HIM INTO A PIT WITHOUT FOOD AND WATER, AND WAITED FOR HIM TO DIE.

BUT TRADERS CAME BY, GOING FROM GILEAD INTO EGYPT, AND THE BROTHERS SOLD JOSEPH TO THEM FOR TWENTY PIECES OF SILVER.

THEY DIPPED THE COAT IN GOAT'S BLOOD AND SHOWED IT TO JACOB, SAYING THEY HAD FOUND IT. THE FATHER MOURNED FOR HIS BELOVED, THINKING HE HAD BEEN EATEN BY A BEAST.

BUT JOSEPH STILL LIVED. HE WAS TAKEN TO EGYPT AND SOLD TO POTIPHAR, AN OFFICER OF PHARAOH.

JOSEPH FOUND FAVOR IN THE EYES OF POTIPHAR AND SERVED HIM WELL.

BUT POTIPHAR'S WIFE HATED THE YOUNG SLAVE AND TOLD LIES TO HER HUSBAND ABOUT HIM.

SO JOSEPH WAS THROWN INTO PRISON.

THERE, THE OTHER PRISONERS TOLD HIM THEIR DREAMS, AND HE TOLD THEM WHAT THEY MEANT. EACH MEANING WAS TRUE.

ONE NIGHT PHARAOH HAD TWO DREAMS. IN ONE, HE SAW SEVEN FAT COWS COME OUT OF THE RIVER AND FEED IN THE MEADOW.

BUT SEVEN THIN COWS FOLLOWED AND ATE UP THE FIRST SEVEN.

IN THE SECOND DREAM, HE SAW SEVEN STRONG EARS OF CORN COME OUT OF A STALK, ONLY TO BE EATEN BY SEVEN THIN EARS. PHARAOH AWOKE DISTURBED.

NO ONE COULD INTERPRET THE DREAMS. THEN SOMEONE REMEMBERED JOSEPH THE DREAMER, AND PHARAOH SENT FOR HIM.

JOSEPH SAID: "YOUR DREAMS, O PHARAOH, TELL YOU THAT THERE WILL BE SEVEN YEARS OF PLENTY FOLLOWED BY SEVEN YEARS OF FAMINE. YOU MUST STORE UP FOOD DURING THE YEARS OF PLENTY AGAINST THE LEAN YEARS."

"GOD HAS SHOWN YOU ALL THIS," SAID PHARAOH, "SO I SHALL PUT YOU IN CHARGE OF THIS WORK. ONLY I SHALL BE GREATER THAN YOU IN ALL OF EGYPT."

SO JOSEPH WAS MADE GOVERNOR OF EGYPT, AND HIS MEN GATHERED UP THE FOOD INTO ALL THE CITIES FROM ALL THE FIELDS.

MEANWHILE, JACOB STILL MOURNED HIS LOST SON! THE BROTHERS SAW HIS GRIEF AND REGRETTED WHAT THEY HAD DONE.

SOON THERE CAME THE YEARS OF FAMINE AND THE PEOPLE CAME TO JOSEPH FOR FOOD. AMONG THEM WERE HIS BROTHERS, AND THEY KNEW HIM NOT, ALTHOUGH HE RECOGNIZED THEM.

"YOU ARE SPIES." HE CRIED TO THEM. "WE ARE BUT TWELVE BROTHERS. THE YOUNGEST IS WITH OUR FATHER AS HE IS TOO YOUNG TO TRAVEL. AND ANOTHER IS NO MORE."

"YOU ARE SPIES." JOSEPH SAID. HE TOOK SIMEON CAPTIVE AND ORDERED THE OTHERS TO BRING BENJAMIN, THE YOUNGEST, TO HIM TO PROVE THEY WERE NOT SPIES.

THE BROTHERS RETURNED TO THEIR FATHER WITH TEARS FOR ANOTHER BROTHER WHO HAD BEEN LOST. THEY FEARED TO GO BACK WITH BENJAMIN.

BUT THEY HAD TO RETURN FOR MORE FOOD, AND THIS TIME THEY BROUGHT THE YOUNGEST. JOSEPH FEASTED THEM AND GAVE THEM GRAIN AND SENT THEM ON THEIR WAY.

BUT JOSEPH'S SOLDIERS STOPPED THEM AND SEARCHED THEIR BAGS. THERE THEY FOUND JOSEPH'S SILVER CUP.

BROUGHT BACK TO JOSEPH, JUDAH SAID: "WE ARE NOT THIEVES. BUT DO NOT TAKE BENJAMIN IN PUNISHMENT. TAKE ME. OUR FATHER'S HEART IS ALREADY BROKEN BECAUSE OF THE LOSS OF ONE BELOVED."

NOW JOSEPH KNEW THAT HIS BROTHERS REGRETTED WHAT THEY HAD DONE. "DO YOU NOT KNOW ME?" HE SAID: "I AM YOUR BROTHER JOSEPH, WHOM YOU SOLD INTO SLAVERY."

THE BROTHERS EMBRACED, WEEPING FOR JOY, RE-UNITED AT LAST. JOSEPH'S DREAMS HAD COME TRUE, FOR THEY HAD ALL BOWED DOWN TO HIM.

AND JOSEPH WELCOMED JACOB AND ALL HIS FAMILY TO COME AND LIVE IN THE LAND OF GOSHEN.

The TERRORIST

A TRUE SPY STORY

St. Petersburg, Russia—July 28th, 1904! Baron De Plehve, chief of the Okhrana, the Czar's secret police, is blown to bits! Again, the secret terrorist organization headed by the most feared man in Russia, Ievno Azeff, has struck!

All but one of this terrorist cell was arrested by the Okhrana!

HALT! YOU ARE UNDER ARREST! DON'T LET THAT MAN ESCAPE!

KER-BLAMM!

The one who escaped was—Azeff, the terrorist chief!

STOP!

CRACK!

ZEENG!

LATER, IN HIS UNDERGROUND HEADQUARTERS...

--THEY ALMOST GOT ME! THERE IS AN INFORMER-- A SPY IN OUR MIDST!

POLICE NAME, AZEFF-- IT IS VALENTINE! OUR LIVES ARE IN DANGER WHILE HE LIVES! WE MUST FIND HIM!

I KNOW HIS

THE OKHRANA HAS UNCOVERED OUR ARSENALS! WE MUST HAVE MORE ARMS-- ESPECIALLY EXPLOSIVES!

WE FORESAW THAT, AND HAVE ALREADY PUT PLANS ONE, TWO AND THREE INTO OPERATION!

BUT, DUE TO THE INFORMER, VALENTINE, THE TERRORIST SUPPLIES WERE DISCOVERED. PLAN ONE: THE EXPLOSIVES...

NITROGLYCERIN-- HIDDEN IN THE HERRING BARREL!

I FEEL ANOTHER BOTTLE!

I KNOW NOTHING! A MAN PAID ME TO DELIVER THESE BARRELS!

--PLAN TWO: ARMS AND AMMUNITION...

A FALSE PRIEST WITH RIFLES FOR THE TERRORISTS, EH? YOU SHALL DIE FOR THIS!

NO NEED TO PROTEST INNOCENCE! VALENTINE HAS NAMED YOU ALL!

--PLAN THREE: PROPAGANDA!

FOOLS! DON'T YOU UNDERSTAND WE KNOW EVERYTHING? WE HAVE VALENTINE!

THOUGH THEIR RANKS WERE DEPLETED, THE TERRORISTS MET AGAIN...

THE PLOT TO ASSASSINATE THE GRAND DUKE SERGEI MUST SUCCEED! HE IS THE CZAR'S UNCLE! BUT WITH VALENTINE TO BETRAY US--!

I SHALL SEARCH OUT VALENTINE FOR YOU, AZEFF! I, BURTZEFF, PROMISE IT!

I AM HAVING A THIEF STEAL THE PRIVATE FILES OF THE OKHRANA! WE SHALL FIND OUT WHO VALENTINE IS! AND WHEN WE DO...

GOOD! NOW, ABOUT THE GRAND DUKE... YOU, IVAN, WILL TOSS THE BOMB! YOU UNDERSTAND?

YES, AZEFF! THE SAME AS ALWAYS!

MEANWHILE, AT SECRET POLICE HEADQUARTERS...

AZEFF IS THE HEAD OF THE TERRORISTS! WE MUST GET HIM—HE IS DANGEROUS! VALENTINE HAS REPORTED A PLOT AGAINST THE GRAND DUKE SERGEI!

THIS MAN

ONCE AZEFF IS ARRESTED, THE TERRORIST CELLS WILL COLLAPSE!

HERE, IVAN, THE BOMB! THINGS ARE GETTING TOO HOT HERE FOR ME—I MUST GO TO PARIS! THERE IS THE DUKE—YOU MUST NOT FAIL!

I SHALL NOT FAIL! AND—GOOD LUCK, MY CHIEF!

SO, WHILE AZÉFF HURRIED OFF TO MAKE HIS PARIS TRAIN...

HE HAS BLOWN UP THE GRAND DUKE! KILL HIM!

CRACK!!

KER-BLAM!

LONG LIVE AZEFF!

TRUE TO HIS OATH, BURTZEFF, SEARCHING FOR VALENTINE, RECEIVED A THIEF!..

THERE ARE THE SECRET FILES I STOLE FROM THE OKHRANA, BURTZEFF! NOW—MY FEE!

AH! IF ONLY AZEFF WERE HERE! HE WOULD SUPERVISE THE KILLING OF THE TRAITOR, VALENTINE!

BUT BURTZEFF MADE A HORRIFYING DISCOVERY...

IT CANNOT BE! ACCORDING TO THE SECRET FILES OF THE OKHRANA, THE TRAITOR VALENTINE IS AZEFF HIMSELF!

WITH THIS DISCLOSURE, BOTH THE OKHRANA AND THE TERRORISTS COLLAPSED! A HIGH OFFICER OF BOTH ORGANIZATIONS, IEVNO AZEFF HAD BETRAYED EACH! DESPITE THE PERILS OF HIS DOUBLE-DEALING, THIS DEADLY, DARING AND SUCCESSFUL SPY DIED PEACEFULLY IN BED IN BERLIN, APRIL 24, 1918!

The FLYING MACHINE

IN THE YEAR A.D. 400, THE EMPEROR YUAN HELD HIS THRONE BY THE GREAT WALL OF CHINA, AND THE LAND WAS GREEN WITH RAIN, READYING ITSELF TOWARD THE HARVEST, AT PEACE, THE PEOPLE IN HIS DOMINATION NEITHER TOO HAPPY NOR TOO SAD. EARLY ON THE MORNING OF THE FIRST DAY OF THE FIRST WEEK OF THE SECOND MONTH OF THE NEW YEAR, THE EMPEROR YUAN WAS SIPPING TEA AND FANNING HIMSELF AGAINST A WARM BREEZE WHEN A SERVANT RAN ACROSS THE SCARLET AND BLUE GARDEN TILES, CALLING...

OH, *EMPEROR, EMPEROR, A MIRACLE!*

YES, THE AIR *IS* SWEET THIS MORNING.

ADAPTED FROM A STORY BY
RAY BRADBURY

B. Krigstein

THE SERVANT SHOOK HIS HEAD, BOWING QUICKLY...

NO, NO, A *MIRACLE!*

AND THIS *TEA* IS GOOD IN MY *MOUTH.* SURELY *THAT* IS A MIRACLE.

NO, *NO,* YOUR EXCELLENCY.

LET ME GUESS, THEN. ER... THE *SUN* HAS RISEN AND A *NEW DAY* IS UPON US. OR THE *SEA* IS *BLUE. THAT,* NOW, IS THE FINEST OF *ALL* MIRACLES.

EXCELLENCY, A *MAN* IS *FLYING!*

WHAT?

THE EMPEROR STOPPED HIS FAN...

I *SAW* him in the *AIR*, a *MAN* flying with *WINGS*. I HEARD A *VOICE* CALL OUT OF THE SKY, AND WHEN I LOOKED *UP*, THERE HE *WAS*, A *DRAGON* IN THE HEAVENS WITH A *MAN* IN ITS MOUTH, A DRAGON OF *PAPER* AND *BAMBOO*, COLORED LIKE THE *SUN* AND THE *GRASS*.

IT IS *EARLY*, AND YOU HAVE JUST WAKENED FROM A *DREAM*.

IT IS *EARLY*, BUT I HAVE *SEEN* WHAT I HAVE *SEEN!* COME, AND *YOU* WILL SEE IT, *TOO*.

SIT DOWN WITH ME HERE. DRINK SOME *TEA*. IT MUST BE A *STRANGE* THING, IF IT IS *TRUE*, TO SEE A *MAN FLY*. YOU *MUST* HAVE TIME TO *THINK* OF IT, EVEN AS *I* MUST HAVE TIME TO *PREPARE MY-SELF* FOR THE *SIGHT*.

THEY DRANK TEA. THE EMPEROR ROSE THOUGHTFULLY AS THE SER-VANT PLEADED...

PLEASE. OR HE WILL BE *GONE*.

NOW YOU MAY SHOW ME WHAT YOU HAVE SEEN.

THEY WALKED INTO A GARDEN, ACROSS A MEADOW OF GRASS, OVER A SMALL BRIDGE, THROUGH A GROVE OF TREES, AND UP A TINY HILL...

THERE!

THE EMPEROR LOOKED INTO THE SKY...

AND IN THE SKY, LAUGHING SO HIGH THAT YOU COULD HARDLY HEAR HIM LAUGH, WAS A MAN; AND THE MAN WAS CLOTHED IN BRIGHT PAPERS AND REEDS TO MAKE WINGS AND A BEAUTIFUL YELLOW TAIL, AND HE WAS SOARING ALL ABOUT LIKE THE LARGEST BIRD IN A UNIVERSE OF BIRDS, LIKE A NEW DRAGON IN A LAND OF ANCIENT DRAGONS...

I FLY! I FLY!

YES! YES...

THE EMPEROR YUAN DID NOT MOVE. INSTEAD HE LOOKED AT THE GREAT WALL OF CHINA NOW TAKING SHAPE OUT OF THE FARTHEST MIST IN THE GREEN HILLS, THAT WONDERFUL WALL WHICH HAD PROTECTED THEM FOR A TIMELESS TIME FROM ENEMY HORDES AND PRESERVED PEACE FOR YEARS WITHOUT NUMBER...

TELL ME, HAS ANYONE *ELSE* SEEN THIS FLYING MAN?

I AM THE *ONLY ONE* EXCELLENCY.

THE EMPEROR WATCHED THE HEAVENS ANOTHER MINUTE AND THEN SAID...

CALL HIM *DOWN* TO ME.

HO, COME *DOWN*, COME *DOWN!* THE *EMPEROR WISHES TO SEE YOU!*

THE EMPEROR GLANCED IN ALL DIRECTIONS WHILE THE FLYING MAN SOARED DOWN THE MORNING WIND. HE SAW A FARMER, EARLY IN HIS FIELDS, WATCHING THE SKY, AND HE NOTED WHERE THE FARMER STOOD...

THE FLYING MAN ALIT WITH A RUSTLE OF PAPER AND A CREAK OF BAMBOO REEDS. HE CAME PROUDLY TO THE EMPEROR, CLUMSY IN HIS RIG, AT LAST BOWING BEFORE THE OLD MAN...

WHAT *HAVE* YOU *DONE?*

I HAVE *FLOWN* IN THE *SKY,* YOUR EXCELLENCY.

WHAT HAVE YOU *DONE?*

I HAVE JUST *TOLD* YOU!

YOU HAVE TOLD ME *NOTHING AT ALL.*

THE EMPEROR REACHED OUT A THIN HAND TO TOUCH THE PRETTY PAPER AND THE BIRDLIKE KEEL OF THE APPARATUS. IT SMELLED COOL, OF THE WIND...

IS IT NOT *BEAUTIFUL,* EXCELLENCY?

YES, *TOO* BEAUTIFUL,

IT IS THE *ONLY* ONE IN THE *WORLD!* AND *I* AM THE *INVENTOR!*

THE *ONLY* ONE IN THE WORLD?

I *SWEAR* IT!

WHO ELSE *KNOWS* OF THIS?

163

NO ONE. NOT *EVEN* MY *WIFE*, WHO WOULD THINK ME *MAD WITH THE SUN*. SHE THOUGHT I WAS MAKING A *KITE*. I ROSE IN THE NIGHT AND WALKED TO THE CLIFFS FAR AWAY. AND WHEN THE MORNING BREEZES BLEW AND THE SUN ROSE, I GATHERED MY COURAGE, EXCELLENCY, AND LEAPED. I *FLEW!* BUT MY *WIFE* DOES NOT *KNOW* OF IT.

WELL FOR HER, THEN. COME ALONG.

THEY WALKED BACK TO THE GREAT HOUSE. THE SUN WAS FULL IN THE SKY NOW, AND THE SMELL OF THE GRASS WAS REFRESHING. THE EMPEROR, THE SERVANT, AND THE FLIER PAUSED WITHIN THE HUGE GARDEN. THE EMPEROR CLAPPED HIS HANDS.

HO, GUARDS!

THE GUARDS CAME RUNNING...

HOLD THIS MAN.

THE GUARDS SEIZED THE FLIER...

CALL THE EXECUTIONER!

WHAT'S THIS? WHAT HAVE I DONE?

THE FLIER BEGAN TO WEEP, SO THAT THE BEAUTIFUL PAPER APPARATUS RUSTLED...

HERE IS A MAN WHO HAS MADE A CERTAIN *MACHINE*, AND YET HE *ASKS* US WHAT HE HAS *CREATED*. HE DOES *NOT KNOW HIMSELF*. IT IS ONLY NECESSARY THAT HE *CREATE*, WITHOUT KNOWING *WHY* HE HAS DONE SO, OR *WHAT* THIS THING WILL *DO*.

THE EXECUTIONER CAME RUNNING WITH A SILVER AX. HE STOOD WITH HIS NAKED, LARGE-MUSCLED ARMS READY, HIS FACE COVERED WITH A SERENE WHITE MASK...

ONE MOMENT...

THE EMPEROR TURNED TO A NEARBY TABLE UPON WHICH SAT A MACHINE THAT HE HIMSELF HAD CREATED. HE TOOK A TINY GOLDEN KEY FROM AROUND HIS OWN NECK. HE FITTED THIS KEY TO THE TINY, DELICATE MACHINE AND WOUND IT UP...

THEN HE SET THE MACHINE GOING...

THE MACHINE WAS A GARDEN OF METAL AND JEWELS. SET IN MOTION, BIRDS SANG IN TINY METAL TREES, WOLVES WALKED THROUGH MINIATURE FORESTS, AND TINY PEOPLE RAN IN AND OUT OF SUN AND SHADOW, FANNING THEMSELVES WITH MINIATURE FANS, LISTENING TO THE TINY EMERALD BIRDS, AND STANDING BY IMPOSSIBLY SMALL BUT TINKLING FOUNTAINS...

THE EMPEROR SAID...

IS *IT* NOT BEAUTIFUL? IF YOU ASKED ME WHAT *I* HAVE DONE HERE, I COULD *ANSWER* YOU *WELL*. I HAVE MADE *BIRDS* SING, I HAVE MADE *FORESTS* MURMUR, I HAVE SET *PEOPLE* TO WALKING IN THIS WOODLAND, ENJOYING THE LEAVES AND SHADOWS AND SONGS. *THAT* IS WHAT *I* HAVE DONE.

THE FLIER, ON HIS KNEES, THE TEARS POURING DOWN HIS FACE, PLEADED...

BUT *I* HAVE DONE A *SIMILAR* THING! I HAVE FOUND *BEAUTY*. I HAVE *FLOWN* ON THE *MORNING WIND*. I HAVE LOOKED DOWN ON ALL THE SLEEPING HOUSES AND GARDENS. I HAVE SMELLED THE SEA AND EVEN *SEEN* IT, BEYOND THE HILLS, FROM MY HIGH PLACE. AND I HAVE SOARED LIKE A BIRD. OH, I CANNOT *SAY* HOW BEAUTIFUL IT IS UP THERE, IN THE SKY, WITH THE WIND ABOUT ME, BLOWING ME LIKE A FEATHER. *THAT* IS *BEAUTIFUL*, EMPEROR, THAT IS *BEAUTIFUL*, TOO!

YES. I KNOW IT *MUST* BE *TRUE*. FOR I FELT MY *HEART* MOVE WITH YOU IN THE AIR AND I *WONDERED*: WHAT IS IT *LIKE*? HOW DOES IT *FEEL*? HOW DO THE DISTANT POOLS LOOK FROM SO HIGH? AND HOW MY HOUSES AND SERVANTS? LIKE ANTS? AND HOW THE DISTANT TOWNS, NOT YET AWAKE?

THEN *SPARE ME!*

BUT THERE ARE TIMES WHEN ONE MUST *LOSE* A LITTLE BEAUTY IF ONE IS TO *KEEP* WHAT LITTLE BEAUTY ONE *ALREADY* HAS. I DO NOT FEAR *YOU, YOURSELF*, BUT I FEAR *ANOTHER MAN*.

WHAT MAN?

SOME *OTHER* MAN WHO, SEEING YOU, WILL BUILD A THING OF BRIGHT PAPERS AND BAMBOO LIKE THIS. BUT THE *OTHER* MAN WILL HAVE AN *EVIL FACE* AND AN *EVIL HEART*, AND THE *BEAUTY* WILL BE *GONE*. IT IS *THIS* MAN I FEAR!

WHY? WHY?

WHO IS TO SAY THAT SOMEDAY *JUST* SUCH A MAN, IN *JUST* SUCH AN APPARATUS, MIGHT NOT *FLY IN THE SKY AND DROP HUGE STONES UPON THE GREAT WALL OF CHINA?*

NO ONE MOVED OR SAID A WORD...

OFF WITH HIS HEAD!

THE EXECUTIONER WHIRLED HIS SILVER AX...

BURN THE KITE AND THE INVENTOR'S BODY AND BURY THEIR ASHES TOGETHER...

THE GUARDS RETREATED TO OBEY...

THE EMPEROR TURNED TO HIS SERVANT WHO HAD SEEN THE MAN FLYING...

HOLD YOUR *TONGUE*. IT WAS *ALL A DREAM*, A MOST *SORROWFUL* AND *BEAUTIFUL DREAM*. AND THAT *FARMER* IN THE DISTANT FIELD WHO *ALSO* SAW, TELL HIM IT WOULD *PAY* HIM TO *CONSIDER* IT *ONLY A VISION*. IF *EVER* THE *WORD* PASSES AROUND, *YOU AND THE FARMER DIE WITHIN THE HOUR.*

YOU ARE *MERCIFUL* EMPEROR.

THE OLD MAN SAW, BEYOND THE GARDEN WALL, THE GUARDS BURNING THE BEAUTIFUL MACHINE OF PAPER AND REEDS THAT SMELLED OF MORNING WIND. HE SAW THE DARK SMOKE CLIMB INTO THE SKY...

NO, *NOT MERCIFUL*. NO, ONLY *VERY MUCH BEWILDERED* AND *AFRAID*.

HE SAW THE GUARDS DIGGING A TINY PIT WHEREIN TO BURY THE ASHES...

WHAT IS THE LIFE OF *ONE* MAN AGAINST A *MILLION OTHERS*? I MUST TAKE *SOLACE* FROM THAT THOUGHT.

HE TOOK THE KEY FROM ITS CHAIN ABOUT HIS NECK AND ONCE MORE WOUND UP THE BEAUTIFUL MINIATURE GARDEN. THE TINY GARDEN WHIRRED ITS HIDDEN AND DELICATE MACHINERY AND SET ITSELF INTO MOTION; TINY PEOPLE WALKED IN FORESTS, TINY FOXES LOPED THROUGH SUN-SPECKLED GLADES, AND AMONG THE TINY TREES FLEW LITTLE BITS OF HIGH SONG AND BRIGHT BLUE AND YELLOW COLOR, FLYING, FLYING, FLYING IN THAT SMALL SKY. AND THE EMPEROR SAID, CLOSING HIS EYES...

OH, *LOOK* AT THE *BIRDS*, LOOK AT THE *BIRDS!*

THE DEN WAS QUIET. THE FRAGRANT ODOR OF OPIUM FLOATED TO THE CEILING AND LIKE A HEAVY CURTAIN IT DEADENED THE CHINATOWN STREET NOISES, PUSHED THEM FURTHER AND FURTHER AWAY TO THE REALM OF THE UNREAL... AND THE SMOKERS LAY MOTIONLESS, REVELING IN THEIR OWN FANCIFUL WORLD OF DREAMS. LISTEN NOW AS *CHEN CHU YANG* TELLS YOU HIS STORY IN HIS OWN WORDS.

PIPE-DREAM

MY NAME IS *CHEN CHU YANG*, AND IT IS WITH MUCH SORROW IN MY HEART THAT I TELL YOU THIS TALE. BUT WITHIN ME A SMALL VOICE SAYS THAT IT MUST BE TOLD... AND SO BE IT.

B. Krigstein

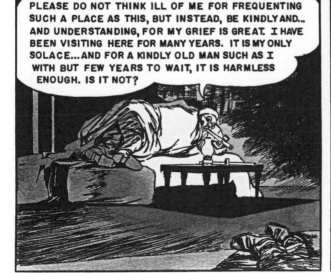

PLEASE DO NOT THINK ILL OF ME FOR FREQUENTING SUCH A PLACE AS THIS, BUT INSTEAD, BE KINDLY AND... AND UNDERSTANDING, FOR MY GRIEF IS GREAT. I HAVE BEEN VISITING HERE FOR MANY YEARS. IT IS MY ONLY SOLACE... AND FOR A KINDLY OLD MAN SUCH AS I WITH BUT FEW YEARS TO WAIT, IT IS HARMLESS ENOUGH. IS IT NOT?

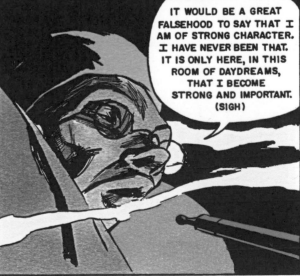

IT WOULD BE A GREAT FALSEHOOD TO SAY THAT I AM OF STRONG CHARACTER. I HAVE NEVER BEEN THAT. IT IS ONLY HERE, IN THIS ROOM OF DAYDREAMS, THAT I BECOME STRONG AND IMPORTANT. (SIGH)

"MY STORY GOES BACK PERHAPS A DOZEN SUMMERS. MY WIFE WAS A GOOD WOMAN...A *STRONG* WOMAN. SHE BORE THE BURDEN THAT I WAS TOO WEAK TO CARRY."

IS IT NOT A MOST BEAUTIFUL AFTERNOON, WIFE? I THINK I SHALL WALK IN THE PARK. IT IS GOOD FOR MY SOUL.

YES, HUSBAND. BUT DO BE CAREFUL!

"SUCH A *GOOD* WOMAN. NEVER CAN I RECALL A WORD OF COMPLAINT FROM HER...EVEN THOUGH SHE BUT KNEW IT WAS NOT TO THE PARK I WALKED...BUT TO THIS HOUSE OF DREAMS. I REMEMBER WELL HOW I CHIDED MYSELF THAT BLACK DAY...UNTIL MY BRAIN WAS LULLED."

"NEVER BEFORE THAT DAY HAD MY DREAMS CONCERNED MY GOOD WIFE. BUT I WAS FILLED TO OVERFLOWING WITH LOVE FOR HER...AND IT WAS BEYOND MY CONTROL..."

"I DREAMED OF HER WONDROUS FAITH AND DEVOTION TO MYSELF AND OUR CHILDREN...AND FOR NO REASON, I DREAMED OF THE SADNESS THAT WOULD BE MINE, WERE SHE TO DIE..."

"IN GREAT DETAIL I DREAMED THE BIRDS WOULD NOT SING, AND THE FLOWERS WOULD BOW THEIR FRAGRANT HEADS TO JOIN ME IN MY SORROW..."

"AI! IT HAD INDEED BEEN A SAD DREAM. BUT IT HAD MADE ME KEENLY AWARE THAT I WAS A FORTUNATE MAN... A *VERY* FORTUNATE MAN TO POSSESS SUCH A TREASURE! AND I HAD RETURNED HOME WITH A LIGHTNESS OF HEART THAT WAS MOST PLEASING. BUT IT PROVED TO BE A BLACK DAY...FOR THE FIRST OF MY GREAT SORROWS HAD FALLEN..."

MY CHILDREN! WHAT IS ALL THIS? WHY DO YOU CRY?

OH, MY FATHER! THE WIND BLOWS CRUEL! *MOTHER HAS DIED!*

"HAD I NOT REASON TO GRIEVE? WHAT WAS TO BECOME OF US? I WAS AWARE OF MY DUTY TO MY TWO CHILDREN, OH YES! AND BY THE BEARD OF MY SIRE, I VOWED THAT DAY TO BEGIN ANEW..."

MY CHILDREN, IT IS WITH MUCH JOY THAT I SPEAK OF THIS! I GO TODAY TO SEEK A POSITION IN THE WORLD OF BUSINESS!

OH, FATHER! YOU MAKE US VERY PLEASED!

"AH, BUT IT IS SAD. MY SO HONORABLE INTENTIONS FADED LIKE SMOKE BEFORE THE WIND. AND WERE IT NOT FOR THE EFFORTS OF MY SON, WE WOULD NOT HAVE HAD FOOD IN OUR MOUTHS, NOR EVEN A ROOF ABOVE OUR HEADS..."

HERE, MY FATHER, IS MONEY WITH WHICH TO PAY THE RENT!

AH, MY SON! GREATLY BLESSED AM I, A WEAK OLD MAN, TO HAVE FATHERED ONE WHO PROVIDES AS YOU!

"BUT AGAIN, MY GLADNESS WAS SHORT-LIVED. THE WAR WAS CALLING FOR MEN... AND MY SON WAS NO EXCEPTION."

BUT I HAVE BEEN DRAFTED, FATHER! WHO, NOW, WILL CARE FOR YOU AND MY SISTER?

SURELY THERE IS NO CAUSE FOR YOU TO WORRY! I, NOW, WILL UPHOLD THE DUTY WHICH FOR SO LONG I HAVE SHIRKED!

"THAT NIGHT I VISITED THIS PLACE. IN MY HEART I CRIED FOR MY SON WHO WOULD LEAVE US... AND SO DID I CRY IN MY SMOKE DREAMS..."

"I SAW IN MY DREAMS THE ANGUISH THROUGH WHICH HE MUST PASS, THE HAUNTING FEAR WHICH I KNEW WOULD CROWD HIS EVERY HOUR..."

"I SAW THE FACE OF THE ENEMY! I FELT THE IMPACT OF SHELLS EXPLODING, SAW THE GREAT BLOODSHED..."

"...AND I DREAMED MY ONLY SON WOULD DIE..."

"(SIGH) THE HOUR WAS LATE WHEN I ARRIVED HOME. I HAD PLEDGED MYSELF TO CARE FOR MY DAUGHTER IN MY SON'S ABSENCE. THIS TIME, SURELY, I WOULD NOT FAIL! YET I WAS GREETED WITH BUT ANOTHER GREAT SORROW..."

NO! NO, THIS CANNOT BE! MY SON DEAD?!

THAT'S RIGHT, SIR! HAD AN AUTO ACCIDENT ON THE WAY HOME FROM HIS GOING-AWAY PARTY!

"THE GODS WERE SURELY PUNISHING ME FOR MY LACK OF HONOR! AMENDS WOULD HAVE TO BE MADE BY MY HUMBLE BEING TO ATONE FOR THE MISFORTUNES I HAVE CAUSED. AT ALL COSTS I HAD TO PROTECT AND CHERISH THE WELFARE OF MY TREASURED DAUGHTER..."

"YEA, THOUGH I TRIED WITH ALL MY POWER TO CONVINCE MY DAUGHTER OF HER FOLLY, I WENT UNHEARD... FOR NO MAN ON THE EARTH CAN SPEAK LOUD ENOUGH FOR A GIRL TO HEAR WHEN HER HEAD IS IN THE CLOUDS. IS IT NOT SO?"

BUT HE IS NOT FOR YOU, MY CHILD! HE IS NOT A GOOD MAN... HE IS ALL WICKEDNESS!

YOU ARE SO WRONG, FATHER! HE *LOVES* ME! IS THAT NOT PROOF ENOUGH OF HIS GOOD HEART?

AH... NOW MY BRIGHTEST JEWEL HAS BEEN TAKEN FROM ME! I WISH GLADNESS FOREVER, MY DAUGHTER. MAY YOUR JOY INCREASE A THOUSAND FOLD!

THANK YOU, MY FATHER! THIS IS INDEED THE HAPPIEST MOMENT IN MY LIFE. I SHALL HAVE NO REGRETS!

"BUT SHE HAD REGRETS. IN THE SPAN OF SIX MONTHS THERE WERE MANY."

OH, MY FATHER! IT IS UNBEARABLE! I AM BUT A *SLAVE* TO HIM! HE TREATS ME AS I WERE A STRANGER, AND NEVER EVEN DOES HE HAVE A SMILE OR A KIND WORD FOR ME! WHATEVER SHALL I DO?

THERE IS NOTHING YOU MUST DO, MY CHILD. IT IS TOO LATE. YOU HAVE A HUSBAND AND YOU MUST REMAIN WITH HIM!

BUT, FATHER! HE IS CRUEL! SEE? THESE BRUISES? HE HAS STRUCK ME MANY TIMES!

IT IS OF NO CONSEQUENCE. YOU ARE A GIRL OF CHINA, AND MY DAUGHTER. YOU MUST DO NOTHING TO BRING A DISGRACE UPON US! YOU HAVE TAKEN A VOW TO BE WITH THE MAN OF YOUR CHOICE. YOU CANNOT RETRACE THE PATH YOU YOURSELF HAVE MADE!

TRUE, IT WILL BE A DIFFICULT TASK... BUT THERE IS NO OTHER COURSE THAT, WITH HONOR, YOU COULD TAKE! I GRIEVE DEEPLY BUT... IT STILL DOES NOT CHANGE! YOU CAN ONLY BE FREE WHEN HE IS DEAD!

(SIGH) YES, MY FATHER! YOUR WORDS ARE WISE... AND TRUE! I MUST DO NOTHING! I MUST RESIGN MYSELF TO MY FATE!

"I HAD WATCHED, TEARS WETTING MY CHEEKS, AS SHE HAD SLOWLY WALKED FROM ME, TO RETURN TO HER MASTER. DID IT NOT SEEM UNFAIR THAT ONE SO YOUNG, SO FAIR, SHOULD SUFFER SO? IT WAS THEN THAT I KNEW I HAD TO ASSERT MYSELF TO RELIEVE MY DAUGHTER OF HER MISERY..."

"SURELY *SOMETHING* HAD TO BE DONE! THE GODS HAD GIVEN ME THIS CHANCE SO THAT I MIGHT REDEEM MYSELF! BUT *WHAT* COULD I, A WEAK OLD MAN, DO? IN MY WORRY, I HAD VISITED THIS ROOM OF ENCHANTMENT, AND AS THE AROMATIC VAPORS STUPEFIED MY SENSES, MY IMAGINATION WAS GIVEN ITS FREEDOM..."

"AH, THIS DREAM I WELL REMEMBER. I DREAMED THAT I WAS STRONG AND BRAVE. I DREAMED OF MY DAUGHTER'S SADNESS, OF HER YOUTH THAT WOULD WITHER AS THE AUTUMN LEAF, OF HER TEARS THAT FLOWED LIKE THE RIVER FROM EYES FILLED WITH DISILLUSION..."

"IN MY DREAM I ARGUED IMPORTANTLY WITH HER MATE. I SAW THE VICIOUS EYES, THE LIPS CURLED IN WRATH, AND I WAS NOT AFRAID..."

"...FOR I HAD THE LION'S HEART! AND WHEN TO HIS SURPRISE, HE SAW HIS WORDS WERE USELESS, WE STRUGGLED MIGHTILY..."

"...AND HIS YOUTHFUL STRENGTH WAS PUT TO ITS GREATEST TEST! IN THE FURY THERE SUDDENLY APPEARED IN MY HAND A HUGE AXE WITH WHICH I STRUCK HIM A HEAVY BLOW..."

"I SHUDDER NOW TO RECALL HOW HE HAD FALLEN TO THE FLOOR, GUSHING RED, AND HOW I, IN MY ANGER, SMOTE HIM A DOZEN MORE TIMES TILL THERE WAS BUT LITTLE LEFT OF HIM FOR ONE TO VIEW..."

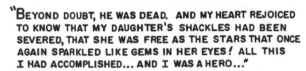

"BEYOND DOUBT, HE WAS DEAD. AND MY HEART REJOICED TO KNOW THAT MY DAUGHTER'S SHACKLES HAD BEEN SEVERED, THAT SHE WAS FREE AS THE STARS THAT ONCE AGAIN SPARKLED LIKE GEMS IN HER EYES! ALL THIS I HAD ACCOMPLISHED... AND I WAS A HERO..."

"WHEN I RETURNED FROM THE NEBULOUS WORLD, I WAS GREATLY AGITATED. TO BE SURE, IT WAS AN EXCELLENT DAY-DREAM, BUT SUDDENLY MY TWO GREAT SORROWS OCCURRED TO ME! AND I RECALLED THAT BEFORE THE DEATH OF MY WIFE, I *HAD DREAMED HER DEAD!*"

"AND I RECALLED THAT BEFORE THE DEATH OF MY ONLY SON ...I HAD DREAMED *HIM* DEAD! COULD MY DREAMS POSSIBLY BE *MORE* THAN MERE FANCIES? COULD THE GREAT GODS WORK IN SUCH A MANNER TO AWAKEN ME TO MY TRUE SELF? YOU CAN EASILY SEE MY EXCITEMENT! I HAD TO KNOW IF I WERE RIGHT! WITH MUCH HASTE I HURRIED TO MY DAUGHTER..."

"AND, *LO!* WHEN I ARRIVED, THERE WERE POLICEMEN AND CROWDS ALL BUSTLING AND EXCITED..."

MY DAUGHTER, YOU CRY! TELL ME, WHAT HAS TRANSPIRED HERE?

MY HUSBAND HAS BEEN *KILLED*, MY FATHER! I DO NOT KNOW BY WHOM!

SURELY THEN, YOU SHOULD BE JOYFUL! NO ONE GRIEVES AT THE PASSING OF A WICKED SOUL... AND YOU ARE *FREE!* AND *I* HAVE AT LAST EMERGED TO FIND THE SUCCESS AND IMPORTANCE THAT DESTINY HAD PLANNED FOR ME!

YES, MY FATHER!

AH, YES... THAT WAS MANY YEARS AGO. WHY AM *I* HERE, YOU ASK? WHERE IS THE SUCCESS AND IMPORTANCE I WAS TO RECEIVE, YOU ASK? (SIGH) NEVER SHALL I OBTAIN THAT GLORY!

IT IS ONLY HERE IN THIS PLACE THAT I SMOKE AND FIND CONSOLATION! YOU AND I KNOW THAT IT WAS MY *DREAM* THAT CAUSED MY DAUGHTER'S MAN TO DIE... YET THE POLICE WOULD NOT BELIEVE HER INNOCENT! *SHE WAS PUT TO DEATH FOR HIS MURDER!*

(SIGH) AH, WELL... IT IS TIME FOR ANOTHER DREAM... IS IT NOT?

The CATACOMBS

PIETRO MIUTA...

...GRABBED THE SACK WITH ITS LOAD OF SILVER...

...AND, WITH GINO ALCARI FOLLOWING...

...BROKE FOR THE FRONT DOOR!

AS THE FRIGHTENED PAIR FLED DOWN THE STREET, THE STARTLED CRIES OF THE ROBBED OLD MAN SHATTERED THE STILLNESS, THEN DRIFTED OFF INTO THE SILENT DARKNESS...

STOP, YOU THIEVES! STOP!

GINO AND PIETRO VANISHED INTO THE NIGHT, DOWN NARROW STREETS AND LITTERED ALLEYS TILL THEY REACHED A BLEAK LITTLE FLAT IN THE SLUMS...

WE'VE MADE A RICH HAUL THIS TIME, GINO!

SOLID SILVER! WORTH THREE, MAYBE *FOUR THOUSAND LIRE!*

GLEEFULLY, GINO REACHED INTO A CABINET FOR A BOTTLE OF WINE...

"BUT IT IS *MORE* THAN SILVER! IT IS *ANTIQUE!* SOME RICH AMERICAN MAY PAY AS HIGH AS *SIX THOUSAND!*"

"*HAH!* BY HEAVEN, THIS CALLS FOR A DRINK!*"

THEY DRANK GREEDILY OF THE CHEAP RED WINE THEN, SUDDENLY, PIETRO SPAT OUT A MOUTHFUL OF THE LIQUID...

NOT GOOD ENOUGH FOR YOU? NEXT TIME I'LL STEAL *CHAMPAGNE* FOR YOUR MAJESTY!

"THE POLICE, GINO! THE *POLICE!*"

INSTANTLY, GINO WHIRLED TOWARD THE DOOR, KNOCKING HIS CHAIR TO THE FLOOR IN HIS HASTE! HIS FACE WAS CONTORTED WITH A MIXTURE OF BOTH FEAR AND ANGER...

POLICE? WHERE?

NO, YOU IDIOT! NOT YET! BUT WHEN THE ROBBERY IS REPORTED, WHO DO YOU THINK THEY WILL SUSPECT? *US*, OF COURSE! THEY'VE HAD US LOCKED UP FOR THIS KIND OF THING BEFORE, YOU KNOW!

GINO PALED. HIS HANDS CLENCHED AND UNCLENCHED NERVOUSLY AS HE RIGHTED HIS CHAIR...

"WHAT... WHAT CAN WE DO? WE JUST CAN'T THROW IT *AWAY*... NOT AFTER THE CHANCES WE TOOK *GETTING* IT, PIETRO!"

"I DON'T KNOW. WE'LL HAVE TO *HIDE* IT, I GUESS! BUT *WHERE?!*"

TOGETHER, THEIR BROWS KNITTED IN CONCENTRATION, THEY SAT MULLING OVER THIS NEW PROBLEM...

THINK, PIETRO! THINK OF SOMEPLACE TO HIDE THE SILVER!

"I *AM* THINKING! AH! I HAVE IT, GINO! THE *CATACOMBS!*"

"THE... CATACOMBS? I... I DON'T LIKE TO GO THERE! IT'S SCARY... AND COLD... AND SO *DARK!*"

WE WON'T HAVE TO STAY... JUST HIDE THE SILVER TILL IT'S FORGOTTEN ABOUT! WE'LL TAKE A LANTERN, MY FRIEND, AND WINE TO WARM US... *PLENTY OF WINE!*

THE SUN HAD NOT YET RISEN WHEN THE TWO THIEVES REACHED THE CATACOMBS ENTRANCE. PIETRO CARRIED THE SACK OF SILVER AND THE LANTERN, WHILE GINO, TREMBLING IN THE DAMP MORNING AIR, CLUTCHED SEVERAL BOTTLES OF RED WINE IN HIS ARMS...

"I DON'T LIKE THIS, PIETRO! I DON'T LIKE IT AT ALL!"

"FOOL! WOULD YOU RATHER SPEND TEN YEARS BEHIND BARS?!"

THEY LOOKED APPREHENSIVELY INTO THE BLACK OPENING...

"I'VE HEARD A MAN COULD GET LOST IN THERE. WOULD YOU KNOW THE WAY OUT AGAIN?"

"I'M NOT SURE. IF THERE WAS SOMETHING WITH WHICH TO MARK A TRAIL..."

PIETRO SUDDENLY GRINNED, SNATCHED A BOTTLE FROM GINO'S ARM AND BROKE OFF ITS NECK...

WHAT ARE YOU DOING?

WE'LL LEAVE A TRAIL OF RED WINE, GINO... SOMETHING WE CAN FOLLOW BACK!

GINGERLY, THEY STEPPED INTO THE DARK, MUSTY PASSAGE...

MAKE IT A THIN TRAIL, SO THERE'LL BE ENOUGH TO LAST!

I'LL BE SURE THERE'S ENOUGH LEFT TO DRINK, PIETRO!

THEY MOVED SLOWLY, AIMLESSLY, THROUGH THE DARK GLOOM OF MYRIAD PASSAGES...NOW TO THE RIGHT, THEN LEFT, RIGHT, AND DOWN TO ANOTHER LEVEL...

HOW MUCH FURTHER?

THE DEEPER IN WE GO, THE LESS CHANCE OF OUR LOOT BEING DISCOVERED, GINO!

THEY CONTINUED ON, DEEPER AND DEEPER INTO THE MAZE OF TUNNELS, AS GINO DRIBBLED THE WINE ONTO THE GRAY DUST UNTIL THERE WAS LITTLE LEFT...

...STOP NOW, PIETRO! I WANT TO DRINK THE REST... I'M CHILLED TO THE MARROW!

NO...A LITTLE FURTHER! JUST THINK...WE'LL SELL THE SILVER IN A MONTH OR SO, AND YOU'LL HAVE ALL THE WINE YOU CAN DRINK!

AT PIETRO'S URGING, THEY WENT ON UNTIL THEY CAME TO A CHAMBER LARGER THAN THE REST. GINO FOLLOWED THE LANTERN BEAM, THEN GRABBED HIS FRIEND'S ARM, HIS STARTLED CRY ECHOING THROUGH THE VAST LABYRINTH...

"LOOK! THERE IN THE WALL!"

IT'S ONLY A *MUMMY*, GINO! WHAT HARM CAN COME FROM A MAN DEAD MORE THAN SIXTEEN HUNDRED YEARS?

LET'S HIDE THE SILVER AND GET OUT OF HERE, PIETRO!

COME, GINO...IT WILL BE SAFER FURTHER ON!

NO! I USED THE LAST OF THE WINE MORE THAN FIFTY FEET BACK! I GO NO FURTHER!

AS GINO LOOKED ABOUT AND SHUDDERED, PIETRO DELIBERATELY DUMPED THE SACK OF SILVER ON THE STONE FLOOR...

I DREAD HAVING TO COME *BACK* TO THIS PLACE FOR OUR TREASURE!

A MAN WILL DO *ANYTHING* FOR ENOUGH MONEY, GINO!

THE LOUD METALLIC CLATTER SHATTERED THE SILENCE! GINO JUMPED AND TURNED, HIS FACE ASHEN IN FRIGHT...

NERVOUSLY, GINO BENT TO GATHER UP THE SILVER, AND AS HE DID, PIETRO SLIPPED A SWITCHKNIFE FROM HIS POCKET. HE FLICKED OPEN A LONG, SCALPEL-SHARP BLADE...

MADRE! CAN'T YOU BE MORE CAREFUL?!

I'M SORRY, GINO! IT WAS AN ACCIDENT! COME... HELP ME PICK IT UP!

"FIVE OR SIX THOUSAND LIRE, PIETRO! JUST THINK OF IT!"

"I *AM* THINKING OF IT, GINO!"

THE 'CLICK' OF THE BLADE BEING OPENED MADE GINO TURN IN TIME TO SEE THE CRUEL, GREEDY LOOK ON PIETRO'S FACE...IN TIME TO SEE THE BLADE FLASH UP...

DESPERATELY, GINO TRIED TO BRUSH PAST PIETRO... TRIED VAINLY TO DODGE THE VICIOUS BLADE WHICH FLASHED DOWN, PLUNGED TO THE HILT IN HIS BACK...

PIETRO! DON'T! MADRE! WHY?!

I TOLD YOU, GINO! A MAN WILL DO *ANYTHING* FOR MONEY!

SCREAMING IN BITTER AGONY, GINO THRASHED TO HIS FEET AND BLINDLY STUMBLED OFF INTO THE PASSAGE-WAY...

"GO AHEAD! RUN! YOU WON'T LIVE ONE MINUTE!"

AS GINO'S STUMBLING FOOTSTEPS AND STRANGLING SOBS FADED INTO THE BLACK DISTANCE, THE TREACHEROUS PIETRO SET ABOUT GATHERING THE SCATTERED SILVER...

HEH, HEH! THE RICHEST HAUL I'VE EVER MADE, AND THAT STUPID FOOL REALLY THOUGHT I LED HIM TO THIS CREEPY HOLE JUST TO *HIDE* IT! HA HA HA HA HA HA HA

CHUCKLING, HE SLUNG THE SACK OVER HIS SHOULDER AND LEFT THE CHAMBER...

"BY THE TIME THEY FIND HIS BODY... IF THEY EVER DO...THERE'LL BE NO TELLING IT FROM THE OTHER MUMMIES!"

HE WALKED ON, SHARPLY SCANNING THE FLOOR BY THE LANTERN GLOW...

"HEY! I'VE GONE MORE THAN FIFTY FEET! I SHOULD HAVE FOUND THE TRAIL OF WINE BY NOW!"

HE STOPPED, THEN RETURNED TO THE CHAMBER, AND WITH HIS FACE REVEALING DEEP ANXIETY, HE TRIED ONE PASSAGE, THEN ANOTHER...

AGAIN HE WAS UNABLE TO PICK UP THE TRAIL, AND HE RETURNED TO THE CHAMBER ONCE MORE TO TRY STILL ANOTHER PASSAGE! IN THE WANING LANTERN LIGHT, HE BECAME ALMOST FRENZIED...AND THEN...

AH! THE TRAIL! FROM HERE ON IT WILL BE EASY!

SKITTISHLY, PIETRO HURRIED THROUGH THE ENDLESS MAZE OF VAULTS AND GALLERIES, HIS BREATHING HEAVY NOW, HIS FOOTFALLS ECHOING ALL ABOUT HIM...

"HOW GOOD IT WILL BE TO BREATHE FRESH AIR AGAIN...AND SEE THE SUNLIGHT!"

HE FOLLOWED THE THIN TRAIL TO ITS END...BUT IT DID NOT END AS IT SHOULD HAVE! PIETRO STOPPED DEAD IN HIS TRACKS AT THE YAWNING MOUTH OF THE PASSAGE, GAPED INTO A BURIAL CHAMBER AND CHOKED BACK A CRY OF HORROR...

SLOWLY, UNBELIEVINGLY, PIETRO MOVED TO THE BLOODLESS BODY LYING IN THE CHAMBER'S DUST, AND WHILE ALL AROUND THE EMPTY-SOCKETED EYES GAPED DOWN ON HIM, HE RAISED THE LIFELESS FORM AND PLEADED...

"GINO...LISTEN TO ME, GINO! I'M SORRY...GINO, I'M SORRY! WE CAN FIND OUR WAY OUT...TOGETHER. COME, I'LL HELP YOU UP...PLEASE, GINO...THE LANTERN'S GETTING DIM..."

"HURRY, GINO...WE MUST FIND THE RIGHT TRAIL BEFORE THE LANTERN GOES OUT! HEH...HEH...I...THOUGHT YOUR BLOOD WAS THE TRAIL..."

"HEH...I THOUGHT IT WAS THE WINE TRAIL...IT WAS YOUR BLOOD! GINO... THE LIGHT IS FADING! FIND THE RIGHT TRAIL FOR US...HURRY, GINO! HURRY!"

"WHEN WE GET OUT, WE'LL BE FRIENDS AGAIN, EH? GINO, HURRY! EH...EH... HURRY! EH...THE LIGHT, GINO...YOU CAN FIND THE TRAIL, CAN'T YOU, GINO? EH...EH...GINO? GINO?"

...AND THEN...

...THE LIGHT WENT OUT!

KEY CHAIN

UNGER HESITATED BEFORE THE LITTLE HOLE-IN-THE-WALL SHOP. HE SHOOK HIS HEAD. IT WAS THE OLDEST TRICK IN THE WORLD. NO LOCKSMITH WOULD FALL FOR IT. HE KNEW IT. HE KNEW HE'D HAVE TO FIND SOME OTHER WAY TO HAVE A DUPLICATE MADE OF THE SOFT LEAD KEY HE HELD IN HIS TREMBLING HAND...

UNGER PUT THE LEAD KEY BACK INTO HIS POCKET AND LIT A CIGARETTE. HE STUDIED THE LOCKSMITH SHOP. IT WAS ONE OF THOSE LITTLE CUBICLE-TYPE STORES THAT NESTLED SNUGLY BETWEEN TWO LARGER ONES AS IF SEEKING THEIR PROTECTION AND WARMTH. HIS TRAINED EYES NOTED THE FRONT DOOR... NOTED NO BURGLAR ALARM METAL DECORATIONS ON THE GLASS...

HMMPH! OF COURSE NOT! WHAT'S TO STEAL IN A TWO-BIT LOCKSMITH SHOP LIKE THAT?

HE GLANCED AT THE LOCKSMITH STANDING IN THE FRONT WINDOW, BUSY AT HIS KEYMAKING MACHINE... THE MACHINE UNGER NEEDED SO DESPERATELY TO USE...

HIS GAZE FELL UPON THE BOARD OF KEY BLANKS HANGING BEHIND THE LOCKSMITH. SOMEWHERE ON THAT BOARD WAS THE BLANK THAT UNGER WOULD USE TO REPRODUCE A STURDY DUPLICATE OF THE USELESS LEAD CAST IN HIS POCKET...

AND THE LEAD KEY *WAS* USELESS IN ITS *PRESENT* FORM. IF UNGER WOULD TRY TO *USE* IT, IT WOULD *BEND* AND *SNAP* AND *SPOIL* HIS WEEKS OF *PLANNING* ...HIS WEEKS OF *PATIENT WAITING* ...WAITING FOR HIS *CHANCE*. HE REMEMBERED HOW HE'D CHECKED *IN* AT THE LUXURIOUS APARTMENT HOTEL ...

WILL YOU BE *STAYING* WITH US *LONG*, MR... ER... MR. MILLER?

I HOPE...*PERMA-NENTLY!* MY FIRM JUST OPENED A *BRANCH OFFICE* HERE AND I'VE BEEN SENT DOWN TO *RUN* IT!

HE'D TAKEN HIS *LAST THOUSAND DOLLARS* AND HE'D MADE AN *INVESTMENT* WITH IT. HE'D BOUGHT *RESPECTABILITY* WITH IT...

ER... AH... HELLO! MY NAME IS *MILLER!* *JOHN* MILLER. I'VE JUST MOVED IN! WE'RE HEH...HEH...*NEIGHBORS,* YOU MIGHT SAY!

WELL, COME *IN*, MR. MILLER! HOW ABOUT A *DRINK?*

HE'D DRESSED IN CONSERVATIVE CLOTHES AND HE'D LED A CONSERV-ATIVE LIFE. FOR THREE WEEKS HE'D COME AND GONE IN THAT HOTEL AS A RESPECTABLE BUSINESS MAN...

GOOD *EVENING,* MRS. HODGES! *LOVELY* EVENING...

GOOD EVENING, MR. MILLER! ER... DO YOU PLAY *BRIDGE*, MR. MILLER?

AND FOR *THREE WEEKS* UNGER'D CASED THE JOINT...SEARCHING FOR HIS *PREY*...SEARCHING FOR HIS *MARK*...

ONE TWO NO CLUBS! TRUMP!

PASS...

THAT'S A *LOVELY* DIAMOND *NECKLACE,* MA'AM!

...UNTIL HE'D *FOUND* HER...

OH...UH... *THANK* YOU, MR. MILLER. IT'S...HEH, HEH... *YOUR BID!*

FORGIVE ME FOR BEING SO *INTERESTED*, MRS. HODGES. YOU SEE, *DIAMONDS* ARE *MY BUSINESS!*

...AND HE'D FOUND HER AN *EAGER* AND *WILLING* PREY...

OH? IS THAT *SO*, MR. MILLER. THEN *SOMEDAY* YOU MUST LET ME SHOW YOU *ALL* OF MY *DIAMOND COLLECTION.* *YOU* WOULD *APPRECIATE* IT!

I *WOULD*, MRS. HODGES! I *REALLY* WOULD!

IT'S... *YOUR BID,* MR. MILLER!

MR. HODGES'D BEEN *WRONG!* UNGER'D ALREADY *MADE* HIS BID! AND MRS. HODGES HAD *ANSWERED.* LATER...

THERE'S *NO FINER DIAMOND* THAN A *FLAWLESS BLUE-WHITE!* NO *FINER!* A *MAG-NIFICENT RING,* MRS. HODGES!

THEY'RE THE *ONLY* DIAMONDS I'LL *BUY,* MR. MILLER! THIS IS ALL I HAVE *HOME* AT THE MOMENT.

THE *REST* ARE IN MY *VAULT!* ALL TOLD, ABOUT $125,000 *WORTH!*

I HOPE YOU ARE PROPERLY *INSURED,* MRS. HODGES. IT WOULD BE SUCH A *PITY* IF...

I HAVE POLICIES ON *ALL* MY JEWELRY, MR. MILLER. HAVE *NO FEAR!*

YOU SAY YOU *BOUGHT* THIS TIARA IN *1934,* MRS. HODGES? *DID* YOU INSURE IT *THEN?*

THE MOMENT I BROUGHT IT *HOME,* I CALLED MY BROKER!

THEN YOU *INSURED* IT FOR ITS *1934* VALUE. HAVEN'T YOU EVER HAD IT *REVALUED,* MRS. HODGES?

WHY, *NO,* I... I...OH, *DEAR!*

DON'T YOU *SEE,* MRS. HODGES? THIS TIARA IS PROBABLY WORTH *TWICE* AS MUCH *TODAY* AS YOU *ORIGINALLY* PAID FOR IT. YOU MUST BE *HOPE-LESSLY UNDER-INSURED!*

WHAT WILL I *DO,* MR. MILLER?

I'D BE *GLAD* TO EXAMINE *ALL* OF YOUR DIAMONDS, MRS. HODGES! I'D BE *GLAD* TO GIVE YOU AN *ESTIMATE* OF THEIR *CURRENT VALUE!* *THEN* YOU CAN BE *ADEQUATELY PROTECTED...*

WOULD YOU, MR. MILLER? OH *WOULD* YOU DO THAT? I'LL BRING THEM HOME FROM MY VAULT BOX *TOMORROW...*

TILL *TOMORROW NIGHT,* THEN, MRS. HODGES!

YES, UNGER'D *MADE* HIS *BID...* FOR A *GRAND SLAM!* HE'D HURRIED BACK TO HIS OWN APARTMENT AND UNWRAPPED THE PACKAGE OF PLASTILENE CLAY...

...AND HE'D SLIT THE BRICK OF CLAY NEATLY IN TWO...

HE'D LEFT THE CLAY ON THE COFFEE TABLE AND HE'D GONE OUT, THROUGH THE LOBBY, PAST THE FRONT DESK... THE PERFECT GENTLEMAN...

GOOD EVENING, MR. MILLER!

GOOD EVENING, ROY!

...AND HE'D RETURNED SOME TIME LATER, *ROARING DRUNK*...

WHERE'SH EVVYBODDY? HEY! ROY! FRONT! HEY! ...HIC...

P-PLEASE, MR. MILLER! YOU'LL DISTURB THE OTHER TENENTS!

I FERGOT MY KEY... HIC...ROY! I'M...LOCKED UP! ER... OUT!

I'LL LET YOU *IN*, MR. MILLER. I'LL GET THE *PASS-KEY!* PLEASE BE QUIET!

IT HAD ALL WORKED SO NICELY...SO PERFECTLY. ROY'D GOTTEN THE PASS-KEY...THE WONDERFUL MASTER KEY THAT WOULD UNLOCK THE DOOR TO A QUARTER OF A MILLION DOLLARS FOR UNGER...

THERE YOU ARE, MR. MILLER!

YOU'RE A *GOO'* KID, ROY! YOU'RE A *DOLL!* YOU... YOU...

AND UNGER'D COLLAPSED SO REALISTICALLY...

MR. *MILLER?* YOU *ALL RIGHT?*

YOU...YOU BETTER FIX ME SOME *COFFEE,* ROY!

AND SO, WHILE ROY'D PUTTERED IN THE KITCHEN, UNGER'D PRESSED THE IMPRESSIONS OF THE MASTER PASS-KEY INTO THE WRITING SLABS OF CLAY...ONE FOR EACH SIDE...

AND WHEN ROY'D LEFT, UNGER'D MELTED SOME LEAD, AND HE'D PUT THE TWO SLABS TOGETHER AS A MOLD, AND HE'D POURED THE CAST...

...THE CAST HE NOW HELD IN HIS TREMBLING HAND...USELESS...BUT WITH A $250,000 POTENTIAL...

OH-OH! THE OLD GUY'S CLOSIN' UP SHOP!

UNGER WATCHED THE OLD MAN POCKET THE KEY TO THE SHOP AND START TOWARD HIM. IT WAS *NOW* OR *NEVER*...

OOPS! I...I *BEG* YOUR PARDON!

MY FAULT! *SORRY!* I WASN'T LOOKING WHERE I WAS GOING!

UNGER WATCHED THE OLD MAN HOBBLE DOWN THE STREET INTO THE GATHERING DARKNESS. HE SMILED DOWN AT THE KEY TO THE LOCKSMITH SHOP HE'D PICKED FROM THE OLD MAN'S POCKET...

HEH, HEH!

WHEN DARKNESS CAME, HE LET HIMSELF INTO THE SHOP...

HE LOCKED THE DOOR BEHIND HIM AND PUT THE KEY TO THE SHOP ON THE WORKBENCH BESIDE THE KEY-MAKING MACHINE AND TOOK OUT THE LEAD CAST...

HE TURNED TO THE BOARD...THE BOARD UPON WHICH HUNDREDS OF BLANKS HUNG...

HE FOUND THE MATCHING BLANK. HE REACHED FOR IT. THE BOARD CAME LOOSE FROM THE WALL, CRASHING DOWN, SPILLING THE BLANKS UPON THE CRAMPED FLOOR...

HE FROZE. OUTSIDE THE SHOP, FOOTSTEPS ECHOED. A COP... ON HIS BEAT...

THE FOOTSTEPS FADED AWAY INTO THE NIGHT. UNGER SIGHED WITH RELIEF AND BENT TO PICK THE BLANK HE NEEDED...KNOCKING OVER A BOX OF DISCARDED BADLY-MADE KEYS...

HE CURSED SOFTLY. HE FOUND THE CORRECT BLANK AND STOOD UP. HE TURNED TO THE MACHINE, ACCIDENTLY BRUSHING THE KEY TO THE SHOP DOOR FROM THE BENCH...

HE LOOKED DOWN AT THE PILE OF KEYS COVERING THE TINY SHOP FLOOR. A COLD CHILL CREPT UP HIS SPINE. HE LOOKED AT THE FRONT DOOR HE'D LOCKED...

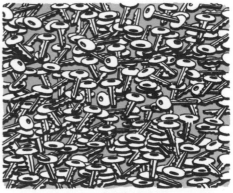

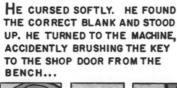

HOW WAS HE GOING TO GET OUT?

HIS MISSION FORGOTTEN, HE BEGAN TO TRY KEY AFTER KEY... PICKING THEM FROM THE PILE AND INSERTING THEM IN THE FRONT DOOR LOCK...FAILING...TRYING AGAIN...FAILING...GROWING MORE AND MORE DESPERATE...

FEAR GRIPPED HIM. HE FROZE AS THE FOOTSTEPS RETURNED. THE COP AGAIN! UNGER COWERED IN THE SHADOWS...

THE POLICEMAN PASSED. UNGER'S SLEEVE CAUGHT THE HANDLE OF A BENCH DRAWER, PULLING IT OUT, SPILLING ITS CONTENTS UPON THE FLOOR. MORE KEYS...

FOR A WILD MOMENT, HE ALMOST SMASHED THE GLASS BUT THE FOOTSTEPS RETURNED. HE COULDN'T DO THAT! THE COP WOULD HEAR IT...

HE GROVELED AMONG THE MASS OF KEYS ON THE FLOOR...TRYING ONE... DISCARDING IT ONTO THE BENCH... TRYING AGAIN...

HE TRIED AND FAILED FOR AN HOUR...

HIS LEGS ACHED FROM HIS CRAMPED POSITION. HE STOOD UP, SWAYING, STUMBLING AGAINST THE BENCH, KNOCKING THE KEYS HE'D TRIED BACK ONTO THE FLOOR...

THE KEYS GLITTERED. THE WALLS SEEMED TO CLOSE IN. UNGER GIGGLED. HE STARTED ALL OVER AGAIN...TRYING... FAILING...TRYING...

THE OLD MAN FOUND HIM IN THE MORNING, SITTING IN THE MIDDLE OF THE TINY SHOP'S FLOOR. EVERY DRAWER HAD BEEN OPENED AND EMPTIED...EVERY KEY IN THE SHOP SPILLED OUT. UNGER SAT AMONG THEM...CRYING SOFTLY...HIS EYES GLAZED AND STARING...

SOB...SOB...

THEY CAME AND TOOK HIM AWAY. HE NEVER HEARD THE OLD MAN REMARK...

I *FIGURED* HE WAS UP TO SOMETHIN', HANGIN' AROUND LIKE THAT LAST NIGHT. I *MADE BELIEVE* I LOCKED UP. THOUGHT I'D *DISCOURAGE* HIM. WHEN HE *PICKED* MY *POCKET*, I *FIGURED* HE WAS *DESPERATE*. WHAT WOULD A GUY *WANT* IN AN OLD LOCKSMITH'S SHOP ANYWAY? *'SPECIALLY* ONE WITH A *BUSTED FRONT DOOR LOCK THAT DON'T EVEN WORK...*

MASTER RACE
YOU CAN NEVER FORGET, CAN YOU, CARL REISSMAN? EVEN HERE...IN AMERICA...TEN YEARS AND THOUSANDS OF MILES AWAY FROM YOUR NATIVE GERMANY... YOU CAN NEVER FORGET THOSE BLOODY WAR YEARS. THOSE MEMORIES WILL HAUNT YOU FOREVER... AS EVEN NOW THEY HAUNT YOU WHILE YOU DESCEND THE SUBWAY STAIRS INTO THE QUIET SEMI-DARKNESS...
B. Krigstein
YOUR ACCENT IS STILL THICK ALTHOUGH YOU HAVE MASTERED THE LANGUAGE OF YOUR NEW COUNTRY THAT TOOK YOU IN WITH OPEN ARMS WHEN YOU FINALLY ESCAPED FROM BELSEN CONCENTRATION CAMP. YOU SLIDE THE BILL UNDER THE BARRED CHANGE-BOOTH WINDOW. . .
TWO TOKENS, PLEASE.
YOU MOVE TO THE BUSY CLICKING TURNSTILES... SLIP THE SHINY TOKEN INTO THE THIN SLOT...AND PUSH THROUGH. . .
THE TRAIN ROARS OUT OF THE BLACK CAVERN, SHATTERING THE SILENCE OF THE ALMOST DESERTED STATION...
YOU STARE AT THE ONRUSHING STEEL MONSTER...
A
YOU BLINK AS THE FIRST CAR RUSHES BY AND ILLUMINATED WINDOWS FLASH IN AN EVER-SLOWING RHYTHM...

AND THE TRAIN GRINDS TO A HISSING STOP...

YOU MOVE TO THE DOOR AS IT SLIDES OPEN. A PASSENGER EMERGES AND YOU FEEL HIS EYES UPON YOU AND YOU SHUDDER. WHY ARE YOU FRIGHTENED, CARL? THAT WAS A *LONG TIME AGO!* THIS IS *AMERICA.* YOU'RE *SAFE* NOW! YOU'RE *FREE*...

EXCUSE ME...

BUT YOU *ARE* AFRAID, *AREN'T* YOU, CARL? YOU'LL *ALWAYS* BE AFRAID. YOU'LL *KEEP REMEMBERING*... REMEMBERING THE *HORROR*...THE *HATE*...THE *SUFFERING*...AND YOU'LL *STAY* AFRAID. YOU STEP INTO THE ALMOST—EMPTY CAR AND YOU SIGH INTO A SEAT...

THE DOORS SLAM SHUT. THE TRAIN LURCHES AND ROLLS AHEAD, THUNDERING OUT OF THE STATION AND BACK INTO THE BLACK CHASMS TUNNELING BENEATH THE CITY. YOU UNFOLD YOUR PAPER...

YOU TRY TO READ, BUT THE WORDS ARE MEANINGLESS. NOTHING HAS MEANING ANY MORE... NOTHING BUT THE SICKENING SENSATION THAT HAS PLAGUED YOU FOR OVER TEN LONG YEARS. THE CONCENTRATION CAMP HAS LEFT ITS MARK UPON YOU, HASN'T IT, CARL REISSMAN?

YOU LOOK AROUND AT YOUR FELLOW PASSENGERS SITTING ALONE IN THEIR OWN LITTLE WORLDS OF FEAR. YOU STUDY THEIR FACES...THEIR FEATURES...THEIR EYES... LOOKING... ALWAYS LOOKING. WHAT ARE YOU *LOOKING* FOR CARL? WHO *IS* IT YOU'RE *AFRAID* OF?

THE TRAIN GROANS INTO ANOTHER STATION AND JERKS TO A STOP. THE DOORS HUM WIDE. YOU LOOK DOWN AT YOUR PAPER, ONLY *SENSING* PEOPLE GETTING OFF...

...SOMEONE GETTING ON...

AND THEN...DOWN DEEP INSIDE YOU... YOU FEEL THE CHILL...THE COLD CHILL ...THE CHILL OF DEATH. YOU STARE AT THE PAPER ON YOUR LAP, UNABLE TO RAISE YOUR EYES...AFRAID TO SEE WHAT YOU KNOW IS THERE. BUT, AFTER A FEW TERRORIZED MOMENTS, YOU CAN'T STAND IT! YOU *DO* LOOK UP! AND YOU *SEE* HIM...

CHOKE!

HE SITS STIFFLY, READING HIS PAPER, NOT LOOKING AT YOU, NOT NOTICING YOU. BUT *YOU'VE* SEEN *HIM*, CARL! YOU'VE SEEN HIS *FACE*... THE ONE YOU *KNEW* SOMEDAY YOU'D SEE AGAIN... THE FACE YOU'VE BEEN *AFRAID* TO SEE FOR *TEN LONG YEARS*. YOUR MOUTH TWITCHES. YOUR HANDS OPEN AND CLOSE, WET WITH PERSPIRATION...

NO! *NO!* HE *CAN'T* HURT ME NOW! HE *CAN'T!* HE *WOULDN'T!*

THE TRAIN SCREAMS AROUND A CURVE IN ITS SUBTERRANIAN ROUTE ...AND THE SCREAM IS SHRILL AND SHARP...SETTING YOUR TEETH ON EDGE...REACHING BACK INTO THE PAST...

...TO ANOTHER SHRILL SCREAM...THE SCREAM OF A LITTLE MAN WITH WILD EYES AND BLACK HAIR AND A SMALL BLACK MOUSTACHE...

SIEG HEIL...SIEG HEIL...SIEG HEIL!

REMEMBER, CARL? REMEMBER THE LITTLE MAN IN THE UNIFORM WHO STOOD FIRST BEFORE SMALL GROUPS... THEN BEFORE CROWDS...AND FINALLY BEFORE MULTITUDES...AND SCREAMED AND SCREAMED THEM INTO AN HYSTERICAL MISSION OF WORLD CONQUEST. *YOU* WERE THERE...IN ONE OF THOSE CROWDS. REMEMBER?

SIEG HEIL!

AND WHEN THE LITTLE MAN HAD STOPPED SCREAMING AND THE CROWD HAD DISPERSED, REMEMBER THE SICKENING FEELING YOU HAD...THE REVULSION AND NAUSEA YOU FELT AS YOU TRUDGED HOME?...

THERE WERE *OTHERS* LIKE YOU, CARL...

...*OTHERS* WHO WERE *SICK* AND *REVOLTED* AND *NAUSEATED* AT THE SCREAMING PROPOSALS OF THIS LITTLE MAN. BUT *THEY* COULDN'T STOP THE TIDE, *COULD* THEY, CARL? *THEY* COULDN'T STEM THE FLOW OF HATE THAT POURED THROUGH THE STREETS WITH CLUBS AND GUNS AND THE ECHOES OF THE LITTLE MAN'S SCREAMS URGING IT ON...

NO ONE COULD STOP THE BOOKS FROM BEING BURNED...

...OR THE SHOP WINDOWS FROM BEING SMASHED AND THEIR CONTENTS RANSACKED...

... OR THE SANCTITY OF HOMES FROM BEING VIOLATED...

IT WAS A MADNESS...A WAVE THAT SWEPT THROUGH YOUR HOMELAND LIKE A PLAGUE...A TIDAL WAVE OF FRENZIED HATE-FEARS AND BLOOD-LETTING AND EXPLODING VIOLENCE... A WILD UNCONTROLLED WAVE THAT SWEPT YOU AND YOUR KIND ALONG WITH IT...

WHAT HAPPENED TO YOU, CARL? WHEN WERE YOU CAUGHT UP IN THIS TIDE? WHEN DID YOU FIRST SEE BELSEN CONCENTRATION CAMP AND THE HUMAN MISERY THAT SOBBED WITHIN ITS BARBED-WIRE WALLS?...

DO YOU REMEMBER, CARL? DO YOU REMEMBER THE AWFUL SMELL OF THE GAS CHAMBERS THAT HOURLY ANNIHILATED HUNDREDS AND HUNDREDS OF YOUR COUNTRYMEN?...

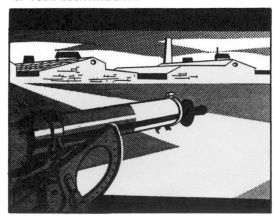

DO YOU REMEMBER THE STINKING ODOR OF HUMAN FLESH BURNING IN THE OVENS... MEN'S...WOMEN'S...CHILDREN'S...PEOPLE YOU ONCE KNEW AND TALKED TO AND DRANK BEER WITH?...

Do you remember the unmerciful tortures...the screams in the night...the pitiful wailing of the doomed? Do you remember the mad experiments with human guinea pigs...the wanton waste of human life?...

...The bulbs that burned in lamps on desks in the concentration camp offices...glowing through their human-skin-shades?...

Look, Carl! Look at the face of this man sitting across from you in this now deserted subway car! Look... and remember! Remember the guards that gleefully carried out the sadistic orders of the master race...whipping...kicking... beating!... The guards that eagerly dragged the women and children to the waiting, smoking ovens!...

Remember the guards that pushed and shoved...heaping the helpless camp inmates into the fresh dug mass graves...

... Laughing wildly as they buried their victims alive...shoveling the dirt down upon them, muffling their pathetic screams ...muffling their pathetic lives!...

LOOK AT THIS MAN AND REMEMBER, CARL! REMEMBER HIS FACE... THE LOOK THAT CAME INTO HIS EYES WHEN THE NEWS CAME THAT THE RUSSIANS WERE ONLY A FEW KILOMETERS AWAY! IT WAS OVER FOR YOU, THEN, CARL! THE KILLING AND MAIMING AND TORTURING WAS SUDDENLY OVER FOR YOU!

AND YET IT WASN'T OVER, BECAUSE HE LOOKED AT YOU AND SWORE...

SOMEDAY, I'LL GET YOU, REISSMAN! I'LL GET YOU... IF IT'S THE LAST THING I DO!

AND THEN YOU WERE FREE... RUNNING PELL-MELL ACROSS EUROPE, HIDING YOUR CLOTHES, LOSING YOURSELF IN AMONG THE STREAMS OF REFUGEES THAT CHOKED THE ROADS AND HIGHWAYS BEFORE THE ADVANCING ALLIED ARMIES...

AND YET YOU WEREN'T FREE, CARL! EVEN THOUGH YOU SOMEHOW GOT TO AMERICA, YOU NEVER FORGOT! YOU NEVER FORGOT HIS PROMISE! SO YOU CARRIED THE FEAR WITH YOU FOR TEN YEARS AND NOW IT'S CAUGHT UP WITH YOU! HE'S THERE... SITTING OPPOSITE YOU... FEELING YOUR FRIGHTENED STARING EYES UPON HIM...

AND NOW HE'S LOOKING AT YOU. HE'S LOOKING AT YOUR HAIR... AT YOUR LIPS... YOUR NOSE... DEEP INTO YOUR FRIGHTENED EYES. AND A SPARK OF FAR-AWAY, LONG-AGO RECOGNITION IGNITES HIS FACE...

YOU!

CHOKE...

HE RISES SLOWLY, HIS MOUTH SET IN A GRIM TAUT LINE. HIS EYES CLOUD WITH HATE, HIS FISTS CLENCH...

REISSMAN!

...IT'S YOU!

NO! NO! GOTT IN HIMMEL!

THE TRAIN GRINDS TO A STOP. THE DOORS SLIDE OPEN. HE'S COMING *TOWARD* YOU, CARL! *RUN!* THIS IS YOUR *CHANCE!* RUN!...

RUN... AS YOU *RAN FROM BELSEN*, CARL! *RUN*... AS YOU *RAN ACROSS EUROPE*, FLEEING THE LIBERATING ALLIED ARMIES! RUN, *NOW*, CARL... AS YOU *REFUSED* TO RUN WHEN THAT *MAD WAVE SWEPT OVER GERMANY...SWEEPING YOU ALONG IN ITS BLOODY WAKE!*...

I SWORE...

I SWORE I'D GET YOU, REISSMAN!

NO!

HAVE PITY!

RUN DOWN THE LONG, EMPTY, DESERTED STATION PLATFORM, CARL! *RUN* FROM THIS PERSONIFICATION OF THE MILLIONS OF YOUR COUNTRYMEN WHO *COULDN'T* RIDE THE TIDE *YOU* CHOSE TO RIDE...WHO WERE *CAUGHT* IN ITS *UNDERTOW*...

IT'S *NO USE*, REISSMAN!

PLEASE...

...WHO WERE *PERSECUTED* AND *JAILED* AND *BURNED IN OVENS* AND *GASSED* AND *BURIED ALIVE* IN MASS GRAVES...

RUN FROM THIS SURVIVOR OF A HUMAN HELL ON EARTH...THIS SURVIVOR OF A GERMAN CONCENTRATION CAMP...*BELSEN CONCENTRATION CAMP*...

THE CAMP THAT YOU COMMANDED!

WHAT *HAPPENED?*

I DON'T *KNOW!* HE GOT OUT *AHEAD* OF ME AND BEGAN TO *RUN!*

HE *RAN UP THE PLATFORM* AND THEN *JUMPED* UNDER THE WHEELS OF THE TRAIN COMING IN THE *OTHER WAY...*

EVER *SEE* HIM BEFORE?

NO! HE...

HE WAS A *PERFECT STRANGER...*

MURDER DREAM

I WANDERED ABOUT THE LONELY LONDON STREETS TONIGHT, CHILLED TO THE MARROW OF MY BONES BY THE DENSE, DANK, CHOKING FOG...

I WAS MORE TIRED THAN I'D EVER BEEN IN MY LIFE, YET I *FEARED SLEEP.* I *FEARED THE DREAM!* SOMEWHERE IN THE VAST, GREY, MISTY SHROUD, BIG BEN TOLLED MIDNIGHT...

AT LAST... TOO EXHAUSTED TO STAND... MY EYES SMARTING... BEGGING FOR REST... I RETURNED TO MY BLEAK HOTEL ROOM...

...UNDRESSED, LEAVING MY CLOTHES WHERE THEY FELL...

...AND SPRAWLED UPON THE BED...

SLEEP CAME AT ONCE... AND THEN THE DREAM...THE DREAD DREAM I'VE HAD FOR THE PAST THREE NIGHTS COMES AGAIN... AND I AM POWERLESS TO STOP IT...

I AM APPROACHING OUR COTTAGE... BAGS IN HAND. I AM RETURNING FROM LONDON, MY AUSTIN PARKED OFF THE ROAD. IT'S ALL SO *CLEAR.* THE *SOUND* IS SO CLEAR...THE *SOUND* OF *CATHY SCREAMING...*

HOWARD! HELP ME! YAAAAAAHHHH...

I HEAR IT SO *CLEARLY*... CATHY'S TERRIFIED HEART-RENDING SCREAM. I'M *RUNNING* NOW... REACHING OUT TOWARD THE DOOR. I'M CLOSER TO IT THAN I HAVE BEEN IN THE PAST TWO NIGHTS...

I'M COMING, CATHY.

BUT *I CAN'T REACH IT!* I AWAKEN WITH HER NAME ON MY LIPS, MY BEDCLOTHES DRENCHED WITH COLD SWEAT. I BURY MY FACE IN MY HANDS, SOBBING ALOUD...

CATHY! WHAT *IS* IT CATHY? *WHY* AM I *DREAMING* THIS? WHAT DOES IT *MEAN?*

I TRY TO DRIVE THE DREAM FROM MY MIND. I LIE BACK AND THINK OF THE COTTAGE AND THAT FIRST DAY CATHY LAID EYES UPON IT... STANDING SILENT AND STILL ON THAT BLEAK, WINDSWEPT MOOR SOME EIGHTY MILES NORTH OF LONDON...

OH, HOWARD! IT'S *JUST* WHAT I'VE *ALWAYS* WANTED!

IT *IS* QUAINT!

HOW I *LOVED* HER, *MY CATHY!* HOW I LOVE HER *STILL!* I REMEMBER THE KNOCKING ON THE COTTAGE DOOR... THE GROAN OF CHAIRSPRINGS INSIDE... THE SLOW PAD OF BOOTS ON CARPETED FLOOR... THE SHABBILY DRESSED MAN PEERING OUT... HIS STARING EYES...

WE SAW THE *"FOR SALE"* SIGN, MAY WE *LOOK* AT THE PLACE! MY NAME'S *HOWARD LEIGHTON!* THIS IS MY WIFE *CATHY!*

IT WAS A COZY HOUSE, EVIDENTLY NEGLECTED, BUT CATHY WAS ENTHRALLED WITH IT...

IT'S *CHARMING*, HOWARD... YOU JUST WAIT TILL I PUT MY *OWN* LITTLE TOUCHES ABOUT!

I DON'T SUPPOSE THERE'LL BE ANY POINT TRYING TO *DISSUADE* YOU, DEAR, SO *NOW* THE QUESTION IS, CAN WE *AFFORD* IT...

I REMEMBER HIS EYES BORING INTO MINE AS WE DISCUSSED PRICE...

SEVEN HUNDRED QUID. THE FURNITURE GOES WITH THE HOUSE. *CLAUDE GRYMES.* I GO WITH THE HOUSE, *TOO.*

OH, THEN *YOU* MUST BE THE *CARE-TAKER.* I'M NOT AT ALL SURE I CAN *AFFORD* YOU, GRYMES!

ONLY *EIGHT BOB A WEEK*... FOR *TOBACCO*, MISTER. I *SLEEP* OVER THE *STABLE!*

I DON'T *KNOW*...

THAT'S *LITTLE ENOUGH*, HOWARD, AND I *WON'T* HAVE TO BE HERE *ALONE* WHEN YOU GO TO LONDON ON BUSINESS.

EVEN AS MY THOUGHTS RAMBLE ON THROUGH THESE MEMORIES, DARKNESS GIVES WAY TO DAWN. AND SO I RISE, TOO WORN AND HAGGARD TO TEND TO THE BUSINESS THAT BROUGHT ME TO LONDON...

THE DAY PASSES TOO QUICKLY AND IT IS NIGHT ONCE MORE. I AM IN BED AGAIN WAITING... WAITING FOR *SLEEP* TO COME AND THAT *AWFUL AWFUL DREAM*...

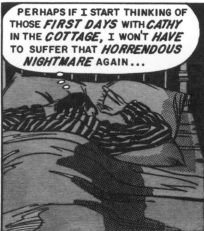

PERHAPS IF I START THINKING OF THOSE *FIRST DAYS* WITH *CATHY* IN THE *COTTAGE,* I WON'T *HAVE* TO SUFFER THAT *HORRENDOUS NIGHTMARE* AGAIN...

CATHY *DID* DO WONDERS WITH THE PLACE, FIXING IT UP. HER HANDS WORKED *MAGIC* WITH THE DECORATING ... THE FLOWER GARDEN. THEN, ONE DAY, THE *LETTER* CAME...

IT'S A *GREAT OPPORTUNITY,* DEAR... BUT I'LL *HATE* LEAVING YOU *ALONE*...

GRYMES HERE WILL LOOK AFTER ME, HOWARD. BESIDES, LONDON IS *ONLY* THREE HOURS AWAY...

CATHY LOOKED SO BEAUTIFUL, SO HAPPY, AS SHE WAVED GOODBYE FROM THE GARDEN. I FELT I LOVED HER MORE AND MORE WITH EACH PASSING DAY...

AWAKENESS GIVES WAY TO SLEEP. MEMORY DRIFTS INTO DREAM... THAT HORRIBLE DREAM AGAIN. I HEAR HER SCREAMING... CATHY'S SCREAMING FROM THE COTTAGE. I'M THERE AGAIN... RACING TOWARD THE DOOR... CLOSER NOW... CLOSER... YET NEVER SEEM TO BE ABLE TO REACH IT...

I'M COMING, CATHY!

THE SCREAM ECHOES OVER THE GRIM GREY MOOR... AGONIZED... UNENDING. MY POOR, TERRIFIED SCREAMING CATHY. LORD, HOW I LOVE HER. WITH SUPERHUMAN EFFORT, I HURL MYSELF AGAINST THE DOOR... TWIST THE KNOB... HEAVE MY WEIGHT AGAINST IT...

I'M COMING...

FOR AN INTERMINABLE MOMENT, I AM TORTURED... FRUSTRATED... UNABLE TO BRING MY DREAM-VISION BEYOND THAT POINT. TIME AND MOTION ARE SUSPENDED. I'M BETWEEN WAKEFULNESS AND SLEEP. *I MUST KNOW!* I FLING WIDE THE DOOR... AND BEHOLD A SIGHT MORE HORRIBLE THAN I'VE EVER, IN MY WILDEST NIGHTMARES, IMAGINED...

NO... CHOKE... *NO!* LET HER ALONE!

THE SCREAM FADES. THE DREAM VANISHES. I AM AWAKE, SITTING BOLT-UPRIGHT, CLAWING AT MY FACE, TRYING TO FORCE THE FINISH INTO MY MIND...

WHAT *WAS* IT! OH, LORD! WHAT DID I *SEE?* WHAT WAS HAPPENING TO *CATHY?*

SUDDENLY I KNOW WHAT I MUST DO. THE DREAM IS AN OMEN... A WARNING. I LEAP FROM BED, FUMBLE FOR THE LAMP SWITCH...

CATHY IS IN *DANGER!* I MUST *GO* TO HER...

BUT MY HAND FALLS AWAY. I SLUMP BACK ONTO THE BED. I REACH FOR MY CIGARETTES IN THE DARKNESS... LIGHT ONE... DRAG DEEPLY... REFLECTING...

NO! IT'S *FOOLISH!* IT'S *ONLY* A *STUPID DREAM!* CATHY IS IN *NO DANGER.* I *KNOW* IT! I *KNOW* IT!

I LIE THERE UNTIL THE CIGARETTE BURNS DOWN AND I CRUSH IT OUT. I AM DETERMINED TO STAY AWAKE BUT MY EYES ARE UNBEARABLY HEAVY. SLEEP REACHES OUT AND SMOTHERS ME IN ITS VELVET GRIP. THE SCREAM ERUPTS TO GREET ME...

EEEEEGHHH!

STOP! LET HER ALONE, YOU MANIAC!

I'M INSIDE THE COTTAGE NOW... DASHING FORWARD... CATHY ON HER KNEES... HER FACE DISTORTED WITH FRIGHT... HER EYES GLAZED IN TERROR... PLEADING WITH ME TO SAVE HER. AND GRYMES, HIS CLAWS IN HER HAIR, THAT MANIACAL LOOK IN HIS EYES, IS STANDING OVER HER, AN AX POISED...

GET AWAY FROM HER!

HOWARD... HOWARD, HELP ME...

HE SEES ME THEN, AND LETS CATHY GO. I DIVE AT HIM, GRABBING FOR THE AX...

...BUT HIS MADMAN'S STRENGTH SENDS ME SPINNING ACROSS THE ROOM...

THEN HE COMES AT ME, THE AX HELD HIGH, HIGH...

HIS TEETH ARE BARED, DROOLING WITH EXERTION. HIS WILD EYES GLEAM. HE GRUNTS AS HE BRINGS THE AX DOWN...

AGAIN CATHY SCREAMS... BUT THIS TIME HER TERROR IS FOR ME...

EEEEEEEAAHHH...

THERE IS A SPLITTING EXPLOSIVE LIGHT. I AM AWAKE, A RINGING IN MY EARS. I SIT UP IN MY SWEAT-DRENCHED BED, SHIVERING...

CATHY! THAT *FIEND* WAS *TRYING TO KILL CATHY!* AND THEN HE TURNED ON *ME!* DID HE..? DID HE..?

I LIE BACK, STARING AT THE CEILING. OBLIVION CREEPS IN ONCE MORE... BLACKNESS... AND THE DREAM. I *MUST FIND OUT*... I MUST KNOW THE *MEANING* OF THIS AWFUL DREAM. THE WILD KALEIDOSCOPE BEGINS... THE SCREAM... RACING TO THE COTTAGE DOOR... FLINGING IT WIDE...

... CATHY ON HER KNEES... GRYMES WITH THE AX... BURNING EYES... SALIVA DRIPPING FROM HIS LIPS... COMING AT ME...

...CATHY'S SCREAM... THE AX FLASHING... GRYMES... HOWARD... BLINDING WHITE... RED... BLACK...

THE SCREAM FADES. LIGHT CREEPS IN. I SEE A *COFFIN*... *CATHY* SITTING ON THE FLOOR *BESIDE* IT... SOBBING... SOBBING. I CAN HEAR HER SOBBING AND I AM THERE, TRYING TO PEER *INTO* THE COFFIN... TRYING TO *SEE*... TRYING TO SEE *WHO'S IN IT*...

SOB...
SOB...

THEN, SUDDENLY, I AM AWAKE AGAIN. FRANTICALLY, I DRESS... PACK... CHECK OUT OF THE HOTEL... AND SOON THE MILES ARE FLYING BY BENEATH THE WHEELS OF MY AUSTIN...

I'VE GOT TO *SEE*... I'VE GOT TO SEE MY CATHY... MAKE SURE SHE'S ALL RIGHT!

THE SHADOWS OF DAWN DESCEND SILENTLY FROM THE GREY SKY, MEET NEAR THE DANK, BLACK BOG BY RISING WHISPS OF MIST. THE FOG FLOATS LOW AND WRAITHLIKE ABOUT THE COTTAGE AS I QUIT THE CAR AND RUSH IN. *CATHY IS THERE... AND JUST AS IN MY DREAM... SHE SITS BESIDE A COFFIN... SOBBING...*

CATHY...

HUH?!

AND HOWARD LEIGHTON IS IN THE COFFIN...

CATHY...

CHOKE... *YOU!!*

I STAGGER TOWARD HER WITH FALTERING, JERKY STEPS. HER FACE IS TAUT WITH TERROR. HER *HUSBAND*... CATHY'S *HOWARD*... LIES *DEAD*... AND I *KNOW*...

CATHY...

KEEP AWAY! KEEP AWAY FROM ME!

TO MURDER CATHY LEIGHTON JUST AS I MURDERED HER HUSBAND...

I *KNOW* THAT I HAVE DREAMED A *MANIAC'S* DREAM. I *KNOW* THAT *I* AM *CLAUDE GRYMES*. AND AS THE SCREAMING BEGINS AGAIN AND I HOLD CATHY'S HAIR IN MY STRONG CLAWING HAND, MY AX POISED, I *KNOW*... OH LORD... THAT I *CAN'T STOP MYSELF*... THAT I'VE *COME BACK TO THE COTTAGE*...

YAAAEEEEEEEE

IN THE BAG

THE NAME'S McLEOD... BADGE 331074. I'M A PLAIN-CLOTHES COP. THEY GOT ME PATROLLING THE TOUGHEST SECTION IN TOWN. IT'S A QUIET NIGHT THOUGH, AND I'M NOT COMPLAINING... 'CEPT THAT THIS ICY DRIZZLE'S CHILLING ME TO THE BONE...

THE SERGEANT MIGHT AS WELL HAVE MADE MY BEAT THE MORGUE, THAT DEAD IT IS TONIGHT. THE ONLY SOUND IS THE SWISHY-HISS OF TIRES NOW AND THEN AS A LONE CAR MOVES DOWN THE BLACK, SHINY STREET...

IT'S SURE LONELY, AND I GET TO THINKING ABOUT STACEY'S JOINT AND HOW COZY HIS BAR ALWAYS IS AND HOW GOOD A SHOT WOULD FEEL WARMING MY INSIDES. I TURN THE CORNER AND HEAD FOR IT WHEN I SPOT THE LITTLE GUY EDGING DOWN THE WET SIDEWALK...

B. Krigstein

HE KINDA STUMBLES ALONG AS HE COMES TO THE BUILDINGS. HE'S WEARING ONE OF THOSE LEATHER JACKETS AND HE'S CARRYING SOMETHING... A BAG... A CANVAS BAG WITH MAYBE A BIG ROUND MELON IN IT...

I TAKE A SQUINT AT HIM AS WE PASS EACH OTHER UNDER A LAMP-POST. HE'S GOT SUNK-IN CHEEKS AND A WIDE-EYED LOOK... LIKE HE'S SCARED OF SOMETHIN'...

AND THEN I NOTICE THE BAG AGAIN... AND I SEE IT'S GOT A BIG RED RUST-COLORED STAIN ON THE BOTTOM. IT LOOKS LIKE... LIKE... LIKE DRIED BLOOD, MAYBE...

HEY! MAC! JUST A *MINUTE!*

THE LITTLE GUY DON'T STOP. HE KEEPS ON GOING. I BUZZ HIM AGAIN. I KNOW HE HEARS ME...UNLESS HE'S STONE DEAF...

HOLD IT, BUDDY! I WANT T' TALK TO YOU...

I YANK MY BADGE. I'M WALKING AFTER HIM NOW AND HE'S STARTING TO WALK EVEN FASTER...

I'M A COP, CHUM! TWENTY-FIRST PRECINCT! WHAT'S IN THE BAG!

I START WONDERIN' IF MAYBE I'VE BEEN A COP TOO LONG...IF MAYBE I GOT TOO MUCH IMAGINATION...IF MAYBE THE RUST-COLORED STAIN AIN'T BLOOD AFTER ALL! YEAH? THEN WHAT'S THE CREEP RUNNIN' FOR?...

HEY!

HE GIVES ME ONE WILD LOOK, TURNS GHOST-WHITE AND TAKES OFF. I TROT ALONG AFTER HIM, THINKIN' MAYBE THE POOR SUCKER IS JUST SCARED 'CAUSE HE WORKS FOR A BUTCHER AND SWIPED A ROLLED ROAST OR SOMETHING BLOODY LIKE THAT...

HE REACHES A CORNER AND DODGES AROUND. BY THE TIME I GET THERE, HE AIN'T IN SIGHT. THERE'S A CAR PARKED AT THE CURB AND I FIGURE HE'S BEHIND IT...

LISTEN, MISTER. IF YOU AIN'T DONE NOTHIN' WRONG... REALLY WRONG...YOU'RE CRAZY FOR RUNNIN'! I'LL GET YOU SOONER OR LATER...

THE GUY DON'T LET OUT A PEEP. I START AROUND THE CAR AND OFF HE GOES, LAMMING OUT LIKE HE'S CARRYING A HOT POTATO...AND I BEGIN THINKING THAT MAYBE THAT BLOODY-BOTTOMED SATCHEL IS SOMETHING HOT...

IN MY TIME ON THE FORCE, I'VE RUN INTO ALL KINDS OF CRAZY BIRDS...PERVERTS...MANIACS...HOMICIDAL FIENDS. I BEGIN PICTURING THIS GUY LURKING IN SOME DARK ALLEY WITH AN EMPTY SACK AND A BIG KNIFE...WAITING...

AND I REMEMBER AN OLD GEEZER NAMED FISCH WHO CARVED UP OLD LADIES. I SEE THIS CREEP JUMPING SOME POOR OLD GAL AND DRAGGING HER INTO THE ALLEY...

...AND HACKING HER UP AND STUFFING HER HEAD IN THAT SATCHEL...THAT BLOODY-BOTTOMED SATCHEL...

THINKING THESE THINGS MAKES ME HATE THE SCURRYING LITTLE RAT. I GOTTA CATCH HIM NOW... CATCH HIM AND FIND OUT FOR SURE. HE TURNS INTO AN ALLEY... AND I'M RIGHT BEHIND HIM, GIVING IT ALL I'VE GOT...

THE POOR IDIOT'S MADE A BIG MISTAKE. THE ALLEY'S BLIND. I GOT HIM TRAPPED. I PULL OUT MY .45 AND MY POCKET FLASH AND START PENCILING THE BEAM AROUND...

> GET THIS *STRAIGHT*, MISTER! YOU RUN *THIS* TIME, AND YOU GET A *SLUG* IN YOUR BACK...

THE LIGHT PICKS HIM UP CRINGING IN A CELLAR DOORWAY... WHITE AND SHIVERING... GASPING FOR AIR. HE WRAPS HIS ARMS AROUND THE SATCHEL AND HUGS IT TO HIM LIKE A LITTLE GIRL WITH A DOLL...

> OKAY, MAC! LET'S HAVE A *LOOK!*

> NO! NO! IT'S *MINE!*

HE STARTS CRYING. I FIGURE HE CAN'T PULL A SHIV ON ME WHILE HE'S HUGGING THE BAG, SO I HOLSTER MY GUN AND MOVE IN, KEEPING MY LIGHT ON HIM...

> I *CAN'T* TAKE *NO* FOR AN *ANSWER*, BUDDY! I'M THE *STUBBORN* TYPE. NOW, HAND *IT* OVER!

> SOB... SOB...

THIS LITTLE CHARACTER IS STRONGER THAN HE LOOKS. I TRY WRENCHING THE BAG AWAY BUT HE'S GOT IT IN A DEATH GRIP...

> C'MON... YOU DUMB... ⊕#\"¿X!!

> WAIT! FIRST... FIRST LET ME *TELL* YOU WHAT IT IS... AND WHY I *DID* IT!

I CAN SEE HE'S SCARED SILLY SO I LET GO. HE STARTS TALKING AND I STUDY HIS EYES, TRYIN' TO SEE IF MAYBE HE'S A HOPHEAD...

> I *HATED* HIM! HE WAS ALWAYS *PICKING* ON ME. "MR. DOMINICK, YOU'RE *TWO MINUTES LATE!*" "MR. DOMINICK, THESE *FIGURES* AREN'T VERY *NEAT!* MR. DOMINICK, YOUR *TIE*... YOUR *HAIR*... YOUR *APPEARANCE!*"

HE WAS A *JOHNNY-COME-LATELY!* I WORKED A *LONG TIME* FOR THE COMPANY BEFORE *HE* CAME. BUT HE WAS *YOUNG*... *AMBITIOUS*... HE HAD A *GOOD HEAD* ON HIS SHOULDERS. HE BECAME *HEAD BOOKKEEPER*... MY BOSS!

> EVERY DAY HE NEEDLED ME! NAGGING... NAGGING. I'D GET *SICK* INSIDE... AND *DIZZY*, SOMETIMES... AND I WOULDN'T KNOW WHAT I WAS *DOING*. BUT, HE WOULDN'T *LET UP!* HE WAS *SHREWD*... *CLEVER*... *SMART!*

> SO I BOUGHT AN *AXE*... HEH, HEH... AND TONIGHT I *WAITED* FOR HIM! HE... HE'S *NOT SHREWD ANYMORE!* HE HASN'T *GOT* A *GOOD HEAD ON HIS SHOULDERS ANYMORE!*

> I'VE GOT IT!

THE LITTLE GUY'S EYES ARE BLAZING AND HIS LIPS ARE TWISTED UP IN A VICIOUS SNARL AND SALIVA IS RUNNING DOWN HIS CHIN. MY STOMACH CRAWLS AS I LOOK DOWN AT THE ROUND-SHAPED SATCHEL...

HA HA HA MEN HA HA HA HA HEAD

CHOKE...YOU *MEAN*...IN THAT BAG...HIS...HIS *HEAD*?

I HAD TO TAKE IT AWAY FROM HIM! YOU CAN *SEE* THAT, CAN'T YOU? *I HAD TO CUT OFF HIS ROTTEN SNEERING SCHEMING HEAD!*

YOU... YOU'RE *CRAZY AS A LOON!*

I FEEL SICK JUST LOOKING AT THE BAG, 'CAUSE NOW I KNOW WHAT'S IN IT... A HEAD... A COLD, STARING, GRIZZLY-GREEN HEAD. AND THEN, SUDDENLY, THE IDIOT IS KICKING AND SCREAMING AND THE FLASHLIGHT IS FLYING FROM MY HAND AND SMASHING ON THE WET CEMENT...

WHY...YOU...

HE COMES UP WITH HIS KNEE IN MY GUT AND WHILE I'M SINKING DOWN IN AGONY, HE TAKES OFF AGAIN...

BY THE TIME I GET MY GUN OUT AND START SHOOTING, I'M SENDING LEAD AT NOTHING. HE'S GONE...

I FIGHT OFF THE NAUSEA AND THE PAIN AND IT'S THE LONGEST DARN ALLEY I EVER LIMP DOWN...BUT NOW I'M ON THE STREET AND I SPOT THE DOLLY TWIN...THE PROWL CAR...

HEY! *SULLIVAN! BERGER!* IT'S *ME... McLEOD*...

THE PROWL CAR EASES UP. I SLIDE IN...

DID YOU SEE A *LITTLE RUNT*...FIVE-FOOT-FOUR, MAYBE...CARRYING A *CANVAS BAG?*

YEAH! HE PASSED US A *MINUTE* AGO... HEADING *SOUTH!*

GO *SOUTH*, SULLIVAN, *FAST!* THAT *SCREWBALL* IS A *HOMICIDAL MANIAC*. HE JUST HACKED THE *HEAD* OFF SOME GUY AND IT'S *IN THAT BAG!*

RIGHT...

SULLIVAN GUNS THE PROWL CAR... U-TURNING IT AND TAKING OFF SOUTH AT SIXTY. ONLY THERE AIN'T NO SIGN OF THE CRAZY KILLER...

EMPTY... JUST *EMPTY STREETS*...

I'LL RADIO IN AN ALARM!

I STICK WITH THE PROWL CAR FOR MAYBE TEN MINUTES AS IT CRUISES THE SIDE STREETS. THEN I GET ANXIOUS...

LE'ME *OUT* AT THE *NEXT CORNER,* SULLIVAN. I'M GOING TO TRY IT ON *FOOT!*

OKAY, McLEOD.

I CLIMB OUT AND WATCH THEM PULL AWAY INTO THE MIST...

I PULL MY COLLAR AROUND MY NECK AND START DOWN THE SHIMMERING SIDEWALK ...

AND THEN I HEAR IT...THE CLICK-CLACK OF FEET ECHOING OUT OF THE DRIZZLE...QUICK-MOVING FEET... MOVING TOWARD ME...

I DUCK BACK INTO A DOORWAY AND WAIT. HE COMES THROUGH THE MIST LIKE A SHADOW... A SHADOW CARRY-ING A MELON-SHAPED CANVAS BAG...

I *GOT* YOU... YOU CRAZY @#*!

I PULL OUT MY .45. HE COMES CLOSER...SWINGING THE BAG LIKE HE WAS HAPPY... HUMMING SOFTLY...

I *GOT* YOU...

I STEP OUT OF THE DOORWAY AS HE PASSES ME...

HEY! DOMINICK!

HE SPINS AROUND! I'M NOT TAKIN' ANY CHANCES. I SQUEEZE THE TRIGGER, BLASTING HIS FACE AWAY IN A RED SMEAR...

HE PITCHES FORWARD. THE CANVAS BAG DROPS WITH A THUD...

I STAND OVER HIS TWITCHING BODY
UNTIL IT DON'T TWITCH ANYMORE...

THEN I LOOK AT THE CANVAS
SATCHEL LYING IN THE PUDDLE...

THE PROWL CAR SCREAMS UP...

WE HEARD
SHOTS! OH,
IT'S *YOU*,
MCLEOD!
*WHAT
HAPPENED?*

I *GOT* HIM! I
GOT THE *MANIAC*,
SULLIVAN! I *HAD*
TO *SHOOT* HIM!
HE TRIED TO...

I CAN SEE SULLIVAN'S FACE TURN WHITE.
AND I CAN HEAR BERGER WHISPERING...

IT...IT *CAN'T* BE HIM!

OF COURSE, IT'S HIM!
LOOK! THERE'S THE
BAG! HE'S GOT A HEAD
IN THAT BAG! I KNOW IT!

NOT *HIM*, MCLEOD!
NOT *THIS* GUY!
CAR *2* JUST RADIOED THAT
THEY GOT YOUR MANIAC A
FEW MINUTES AGO...

I LOOK DOWN AT THE STILL FIGURE LYING FACE-DOWN
ON THE BLOODY, WET SIDEWALK. I LOOK AT THE
CANVAS BAG...

IT'S *GOT* TO BE! IT'S *GOT* TO! IT'S
ROUND! IT'S GOT A *HEAD!* IT...

I UNZIP THE SATCHEL. THE ROUND RED SPHERE
MOANS OUT ONTO THE GUTTER...

A BOWLING BALL! OH, LORD...
IT'S *ONLY* A BOWLING BALL!

YOU...YOU
BETTER GIVE ME
YOUR *GUN*, MCLEOD.

POETIC JUSTICE

LIVE NOW, FOR A SHORT WHILE, IN THE LONG AGO. COME BACK TO THE YEAR 1122 B.C., TO ANCIENT CHINA...TO A HAPPY LAND...A LAND OF CULTURE AND LEARNING... A LAND FILLED WITH THE LOVE OF NATURE AND THE SONGS OF THE POETS. CHINA HAS BEEN HAPPY BECAUSE IT HAS BEEN FREE, RULED BY THE LAST OF HIS LINE, THE KINDLY AND FATHERLY OLD EMPEROR, WU MING. BUT TODAY, IN *THE TEAHOUSE OF THE LOTUS BUD*, THERE IS MUCH SADNESS. FOR THE EMPEROR WU MING IS DEAD AND THE POETS SING IN MOURNING OF HIS PASSING...

THE LOTUS BLOSSOM ON THE TREE HAS BLOOMED FOR MANY GOLDEN YEARS. BUT NOW ITS PETALS, DRY, HAVE FALLEN AND WITH IT, WET, OUR SALTED TEARS.

YOUR SONG IS SWEET, CHOU PO, FOR ITS WORDS ARE THE WORDS THAT ARE IN ALL OF OUR HEARTS!

LET ME NOW READ MY SONG, MY FRIENDS...

THERE IS NO REASON FOR THE POETS THAT SIT NOW IN *THE TEAHOUSE OF THE LOTUS BUD* TO EXPECT CHINA TO CHANGE. THIS IS THE WAY IT HAS BEEN FOR CENTURIES...POETS GATHERING IN TEAHOUSES AND SINGING THEIR SONGS TO EACH OTHER...

THE RIVER OF TIME FLOWS ONWARD, UNENDING, AND A GRASSY BANK THAT LINES ITS SHORE IS CARRIED AWAY BY TIME'S CURRENT, UNBENDING, ONE LIFE, WORN AWAY, 'TIL IT IS NO MORE!

IN THE NAME OF THE EMPEROR, YOU ARE ALL UNDER ARREST!

BUT CHINA *HAS* CHANGED...*OVERNIGHT*...

UNDER *ARREST?* FOR *WHAT?* WE DID NO *WRONG!*

WE ARE POETS...

YOU HAVE VIOLATED THE *NEW EDICT* OF THE EMPEROR, *SHU WANG,* AND YOU MUST *DIE!*

SUDDENLY, ALL IS QUIET IN *THE TEAHOUSE OF THE LOTUS BUD*...

NEW EDICT? WE KNOW OF NO NEW EDICT!

THE EMPEROR HAS DECLARED THAT IT IS A *CRIME* FOR ANY MAN TO SIT ABOUT IDLY... TO WASTE HIS TIME READING VERSE. OUR EMPEROR MADE THAT LAW ONLY THIS MORNING...

THE POETS ARE STUNNED...

THIS MORNING! BUT THAT IS *UNREASONABLE!* WE HAVE HAD NO CHANCE TO *LEARN* OF THE NEW LAW!

SUCH A THING IS *UNHEARD OF!* OUR FATHERS HAVE SPOKEN POETRY FOR *CENTURIES!*

NEVERTHELESS, THAT IS THE LAW, AND YOU WILL ALL BE *PUNISHED*...

THE POETS ARE OUTRAGED, AND BECAUSE THEY ARE MANY AND THE GUARDS ARE FEW, THEY FLING THEMSELVES UPON THEIR OPPRESSORS...

DEATH FOR SO UNJUST A REASON!? NEVER! WE WOULD RATHER DIE *FIGHTING!*

IN THE NAME OF THE EMPEROR...

BUT THE YOUNG POET NAMED CHOU PO... A SMALL, SLENDER, SENSITIVE YOUTH... DOES NOT JOIN HIS FELLOWS IN THEIR STRUGGLE. HE REMAINS BACK AS THEY OVERWHELM THEIR WOULD-BE EXECUTORS...

WHEN THE EMPEROR'S GUARDS ARE FALLEN, THE POETS RUN FROM *THE TEAHOUSE OF THE LOTUS BUD*. THEY RUN FAR, UNTIL THERE IS NO BREATH LEFT FOR RUNNING...

AND WHEN THEY STOP, THEY TURN ANGRILY TO THE ONE CALLED CHOU PO...

WELL, CHOU! YOU ARE THE *ONLY* ONE AMONG US WHO *BEARS NO MARK!*

I DID NOT *FIGHT,* SU LING! WHAT DID YOU *GAIN* BY FIGHTING?

GAIN? DID YOU NOT *HEAR* CHOU?! THEY WOULD HAVE *BURIED US ALIVE!* WE HAVE GAINED OUR *FREEDOM!* OUR VERY *LIVES!*

YOUR *LIVES*, YES, BUT YOUR *FREEDOM, NO!* YOU ARE *FUGITIVES* NOW AND THE NEW EMPEROR'S LAW *STILL* HANGS ABOUT OUR NECKS!

BUT UNLESS WE *FIGHT*, IT WILL HANG ABOUT THE NECKS OF OUR *CHILDREN*... AND OUR *CHILDREN'S CHILDREN*... IF INDEED, WE *LIVE* TO HAVE WIVES AND FAMILIES!

WE *ARE* GOING TO FIGHT, CHOU... TO OUR *DEATHS*, IF WE MUST... TO *FREE* CHINA OF THIS *TYRANT!* ARE YOU *WITH* US?

IT IS WRITTEN: "DO NOT TRY TO MOVE THE MOUNTAIN. THE WAY AROUND IS FAR LESS PAINFUL." THERE ARE *HUNDREDS* OF PALACE GUARDS. YOU WILL BE *FOOLS* TO FIGHT THEM. THEY ARE BUT THE *PEBBLES*. YOU WILL *DIE IN VAIN* AND THE *MOUNTAIN* WILL *REMAIN!* NO, I WILL NOT DIE IN *VAIN!*

THE POETS ARE FURIOUS AT CHOU PO'S WORDS. THEY ORDER HIM AWAY AND INSULT HIM AND THROW STONES AT HIM...

NEVER LET US *SEE* YOU AGAIN!

YOUR NAME WILL BE AS *POISON* TO OUR LIPS!

A MAN WHO WILL NOT *FIGHT* IS *NO MAN AT ALL!*

YOU ARE A *COWARD*, CHOU PO!

SADLY, CHOU PO HURRIES AWAY... BRUISED AND HURT...

GO FIGHT, THEN! *GO DIE!* BUT WHO WILL BE LEFT TO REMIND TOMORROW'S CHILDREN THAT CHINA ONCE KNEW *FREEDOM?* WHO WILL TEACH THEM WHAT FREEDOM *MEANS?*

FOR DAYS AFTER THAT, THE POETS MEET IN SECRET. FINALLY, ARMED WITH SCYTHES AND STONES AND CLUBS, THEY MARCH ON THE PALACE OF THE DESPOTIC SHU WANG...

WHEN THE EMPEROR *SEES* US, HE WILL *KNOW* ALL CHINA IS ANGRY!

AND HE WILL BE *AFRAID!*

A LOOKOUT ON THE PALACE WALL SEES THE ARMED BAND APPROACHING, AND HE RUNS TO TELL THE EMPEROR. BUT THE EMPEROR IS *NOT* AFRAID...

AH... *VISITORS*... AND *ARMED*, EH? LET THEM *ENTER* THE COURTYARD! FIND OUT WHAT THEY *WANT!*

THE GREAT GATES ARE THROWN OPEN, AND THE POET HORDE STRIDES ONTO THE PALACE GROUNDS. THE LONE GUARD FACES THEM...

WHY DO YOU *COME* HERE?

WE HAVE COME TO PROTEST THE EMPEROR'S NEW LAW...TO HAVE IT NULLIFIED *PEACE-FULLY*, IF WE *CAN*...OR BY *FORCE*, IF WE *MUST!*

SUDDENLY, A VOICE ECHOES FROM A BALCONY OVERHEAD. THE POETS LOOK UP, AND THERE IS THE EMPEROR IN HIS ROBES OF GOLD CLOTH... THE TYRANT, ROARING HIS WRATH...

YOU HAVE COME FOR BUT *ONE* THING...*TO DIE!* LET ALL CHINA KNOW THAT THE GODS HAVE GIVEN ME THE RIGHT TO MAKE *ANY* LAW! *CLOSE THE GATES! SEIZE THEM!*

THE GATES ARE SWUNG CLOSED. PALACE GUARDS POUR FROM THEIR HIDING PLACES. THE EMPEROR SMILES AS THE OVERPOWERED POETS ARE CUT DOWN LIKE FLIES...

AND WHEN THE CARNAGE IS COMPLETE AND EACH AND EVERY ONE OF THE HEROIC POETS LIES SILENT AND STILL, THE EMPEROR SNARLS...

TAKE THEIR BODIES TO THE CITY, AND GIVE THEM TO THEIR FAMILIES. AND WHEN YOU ARE ASKED WHY THEY DIED, TELL THE PEOPLE IT WAS BECAUSE THEY QUESTIONED THE LAW OF THEIR EMPEROR...

SO BRAVE MEN FOUGHT TO RIGHT A WRONG AND NOW THEY ARE DEAD AND THERE IS STILL WRONG. THE YOUNG POET, CHOU PO WAS *RIGHT!* THEY *DID* DIE IN VAIN! SEE HIM NOW AS HE LOOKS UPON THEIR MOURNERS WITH HEAVY HEART...

YOU CALLED ME A *COWARD* BECAUSE I *WOULD NOT WASTE MY LIFE IN VAIN!* IT IS WRITTEN: "HE IS CALLED A FOOL WHO FAILS A HERO'S MISSION. HE IS CALLED A COWARD WHO WILL NOT BE A FOOL." I AM *NO COWARD*...AND I WILL *BE NO FOOL!*

SOME WEEKS LATER, THERE IS MUCH EXCITEMENT IN THE CITY OF THE TYRANT SHU WANG...

A *PROCESSION* COMES! A *GREAT* PROCESSION!

THERE ARE *GUARDS* AND *NOBLEMEN!* IT MUST BE THE EMPEROR!

CLEAR THE WAY!

AND INDEED IT IS THE EMPEROR, COME TO SHOW HIMSELF TO HIS PEOPLE THAT THEY MIGHT KNOW AND FEAR HIM. BUT AS HE IS CARRIED PAST THE CRINGING THRONG, THERE IS ONE WHO DOES NOT SEEM TO FEAR HIM. A YOUNG WOMAN RUNS TO HIS GILDED CHAIR...

STOP HER! SHE IS TRYING TO *ASSASSINATE* OUR EMPEROR!

NO! SHE DARES TO APPROACH OUR ALMIGHTY RULER WITH A *FLOWER! SEIZE HER!*

THE PRETTY GIRL'S AUDACITY BRINGS A QUICK END TO THE PROCESSION. THE INFURATED EMPEROR ORDERS HER ARREST, AND LATER, IN HIS THRONE ROOM, SHE IS BROUGHT BEFORE HIM...

HOW DARE YOU! MY SUBJECTS WERE WARNED TO *KEEP THEIR DISTANCE!* I WANT THEM TO BE *AFRAID* OF ME... AFRAID TO BREAK MY *LAWS!*

BUT THE YOUNG WOMAN DOES NOT FLINCH. SHE SMILES SWEETLY AND HER WORDS ARE SOFT, LIKE GENTLE FLUTE NOTES...

MY *FEAR* OF YOU, OH, MIGHTY EMPEROR, WAS QUICKLY *BANISHED* WHEN I BEHELD YOUR *BEAUTY!* I COULD NOT CONTROL MY *FEELINGS!*

YOU... YOU ... RISE UP, LITTLE ONE!

THE DESPOT'S ANGER VANISHES AT THE LOVELY GIRL'S SWEET WORDS AND HE SMILES IN SPITE OF HIMSELF AS HE DRAWS THE TERRIFIED CREATURE TO HIM...

YOU FIND YOUR EMPEROR *BEAUTIFUL TO BEHOLD?*

MORE BEAUTIFUL THAN THE *FLOWER* WHICH I TRIED TO *GIVE* YOU, OH, EMPEROR!

THE EMPEROR LOOKS UPON THE GIRL AND FINDS HER MOST PLEASING TO THE EYE. AND WHEN HE SEES THAT HIS COUNSELLORS, TOO, ARE FEASTING THEIR EYES UPON HER, HE BEAMS... THEN SPEAKS...

FOR AN OFFENSE SUCH AS *YOURS*, I COULD HAVE YOU *TORN APART* BY *WILD HORSES*. BUT I SHALL NEED... AH... TIME TO *CONSIDER! GO TO MY CHAMBERS! WAIT THERE FOR ME! WE WILL SEE!*

IN A WHILE, THE EMPEROR ENTERS HIS CHAMBERS AND FINDS THE GIRL WAITING FOR HIM. SHE BOWS LOW, BUT HER SOFT EYES ARE EVER UPON HIM AND HE SEES IN THEM AN INVITATION...

I SOUGHT *FEAR* FROM ALL OF MY SUBJECTS, AND YET... YET I DELIGHT THAT I HAVE STIRRED *LOVE INSTEAD*... IN *YOU!*

COME *CLOSER*, SO THAT YOU MAY KNOW THE *FULL EXTENT* OF MY LOVE FOR YOU, OH, EMPEROR...

IT IS FULLY AN HOUR LATER THAT THE DOOR TO THE EMPEROR'S CHAMBERS OPENS, SURPRISING THE COUNSELLORS WHO WERE CLUSTERED ABOUT IT, LISTENING...

SH-H-H-H! THE EMPEROR IS *ASLEEP!*

COUGH...

AHEM...

THE EMBARRASSED YOUNG WOMAN BOWS LOW AND HURRIES DOWN THE LONG PALACE HALL...

SHOULD WE LET HER *GO?*

WOULD YOU DARE *WAKE* THE EMPEROR AND *ASK*...?

HE WILL *FIND HER* IF HE WANTS HER AGAIN!

AND SO, THE FRAIL CREATURE PASSES, UNCHALLENGED, THROUGH THE PALACE GATES...

... DOWN THE LONG WINDING ROAD...

...TO *THE TEAHOUSE OF THE LOTUS BUD*...

...WHERE, ONCE SAFELY INSIDE, THE BLACK WIG IS QUICKLY REMOVED...

AND THE GLEAMING DAGGER IS WASHED CLEAN...

...WHILE, BACK IN THE PALACE THE TYRANT LIES DEAD FROM WOUNDS THAT HAD SILENTLY BEEN ADMINISTERED BY A *SMALL, SLENDER, SENSITIVE POET DISGUISED AS A WOMAN*...

...A POET KNOWN AS CHOU PO WHO WOULD NOT BE A *FOOL*, AND WOULD NOT DIE IN *VAIN!*

WHERE ON THE BATTLEFIELD, IS THERE ROOM FOR A COWARD? ANTONIO BARTO WANTED TO SERVE, BUT HE SHRANK FROM VIOLENCE AND PHYSICAL CONTACT WITH THE ENEMY! HE HOPED HIS DREAD SECRET WOULD BE KEPT FROM THE MAN HE IDOLIZED...THE GREAT PATRIOT WHO WAS LEADING ITALY TO FREEDOM AND VICTORY...

GARIBALDI

THIS WAS THE GREAT TRAVELING ARMY OF GARIBALDI THAT CUT ACROSS ITALY, FREEING IT OF ITS ENEMIES AND DRAWING TOGETHER THE VARIOUS PRINCIPALITIES INTO A UNITED COUNTRY... WARRIORS ALL AND VALIANT MEN...

WHAT LOYAL ITALIAN WOULDN'T FOLLOW HIM, WOULDN'T FIGHT FOR HIM, WOULDN'T DIE FOR HIM? THERE WAS ONE! WHISPER HIS NAME... HIDE IT AS HE HIMSELF HID HIS SECRET...THE SECRET THAT HE WAS AFRAID! THIS WAS ANTONIO BARTO...

SO IT WAS WITH YOUNG ANTONIO! HE WANTED TO SERVE AND FOLLOW GARIBALDI, BUT DIDN'T WANT TO MEET THE ENEMY IN HAND-TO-HAND COMBAT! SO THIS IS HOW HE SERVED...

THIS WAS THE PATRIOT! *THIS* WAS THE SOLDIER...PREPARING FOOD AND SERVING IT TO THE WARRIORS WHO DID THE ACTUAL FIGHTING... AND HIDING HIS SECRET...

BUT THERE WAS A FACT THAT HE COULDN'T HIDE! ONE MAN SEEMED TO KNOW EVERYTHING ABOUT EVERY MAN WHO SERVED UNDER HIM! THAT MAN WAS GARIBALDI...

THE PASTA IS READY, SERGEANT!

VERY WELL! ANNOUNCE MEAL CALL!

THE FOOD, AS USUAL, IS PERFECT, BARTO!

GRAZIE, SIGNOR!

WAS THERE RIDICULE IN GARIBALDI'S COMPLIMENT... SARCASM IN HIS MANNER...DISDAIN IN HIS EYES? BUT AS HE ALWAYS DID, ANTONIO REASSURED HIMSELF AND BOLSTERED UP HIS FALTERING COURAGE!

BUT ANTONIO'S MOMENT OF GLORY WAS BRIEF! WHEN THE ARMY WAS ON THE MARCH TOWARD THE ENEMY, HIS COURAGE WOULD FALTER...

I SERVE THE *BEST* I CAN! I KEEP THE KITCHEN WELL! IT WILL HELP SERVE GARIBALDI AND ITALY! THAT'S BEING A *PATRIOT* ISN'T IT?

AND HE WOULD FOLLOW AT THE REAR WITH HIS PANS...THE TRAVELING KITCHEN...

THE GREATEST IN THE RANKS...AND THE LEAST...BOTH IN ONE ARMY! EACH AWARE OF THE OTHER...AND EACH SILENT AS THEY TRAVELED ON...

AND WAITING FOR THEM BOTH WAS... *THE ENEMY!*

THE VAST TROOPS OF THE ENEMY WAITED UNTIL THE LONG COLUMN HAD PASSED BY! UNTIL THE LEADER, THE CRACK RIFLEMEN, THE EXPERT CANNONEERS, THE CAVALRY, HAD ALL GONE PAST...AND THEN THEY ATTACKED...*AT THE REAR!*

THE CHARGE WAS AWESOME! RIFLES CRACKLED! TRUMPETS BLARED THE CHARGE! CANNON FROM DEEP IN THE MOUNTAINS ROARED...AND ANTONIO BARTO FOUND HIMSELF FACING THE ONE THING HE DREADED...*COMBAT...*

ALL AROUND HIM, HIS COMRADES PICKED UP GUNS AND FOUGHT BACK, TRYING TO HOLD OUT UNTIL GARIBALDI COULD SWING BACK AND TAKE UP THE BATTLE! BUT ANTONIO STOOD THERE, UNCERTAIN AND PARALYZED WITH FEAR...

IF I RUN AND ESCAPE...IT WOULD MEAN COURT-MARTIAL... AND THE SENTENCE OF DEATH! BUT WORSE EVEN THAN THAT, THEY'D LAUGH AT ME FOR MY COWARDICE...AND GARIBALDI WOULD HEAR THAT LAUGHTER!

BUT THERE'S NOTHING ELSE I CAN DO! I CAN'T FIGHT! AND THE ENEMY'S RIGHT ON TOP OF ME!

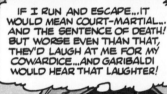

WHAT SHALL I DO?

MY KITCHEN! WHAT ARE THEY DOING TO MY KITCHEN?

THEY'RE *WRECKING* IT! MY STOVE! EVERYTHING RUINED! HOW CAN I FEED THE FIGHTING SOLDIERS...THEY CAN'T DO THAT! NO ENEMY CAN WRECK IT!

FEAR? UNCERTAINTY? COWARDICE? THEY WERE MERE WORDS NOW AS ANTONIO SAW HIS BELOVED KITCHEN WRECKED BY THE ENEMY! THERE WAS ONLY ONE THING TO DO... *FIGHT!*

FIGHT...TO DESTROY THOSE WHO INVADED HIS DOMAIN!

FIGHT...BECAUSE THAT IS THE ONLY THING LEFT TO DO!

FIGHT...BECAUSE THIS IS YOURS, ANTONIO BARTO, AND YOU MUST FIGHT FOR WHAT IS YOURS!

AND WHEN THERE WERE NO MORE BULLETS LEFT IN HIS RIFLE, HE STILL USED IT TO MOW DOWN ALL THOSE WHO STILL DARED TO REMAIN WITHIN THE PROVINCE THAT BELONGED ONLY TO HIM...

HE WAS AWARE OF NOTHING BUT THE FURY WITHIN HIMSELF, THE ANGER, THE FIGHTING RAGE! AND THAT FURY DROVE HIM ON TO KEEP FIGHTING SO THAT HE DIDN'T EVEN KNOW IT WHEN HELP CAME AT LAST! BUT THERE WAS ONE VOICE HE *DID* HEAR...

ENOUGH, BARTO! IT IS OVER!

THEN, THE SAVAGE TEMPER WORN, ANTONIO BARTO BROKE DOWN! HE COULD NOT KEEP HIS SECRET ANY LONGER FROM THE ONE MAN HE COULD NOT FOOL! BITTER TEARS BLINDED HIM AND HIS CONFESSION GUSHED FORTH...

BUT... I *AM* A COWARD!

WE ARE ALL ALIKE, MY BOY! NO MAN LIKES TO ATTACK ANOTHER... UNTIL THAT OTHER INVADES, ATTACKS, WRECKS WHAT IS OURS! *THAT* IS WHY WE ARE FIGHTING...FOR THE LIBERTY THAT IS OURS AND *THAT* NO ONE CAN WRECK!

AND THEY MARCHED ON TO CONTINUE THE FIGHT... AND GARIBALDI WAS SURE NOW OF THE PATRIOT WHOM HE HAD NEVER DOUBTED, BUT WHO NEEDED THIS EXPERIENCE TO PROVE TO HIMSELF THAT HE WAS A BRAVE SOLDIER WORTHY OF SERVING UNDER GARIBALDI!

I AM NOT WORTHY OF SERVING YOU, SIGNOR! I LET THEM WRECK MY KITCHEN! I AM A *COWARD!*

NO, BARTO! I AM PROUD OF YOU!

WHEN THE MYSTERIOUS PROFESSOR DUBOIS UNDERTOOK THE TASK OF OVERCOMING THE FEARS OF IRWIN BOTTS, HE MET WITH GREAT SUCCESS! BUT WHEN THE HYPNOTIST TRIED TO MIX BUSINESS WITH TREACHERY, HE FOUND THAT HE'D DONE HIS JOB *TOO* WELL!

THE HYPNOTIST!

HE'S COMING RIGHT AT ME!

B. Krigstein

OOHHH! OH, NO! NO, NO! PLEASE!!

WHA...!

IT'S ONLY MY SHADOW!

IRWIN BOTTS WAS OVERCOME WITH SHAME BY THE TIME HE REACHED HOME...

WHY DO I HAVE TO BE SO TIMID? IF THERE WERE ONLY SOME WAY TO MAKE MYSELF DIFFERENT... BRAVE!

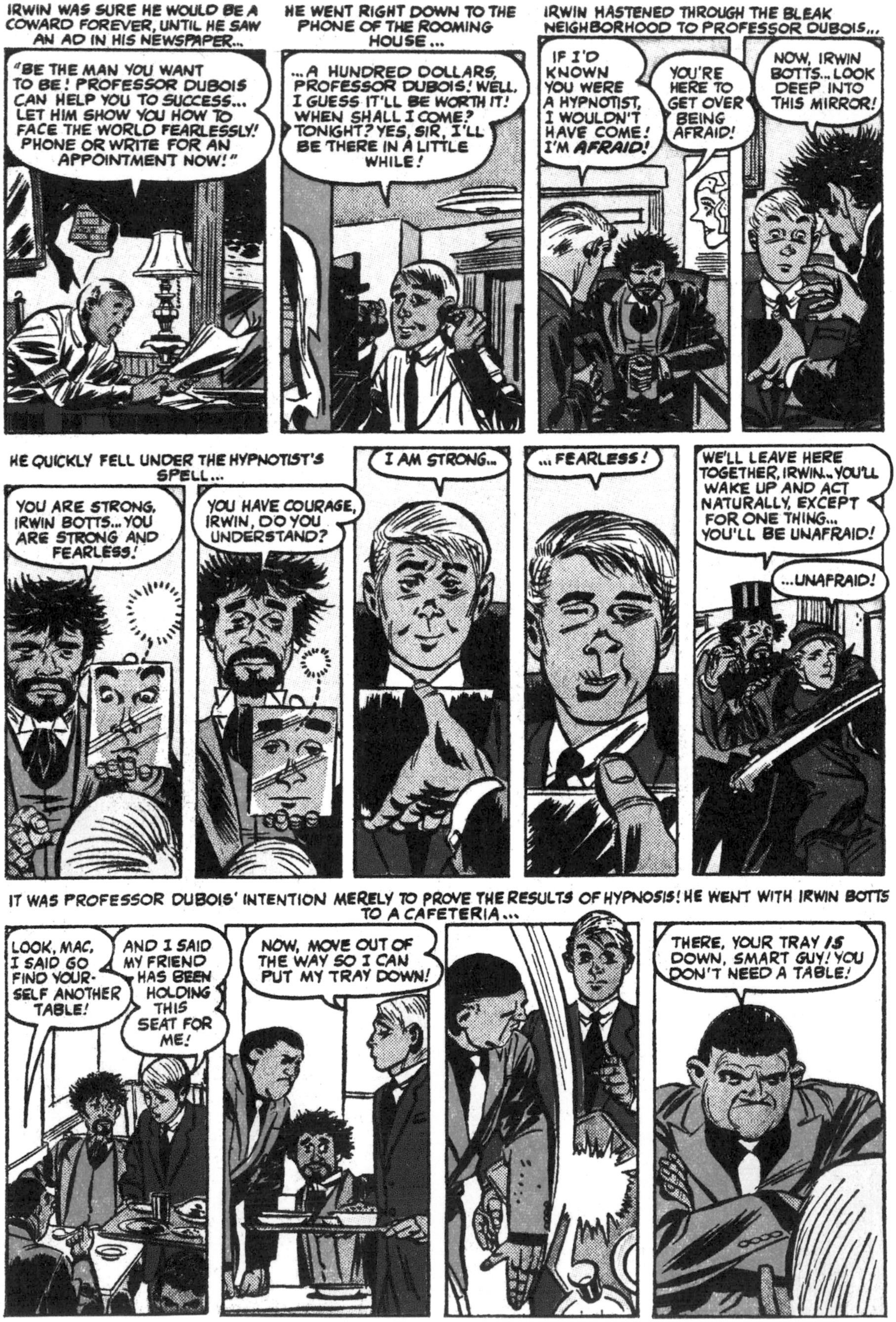

IRWIN WAS SURE HE WOULD BE A COWARD FOREVER, UNTIL HE SAW AN AD IN HIS NEWSPAPER...
"BE THE MAN YOU WANT TO BE! PROFESSOR DUBOIS CAN HELP YOU TO SUCCESS... LET HIM SHOW YOU HOW TO FACE THE WORLD FEARLESSLY! PHONE OR WRITE FOR AN APPOINTMENT NOW!"
HE WENT RIGHT DOWN TO THE PHONE OF THE ROOMING HOUSE...
...A HUNDRED DOLLARS, PROFESSOR DUBOIS! WELL, I GUESS IT'LL BE WORTH IT! WHEN SHALL I COME? TONIGHT? YES, SIR, I'LL BE THERE IN A LITTLE WHILE!
IRWIN HASTENED THROUGH THE BLEAK NEIGHBORHOOD TO PROFESSOR DUBOIS...
IF I'D KNOWN YOU WERE A HYPNOTIST, I WOULDN'T HAVE COME! I'M AFRAID!
YOU'RE HERE TO GET OVER BEING AFRAID!
NOW, IRWIN BOTTS... LOOK DEEP INTO THIS MIRROR!
HE QUICKLY FELL UNDER THE HYPNOTIST'S SPELL...
YOU ARE STRONG, IRWIN BOTTS... YOU ARE STRONG AND FEARLESS!
YOU HAVE COURAGE, IRWIN, DO YOU UNDERSTAND?
I AM STRONG...
...FEARLESS!
WE'LL LEAVE HERE TOGETHER, IRWIN... YOU'LL WAKE UP AND ACT NATURALLY, EXCEPT FOR ONE THING... YOU'LL BE UNAFRAID!
...UNAFRAID!
IT WAS PROFESSOR DUBOIS' INTENTION MERELY TO PROVE THE RESULTS OF HYPNOSIS! HE WENT WITH IRWIN BOTTS TO A CAFETERIA...
LOOK, MAC, I SAID GO FIND YOURSELF ANOTHER TABLE!
AND I SAID MY FRIEND HAS BEEN HOLDING THIS SEAT FOR ME!
NOW, MOVE OUT OF THE WAY SO I CAN PUT MY TRAY DOWN!
THERE, YOUR TRAY IS DOWN, SMART GUY! YOU DON'T NEED A TABLE!

IRWIN'S FIST FLASHED OUT SO FAST...

...THAT NOBODY KNEW WHAT HAPPENED!

MAGNIFICENT, IRWIN!

BUT WE'D BETTER GET OUT OF HERE!

WHEN THEY GOT BACK TO PROFESSOR DUBOIS OFFICE...

I'VE DECIDED THAT YOUR STRENGTH AND COURAGE MUST NOT BE WASTED! I'M GOING TO MAKE YOU MIDDLEWEIGHT BOXING CHAMP OF THE WORLD!

I SHALL MANAGE YOU AND WE SHALL **BOTH** BE RICH!

IT WAS SOME TIME BEFORE PROFESSOR DUBOIS COULD ARRANGE A FIGHT FOR IRWIN...

WE HAVE A CHANGE IN TONIGHT'S PRELIMINARY BOUT, OWIN' TO THE ILLNESS OF HOWIE KIRK! REPLACIN' KIRK IS A NEW-COMER TO PROFESSIONAL BOXIN', IRWIN BOTTS! HIS OPPONENT, MICKEY DAVIS!

NOW, LOOK INTO THE MIRROR...IRWIN, YOU WILL BEAT DAVIS TONIGHT! YOU WILL WIN IN THE FIRST ROUND!

IN THE FIRST ROUND!

AT THE SOUND OF THE BELL, IRWIN SPRANG FORWARD...

IRWIN'S FIST FLASHED OUT SO FAST...

...THAT HIS OPPONENT DIDN'T KNOW WHAT HAPPENED!

SEVEN... EIGHT... NINE... TEN!

THE CROWD ROARED AND AND CHEERED ITSELF HOARSE...

THE WINNAH!

THE PROFESSOR RUSHED IRWIN TO THE DRESSING ROOM...

DID YOU HEAR THE CHEERS, IRWIN? WE'RE ON OUR WAY! SOON YOU WILL CHALLENGE KID ROGAN FOR THE CROWN!

THEN WE'LL BE RICH, IRWIN ...VERY RICH!

THE MAIN EVENT WAS FORGOTTEN AS THE SPORTS WRITERS SOON CROWDED INTO THE DRESSING ROOM...

DAVIS HAD HIS EYE ON THE TITLE... HE'D *NEVER* BEEN KNOCKED OUT TILL *TONIGHT!*

IRWIN HAD *HIS* EYE ON THE MIDDLEWEIGHT CROWN, TOO... AND HE'S GOING TO *WIN* IT!

WHAT'S THE MATTER WITH BOTTS? HE JUST SITS STARING...

IT'S IRWIN'S GREAT POWER OF CONCENTRATION... HE THINKS CONSTANTLY OF STRATEGY!

BATTLING BOTTS, AS THE NEWSPAPERS STARTED TO CALL HIM, TRAINED FOR HIS NEXT FIGHTS SITTING DOWN...

AFTER HE WON A FEW MORE BOUTS BY ONE-PUNCH KAYOES, THE PUBLIC CLAMORED FOR A MATCH BETWEEN BOTTS AND PETE JORDAN, THIRD RANKING CONTENDER FOR THE CROWN...

YOU CANNOT LOSE, IRWIN... YOU HAVE GREAT COURAGE, IRWIN... YOU WILL BE CHAMPION!

POW!

I CANNOT LOSE...

YOU WILL KNOCK JORDAN OUT, IRWIN!

...I'LL KNOCK JORDAN OUT!

BOFF!

...KNOCK JORDAN OUT!

BATTLING BOTTS SOON DEFEATED ROCKY KNOWLES AND JACK FARLEY AND HE WAS NOW READY TO TAKE ON THE CHAMP... KID ROGAN...

ROGAN... IRWIN'S ONLY OBSTACLE TO THE CHAMPIONSHIP!

BONG!

ROGAN DANCED UP TO IRWIN WITH SUPREME CONFIDENCE...

ROGAN SWUNG AND MISSED!

IRWIN'S FIST FLASHED OUT SO FAST...

...THAT ROGAN DIDN'T KNOW WHAT HAPPENED!

THE WINNER AND *NEW* MIDDLEWEIGHT CHAMPION OF THE WORLD... IRWIN "BATTLING" BOTTS!

IRWIN!

WAKE UP, IRWIN! WE'VE MADE IT! YOU BEAT ROGAN!

SNAP!

I'M CHAMP? I-I CAN'T BELIEVE IT, PROFESSOR DUBOIS! WHY, JUST A FEW MONTHS AGO I WAS AFRAID OF MY OWN SHADOW!

YES, IRWIN... CHAMP OF THE WORLD! I HYPNOTIZED YOU INTO VICTORY!

WE'LL BE RICH... VERY RICH!

I KNOW, PROFESSOR DUBOIS...

...AND I'M GRATEFUL!

THE HYPNOTIST AND HIS CHAMPION DID BECOME RICH! AFTER A FEW MONTHS DUBOIS AGREED TO A RETURN MATCH WITH KID ROGAN...

THE ODDS ON BATTLING BOTTS TO WIN OVER ROGAN WERE 15-TO-1! PROFESSOR DUBOIS WAGERED HIS ENTIRE FORTUNE ON THE FIGHT...

IRWIN BOTTS WAS PUZZLED AS HE WAITED FOR HIS SECOND BATTLE WITH KID ROGAN TO BEGIN...

YOU'RE PRETTY CONFIDENT THAT BOTTS WILL WIN THIS FIGHT, DUBOIS?

HE CAN'T LOSE! I'M BETTING EVERY CENT I HAVE ON THIS BOUT!

YOU HEARD WHAT I SAID... I WANT IT ALL ON ROGAN TO WIN! IRWIN DOESN'T KNOW IT, BUT HE'S GOING TO LOSE!

THE OLD DOUBLE-CROSS, EH? YOU CLEAN UP A FORTUNE, DUMP BOTTS AND LIVE IN CLOVER THE REST OF YOUR LIFE!

THE MIRROR, PROFESSOR... WHERE IS IT? AREN'T YOU GOING TO HYPNOTIZE ME?

NO, IRWIN, NEVER AGAIN! I'VE TORN UP YOUR CONTRACT ...I'M THROUGH MANAGING YOU AFTER TONIGHT!

IRWIN RUSHED FROM HIS CORNER AS THE BELL SOUNDED!

IRWIN'S FIST FLASHED OUT...

IT WAS SOME TIME BEFORE THE BEWILDERED... AND BROKE.. PROFESSOR DUBOIS COULD FIND HIS VOICE!

ZOK!

Y-YOU WON WITHOUT MY HELP, WITHOUT BEING HYPNOTIZED!

I GOT SO MAD I FORGOT TO BE AFRAID...

...THEN I REALIZED I DIDN'T NEED TO BE HYPNOTIZED ...IT WAS INSIDE OF ME ALL THE TIME!

BEING CHAMPION ISN'T HALF SO IMPORTANT AS KNOWING I'LL NEVER BE TIMID OR AFRAID AGAIN!

THEY WERE A DEVOTED, ELDERLY COUPLE, OCCUPYING A HOUSE THAT SEEMED TOO LARGE FOR THEIR NEEDS AND NOW, THERE WAS A MELANCHOLY AIR ABOUT THE HOUSE... IN ITS OWN WAY IT COMPLAINED, UNTIL SOMETHING WAS DONE FOR IT!

THE HOUSE THAT LIVED

JONATHAN, YOU NEVER USED TO LET THIS HOUSE GET IN SUCH BAD SHAPE!

I'M NOT YOUNG LIKE I USED TO BE, ELVIRA!

A **MYSTERY TALE** TO HOLD YOU BREATHLESS!

ARE YOU JUST GOING TO SIT HERE TILL THE ROOF FALLS OVER OUR HEADS?

OH, WELL... IF IT'LL MAKE YOU HAPPY, I'LL TRY TO DO SOME REPAIRIN'!

JONATHAN GIBBONS TRIED HIS BEST TO PLEASE HIS WIFE, BUT...

IT'S NO USE, ELVIRA! THIS HOUSE IS JUST TOO MUCH FOR ME TO TAKE CARE OF!

THINGS AREN'T THE SAME AS BEFORE THE BOYS GOT MARRIED! THEY USED TO HELP YOU KEEP THINGS SHIPSHAPE!

JONATHAN RETURNED TO THE HOUSE, THOUGHTFULLY...

YOU KNOW, ELVIRA... I...I'VE COME 'ROUND TO YOUR WAY OF THINKING...

PERHAPS WE'D BE BETTER OFF IN A SMALL APARTMENT!

THAT'S WHAT I'VE BEEN TELLING YOU FOR THE PAST SIX YEARS, JONATHAN!

SEVERAL WEEKS LATER, JONATHAN GIBBONS COMPLETED THE SALE OF HIS HOUSE...

I'M BEING *GENEROUS*...

MORE THAN GENEROUS!

FIVE THOUSAND FOR THIS OLD PLACE IS A LOT OF MONEY!

PLEASE DON'T TALK THAT WAY, MR. WILCOX!

WE *LOVE* THIS HOUSE!

IT...IT'S ALMOST A LIVING PART OF US...OUR CHILDREN *GREW UP* HERE!

WELL - ER - HEM... YOU CAN'T SELL *SENTIMENTAL* VALUE, MRS. GIBBONS! HEH, HEH!

HOWEVER, IT'S A GOOD LOCATION FOR A *BUSINESS* THAT I HAVE IN MIND!

OTHERWISE I WOULDN'T GIVE YOU FIVE HUNDRED FOR IT!

WELL...GOOD-BYE AND...GOOD LUCK!

IT RAINED HARD THE DAY THE ELDERLY COUPLE LEFT THE OLD HOUSE FOR THE LAST TIME...

IT'S NOT *OUR* HOUSE ANY MORE, ELVIRA!

REMEMBER THE WAY IT *WAS*... WHEN THE BOYS AND WE WERE YOUNG?

...WHEN THE HOUSE USED TO ECHO TO THE SOUNDS OF CHILDREN'S GAMES?

THE HOUSE STOOD THERE, A SILENT SENTINEL...

THE WIND, WHISPERING THROUGH ITS BOARDS, SOUNDED LIKE A SIGH...

WH-OO-OSH-SSH-HH

ONE WEEK LATER, RUFUS WILCOX CAME TO LOOK OVER HIS PROPERTY...

LET'S SEE NOW...

FIX IT HERE...

REPAIR IT THERE...

SOON I'LL HAVE A FIRST-CLASS MOTEL...

...AND NEXT TO IT A FILLING STATION...

...DEFINITELY A MONEY-MAKING PROPOSITION!

WINK!

THE NEXT DAY A CREW ARRIVED...

THE WAY THEY LOVED THIS HOUSE, YOU'D THINK IT WAS HUMAN...

THEY STARTED RE-PLACING THE ANCIENT BOARDS...

HMM! OLD TOYS...

THEY HAMMERED...

IMAGINE LOVING PLANKS OF WOOD...

...SCRAPED...

I MIGHT UNDER-STAND IT IF THE HOUSE WERE ELEGANT AND BEAUTIFUL...

...PAINTED...

BUT IT'S NOT... IT'S REALLY UGLY!!

TWO WEEKS WENT BY...

EVERYTHING WILL SOON BE FINISHED! THIS JOB IS USING UP ALL MY MONEY, BUT IT WILL MORE THAN PAY ME BACK!

THAT NIGHT, RUFUS SLEPT AND DREAMED OF THE FUTURE...

MOTELS... Z-Z-Z-Z Z-Z-Z-Z...CHAIN OF THEM...COVER THE EARTH... Z-Z-Z-Z-Z-Z!

WHILE, OUTSIDE, THE CLOUDS GATHERED...

RUMBLE RUMBLE

LIGHTNING CRACKLED...

POW!

RAIN FELL...

AND A STORM RAGED...

CRACK!

THE NEXT MORNING, RUFUS WILCOX WENT TO EXAMINE HIS PROPERTY...

MY GOSH...I-I'M BACK WHERE I STARTED! THE STORM HAS DAMAGED THE HOUSE, AND ALL MY MONEY HAS BEEN WASTED!

I'VE NEVER LIKED THE HOUSE...AND IT DOESN'T LIKE ME! I'M THROUGH... FINISHED!

THE STORM HAD CRUSHED RUFUS' DREAM...

SO, ONCE AGAIN, THE HOUSE STOOD THERE THROUGH THE FALL, THROUGH THE SNOWS OF WINTER...

...ALONE...

HOUSE AND GROUND FOR SALE PHONE: RIVERSIDE 3114 FOR INFORMATION

IT WASN'T TILL SPRING THAT ANYONE THOUGHT OF BUYING THE HOUSE...

...IT COULD BE BEAUTIFUL, HAL, WITH A LITTLE FIXING! LET'S FIND OUT HOW MUCH HE'S ASKING FOR IT!

HAL AND DIANA CURTISS VISITED RUFUS IN HIS ONE-ROOM FLAT...

...BUT ALL WE'VE GOT IS TWO THOUSAND DOLLARS!

WHY, IT COST ME *THREE* TIMES THE PRICE I'M ASKING FOR IT!

...AND WE'D HAVE TO BORROW TO GET THE HOUSE IN SHAPE!

WELL, I'VE NEVER LIKED THE HOUSE... *OKAY!* IT'S YOURS!

AFTER THE SALE WAS COMPLETED...

HMM! INVEST IN A RESTAURANT! WHY NOT?

RESTAURANTS! A CHAIN OF THEM!

I'LL COVER THE EARTH WITH THEM!

HAL AND DIANA WORKED HARD TO REPAIR THE HOUSE...

I WISH WE COULD SPEND MORE TIME ON THIS WORK!

OH, HAL, IT'S SHAPING UP *BEAUTIFULLY!*

THIS HOUSE GROWS ON ME MORE AND MORE!

I *LOVE* IT, HAL!

THEY WERE HAPPY, LIVING THERE...

HOW'S MY HARD-WORKING MAN?

GLAD TO BE HOME!

THE HOUSE RANG WITH *CHILDREN'S* SHOUTS AND GAMES...

GIDDYAP! GIDDYAP! THE PONY EXPRESS IS NEVER LATE!

HI, BIG BOYS!

DADDY! HEY, DADDY! *YOU* BE THE HORSE!

HA! HA! HA!

THE CURTISS FAMILY WERE HAPPY AND THE HOUSE...WELL, IF IT COULD TALK IT WOULD SAY *IT* WAS *HAPPY*, TOO!

DIANA, EVEN IF WE *COULD* AFFORD IT, I WOULDN'T MOVE OUT OF THIS HOUSE FOR *ANYTHING!* I JUST *LOVE* IT!

THE PLANTS CAME TO LIFE, THE LAWN BECAME A RICH GREEN! MAGICALLY, THE HOUSE BECAME EVEN *MORE* BEAUTIFUL THAN IT HAD EVER BEEN BEFORE!

As DUSK STAINS THE WIND-LASHED SKY, WAVES CRASH AGAINST THE JAGGED ROCKS! INSIDE THE LIGHTHOUSE, THE LONELY KEEPER PREPARES TO TURN THE BEACON ON! BUT EVIL LURKS BELOW THOSE CHURNING WATERS...AND THE DECREE OF EVIL IS THAT THE WARNING BEACON REMAIN DARK TONIGHT!

THEY WAIT BELOW

FOR SIX SLOW-DRAGGING MONTHS, *MATT RONSON* HAS BEEN WITHOUT SIGHT OR SOUND OF ANOTHER HUMAN BEING...

I'VE BEEN ALONE TOO LONG...

B. Krigstein

IF I COULD ONLY BE AMONG FOLKS AGAIN...

TO HEAR LAUGHING AND TALK!

I'M TIRED... TIRED!

S-C-RATCH!

I NEED REST!

SPUT-SPUTTER

AHHH...NO CHANCE OF THAT, TILL MY RELIEF COMES!

IT'S *TIME* NOW...

...TIME TO LIGHT THE *BEACON!*

TO LIGHT ...THE...

Z-Z-Z-Z

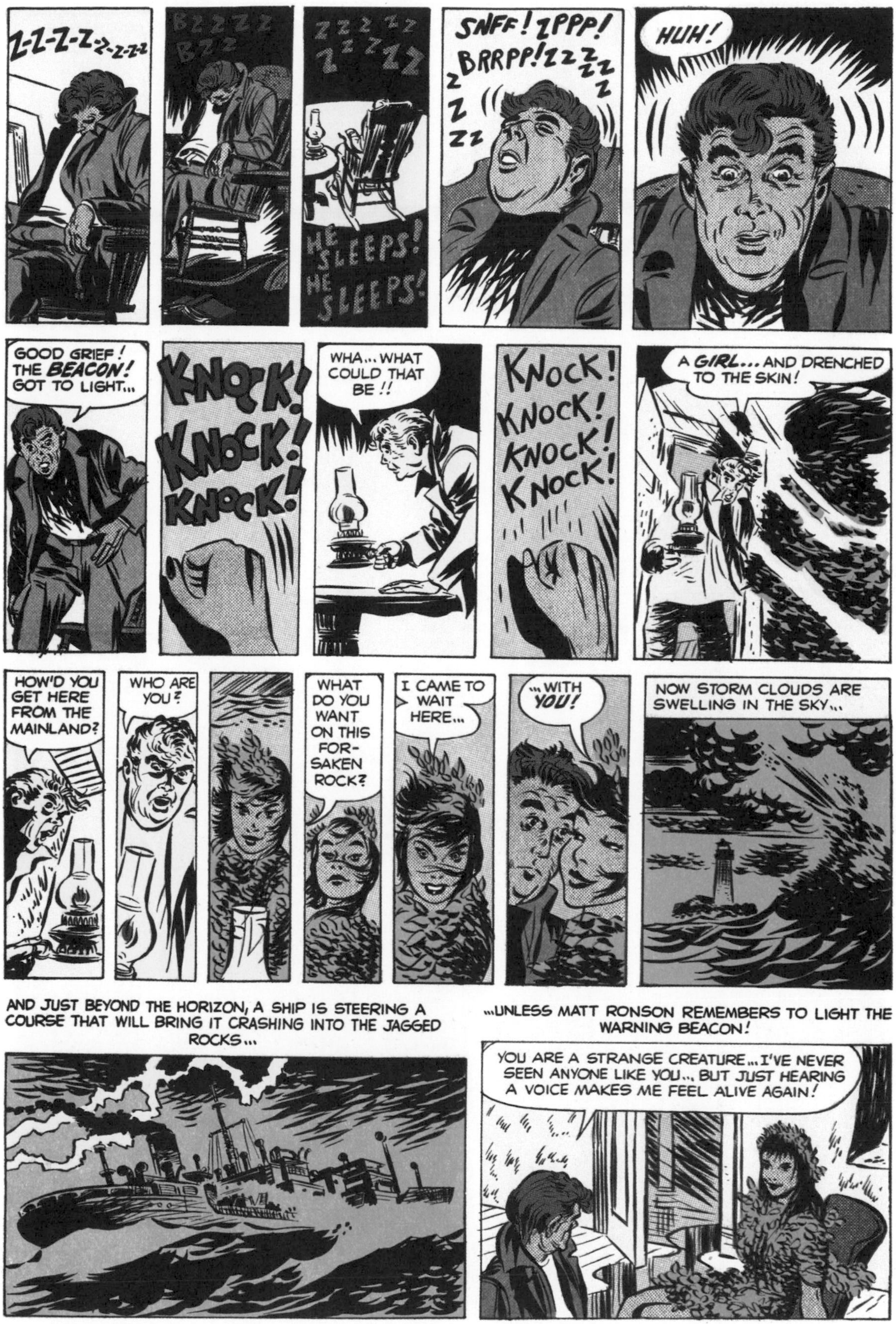
Z-Z-Z-Z-Z-Z-Z-Z-Z
BZZZZ BZZ
ZZZZZZ ZZZZZ
HE SLEEPS! HE SLEEPS!
SNFF! ZPPP! BRRPP! ZZZ ZZZ
HUH!
GOOD GRIEF! THE BEACON! GOT TO LIGHT...
KNOCK! KNOCK! KNOCK!
WHA... WHAT COULD THAT BE!!
KNOCK! KNOCK! KNOCK! KNOCK!
A GIRL... AND DRENCHED TO THE SKIN!
HOW'D YOU GET HERE FROM THE MAINLAND?
WHO ARE YOU?
WHAT DO YOU WANT ON THIS FOR-SAKEN ROCK?
I CAME TO WAIT HERE...
...WITH YOU!
NOW STORM CLOUDS ARE SWELLING IN THE SKY...
AND JUST BEYOND THE HORIZON, A SHIP IS STEERING A COURSE THAT WILL BRING IT CRASHING INTO THE JAGGED ROCKS...
...UNLESS MATT RONSON REMEMBERS TO LIGHT THE WARNING BEACON!
YOU ARE A STRANGE CREATURE... I'VE NEVER SEEN ANYONE LIKE YOU... BUT JUST HEARING A VOICE MAKES ME FEEL ALIVE AGAIN!

WE'RE IN FOR A BAD STORM, MATE!

AYE, CAPTAIN... BUT IT'S NOT THE STORM THAT WORRIES ME...

... IT'S THOSE ROCKS THAT THE CHART SAYS SHOULD LIE DEAD AHEAD!

IF THERE *WERE* ROCKS, THERE'D BE A WARNING BEACON, MATE...

...AND THERE'S *NOTHING* AHEAD BUT DARKNESS!

WITH THE CAPTAIN'S PERMISSION, I'D LIKE TO SOUND THE FOGHORN!

IF IT'LL MAKE YOU HAPPY... START SOUNDING!

OOO

O-OO O

OO O OOO

A FOGHORN CLOSE BY...AND THE BEACON'S STILL DARK! HAVE TO...

NO!

I'LL BE RIGHT DOWN!

WAIT DOWN HERE WITH ME!

GASP!

I-I KNOW *NOW!*

I...I'VE READ ABOUT THEM!

YOU MUST BE ONE OF THOSE *SIRENS* I'VE READ ABOUT!

YOU...YOU...

YOU'VE BEEN *HOLDING* ME DOWN HERE!

THE SHIP MUST CRASH INTO THE ROCKS, SO YOU AND I...AND MY SISTERS...CAN PLUNDER IT!

YOU'LL BE *RICH,* MATT!

RICH!!

In the panels above:

Panel 1: MY JOB...

Panel 2: ...IT'S MY *JOB* TO *WARN* SHIPS...

Panel 3: ...AND I'M *GOING* TO!

Panel 4: *WHAT*, MATT?

Panel 5: *WHAT* ARE YOU *GOING* TO DO?

Panel 6: W-WHERE DID THEY COME FROM?

Panel 7: *NO!*

Panel 8: *NO! NO!*

Panel 9: *WHAT*, MATT?

Panel 10: DON'T COME NEAR...

Panel 15: MATT?

Panel 16: MATT? WHAT? MATT? WHAT?

Panel 18: *CAPTAIN, LOOK...*

Panel 19: A *WARNING* LIGHT!

Panel 20: *REVERSE ENGINES!*

IN THE MORNING, THE MEN FROM THE MAIN-LAND HEAR MATT TELL ABOUT THE BURNING OF THE LIGHTHOUSE, AND HOW THE FIRE WARNED THE SHIP OFF...

BUT WHEN THEY HEAR OF THE SIRENS...

MATT'S BEEN ALONE TOO LONG!

HE'S STARTED SEEING THINGS!

LOOK HERE!

DO YOU STILL THINK I WAS SEEING THINGS?

In the murky depths of a South American jungle, as old as the beginning of time itself, a group of researchers stared at their strange and puzzling find!

DINOSAUR

WHAT DO YOU MAKE OF IT, JAMES?

B. Krigstein

IT'S REPTILIAN, OF COURSE, BUT LOOK AT THE SIZE OF THEM...

...TRULY MONSTROUS!

I KNOW I'LL BE SHOUTED DOWN ON THIS, NOT THAT I'D BLAME YOU... BUT I'D ALMOST BE WILLING TO SAY THAT THESE ARE...

...DINOSAUR EGGS!

WHAT?

PERHAPS YOU SHOULD HEAR ME THRU BEFORE YOU SCOFF, OSBORNE! AFTER ALL, I'M NOT SUGGESTING THAT PREHISTORIC BEASTS ARE NOW PROWLING THIS JUNGLE!

THEN WHAT DO YOU MEAN?

SIMPLY THIS! THESE EGGS ARE FOSSILS, COMPLETELY WITHOUT LIFE, AND RETAINING THEIR SHAPE ONLY BECAUSE OF THE WARM PROTECTIVE MUD IN WHICH THEY HAVE LAIN!

YES...

NATURALLY...

GULP

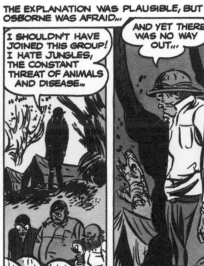

THE EXPLANATION WAS PLAUSIBLE, BUT OSBORNE WAS AFRAID...

I SHOULDN'T HAVE JOINED THIS GROUP! I HATE JUNGLES, THE CONSTANT THREAT OF ANIMALS AND DISEASE...

AND YET THERE WAS NO WAY OUT...

I COULDN'T LET THEM *KNOW* I WAS AFRAID!

I HAD TO THINK OF MY *CAREER*...

AND YET I DON'T WANT TO STAY ON HERE!

BUT WHAT CAN I DO?

BUT THEN A THOUGHT OCCURRED TO OSBORNE...

... AN AVENUE OF ESCAPE...

THERE *IS* A WAY TO GET OUT OF HERE... AND THEY WILL NEVER KNOW THAT *I* HAD A HAND IN IT!

AND LATE THAT NIGHT, WHILE THE OTHERS SLEPT...

THEY'RE ALL FAST ASLEEP, BUT I'LL HAVE TO WORK FAST!

THERE, THAT SHOULD DO IT! IT'S BOUND TO BRING RESULTS!

AND EARLY THE FOLLOWING MORNING...

JAMES, PARKER, OSBORNE! COME QUICKLY... HURRY!

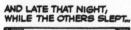

MINUTES LATER THEY WERE GASPING WITH SHOCK... ALL BUT OSBORNE...

WELL, JAMES, WHAT ARE THEY?

THEY'RE THE IMPRINTS OF A GIGANTIC BEAST, A *DINOSAUR*... BUT IT'S IMPOSSIBLE!

THOSE EGGS, JAMES! IS IT POSSIBLE THAT THE WARM MUD, THE SUN'S HEAT... COULD THEY...

I DON'T KNOW...

THAT'S NONSENSE, GENTLEMEN!

HOW COULD AN EGG, MILLIONS OF YEARS OLD, HATCH OUT IN THE TWENTIETH CENTURY?

YOU'RE BEHAVING LIKE SCHOOLBOYS, NOT SCIENTISTS!

I ADMIRE YOUR COOL COURAGE, OSBORNE!

I WISH THE OTHERS AND MYSELF COULD SHARE IT, BUT I'M AFRAID THIS HAS BEEN AN UNNERVING EXPERIENCE!

YES, OF COURSE...

DURING THE NEXT FEW DAYS, FEAR HAD BROUGHT ALL THE ACTIVITIES TO A HALT... AND THE SWAGGERING OSBORNE PLAYED HIS PART TO THE HILT!

OF COURSE, I CAN'T MAKE YOU STAY, BUT IT'S A PITY TO RUN OFF! THERE IS SO MUCH OF SCIENTIFIC VALUE HERE! SO MUCH TO BE HAD!

PLEASE, OSBORNE! DON'T MAKE US FEEL WORSE!

AND WHEN THEY TURNED IN...

I'VE SUCCEEDED! IN AN-OTHER DAY OR SO THEY'LL BE READY TO PACK UP AND QUIT... AND IT WILL APPEAR THEIR DOING... NOT *MINE*!

IT WAS MUCH LATER THAT NIGHT WHEN OSBORNE SUDDENLY AWOKE... EVERY SENSE ALERTED...

SOMETHING'S WRONG...

I CAN FEEL IT!

BETTER CALL THE OTHERS!

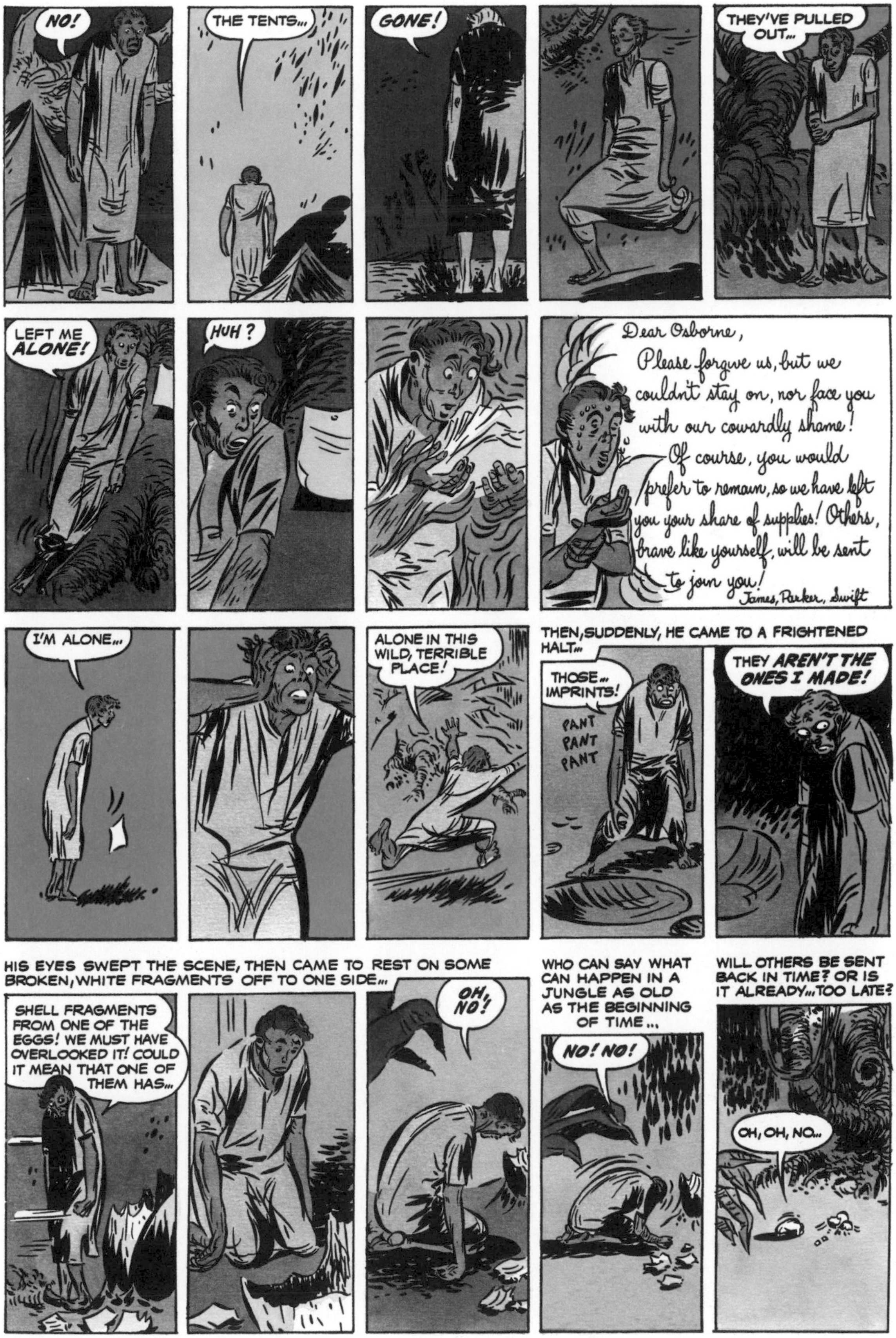
NO!
THE TENTS...
GONE!
THEY'VE PULLED OUT...
LEFT ME ALONE!
HUH ?
Dear Osborne,
Please forgive us, but we couldn't stay on, nor face you with our cowardly shame!
Of course, you would prefer to remain, so we have left you your share of supplies! Others, brave like yourself, will be sent to join you!
James, Parker, Swift
I'M ALONE...
ALONE IN THIS WILD, TERRIBLE PLACE!
THEN, SUDDENLY, HE CAME TO A FRIGHTENED HALT...
THOSE... IMPRINTS!
PANT PANT PANT
THEY AREN'T THE ONES I MADE!
HIS EYES SWEPT THE SCENE, THEN CAME TO REST ON SOME BROKEN, WHITE FRAGMENTS OFF TO ONE SIDE...
SHELL FRAGMENTS FROM ONE OF THE EGGS! WE MUST HAVE OVERLOOKED IT! COULD IT MEAN THAT ONE OF THEM HAS...
OH, NO!
WHO CAN SAY WHAT CAN HAPPEN IN A JUNGLE AS OLD AS THE BEGINNING OF TIME...
NO! NO!
WILL OTHERS BE SENT BACK IN TIME? OR IS IT ALREADY... TOO LATE?
OH, OH, NO...

THE YEAR WAS 1944, THE PLACE THE VAST ATOLL-DOTTED AREA OF THE SOUTH PACIFIC! IN THE BATTLE BETWEEN OUR FORCES AND THOSE OF THE HAUGHTY JAPANESE NAVY, THE HEROES OF MANY AN ENCOUNTER WERE THE FAST, HARD-HITTING, PINT-SIZED *P.T. BOATS!* SMALL IN SIZE, BUT PACKING A TERRIFIC WALLOP, THESE VALIANT SHIPS AND THEIR COURAGEOUS CREWS STRUCK MANY A WORTHY BLOW FOR THE CAUSE OF FREEDOM!

SURVIVAL!

HAVING SET TWO OF THE JAP CRUISERS AFLAME, THE P.T. BOAT NOW SET A ZIGZAG COURSE THROUGH A FURIOUS BARRAGE OF ENEMY FIRE...

BUT SUDDENLY, TRAGICALLY, ITS LUCK RAN OUT...

ABOARD THE JAPANESE FLAGSHIP...

A DIRECT HIT!

SO! BUT IT HAS COST US TWO CRUISERS! A PRICE MUCH TOO HIGH!

HOWEVER, VERY SOON WE WILL EVEN MATTERS! A MASTER PLAN IS BEING READIED! ONE THAT WILL BRING VICTORY!

THUS THE GRIM NIGHT OF BATTLE ENDED! BUT THE FOLLOWING MORNING...

OH-H-HH!

WH-WHAT HAPPENED?

WH-WHERE AM I?

N-NOW I REMEMBER! LAST NIGHT... THE DIRECT HIT! I HUNG ON TO SOME WRECKAGE!

GOT TO FIND COVER! CAN'T STAY IN THE OPEN!

THE DAZED MAN WAS SEAMAN BARRY CAINE...

WITHIN A FEW MINUTES, HE WAS PUSHING HIS WAY THROUGH THE DENSE FOLIAGE!

HUH?

THE YOUNG SEAMAN WAS GRATEFUL FOR THOSE LESSONS IN BASIC JAPANESE AT THE NAVY BASE...

EVERYTHING IN ORDER?

YES, COLONEL YAMATO!

JAPS!

ALL IS IN READINESS! THE BIG CANNON IS WELL-HIDDEN, AND ALL THE OTHERS TOO!

GOOD!

THIS TIME OUR PLAN WILL FOOL WHOLE YANKEE FLEET! WE WILL USE OLD, OBSOLETE BATTLESHIP FOR BAIT!

SO I UNDERSTAND...

AND WHEN YANKEE FLEET PURSUES OLD BATTLESHIP PAST ATOLL, THEN OUR BIG GUNS SHALL TAKE THEM BY SURPRISE!

A TRAP!

LATE THAT NIGHT...

HERE THEY COME! OUR FLEET IS FOLLOWING THAT OLD JAP BATTLEWAGON RIGHT INTO THE LINE OF FIRE! I'LL HAVE TO DO SOMETHING FAST!

SEAMAN FIRST CLASS, BARRY CAINE, DID DO SOMETHING FAST...

OH-H!

NOT MUCH TIME! EVERY SECOND COUNTS!

SECONDS LATER A THUNDEROUS ROAR SHATTERED THE SILENCE, WHILE *ORANGE* FLAMES LEAPED SKYWARD...

AND ABOARD THE AMERICAN FLAGSHIP...

GUN INSTALLATIONS ON THAT ATOLL!

IT WAS MEANT AS A *TRAP!* SIGNAL THE CARRIER!

I CAN HEAR PLANES... *OUR* PLANES! I GUESS THAT AMMO I SET OFF WARNED THEM JUST IN TIME!

WITHIN MINUTES, THE CARRIER'S AIRCRAFT WERE AIR-BORNE, THEIR DEMOLITION BOMBS SHATTERING THE JAPANESE FORTIFICATIONS INTO USELESS RUBBLE...

THE FLAMES LEAPED HIGHER STILL, AND THEN THE PLANES DRONED OFF... ANOTHER ENEMY PLAN DOOMED TO DISMAL FAILURE...

IT WAS ALTOGETHER FITTING THAT A SHARP-EYED P.T. BOAT LOOKOUT SPOTTED BARRY CAINE AND HAULED HIM ABOARD...

YOU'LL BE IN FOR SOME HEAVY DECORATIONS FOR WHAT YOU DID, SAILOR!

BEING ABOARD SHIP IS ENOUGH REWARD, SIR! IN A WAY, IT'S LIKE COMING HOME!

FOR YEARS ROSS HAD PEERED INTO HIS CRYSTAL BALL AND PRETENDED HE COULD READ THE FUTURE! BUT THIS TIME THERE REALLY **WAS** SOMETHING THERE TO SEE!

the LAST LOOK!

ROSS! GET GOING! WE JUST SWINDLED A GUY OUT OF HIS LIFE'S SAVINGS WITH YOUR SWAMI ACT, REMEMBER? WHAT'S WRONG?

I-I'M NOT SURE! BUT I THINK I'M SEEING SOMETHING THAT HASN'T HAPPENED YET! SOMETHING THAT'S **GOING** TO HAPPEN!

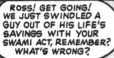

ALL I SEE IS YOUR PHONY CRYSTAL BALL! WHAT ARE YOU TALKING ABOUT?

IT'S GONE!

BUT I **SAW** IT!

I ACTUALLY **SAW** THE **FUTURE**!

I SAW **YOU**!

I COULDN'T BE MISTAKEN ABOUT THAT JACKET YOU'RE WEARING!

I SAW **YOU** IN THE CRYSTAL!

YOU'D JUST KILLED A MAN, AND THE POLICE WERE ABOUT TO GRAB YOU!

ARE YOU TRYING TO SAY YOU'VE TURNED INTO A REAL SWAMI ALL OF A SUDDEN, DON'T MAKE ME LAUGH! WHAT'S THE GAG?

B. Krigstein

IT'S TRUE! YOU'RE GOING TO KILL SOMEONE! I SAW IT!

SNAP OUT OF IT!

WE HAVEN'T GOT TIME FOR HYSTERICS! YOU IMAGINED IT!

THAT'S BETTER! YOU WERE ALWAYS SPINELESS FOR A CON MAN! LET'S GO BEFORE THAT GUY GETS SMART AND HOLLERS FOR THE POLICE!

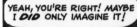

YEAH, YOU'RE RIGHT! MAYBE I DID ONLY IMAGINE IT!

ROSS SAID THE WORDS, BUT HE KNEW THAT HE LIED! SO, FROM THEN ON, HE LIVED WITH FEAR! AND A WEEK LATER, IN ANOTHER TOWN, THE FEAR WOULD NO LONGER LET HIM BE SILENT...

COOPER, I-I'VE BEEN THINKING....MAYBE WE OUGHT TO SPLIT UP...

SPLIT UP?

SO YOU STILL FIGURE I'M GOING TO GET HOOKED FOR MURDER, AND YOU DON'T WANT ANY PART OF IT, EH?

NOW, YOU GET THIS! WE'RE GOING BACK TO WORK! AS SOON AS I LINE UP A NEW VICTIM!

ANY OBJECTIONS?

DON'T! I... ALL RIGHT! JUST GIVE ME A FEW DAYS TO FORGET WHAT I SAW IN THE CRYSTAL!

YOU SAW NOTHING, AND I'M NOT SPLITTING UP ANY MONEY-MAKING DEAL BECAUSE YOU'RE SCARED! OKAY! A FEW DAYS! BUT THAT'S ALL!

AFTER THAT, THE FEAR WAS AN ICY FIST CLAMPED TIGHT ABOUT ROSS'S HEART...

I'VE GOT TO GET AWAY FROM HIM! I'VE GOT TO!

BY THE NEXT NIGHT, ROSS HAD MADE UP HIS MIND!

ALL RIGHT, I ASKED YOU TO SPLIT UP, AND YOU WOULDN'T! NOW WE'LL DO IT MY WAY!

IF YOU WON'T GET OUT, *I* WILL! AND I'LL MAKE SURE THAT YOU NEVER FOLLOW ME!

WHEN YOU COME TO, YOU'LL BE ON YOUR WAY TO JAIL, AND I'LL BE ON MY WAY IN ANY DIRECTION THAT TAKES ME AWAY FROM *YOU!*

HURRIEDLY, TREMBLING, ROSS DRESSED AND PACKED...

POLICE? THERE'S A MAN ASLEEP IN THE HOTEL MAYFAIR, ROOM 403! HE'S WANTED FOR A SWINDLING BACK EAST...

ROSS HAD NO DESIRE TO MEET THE POLICE! HE STUCK TO THE DARK ALLEYS!

SO LONG, COOPER! AND GOOD LUCK! YOU'LL *NEED* IT!

ROSS SMILED...HIS NIGHTMARE WAS ALMOST ENDED, OR SO HE THOUGHT! BUT HE WAS *WRONG!* NEAR THE RAILROAD STATION, IT HAPPENED...

OKAY, DOUBLE-CROSSER! THIS IS AS FAR AS YOU GO! I FIGURED YOU'D COME THRU THE BACK ALLEYS, SO *I* USED THE MAIN STREETS!

AND I GOT HERE FIRST!

YOU NEVER FIGURED I MIGHT GET AWAY FROM THE POLICE, DID YOU?

COOPER! *NO!* YOU WOULDN'T SHOOT ME!

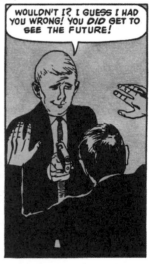

WOULDN'T I? I GUESS I HAD YOU WRONG! YOU *DID* GET TO SEE THE FUTURE!

YOU *DID* SEE ME KILL SOMEONE!

YOU!

NO!!

DON'T!!!

238

NO!

IT WAS NO USE!

COOPER WOULD KILL HIM... ROSS KNEW THAT...

HE HAD *SEEN* IT HAPPEN...

A ROAR, A BLAST OF FIRE...

AND THEN... ROSS WAS STANDING ALONE, HOLDING COOPER'S GUN...

NO, THIS IS ALL WRONG! IN THE CRYSTAL, IT WAS *COOPER* WHO WAS STANDING LIKE THIS!

IT JUST DOESN'T ADD UP! I *SAW* HIM! I SAW *HIM* STANDING OVER A BODY!

ROSS MUMBLED STUPIDLY AS THE POLICE LED HIM INTO THE LIGHT! AND IT WAS THEN, SUDDENLY, THAT HE KNEW THE TRUTH!

SO *THAT'S* IT! NO! OH, NO!

ROSS LOOKED DOWN AT HIMSELF, AND IT WAS ALL SO SIMPLE, REALLY! IF THE POLICE COULD NOT UNDERSTAND HIS BITTER LAUGHTER, WHAT DID IT MATTER? WHAT DID ANYTHING MATTER, NOW?

I *DID* SEE THE FUTURE!

BUT I DIDN'T KNOW THAT WHEN I DRESSED IN THE DARK TONIGHT, I'D *PUT ON* COOPER'S JACKET!

I DIDN'T KNOW THAT THE MAN I SAW IN THE CRYSTAL WAS *MYSELF!* HA!HA!HA!

THE EVENTS OF THE NIGHT WERE STRANGE AND ALARMING! IN FACT THEY WERE...

OUT OF THIS WORLD

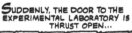

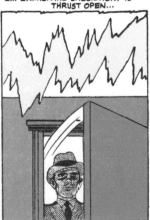

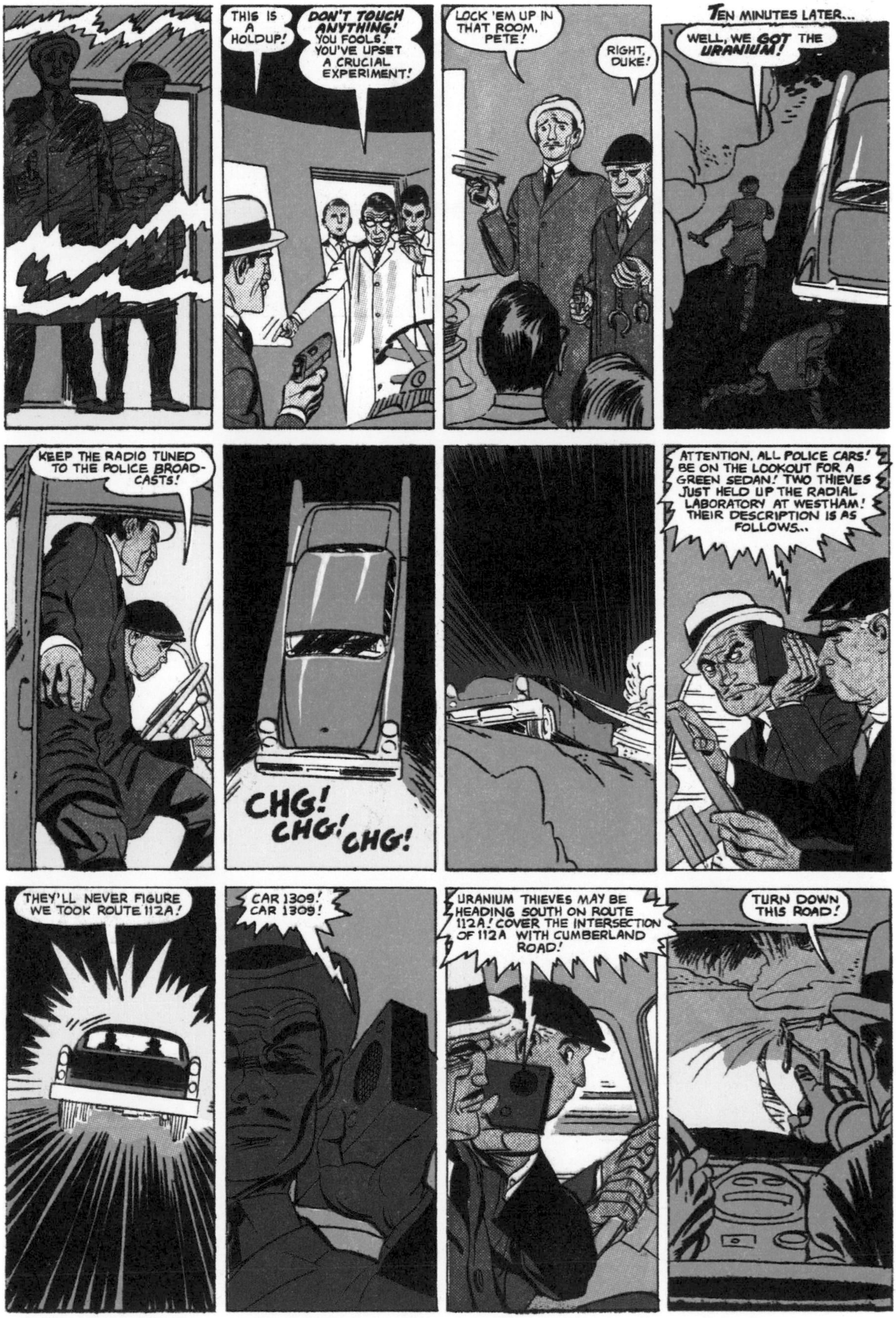
THIS IS A HOLDUP!
DON'T TOUCH ANYTHING! YOU FOOLS! YOU'VE UPSET A CRUCIAL EXPERIMENT!
LOCK 'EM UP IN THAT ROOM, PETE!
RIGHT, DUKE!
TEN MINUTES LATER...
WELL, WE GOT THE URANIUM!
KEEP THE RADIO TUNED TO THE POLICE BROAD-CASTS!
CHG! CHG! CHG!
ATTENTION, ALL POLICE CARS! BE ON THE LOOKOUT FOR A GREEN SEDAN! TWO THIEVES JUST HELD UP THE RADIAL LABORATORY AT WESTHAM! THEIR DESCRIPTION IS AS FOLLOWS...
THEY'LL NEVER FIGURE WE TOOK ROUTE 112A!
CAR 1309! CAR 1309!
URANIUM THIEVES MAY BE HEADING SOUTH ON ROUTE 112A! COVER THE INTERSECTION OF 112A WITH CUMBERLAND ROAD!
TURN DOWN THIS ROAD!

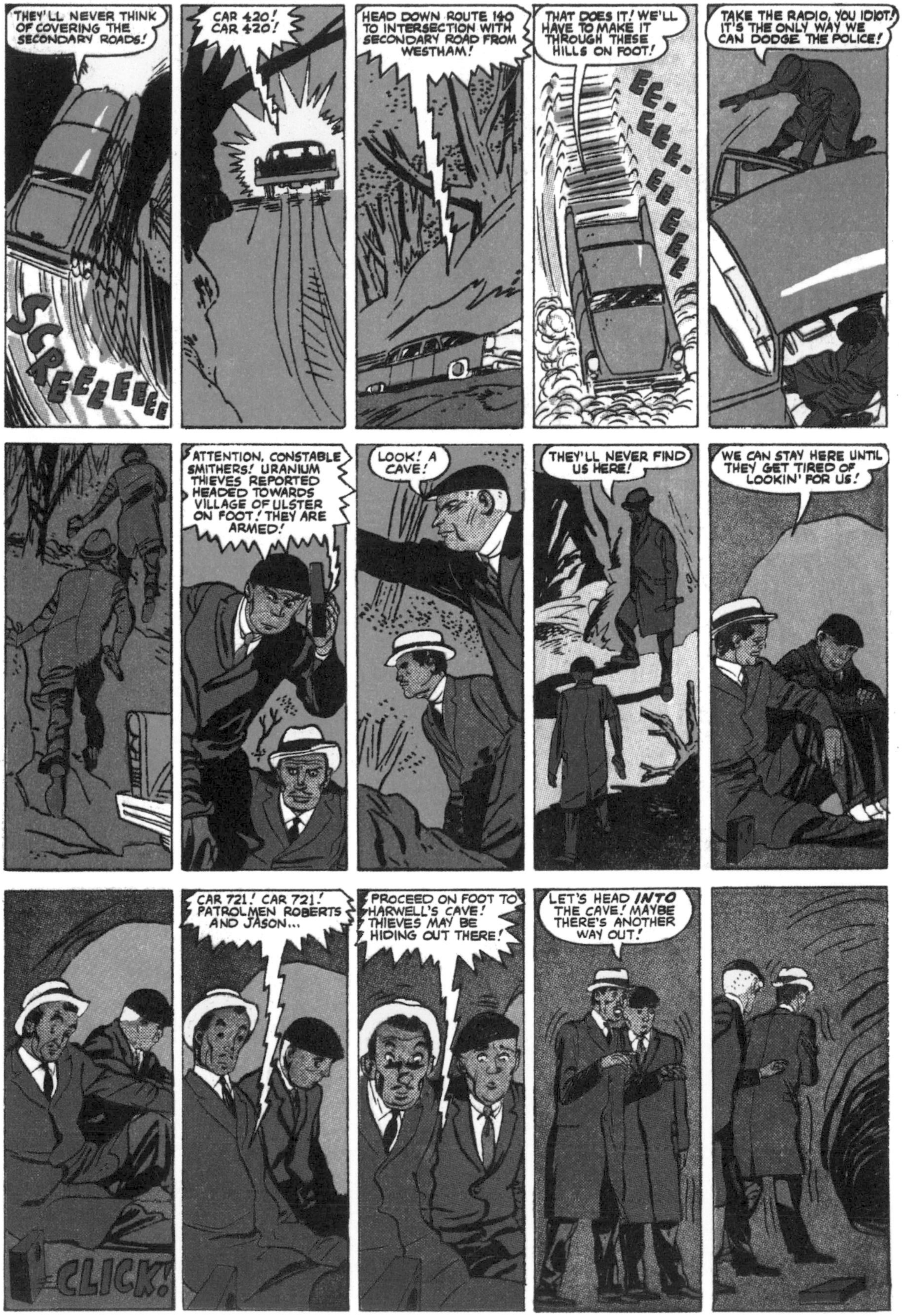
THEY'LL NEVER THINK OF COVERING THE SECONDARY ROADS!
SCREEEEEEEE
CAR 420! CAR 420!
HEAD DOWN ROUTE 140 TO INTERSECTION WITH SECONDARY ROAD FROM WESTHAM!
THAT DOES IT! WE'LL HAVE TO MAKE IT THROUGH THESE HILLS ON FOOT!
EE-EEEE-EEEEEE
TAKE THE RADIO, YOU IDIOT! IT'S THE ONLY WAY WE CAN DODGE THE POLICE!
ATTENTION, CONSTABLE SMITHERS! URANIUM THIEVES REPORTED HEADED TOWARDS VILLAGE OF ULSTER ON FOOT! THEY ARE ARMED!
LOOK! A CAVE!
THEY'LL NEVER FIND US HERE!
WE CAN STAY HERE UNTIL THEY GET TIRED OF LOOKIN' FOR US!
CLICK!
CAR 721! CAR 721! PATROLMEN ROBERTS AND JASON...
PROCEED ON FOOT TO HARWELL'S CAVE! THIEVES MAY BE HIDING OUT THERE!
LET'S HEAD INTO THE CAVE! MAYBE THERE'S ANOTHER WAY OUT!

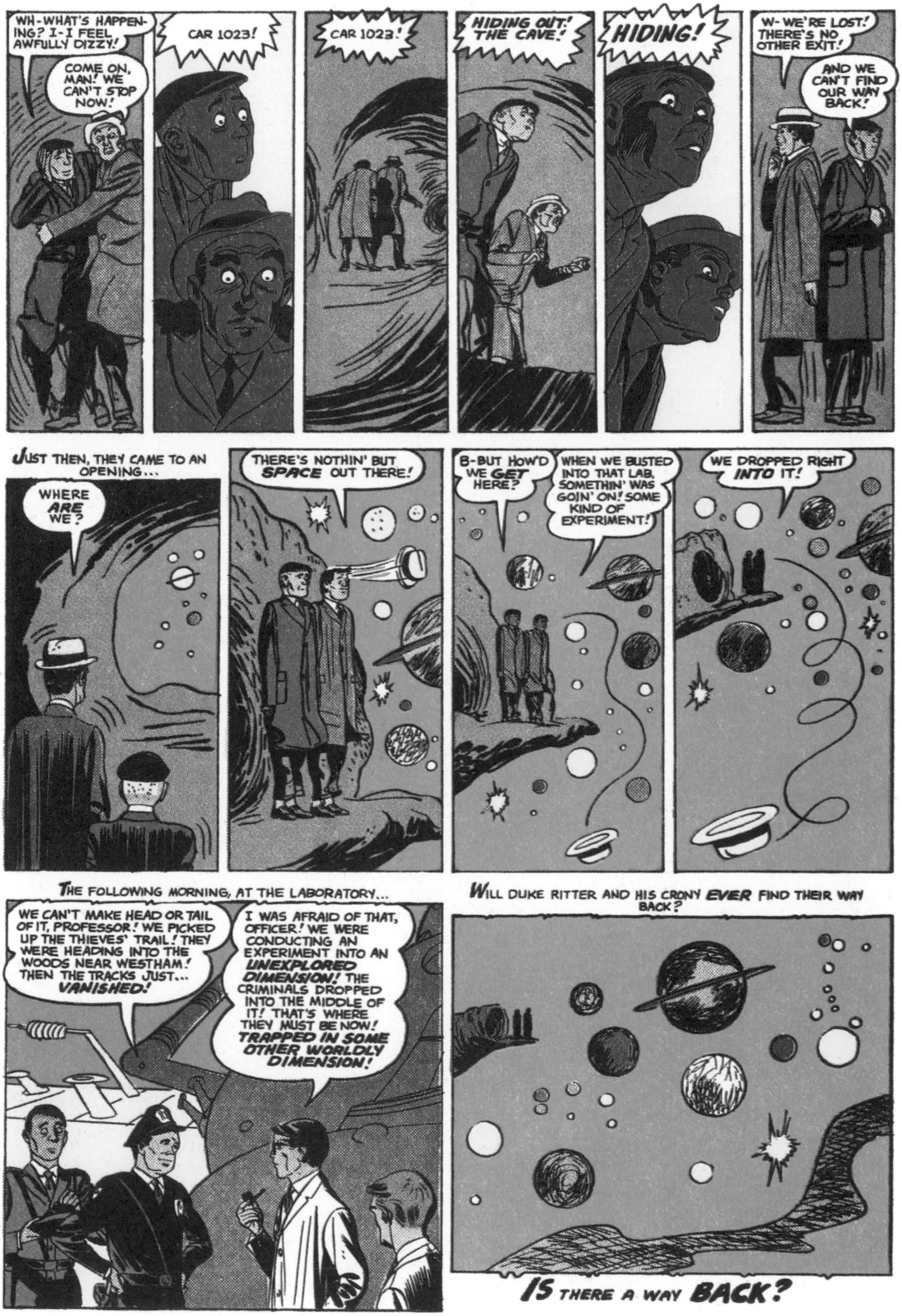
WH-WHAT'S HAPPENING? I-I FEEL AWFULLY DIZZY!
COME ON, MAN! WE CAN'T STOP NOW!
CAR 1023!
CAR 1023!
HIDING OUT! THE CAVE!
HIDING!
W-WE'RE LOST! THERE'S NO OTHER EXIT!
AND WE CAN'T FIND OUR WAY BACK!
JUST THEN, THEY CAME TO AN OPENING...
WHERE ARE WE?
THERE'S NOTHIN' BUT SPACE OUT THERE!
B-BUT HOW'D WE GET HERE?
WHEN WE BUSTED INTO THAT LAB, SOMETHIN' WAS GOIN' ON! SOME KIND OF EXPERIMENT!
WE DROPPED RIGHT INTO IT!
THE FOLLOWING MORNING, AT THE LABORATORY...
WE CAN'T MAKE HEAD OR TAIL OF IT, PROFESSOR! WE PICKED UP THE THIEVES' TRAIL! THEY WERE HEADING INTO THE WOODS NEAR WESTHAM! THEN THE TRACKS JUST... VANISHED!
I WAS AFRAID OF THAT, OFFICER! WE WERE CONDUCTING AN EXPERIMENT INTO AN UNEXPLORED DIMENSION! THE CRIMINALS DROPPED INTO THE MIDDLE OF IT! THAT'S WHERE THEY MUST BE NOW! TRAPPED IN SOME OTHER WORLDLY DIMENSION!
WILL DUKE RITTER AND HIS CRONY EVER FIND THEIR WAY BACK?
IS THERE A WAY BACK?

HE FLITTED THROUGH THE DARKNESS, A SHADOW HIM-
SELF! A MENACING FIGURE WITHOUT HUMAN FEAR OR
HUMAN WEAKNESS! NO WONDER THEY QUAILED BEFORE...

THE PHANTOM OF THE FARM!

BETTER BANK THIS IN THE MORNING, JED! YOU DON'T KNOW WHO CAN PASS DURING THE NIGHT!

I'M NOT WORRIED, MR. CARTER! BESIDES, THIS MONEY'S NOT FOR *BANKING!* IT'S TO PAY OFF PERSONAL DEBTS!

WELL, MADIGAN?

THE EDITORS GUARANTEE THAT THIS IS ONE OF THE MOST *ASTONISHING* STORIES YOU'VE EVER READ!

THE FARMER'S SELLIN' HIS CROP... A NICE, FAT CROP FOR A NICE, FAT PRICE! I'M THINKIN' HOW NICE HIS MONEY WOULD FEEL IN *OUR* POCKETS!

B. Krigstein

TWO YEARS AGO THIS FARM WAS DESTROYED BY A CYCLONE! EVERYTHING STANDING WAS SMASHED! THE ROOF OVER OUR HEAD...GONE...

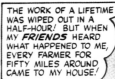

THE WORK OF A LIFETIME WAS WIPED OUT IN A HALF-HOUR! BUT WHEN MY *FRIENDS* HEARD WHAT HAPPENED TO ME, EVERY FARMER FOR FIFTY MILES AROUND CAME TO MY HOUSE!

THEY BROUGHT *THIS! CASH!* IT'S TAKEN ME TWO YEARS OF TOIL TO DO IT...BUT AT LAST I CAN PAY 'EM ALL BACK...THE WAY THEY PUT HELP IN MY HAND! *IN CASH!*

I UNDERSTAND, JED! THE BEST OF LUCK!

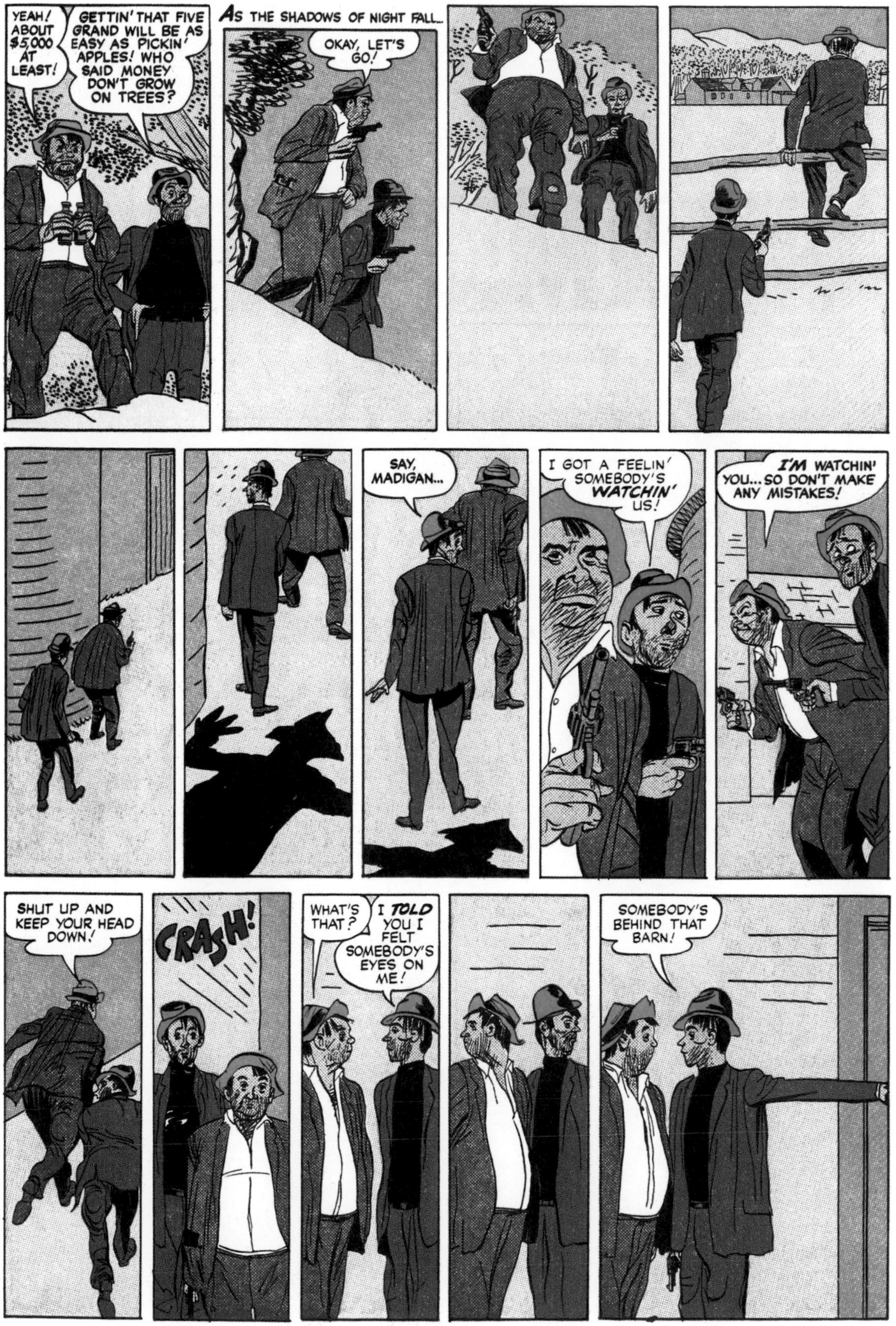
YEAH! ABOUT $5,000 AT LEAST!
GETTIN' THAT FIVE GRAND WILL BE AS EASY AS PICKIN' APPLES! WHO SAID MONEY DON'T GROW ON TREES?
AS THE SHADOWS OF NIGHT FALL...
OKAY, LET'S GO!
SAY, MADIGAN...
I GOT A FEELIN' SOMEBODY'S WATCHIN' US!
I'M WATCHIN' YOU... SO DON'T MAKE ANY MISTAKES!
SHUT UP AND KEEP YOUR HEAD DOWN!
CRASH!
WHAT'S THAT?
I TOLD YOU I FELT SOMEBODY'S EYES ON ME!
SOMEBODY'S BEHIND THAT BARN!

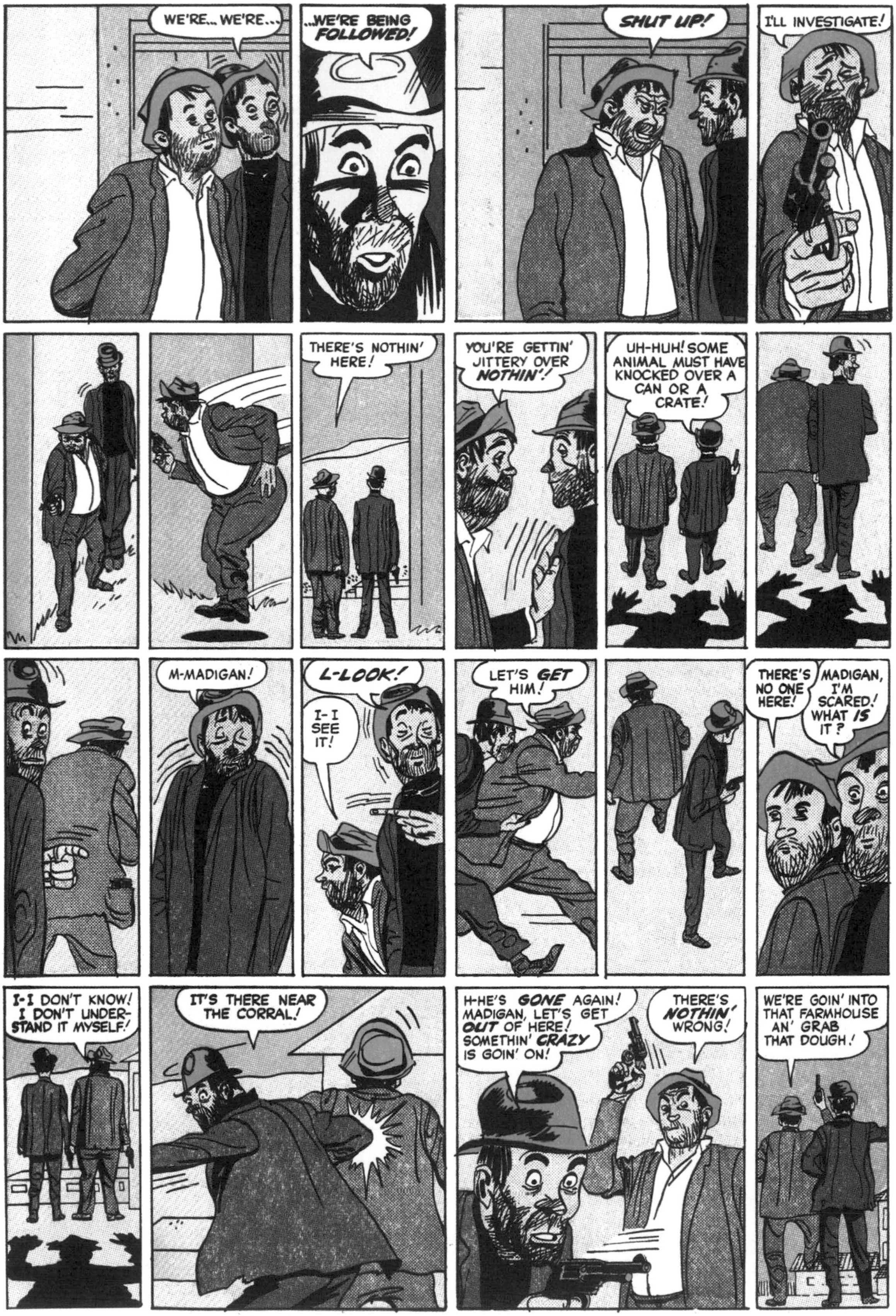

WE'RE... WE'RE...
...WE'RE BEING FOLLOWED!
SHUT UP!
I'LL INVESTIGATE!
THERE'S NOTHIN' HERE!
YOU'RE GETTIN' JITTERY OVER NOTHIN'!
UH-HUH! SOME ANIMAL MUST HAVE KNOCKED OVER A CAN OR A CRATE!
M-MADIGAN!
L-LOOK!
I-I SEE IT!
LET'S GET HIM!
THERE'S NO ONE HERE!
MADIGAN, I'M SCARED! WHAT IS IT?
I-I DON'T KNOW! I DON'T UNDERSTAND IT MYSELF!
IT'S THERE NEAR THE CORRAL!
H-HE'S GONE AGAIN! MADIGAN, LET'S GET OUT OF HERE! SOMETHIN' CRAZY IS GOIN' ON!
THERE'S NOTHIN' WRONG!
WE'RE GOIN' INTO THAT FARMHOUSE AN' GRAB THAT DOUGH!

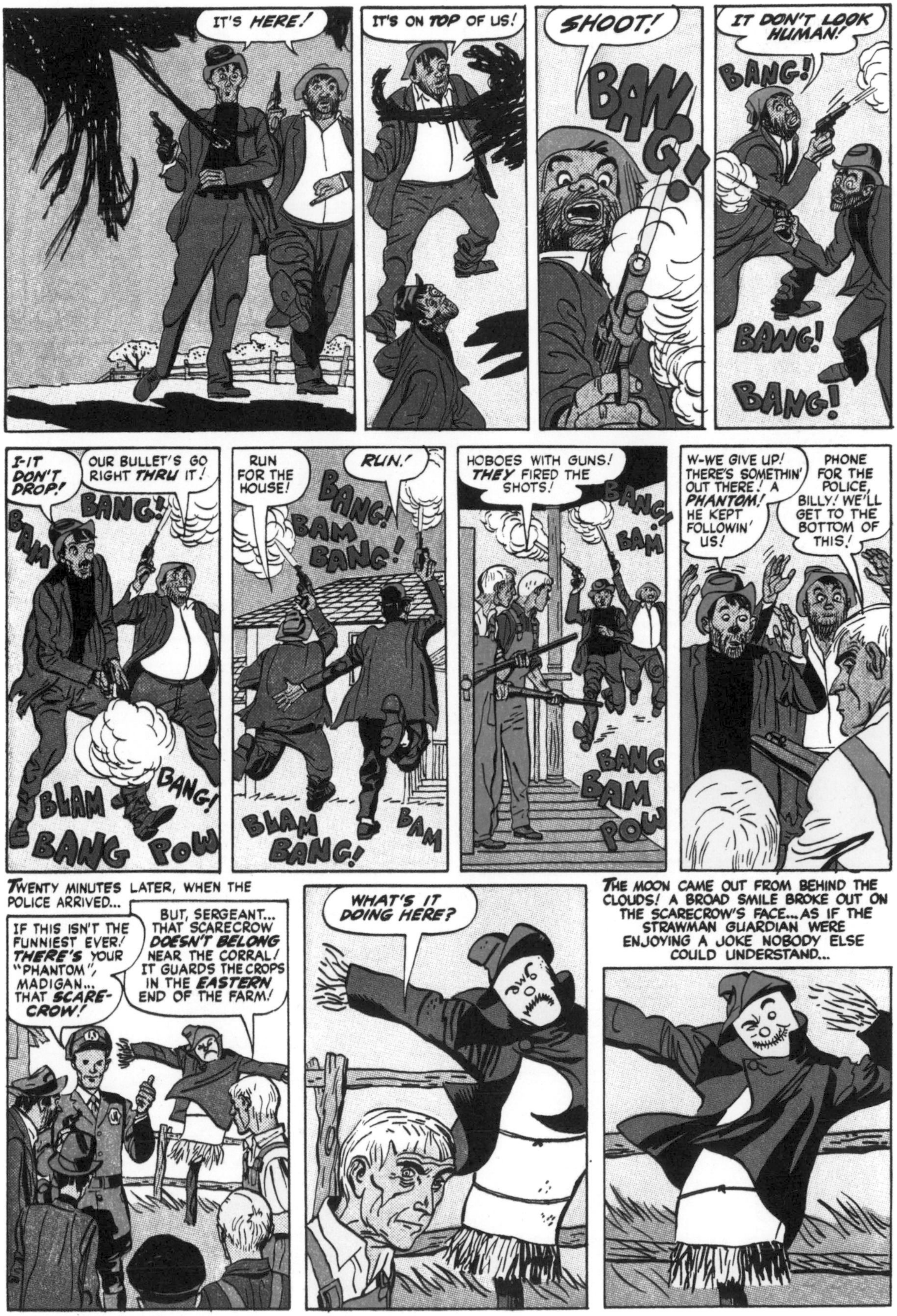
IT'S HERE!
IT'S ON TOP OF US!
SHOOT!
BANG!
IT DON'T LOOK HUMAN!
BANG!
BANG!
BANG!
I-IT DON'T DROP!
OUR BULLET'S GO RIGHT THRU IT!
BAM
BANG!
BLAM
BANG!
BANG
POW
RUN FOR THE HOUSE!
RUN!
BANG!
BAM
BANG!
BLAM
BANG!
BAM
HOBOES WITH GUNS! THEY FIRED THE SHOTS!
BANG!
BAM
BANG
BAM
POW
W-WE GIVE UP! THERE'S SOMETHIN' OUT THERE! A PHANTOM! HE KEPT FOLLOWIN' US!
PHONE FOR THE POLICE, BILLY! WE'LL GET TO THE BOTTOM OF THIS!
TWENTY MINUTES LATER, WHEN THE POLICE ARRIVED...
IF THIS ISN'T THE FUNNIEST EVER! THERE'S YOUR "PHANTOM", MADIGAN... THAT SCARE-CROW!
BUT, SERGEANT... THAT SCARECROW DOESN'T BELONG NEAR THE CORRAL! IT GUARDS THE CROPS IN THE EASTERN END OF THE FARM!
WHAT'S IT DOING HERE?
THE MOON CAME OUT FROM BEHIND THE CLOUDS! A BROAD SMILE BROKE OUT ON THE SCARECROW'S FACE...AS IF THE STRAWMAN GUARDIAN WERE ENJOYING A JOKE NOBODY ELSE COULD UNDERSTAND...

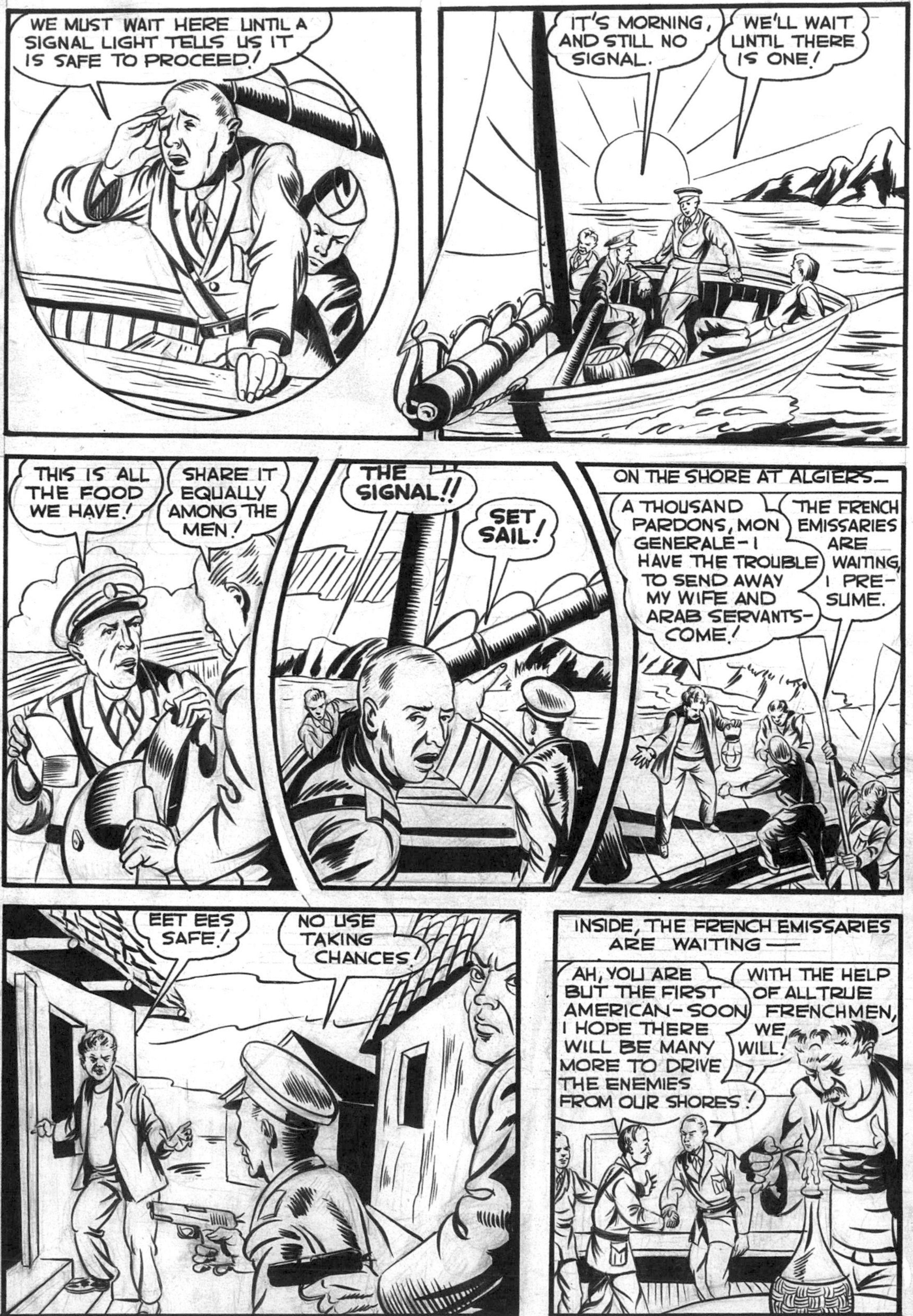
WE MUST WAIT HERE UNTIL A SIGNAL LIGHT TELLS US IT IS SAFE TO PROCEED!
IT'S MORNING, AND STILL NO SIGNAL.
WE'LL WAIT UNTIL THERE IS ONE!
THIS IS ALL THE FOOD WE HAVE!
SHARE IT EQUALLY AMONG THE MEN!
THE SIGNAL!!
SET SAIL!
ON THE SHORE AT ALGIERS—
A THOUSAND PARDONS, MON GENERALE - I HAVE THE TROUBLE TO SEND AWAY MY WIFE AND ARAB SERVANTS - COME!
THE FRENCH EMISSARIES ARE WAITING, I PRESUME.
EET EES SAFE!
NO USE TAKING CHANCES!
INSIDE, THE FRENCH EMISSARIES ARE WAITING —
AH, YOU ARE BUT THE FIRST AMERICAN - SOON I HOPE THERE WILL BE MANY MORE TO DRIVE THE ENEMIES FROM OUR SHORES!
WITH THE HELP OF ALL TRUE FRENCHMEN, WE WILL!
May All New P. 39

Notes and Original Art

1. Page 6 "Buck Saunders and His Pals," *Prize Comics* 34, **Sept. 1943; all stories restored from an original comic book unless otherwise noted**

Classically trained artist Bernard Krigstein (1919-1990) entered the lowly field of comic book illustration out of financial necessity. In mid-1942, two years after he graduated from Brooklyn College with a Bachelor of Fine Arts degree, he was struggling as both a painter and a commercial artist. He found employment as an art teacher and painter for the Arts Project of the WPA, but its funding had been cut off in late 1941 following America's entry into World War II. Realizing he would soon be drafted into the military, Krigstein wanted to leave some money with his wife Natalie before he was shipped overseas, but apart from a few odd jobs (house painter, welder, etc.), there was little work to be found.

Aware of his predicament, Krigstein's cousin Esther Rubenstein told him about the princely sums her then-husband Jerry Gale was making as staff writer for Bernard Baily's comic book studio, one of several in the Times Square area that created content for publishers. Rubenstein arranged for Gale to introduce her cousin to Baily; after showing his samples, Krigstein was hired on the spot. Initially given entrance chores (erasing pencils, filling in blacks, inking backgrounds), he soon graduated to full art duties.

This "Buck Saunders" example is one of several Krigstein installments of the *Prize Comics* feature made before his Army induction. In 1987, armed with a group of comic books, John Benson visited Krigstein and his wife at their Queens apartment to verify some unsigned work. When he came to this story, they had the following exchange:

John Benson: How long did you work for Prize?

Bernard Krigstein: Well, that was when I worked for Bernie Baily. He was the guy who was the agent at Prize. It seems to me about a year. Well, this looks a little familiar to me.

Benson: This is dated September 1943, which would mean that it was done in May or June.

Natalie Krigstein: You were in the Army two and a half years, and you came out in October 1945. So you went in the Spring of '43.

Krigstein: OK, so then I could easily have done this as one of the last stories.

Natalie: Did you ever ink for Baily?

Krigstein: I used to ink my own stories for him. But there are things in here that also make

me think it's possible that there's another hand in the inking. I wouldn't do this. I wouldn't ink these blacks on both sides, like that, both sides of a form [*page 2, panel 3*]. So that makes me feel a little doubtful about that. Though it's possible that I did do that; this is supposed to be a night scene. Also, there's some very fine feathering. I don't know if I was working in such fine feathering at that time. But a few of the things have very fine feathering. That hand is sort of betwixt and between good and bad. That's where I may have been at that time. The way these are drawn kind of makes me feel sympathetic to them. I'm sure there was another inking hand in this. It's amazing that you could pick these stories out of the bin. I think it's probably mine—I think it's very probably mine. This kind of a composition [*page 5, panel 6*]...

Natalie: Composition?

Krigstein: Well, it came so naturally. This is, I think, characteristic of me [*page 6, top*]. It's a cute story [*laughs*].

Natalie: You mean the writing?

Krigstein: Well, everything. I would like to claim this guy jumping up in the air [*last page, panel 1*]. Well, I think I did this story. This is very much like what I would do, very much [*last page, panel 4*]. The mist rising above the waterfall there is a nice composition [*last page, panel 2*]. I hope I thought of it. I think I did do it. There's a lot in there that makes me think I did it, but, again, I think there was another inking hand somewhere in there. It may have been that I left the story unfinished because I was drafted into the Army...There are a lot of nice touches in there. I hope I'm not being too cavalier in claiming these things. Absolutely, there are things in there that are characteristic of my approach. Oh, you know who may have inked some of that stuff? Bernie Baily himself, that fine feathering. Very possible.

2. Page 14 "The Accursed Diamond," *Treasure Comics* 5, **Feb.–March 1946**

While in the Army, Krigstein was struck by comics' popularity among the servicemen—everyone seemed to be reading them—and he discovered the two great influences of his early period: the team of Joe Simon and Jack Kirby, and

Editor's note: All Krigstein quotes taken from a 1963 interview with John Benson and Bhob Stewart, and later (1969-89) Benson correspondence and interviews, including a joint session from the early 1970s with Art Spiegelman. Without the work of these three pioneering comic book historians, we'd be left with very little of Krigstein in his own words.

Opposite: *All-New Short Story Comics* no. 3, May 1943. Original art to page four of "Trail Blazing to Victory" (Courtesy of Allan Bourne)

Mort Meskin ("Nobody talks about Meskin's work. He was the most brilliant inker").

On the very day of his discharge in October 1945, Krigstein returned to Baily's shop and was given "The Accursed Diamond." After turning it in, he received encouragement from Baily staffer Charles Voight, a veteran strip cartoonist from the newspaper Golden Age:

> To my utter astonishment, Baily told me that Voight had praised it very much when he saw it. And I hadn't thought it had any quality, you know. But I enjoyed doing that dumb story very much.

Krigstein remained at Baily's for about a year, appearing in several issues of *Treasure Comics* for Prize Publications, where his early heroes Meskin and Simon & Kirby were also contributing. In the mid-1940s he left Baily for packager Lloyd Jacquet's Funnies, Inc., then became a freelancer for the rest of his career. In 1947 he settled in at Fawcett Publications, doing hundreds of pages for *Nyoka the Jungle Girl* and *Golden Arrow*—important experience, as he related to John Benson and Bhob Stewart:

> These were 32-page stories appearing monthly. I believe I handled the chore almost single-handedly, including the covers. I never signed them; they were hack work of the purest distillation. But they were fun, and helped me learn my trade.

Nyoka the Jungle Girl vol. 3 no. 13, Nov. 1947 ("The Human Leopard")

Krigstein tackled this large amount of work to pay for his family's recent medical expenses. Natalie Krigstein had become severely ill and bedridden for almost a year after the birth of their son, Paul, who was sickly from the start and would die at the age of sixteen months.

By the late 1940s, Krigstein put his painting career on hold and began giving his comics the care and respect typically reserved for fine art and serious illustration.

> I found that comics was *drawing*, and it became the only serious field for me at that time. As far as the germinating of ideas and style goes, my time in comics was the most artistically productive, because of the drawing and composition. I became no longer embarrassed about the so-called limitations, of working in black and white and so forth; I shed all criticisms of the form as I worked in it.

Krigstein began moving into his mature period with three stories published in late 1948. On two of these, "The Iron Octopus," for Hillman, and "The Man with the Golden Hand," for Ray Hermann, his pencils were ruined by the industry's practice of employing inking "specialists," whose main qualification seems to have been the speed with which they accomplished their task. Although the third story, "Eugene Vidocq...First Great Detective" (*Justice Traps the Guilty* 8, Jan.–Feb. 1949), had a more sensitive inker, Krigstein became increasingly resentful at having his intricate pencil drawings compromised by outside hands.

3. Page 20 "Conning the Confidence Man," *Justice Traps the Guilty* 10, June 1949

Justice Traps the Guilty featured an impressive artist roster, including Simon & Kirby (who edited and packaged the title for Prize), Mort Meskin, and Jerry Robinson. Being in their company inspired Krigstein to create work of comparable quality, and to begin to discover the potential of graphic narrative.

Krigstein's files included a few comic books that contained artists whose technique he would study to help him advance both artistically and professionally. Among these were two 1948 *Feature Books* featuring Alex Raymond's *Rip Kirby* (Krigstein had written "Comics Art" on both covers). Some of Raymond's sophistication rubbed off on "Conning the Confidence Man," Krigstein's second and last

Patches no. 9, Aug. 1947 ("Taxi Mister?") Pencils by Mort Leav, inks by Krigstein.

inking on the last page). Still, there is prime evidence we are now in mature Krigstein territory: rich characterizations, advanced breakdowns, authentic costuming, a firm grasp of design and spatial relationships, and the integrity of anatomic details (i.e., the subtle shifts of the heads and expressive hands drawn in true foreshortened perspectives), all of which would reach greater heights over the next decade.

A rare female comics publisher, Ruth Hermann kept her gender concealed from her readers with the masculine pseudonym "Ray." She began in comics in the early 1940s as secretary to publisher Frank Temerson (who published the Continental line of comics among other imprints). By the end of the decade Hermann had her own line of comic books under the banner of Orbit Publications and various off-shoots thereof. She took an interest in the editing and writing, particularly in her romance title, *Love Diary*, where she handled its lovelorn letter column, "Frankly Speaking," and contributed cautionary text features such as "Girls Who Go Wrong," and "Shall I Pet?"

By all accounts warm and generous, Hermann allowed Krigstein the free use of one of her studio desks months before he started working for her. From his desk, Krigstein began to lobby for the job of inking Hermann's most prolific artist, Mort Leav, who drew many of the covers and the lead story in practically every issue of every title. Hermann relied so extensively on Leav that many incorrectly assumed he was her art director.

Convinced that Leav's inks followed his pencils too literally, Krigstein was finally given his chance on two Leav stories in *Patches* 9 (Aug 1947). He was proven right: taking on more of an embellisher's role, he gave Leav's work a visual coherence and consistency it generally lacked. Still, Leav never personally warmed to Krigstein (who years later complained to John Benson that Leav was a "cold fish"), and the collaboration ended there. About a year later, Hermann hired Krigstein as a freelance artist, allowing him to create his first distinguished body of work.

story for *Justice Traps the Guilty*. By studying Raymond, Krigstein tightened his grasp on two vital elements of black-and-white comic book graphics: clothing and drapery (the stylish dressing of figures and the design of folds and wrinkles), and advanced figure drawing, with emphasis on heads and hands to express attitude and emotion.

Raymond's influence can also be detected in Krigstein's polished inking and spotting of blacks, though in other respects the artist remains true to his own vision and avoids the clichés that plague much of Raymond's work. In contrast to the handsome and dashing Rip Kirby, Krigstein's squad chief Marvin Eldridge is a weary middle-aged cop trying to hang on until his pension kicks in; he is repeatedly shown sitting down or leaning against a support. (Eldridge is based on movie actor Barry Fitzgerald, who had recently appeared in a similar role in the 1948 movie *The Naked City*.) Moreover, while Raymond's heavy reliance on live models often made his figures look studio-posed, Krigstein's figures are always true to the nature of the script and dramatic situation. Throughout his career, the abundance of gesture and anatomical detail reveal countless nuances of character and emotion, underscoring his powers of observation, technical skill, and control.

4. Page 29 "The Mistake," *Wanted* 21, July 1949

Krigstein had been signing his work as "B.B. Krig" by this time, and the absence of a signature leads one to suspect he did not ink this entire story (another giveaway is the sloppy

5. Page 36 "Double Trouble," *The Westerner* 22, Aug. 1949

Five of Krigstein's twelve Ray Hermann stories featured cowboy sidekick Nuggets Nugent, and he obviously enjoyed tackling these knockabout farces. Their hamminess owes much to Leav, who created the model for the series, but the similarity ends there. Unlike Leav (considered one of the

A daily episode of *Pepper Young's Family*, an unsold 1949 syndicated strip based on Elaine Sterne Carrington's popular radio soap opera.

field's better artists), Krigstein displayed an unprecedented understanding of classical technique, with its emphasis on form, simplicity, proportion, and restraint. Treating the narratives as legitimate artistic endeavors, he drew on his training and experience to intimately fashion the Western settings and inhabitants, while conceiving each panel as an individual work of art. As he stated during a conversation with John Benson and Art Spiegelman:

> The panel has to exist by itself, otherwise the integrity of the art is in jeopardy. Until the artist arrives at the point where he realizes that by drawing a single panel he has a single work of art that exists by itself as a single statement which can live by itself, only then can all the panels live together. And then you reach a totality that is completely out of the realm of the infantile kind of continuities that comics are filled with.
>
> Each panel must exist by itself. And the thing that makes a comic page different from every other day in the year is that each of these different works of art, at the same time as they have a totally individual life of their own, also exist as a total group, as a unit. This was my inspiring motivation in doing comics. If you can pull out your panel and frame it, exhibit it as a panel, and then have the reader unconscious of that as he's reading the totality, then you've done something, in my estimation. You've raised comic book art to the level of Goya, if you can achieve that.

6. Page 42 "Liar," *Love Diary* 2, Oct. 1949

Even at this early stage of his career, Krigstein was adapting his drawing style to suit each story's subject matter. In contrast to Nuggets Nugent's bright over-the-top antics, Krigstein's romance work for Hermann has a quiet understated sentiment, well-suited to its romantic theme. Tasteful and reserved, subtle body positioning and hand gestures convey character and emotion.

7. Page 50 "Magician of Murder Creek," *The Westerner* 23, Oct. 1949

Krigstein's powers of gesture and expression propel this entertaining Nuggets narrative, with his characters inter-

acting naturally and convincingly. Dog sidekick Geronimo's aping of his master's reactions are later mirrored by Nugent's canine transformation on page five, a sequence that climaxes with the sixth panel's mock pietà.

8. Page 57 "One Way Street," *Wanted* 24, Jan. 1950

Krigstein's style shifts again in this raucous Ray Hermann crime yarn. In the earlier "Liar," he had used conservative, squared-off panel designs framing well-lit illustrations; here the graphics turn angular and threatening, heavily laden with solid blacks and dramatic lighting. The overall effect is grotesque and disturbing, characteristics that return often to Krigstein's work.

9. Page 64 "Death of Nuggets Nugent," *The Westerner* 26, April 1950

Here Krigstein was given a crack at the title's hero, Wild Bill Pecos, whom he imparts with a quiet determination, not allowing him to break into a smile until he discovers Nuggets Nugent still alive. The art showcases Krigstein's virtuosity at figure drawing, with bodies circling one another in near-balletic fashion, reaching a climax on the last page with a multi-figured full-tiered silent panel depicting the reunited duo giving their adversaries a thorough thrashing.

Though Krigstein had become the most accomplished artist on Hermann's staff, he could see there was little room for advancement, with the two Morts—Leav and Lawrence—entrenched as the company's star artists. Gradually curtailing his assignments, he drew his last story for Hermann in early 1950.

10. Page 71 "The World's Strangest Shuffle," *Real Clue Crime Stories* v5 n6, Aug. 1950

Unlike Ray Hermann, Hillman editor Ed Cronin did not initially allow Krigstein to ink his pencils, and he watched helplessly as story after story was butchered by staff artists. While Krigstein enjoyed the challenging scripts at Hillman (which employed some of the better writers in the business), he routinely complained to Cronin about the company's inking practices. This ongoing dispute led the pair to talk for hours about the art of comics, even knocking around the idea of adapting Shakespeare. Only after Krigstein threatened to quit did Cronin relent and allow him to do his own inking, prompting the artist to leave Ray Hermann for good and concentrate solely on his Hillman work.

Photostats of penciled panels to "The One and Only Tex" (*All-Time Sports* vol. 2 no. 7, Oct.–Nov. 1949), a story later inked by a Hillman staff artist. In the late 1950s, Krigstein whited-out the balloons to use the images as samples for illustration work.

There was a sizable four-month gap between "The World's Strangest Shuffle" and Krigstein's previous Hillman story. In fact, he did only one comics story dated between May and August 1950: "Mystery of the Missing Train" (*The Westerner* 27, June 1950), his last for Hermann. This was due to his separate career as a fine artist (which assumed less importance as his interest in comics grew) and his involvement with a proposed syndicated strip, *Pepper Young's Family*. After completing twelve sample dailies, however, Krigstein felt limited by the episodic nature of the strip form and he was almost relieved that it was not accepted:

> Extended dramatic development…is what really always interested me in comics—the fact that one could develop a dramatic idea,

more or less like a play. And it would be kind of absurd to have a one-page serial of a dramatic play appear, say, every week. That's the sort of inhibition that existed for me.

He returned to comic books with heightened purpose on "The World's Strangest Shuffle," and continued his immersion without a break for the next six years.

The story chronicles the final weeks of spoiled playboy and murderer Harold Lowe, who chooses suicide rather than facing his just deserts. While Krigstein found inspiration in both plays and literature, his love of motion pictures infuses this work; it displays "production values" worthy of a big-budget Hollywood movie with leads patterned after screen stars Joan Crawford and Robert Montgomery.

EVERYONE KNOWS CRIME DOESN'T PAY BUT JOHN K MEREDITH, AN AMBITIOUS CONFIDENCE MAN, WENT OUT OF HIS WAY TO PROVE THE OLD AXIOM. IN FACT, IF THE FBI HADN'T CAUGHT HIM, HE MIGHT HAVE GONE DOWN ON RECORD AS THE ONLY CONFIDENCE MAN IN HISTORY WHO WAS FORCED INTO BANKRUPTCY, BUT NOW, LET US JOIN MEREDITH ON AN UNHAPPY DAY IN 1945.....

The script of this unsavory melodrama offered the psychological depth Krigstein had been hoping for. At the penultimate page's climax, a "crane shot" moves back to reveal the vast and impersonal train yards; Lowe is barely noticed in the foreground, a man rendered insignificant by implacable fate. His attempt to "cheat fate"—by choosing death on his own terms—only serves to bring about the final judgment he assumed fate had passed on him.

Although Krigstein believed that the comics medium was capable of achieving expression equal to that of any fine art, he would have a difficult time convincing others. His greatest obstacle was the industry itself, comfortably raking in millions of adolescent dimes by issuing sensationalistic titles with rudimentary plots. At this point still optimistic for the medium and proud of his achievement, with this story he forever discarded the "B.B. Krig" pen name and unveiled the signature previously reserved exclusively for his paintings: *B. Krigstein*.

11. Page 79 "Now I Can Die Easy..." *Crime Detective* v2 n4, Sept.–Oct. 1950

This Hillman tale demonstrates Krigstein's ability to rise to the occasion whenever handed a top-drawer script. Revolving around three gangsters and a host of well-defined incidental players, this entertaining yarn focuses primarily on cheap thug Benny Asley—remarkably virtuous for a thief and murderer—who is brought to life by Krigstein with great sympathy and humor. The artist examines details that would normally have been passed over were it not for the story's relatively luxurious length—nine pages—the most Krigstein was ever allotted during his peak years in comics.

12. Page 88 "The Highwayman," *All True Crime* 42, Jan. 1951; shot from photostats; recolored by Marie Severin

Testing the freelance waters, Krigstein took a break from Hillman for about two months, during which time he drew his first three stories for publisher Martin Goodman's Atlas Comics, edited by Stan Lee. During this period Krigstein had been gradually pulling back from his use of chiaroscuro (the pictorial representation of light and shade), using black solely to create abstract design shapes, relying on color to saturate the remaining forms. While inspiring some powerful imagery, the long-winded Atlas scripts of the time sent Krigstein scurrying back to Hillman.

"The Highwayman" is the first story in this volume recolored by original EC colorist Marie Severin. To prepare the art, original photostats and silverprints were scanned, enlarged, and printed as line art on 11 × 15-inch sheets, then watercolored by Severin, re-scanned, and digitally cleaned up.

13. Page 95 "Blacksmith Belle Malone," *Dead Eye Western* v2 n3, April–May 1951

Returning to Hillman, in this story Krigstein distills his drawings to pure linear expression, completely eliminating shadows and solid black areas, working with color to achieve an iridescence worthy of stained glass.

Several restorations were made to this story's opening page, thanks to a photostat of the pencils found in Krigstein's files. A Hillman blurb had been pasted over the lower left area of the published splash panel, obscuring artwork and, most likely, Krigstein's original signature (the awkward placement of the signature turned on its side leads to that assumption). The photostat of the covered area was digitally "inked" and placed in position.

An additional problem also needed attention. Because this story began the issue, the bottoms of the first two panels had been trimmed to allow room for the publisher's indicia. These have also been restored from the aforementioned photostat, unveiling page one in its entirety.

14. Page 103 "Monster of the Seas," *Airboy* v8 n4, May 1951; shot from photostats; recolored by Marie Severin

Black shapes return to Krigstein's compositions, but are held back almost exclusively until the last page. The art teems with humanity—over a hundred distinctive figures (not to mention a gorilla) swarm through the seven-page narrative. Detailed compositions are accentuated by varied perspectives and tilted planes, set in motion by the impressive splash panel of two ships engaging in combat.

This is one of two complete Hillman photostats found in Krigstein's files, an indication that both were personal favorites (the other, "Black Silver Heart," immediately follows). The story saw print as "Captain Splint's Hairy Helper," but the more dignified original title discovered on Krigstein's photostat has been inserted.

15. Page 110 "Black Silver Heart," *Dead-Eye Western* v2 n4, June–July 1951; shot from photostats; recolored by Marie Severin

"Black Silver Heart" is Krigstein's shining moment at Hillman. Never before had he drawn with such bravura, or invented characterizations so robust. His calligraphic line and unorthodox compositions display an impressive clarity and spatial depth, reflecting his love of the Oriental masters. The opening splash panel is crowded with humanity—22 figures—and the story makes effective use of extreme close-ups, adding to his arsenal of effects. Powerful breakdowns, daring graphic design, sophisticated costuming, and the sheer vitality of his characters all demonstrate Krigstein at his most inspired.

"Black Silver Heart" is the apogee of Krigstein's color-saturated open line style at Hillman. When he felt he had mastered a particular approach, he abandoned it and moved on to the next challenge. His later Hillman work relies more heavily on black areas and ventures into darker textures, as displayed in our next entry.

16. Page 117 "The Kid Talks Tough," *Western Fighters* v4 n2, Jan. 1952

Krigstein singled out this story in his 1963 interview with John Benson and Bhob Stewart: "Cronin gave me very

Opposite: *Real Clue Crime Stories* vol. 4 no. 10, Dec. 1949. Photostat of pencils to page one of "$22,000 Worth of Wheelbarrows," later inked by a Hillman staff artist.

good stories. I remember a Western I did for him where I made some changes in the script. The story had a gun battle on a wooden pathway across a muddy street; that's all I remember about it."

Krigstein was given greater freedom by Ed Cronin than by any of his other editors, and as a result his Hillman period can be seen as his purest and most personal:

> I remember that when I worked for Cronin... [the stories] were not written perfectly for the artist, but I could still manipulate the panels. And I remember rewriting panels, and it was permissible, it was very acceptable. So therefore I never felt chained.

In the printed comic's opening page, Krigstein's signature, unusually, consists of his full name hastily written under panel three. This is due to his original signature once again being covered by a blurb on the splash panel. Using the artist's first-page photostat, his signature (and the art behind it) has been restored to its proper place.

17. Page 123 "Going My Way?" *Marvel Tales* 107, June 1952

Now freelancing primarily at editor Stan Lee's Atlas Comics, Krigstein at first toiled away halfheartedly on its dreary romance line, but sprung to life when moved to horror. Atlas artist Dick Ayers recalled that Stan Lee encouraged his staff to pattern their style after his personal favorite, Joe Maneely, whose work Krigstein described to John Benson as "marvelously ugly." In this and the following story he emulates Maneely's dark overworked textures, and appears to be having fun with it.

18. Page 127 "Ghoul's Gold," *Astonishing* 13, May 1952; shot from photostats; recolored by Marie Severin

Another example of Krigstein's early Atlas horror work, "Ghoul's Gold" is executed in the ersatz Gothic style typical of the era. Though he initially accepted the Atlas/Maneely house style as an artistic exercise, by the end of 1952 his work became increasingly idiosyncratic, with the style of drawing dictated solely by Krigstein's personal reaction to the script.

19. Page 131 "War Horse," *War Action* 12, March 1953; shot from photostats; recolored by Marie Severin

By this time Krigstein was experimenting with a series of different approaches. Parts of "War Horse" show the influence of Winslow Homer's Civil War illustrations, but the story lacks the consistency of Krigstein's finest work. The drawing is painfully lax in several panels, including the first head in the fifth panel of page three, and the missing back half of the second horse in the fifth panel of page five. It's likely that Krigstein briefly employed an outside inker during this time, as his very next story, "The Eagle's Brood" (*War Action* 13), is unsigned and marred by inferior ink-

ing. This dip in quality may have been caused by Krigstein's workload as president of the Society of Comic Book Illustrators (SOCBI), a failed attempt at unionizing comic book artists, writers, and letterers. Not coincidentally, its collapse in the late summer of 1953 also marks the beginning of Krigstein's greatest period.

In researching the colors for this story, Marie Severin contacted Virginia's Washington and Lee University, where Robert E. Lee served as president after the Civil War. Marie asked one of the curators for the color of Lee's horse. The reply: "Confederate gray, naturally."

20. Page 137 "Last Bullet," *Battle* 23, Nov. 1953. Delivered by Krigstein on 12/29/52 (Krigstein's job ledger begins here; from this point on, the story's delivery date will be noted); shot from photostats; recolored by Marie Severin

Alex Toth's concurrent war work at Standard Comics is strongly felt in this story, with its prominent blacks, crisp inking, and a "less is more" approach to graphics. Like Toth, Krigstein reveals much of his character's emotion through the powerful delineation of eyes and hands.

21. Page 142 "Drummer of Waterloo," *Our Army at War* 14, Sept. 1953 (delivered 3/23/53); shot from photostats; recolored by Marie Severin

Krigstein endured his most uncomfortable period in comics during his eight months at DC, as he tried to adapt to the company's slick generic house style and please imperious editor Robert Kanigher. Increasing the tension, Kanigher openly disapproved of Krigstein's union activities, delivering a speech at a SOCBI meeting dismissing the entire organization as a sham. Krigstein stated that Kanigher then proceeded to lure key members away from the union with promises of steady work, hastening the demise of the already shaky alliance. The editor fired Krigstein soon afterwards for missing a deadline and for lying about the reason (he was finishing a job for Atlas, DC's arch-rival). Kanigher summed up his feelings by noting that Krigstein "simply wasn't good enough to be needed, even for short stories." According to wife Natalie, Krigstein was then blacklisted by DC and never worked there again.

"Drummer of Waterloo" is Krigstein's most ambitious DC story (and the only one he considered worthy of photostating for his personal files). Marie Severin's recoloring is particularly welcome here, as the original comic's dark hues obscured much of the draftsmanship.

22. Page 148 "The Untouchable," *Strange Tales* 22, Sept. 1953 (delivered 2/9/53)

The graphics of "The Untouchable" bring us nearer to Krigstein's classic EC technique, which would begin in a few months. His late pre-EC Atlas stories display an advanced exploration of panel breakdown, which for the most part he was unable to continue at EC, where the editor laid out the pages. Here he mixes panel rhythms until the last page's grid of slender panels mark the protagonist's demise. Other

Opposite: Our Army at War no. 14, Aug. 1953. Original art to page five of "Minutemen of Saratoga," Krigstein's final DC story. Art courtesy of Allan Bourne. (Copyright © 2013 DC Comics)

THUS THE THREE YOUNG HORSEMEN...

BLAAM!

..GALLOPED WITH GLEAMING SWORDS...

BLHM!

...THROUGH THE BATTLE-SMOKE OF SARATOGA--AGAINST THE RED-COAT CANNONEERS OF KING GEORGE III ...

ONCE OFF YOUR HORSE, REBEL-- AND WE'LL SPLIT YOU ON A BAYONET LIKE A BARNYARD FOWL!

AYE!

YOU FORGOT, A BARNYARD FOWL HAS TEETH!

THIS BRITISH STEEL WILL EXTRACT YOUR TEETH, YANKEE ROOSTER!

CLANG!

PARRIED ME, EH? ALL YOU'VE WON FOR YOURSELF, REBEL, IS BUT ANOTHER BREATH!

CLANG!

THIS THRUST MUST FINISH HIM--OR I AM DONE!

SWISH!

notable details include the large figure walking out of the opening splash panel, and the elegant blacks, used both for shadow and as an abstract design element.

23. Page 153 "Joseph and His Brethren," *Bible Tales for Young Folk* **2, Oct. 1953 (delivered 4/27/53); shot from original art; recolored by Marie Severin.**

Conceived in a quiet pastoral style, the final Atlas story of Krigstein's pre-EC period is told without dialogue balloons, and his sense of liberation is palpable. Each panel is given an expansive rectangular picture area, each containing a fully realized graphic statement with its own distinct emotion.

Having access to the original art revealed some interesting details. We found that for the first time Krigstein used the iconic "B. Krigstein" signature that graced his EC and post-EC work. This was pasted over during production, with his credit moved to the bottom of the page. It was also discovered that the opening splash drawing continued under the pasted-over title lettering, which was reformatted and raised to provide full view of the art.

24. Page 158 "The Terrorist," *Daring Adventures* **6, May 1954 (story not listed in Krigstein's ledger)**

A rare freelance story from Krigstein's EC period, this expressionistic three-pager was the most inspired of Krigstein's three stories for St. John, with the artist naturally responding to its subversive theme.

25. Page 161 "The Flying Machine," *Weird Science-Fantasy* **23, March 1954; story by Ray Bradbury; adaptation by Al Feldstein (delivered 6/29/53); shot from silverprints; recolored by Marie Severin**

During his Hillman period, Krigstein received a phone call from Harvey Kurtzman, offering the artist a job on the EC war books he had begun editing. Knowing little about EC at the time, Krigstein declined due to their slightly lower pages rates, a decision he grew to regret. Two years later, disillusioned with Atlas and dismissed by DC, he called Kurtzman to see if his offer was still open. Even though EC had a full roster, Kurtzman convinced publisher William M. Gaines to add one last artist to his staff.

Gaines and editors Kurtzman and Al Feldstein had assembled the finest stable of artists in the history of comic books, and Natalie Krigstein could see what working there meant to her husband. "Bernie knew he was working with the best, and he was very proud of that. He felt like he belonged to this exclusive artist's club."

Krigstein's second EC assignment was a powerful adaptation of Ray Bradbury's short story "The Flying Machine." His sensitive calligraphic Eastern-influenced graphics perfectly suited the Bradbury classic. As Bhob Stewart notes, it seemed hard to believe it was adapted from a work of prose: "There is an almost perfect affinity between writer and artist; Krigstein has depicted the emotions and moods that Bradbury created with words." And Jerry Weist wrote in his 1970 fanzine *Squa Tront*, "Here was a free-flowing line that no one had ever attempted before—spontaneous in execution...free in expression, subtle and diverse in its technique and finesse." Stewart praised it as the greatest comics story of all time, and Bradbury himself was moved enough to write EC: "'The Flying Machine' is the finest single piece of art-drawing I've seen in years. Beautiful work: I was so touched and pleased."

All of the EC stories in this volume have been shot from original silverprints found in Krigstein's files. EC did not own a photostat machine and relied on silverprints from its plate maker, Chemical Engraving. These were made at the engravers from the negatives; copies were given to Marie Severin to paint the color guides, and to the editor to catch any last-minute errors. Though not as convenient as in-house photostats, silverprints captured much finer detail.

26. Page 167 "Pipe Dream," *Vault of Horror* **36, April–May 1954; story by Johnny Craig (delivered 11/6/53); shot from silverprints; recolored by Marie Severin**

Johnny Craig's evocative script inspired a graphic response in Krigstein unlike anything that preceded it, a scratchy, grimy Asian-influenced style infused with urban textures, drug-induced imagery, and disturbing bursts of violence. The supposedly juvenile medium of comics was being taken to a psychologically conflicted area some readers were not ready to experience, Marie Severin included:

> I can't remember a thing about coloring "Pipe Dream" the first time. I rushed through it because I found it so depressing. The whole subject was so *dingy* to me. I was just a kid, you know—I didn't want to know anything about *dope*. When I saw it again it brought back all these negative feelings. I suppose I shielded myself from them by doing it quickly. Now that I've lived a while I can appreciate its beauty, and I'm better equipped to color it.

27. Page 173 "The Catacombs," *Vault of Horror* **38, Aug.–Sep. 1954; story by Carl Wessler (delivered 2/17/54); shot from silverprints; recolored by Marie Severin**

Written by the newly hired Carl Wessler, this atmospheric tale of greed made an enormous impression on Krigstein, and after receiving the layout he asked editor Johnny Craig for permission to change the opening:

> The layout of the first page was entirely my idea. What was expected there was one large splash panel and one panel underneath...I made a very rough sketch of how I wanted it done. Johnny's first reaction was that he couldn't do it...then he said he'd have to discuss it with Bill...I got the OK to do it, and it was relettered. "The Catacombs" was my first exciting experiment in really splitting up panels...it was the first time I actually tried to change the pre-lettered

Opposite: Weird Science-Fantasy *no. 23, March 1954. Original art to page four of "The Flying Machine." Courtesy of Heritage Auctions. (Copyright © 2013 William M. Gaines, Agent)*

NO ONE. NOT EVEN MY WIFE, WHO WOULD THINK ME MAD WITH THE SUN. SHE THOUGHT I WAS MAKING A KITE. I ROSE IN THE NIGHT AND WALKED TO THE CLIFFS FAR AWAY. AND WHEN THE MORNING BREEZES BLEW AND THE SUN ROSE, I GATHERED MY COURAGE, EXCELLENCY, AND LEAPED. I FLEW! BUT MY WIFE DOES NOT KNOW OF IT.

WELL FOR HER, THEN. COME ALONG.

THEY WALKED BACK TO THE GREAT HOUSE. THE SUN WAS FULL IN THE SKY NOW, AND THE SMELL OF THE GRASS WAS REFRESHING. THE EMPEROR, THE SERVANT, AND THE FLIER PAUSED WITHIN THE HUGE GARDEN. THE EMPEROR CLAPPED HIS HANDS.

HO, GUARDS!

THE GUARDS CAME RUNNING...

HOLD THIS MAN.

THE GUARDS SEIZED THE FLIER...

CALL THE EXECUTIONER!

WHAT'S THIS? WHAT HAVE I DONE?

THE FLIER BEGAN TO WEEP, SO THAT THE BEAUTIFUL PAPER APPARATUS RUSTLED...

HERE IS A MAN WHO HAS MADE A CERTAIN MACHINE, AND YET HE ASKS US WHAT HE HAS CREATED. HE DOES NOT KNOW HIMSELF. IT IS ONLY NECESSARY THAT HE CREATE, WITHOUT KNOWING WHY HE HAS DONE SO, OR WHAT THIS THING WILL DO.

THE EXECUTIONER CAME RUNNING WITH A SILVER AX. HE STOOD WITH HIS NAKED, LARGE-MUSCLED ARMS READY, HIS FACE COVERED WITH A SERENE WHITE MASK...

ONE MOMENT...

THE EMPEROR TURNED TO A NEARBY TABLE UPON WHICH SAT A MACHINE THAT HE HIMSELF HAD CREATED. HE TOOK A TINY GOLDEN KEY FROM AROUND HIS OWN NECK. HE FITTED THIS KEY TO THE TINY, DELICATE MACHINE AND WOUND IT UP...

THEN HE SET THE MACHINE GOING...

4

19

HEH, HEH! YOU MORBID MEATBALLS WANT MORE, EH?
OKAY, THEN...HERE'S A SUBTERRANEAN SAGA I CALL...

The CATACOMBS

PIETRO MIUTA...

...GRABBED THE SACK WITH ITS LOAD OF SILVER...

...AND, WITH GINO ALCARI FOLLOWING...

...BROKE FOR THE FRONT DOOR!

B. Krigstein

AS THE FRIGHTENED PAIR FLED DOWN THE STREET, THE STARTLED CRIES OF THE ROBBED OLD MAN SHAT-TERED THE STILLNESS, THEN DRIFTED OFF INTO THE SILENT DARKNESS...

STOP, YOU THIEVES! STOP!

6¼ x 9

pages, which was a natural lead-in for me to do it with "Master Race."

In the ensuing pages, Krigstein subdivided certain panels "in order to get more movement and richer dramatic feeling. In other words, I multiplied the amount of action from one to two." It demonstrated the effects shared by graphic narrative and a piece of music: tonal contrasts, staccato and legato rhythms, textural colors, and as Bill Mason pointed out, "the [final] eight panels are a decrescendo into total darkness." Krigstein proved beyond question that the comic book form was capable of expressing complex situations and emotions.

28. Page 179 "Key Chain," *Crime SuspenStories* 25, Oct.–Nov. 1954; story attributed to Jack Oleck (63 panels, delivered 3/8/54); shot from silverprints; recolored by Marie Severin

In one significant respect, working at EC was limiting for Krigstein. He had always done his own panel breakdowns, but was disappointed to find that at EC the editor assumed this task. By the time the artists got the pages they had already been lettered and arranged into panels, left empty for the art. Editor Al Feldstein had no problem with Krigstein's changes as long as he kept the same page count, but Krigstein soon rebelled against this as well, constantly (and futilely) imploring Feldstein for extra pages:

> I wanted panels. I was desperate for panels. And this is what they *didn't* give me, so out of desperation I began subdividing the panels. The point came to where it was simply absurd to have six panels for a certain amount of text. I began to see 12 panels, 18 panels, in the same amount of text. I began to see people doing all sorts of things, and it became just ridiculous to have them doing all this stuff in six panels…Because it's what happens *between* these panels that's so fascinating. Look at all the dramatic action that one never gets a chance to see. Unless the artist would be permitted to delve into that, the form must remain infantile.

The last two pages of "Key Chain" are a prime example of Krigstein's multi-panel technique, but the slower paced pages leading up to them are no less impressive, as we follow the subtle actions of the protagonist deftly and methodically nursing along his scheme. It is this careful, deliberate beginning that makes the frenzy at the end all the more chilling.

"Key Chain" was created in the middle of Krigstein's high point at EC, the first six months of 1954 before the company began to unravel. As he turned in this story, editor Feldstein handed him the six-page layout to "Master Race."

29. Page 185 "Master Race," *Impact* 1, March–April 1955; story by Al Feldstein (delivered 4/5/5; shot from silverprints; recolored by Marie Severin

When Krigstein brought Feldstein's layout back to his home and began reading it, he knew he was given something exceptional, and that the six pages allotted to it were far from adequate. As he told Benson and Stewart:

> I received this six-page story and read it, and it was just the most explosive story that I had come across in my work in the field…and I persuaded Feldstein and Gaines to let me make it into an eight-page story. And I cut the thing apart and re-pasted it and relaid it out and redesigned it in order to realize my ideas of developing the breakdown of the story.

In their landmark critical evaluation, "An Examination of Master Race," John Benson, Art Spiegelman, and David Kasakove write:

> …much of the power that Krigstein brings to the story is due to his choice of a style which is the antithesis of standard comics storytelling. Instead of employing the exaggerated visual comic book phrases usually used to clearly denote action and emotion (speed lines, large beads of sweat, etc.), Krigstein uses a more objective standard of delineation. Instead of frequent close-ups, an often-used technique to get "close" to a character's feelings, Krigstein keeps a physical distance from the characters. Instead of using dramatic motion picture type lighting effects, Krigstein uses patterns of dark and light in much more abstract ways. Instead of a humanizing use of free shapes, Krigstein concentrates on using sharp angles and straight lines whenever possible. Finally, in opposition to the cartoonists's approach, there is the chilling, aloof, precise, clean rendering which is used throughout the entire story. In this contrast of the story lies the strength of Krigstein's interpretation.

In the early 1970s, John Benson and Art Spiegelman visited Krigstein at his studio to show him their evaluation. While having strong disagreements with much of it, he concurred that the story's rendering was no accident:

> I wanted this story to appear in a total light, total and beautiful and clear light. And the more clear and orderly the story, the more "objectively" done, the more the emotional content of it would have weight…I felt that the intensity of the story was best served by total clarity—total beautiful clarity.

Krigstein spent a month on the art, twice as long as usual, widely missing his deadline. After he finally delivered it to

EC, it sat around for nearly six months. Krigstein recalled, "I think they didn't know what to do with it. Every time I came into the office, I'd urge them to run it."

The story finally appeared in early 1955 in the first issue of *Impact*, part of EC's revamped "New Direction" series of titles. The company had been forced to cancel its entire line in response to public attacks on the industry's overreliance on unwholesome themes such as horror and crime. A Comics Code Authority was instituted; for a book to carry its seal of approval, the original art was subjected to inspection to prevent questionable panels (or entire stories) from going to the printer.

EC resisted the Comics Code on the premiere issues of its new titles, but it acquiesced on succeeding issues. "Master Race" went to press just in time—it would have never made it past the censors.

30. Page 193 "Murder Dream," *Tales from the Crypt* 45, Dec. 1954–Jan. 1955; story by Carl Wessler (delivered 5/5/54); shot from silverprints; recolored by Marie Severin

Al Feldstein would occasionally accommodate Krigstein's thirst for panels by beginning a Krigstein layout with a panel sequence instead of the usual large splash panel, a convention Krigstein considered superfluous. As he told Benson and Stewart, "I never liked the idea of a splash panel as a storytelling device. They serve no artistic purpose or dramatic use. There's no reason why a story can't start right out with the opening situation, instead of having a big panel first."

By this time Krigstein's mastery of the form enabled him to subconsciously visualize each story's particular graphic style and panel breakdown:

> I didn't have any method. I would think of these things as I read the script, and the characters, in my mind, simply as I was reading about them, became very rich. So that a word of dialogue was not merely an instrument to carry you from one panel to the other, but to reveal greater depth in what that sentence or word *meant*...seeing, feeling the line of dialogue and then wishing to create that with reverberations, other things, maybe even the *opposite* things from the dialogue happening, which would reveal that character more clearly. So in a sense I was participating in that story very deeply. But it was not a conscious thing. It forms itself in your mind as you're reading it; it's your training. I imagine a director reading a movie script would have the same reaction.

Apart from the opening, "Murder Dream" employs the customary six to eight panels per page, with assured draftsmanship contrasting idyllic settings against surreal visions. Though Carl Wessler's script is careful to telegraph the looming evil of the antagonist early on, one is still unprepared for the excessively cruel fate awaiting Krigstein's stylish young couple.

31. Page 199 "In the Bag," *Shock SuspenStories* 18, Dec. 1954–Jan. 1955; story by Carl Wessler (77 panels, delivered 6/14/54); shot from silverprints; recolored by Marie Severin

Dense with panels and saturated in Zip-a-Tone, this story ends Krigstein's peak EC period. Unable to withstand the moral outcry against horror and crime comics, EC canceled most of its titles by late 1954, and a year later would be out of comics for good. Krigstein hung on until the end, but after "In the Bag" he would employ panel subdivision only a handful of times and his use of tonal sheets would stop completely. The company was forced to lower its page rates from $41 to $35 a page, and Krigstein began to resent the extra work and added expense involved—especially since Gaines and Feldstein would not budge on giving him what he begged for:

> I kept approaching [Feldstein] to give me his regular manuscripts, which I thought were terrific—he had some terrific writers working for him—and I would have wanted to re-break them down in my style. In fact, I wanted to edit a book. I wanted to devote one book to a single story. And if he couldn't give me one book, I asked him to give me, say, 12 pages—just let me expand a five-page story into 12 pages and break it down in my style, because I had all these things that were seething in my mind. And then he would come back and say, 'I'll give you a five-page story, and you can break it down any way you want—within five pages.' It was ridiculous. He wanted me to subdivide it, in other words; to take a six-panel page and create a 15-panel page. Well, that was getting a lot for your money. If you get 15 panels a page, that sounds like a good proposition.

32. Page 205 "Poetic Justice," *Valor* 2, May–June 1955; story by Carl Wessler (delivered 11/12/54); shot from silverprints; recolored by Marie Severin

In this late EC masterwork, Krigstein utilizes Feldstein's conservative breakdowns to create compositions of remarkable breadth and complexity, a moving tribute to the centuries-old Eastern graphic tradition he studied and admired his entire life.

In a 1976 interview with John Benson, Harvey Kurtzman said of Krigstein, "There is no doubt that Bernie is an intense artist. Certainly he's the, I think, *the* outstanding artist in comic books. He had a feel for graphics second to nobody I can think of in the field—a sensitive, intelligent approach to comic graphics. There's no doubt about that." For sheer drawing and graphic invention, "Poetic Justice" must surely rank near the top in Krigstein's catalog.

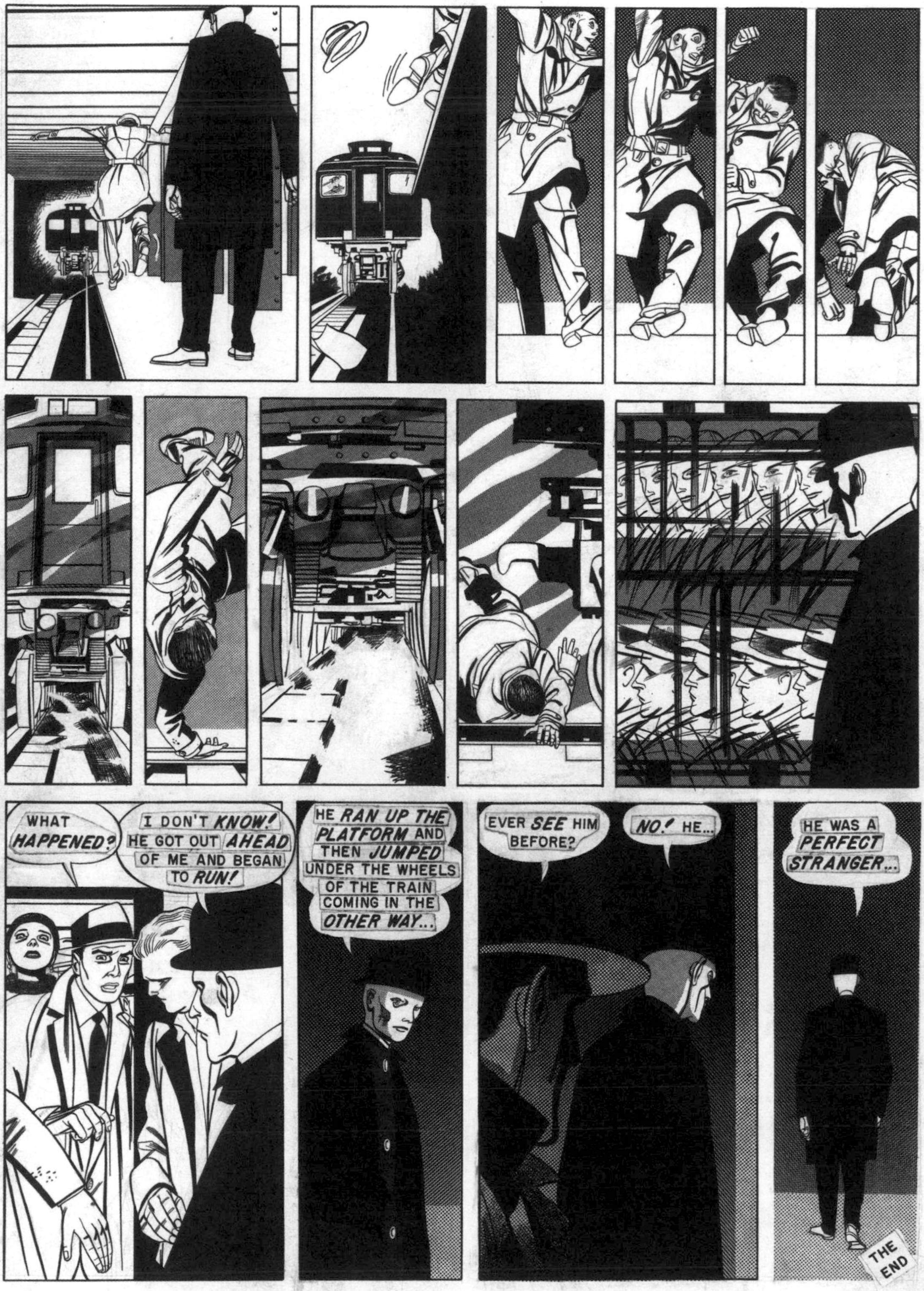

WHAT HAPPENED?
I DON'T KNOW! HE GOT OUT AHEAD OF ME AND BEGAN TO RUN!
HE RAN UP THE PLATFORM AND THEN JUMPED UNDER THE WHEELS OF THE TRAIN COMING IN THE OTHER WAY...
EVER SEE HIM BEFORE?
NO! HE...
HE WAS A PERFECT STRANGER...
THE END

M 8

Book A

SUDDENLY, EMILE LEAPED FORWARD, PULLING HIS SWORD. THIS WAS THE MOMENT HE'D BEEN WAITING FOR...

SAILORS OF FRANCE! HOW LONG WILL YOU ENDURE THE TYRANNY OF A MADMAN!? SAVE YOUR LIVES! MURDER YOUR WOULD-BE MURDERERS! SEIZE THE BON ST. LOUIS!

EMILE! HAVE YOU GONE CRAZY?! YOU'RE ASKING THEM TO MUTINY!?

EXACTLY, MY DEAR BROTHER! RISE SAILORS OF FRANCE! SAVE YOURSELVES! CUT DOWN THE OPPRESSORS! KILL! KILL!

EMILE...

THE LIEUTENANT IS RIGHT! LET'S GET THEM! THE MOMENT IS AT HAND!

THE ENRAGED AND INCITED CREW STORMED THE QUARTER DECK, AS EMILE TURNED AND RAN AN OFFICER THROUGH...

YAAAGGHHH...

IN A MOMENT, THE DECK OF THE BON ST. LOUIS WAS A SCENE OF UTTER CONFUSION. MUSKETS WERE FIRED AT CLOSE RANGE, BLOWING FACES INTO RED SMEARS. CLUBS, SWORDS, DIRKS, BELAYING PINS AND BARE HANDS TORE AT FLESH, CRUSHED BONE, AND SPLATTERED BLOOD...

EMILE SCREAMED THEM ON, FIGHTING BLINDLY. FINALLY, HE STOOD FACE TO FACE WITH HIS BROTHER, THE COUNT, CHARLES. HE RAISED HIS PISTOLS...

EMILE! NO! WAIT! YOU... YOU WOULDN'T SHOOT YOUR OWN BROTHER...

WOULDN'T I, CHARLES? I'D DO ANYTHING TO GET WHAT I WANT!

6

Piracy

Though proud to have been a part of EC, Krigstein harbored regret for the work left undone. In 1963, he told Benson and Stewart:

> If I could have expanded the material there, I felt that I could have done very new and good things. And all these years, frankly, I've been nurturing that frustration...this feeling that something tremendous could have been done if they'd let me do it.

Krigstein worked at EC for two short years, during which he forged a bold new graphic vocabulary never before attempted in the comic book medium. Despite its breakdown practices and limited amount of story pages, EC afforded him the opportunity to create sophisticated, truly adult stories. Once that window was closed, the consummate comic book artist of his day—arguably of all time—was left with his vision of what *could* be, and very few avenues to apply his craft.

33. Page 211 "Garibaldi," *Battleground* 9, Jan. 1956 (delivered 7/19/55); shot from photostats; recolored by Marie Severin

With EC's demise, Krigstein had little choice but to return to Atlas, one of the few companies left standing in the wake of the Comics Code upheaval. He took a conservative approach initially to regain a feel for his old company. "Garibaldi," his second story, has an appropriately dignified flavor, though the artist provides some exciting graphics at the climax—including a short burst of panel subdivision.

34. Page 215 "The Hypnotist," *Astonishing* 47, March 1956 (61 panels, delivered 9/19/55)

As Krigstein progressed at Atlas he grew more engaged and imaginative. This rare late-Atlas five-pager (most were four) begins with a dramatic splash introducing the cowardly Irwin Botts, pleading for his life to his own cast shadow. Like many of Krigstein's best narratives, the plot focuses on the relationship between two players, in this case Botts and the crooked hypnotist who becomes his manager. Evocative settings, vivid characterizations, and contrasting panel rhythms turn a fairly routine story into a convincing psychological roller-coaster ride:

> I thought the plots that Stan Lee was using at the time weren't that bad, but their treatment was very banal. As far as possible I tried to transcend that written treatment to bring out the idea behind the story, and to give them a lighter touch. I was really writing messages and sending them to sea in a bottle, there. Those stories were my attempt at carrying out an object lesson of how comics stories could be broken down. I used them as a medium for dramatizing the breakdown technique, to show

the limitless ways that a comics story could be unfolded. I wanted to show that the form was fluid and dynamic and should not be considered a static form.

35. Page 220 "The House that Lived," *Mystery Tales* 39, April 1956 (58 panels, delivered 11/4/55); restored from an original comic book and photostats

A gentle, good-natured touch pervades "The House that Lived." Though a repeated failure, antagonist Wilcox is painted sympathetically as an eternal optimist: he twice breaks into a spontaneous multi-paneled jig at the prospect of a new scheme.

Krigstein cultivated a looser drawing style during his late Atlas period to allow him to concentrate more fully on the layouts, telling Benson and Stewart, "I spent proportionately more time on the breakdown than the art." Though obviously not labored over, Krigstein's breakdowns, compositions, characterizations, and agile brushwork leave no doubt that a master is at work.

36. Page 224 "They Wait Below," *Uncanny Tales* 42, Jan. 1956 (75 panels, delivered 12/15/55); restored from an original comic book and photostats

At 75 panels, the four-page "They Wait Below" is the most densely paneled story of Krigstein's career. Motion lines and sound effects are employed liberally, adding an extra level of animation to the art. Krigstein used these effects with discretion; on his more conservative layouts for "Garibaldi" and "Survival" they are missing entirely.

After finishing this story, Krigstein tried to get out of comic books; with Atlas rates at $27 a page, he could barely make a living. He left in late December 1955 to work in illustration, but after a good January ($311.20) his total for the next two months was $278.55. In April he quit the commercial art field entirely to help supervise his father's Manhattan clothing factory. Eight months later, in October 1956, family squabbles led him to return to Atlas for a final four months.

37. Page 228 "Dinosaur," *Mystic* 58, April 1957 (delivered 10/7/56); shot from photostats; recolored by Marie Severin

Relieved to be out of the garment district, Krigstein returned to Atlas in October 1956 with a vengeance—doing 13 stories in two months (with the page rate now down to $23). The second story of that breathless run, the beautifully inked "Dinosaur," is one of Krigstein's most nimble post-Code efforts. The contrasting personalities of the four-member research team usher us briskly through its first three pages to its dark ending, as 19 subdivided panels penetrate into the shattered psyche of the abandoned researcher, progressing from disbelief to fear to panic to utter hopelessness.

38. Page 232 "Survival," *Navy Tales* 3, May 1957 (delivered 11/20/56); shot from photostats; recolored by Marie Severin

Opposite: *Piracy* no. 4, April–May 1955. Original art to page six of "Inheritance," one of Krigstein's finest post-Code EC stories. Art courtesy of Lars Teglbjaerg. (Copyright © 2013 William M. Gaines, Agent)

Krigstein's black-and-white graphics take center stage in this story, which embraces the traditional breakdown technique of six panels per page—though on page two he deftly breaks up the rhythm with a subdivided panel sequence.

39. Page 236 "The Last Look," *Marvel Tales* 159, Aug. 1957 (45 panels, delivered 12/19/56); shot from photostats; recolored by Marie Severin

Representing his final explorations into dynamic panel breakdown, our last three stories were done consecutively during Krigstein's final weeks in comics. "The Last Look" employs a strict quarter-note rhythm (four panels per tier), bringing a relentless drive to the murder foretold in the splash panel. Krigstein's pacing and characterizations once again transform a slight plot into a captivating narrative.

40. Page 240 "Out of this World," *Uncanny Tales* 56, Sept. 1957 (47 panels, delivered 1/8/57)

Here Krigstein builds tension by increasing panel rhythms—from page two's four-panel grid to the five-panel grid on page three, climaxing with six panels to start page four, then winding down with four, and finally two. As he explained to Benson and Stewart:

> I was striving to control these effects...building up to dramatic climaxes, and then realizing, as far as it was in my power to do so, all the emotional force of the climax. And I think I succeeded pretty well, because in groping towards something I really feel I stumbled upon an important way to tell stories, to break down stories.

41. Page 244 "The Phantom of the Farm," *World of Fantasy* 9, Dec. 1957 (51 panels, delivered 1/12/57); restored from an original comic book and photostats

Here Krigstein's page meters echo the fear and confusion of his two protagonists, with every tier but two having irregular rhythms. The varying approaches of these last three stories support his contention that the comics form was indeed fluid and dynamic.

Yet while devoting more thought to these thin plots than they certainly merited—for the lowest page rates of his career—Krigstein could not escape the editorial interference that haunted him throughout his time in comics. Standard procedure at Atlas dictated that the artist's pencilled pages be submitted for Stan Lee's approval; they were then lettered and returned to the artist for final inking. Shortly after he sent the pencils to "Phantom of the Farm," an incident occurred that convinced Krigstein to call it a day.

> I received a call from [Lee's] flunky, and was told that Stan wanted to consolidate some of the panels, and add dialogue to those panto-mime panels that I had invented. I refused

to give him permission to do so. I was told that Stan had bought the work, and since he "owned" it he could do whatever he wished with it. My answer was that Stan had been privileged to purchase publishing rights to my art, and if any changes were made, I would sue. I gave him the option of returning the work, and I think I may have been stupid enough to offer to return the money. In any case, the story was published unchanged.

Krigstein's final Atlas stories, "The Lair of the Thunder Lizard" (*Mystical Tales* 8, Aug. 57) and "The Eyes that Wouldn't Close" (*Strange Tales* 61, Feb. 58) are treated ultra-conservatively, strictly six panels to a page; he obviously wanted no more skirmishes. As fellow artist Gil Kane observed, "Krigstein was getting sick and tired of being embroiled and embattled." Despite his years of defending comics as a form worthy of serious study, it was clear that management would forever consider artists nothing more than interchangeable hirelings. To make matters worse, the Comics Code's decimation of the industry severely curtailed available work, with artists treated even more cavalierly. The insulting rate of $23 a page was a final nail in the coffin.

Krigstein left Atlas for good in January 1957, but with a lingering resentment. In 1965, when told by Benson that Stan Lee was spearheading comics' revitalization, he responded bitterly:

> I was delighted to learn that Lee has attained the status of an authority in the comics field. Twenty years of unrelenting editorial effort to suppress the artistic effort, encourage miserable taste, flood the field with degraded imitations and polluted non-stories, treating artists and writers like cattle, and failure on his part to make an independent success as a cartoonist have certainly qualified him for this respected position.

Hoping to continue as an independent, in the late 1950s and early 1960s Krigstein approached several book publishers (including Ballantine, Knopf, and Putnam) with ambitious proposals to adapt literary works to the comics form (*The Red Badge of Courage, Fahrenheit 451, The Book of Job, Treasure Island, War and Peace,* et al.). Each was met with a complete lack of interest. Unable to work without financial support, this master of pictorial narrative was forced to abandon his chosen medium at the peak of his powers.

After six ambivalent years in commercial illustration, Krigstein returned to canvas painting in 1964 and spent the rest of his career teaching at Manhattan's High School of Art & Design. One of his students recalled an occasion when his time in comics came up in conversation. Krigstein uttered, "Oh, that was years ago," and quickly changed the subject.

—G.S.

Opposite: *Valor* no. 2, May–June 1955. Original art to "Poetic Justice." Paste-ups made to comply with the Comics Code Authority (page four, panels four and five; page six, panels seven and eight) have been removed. (Art courtesy of Steven Bialek) Copyright © 2013 William M. Gaines, Agent

POETIC JUSTICE

LIVE NOW, FOR A SHORT WHILE, IN THE LONG AGO. COME BACK TO THE YEAR 1122 B.C., TO ANCIENT CHINA... TO A HAPPY LAND... A LAND OF CULTURE AND LEARNING... A LAND FILLED WITH THE LOVE OF NATURE AND THE SONGS OF THE POETS. CHINA HAS BEEN HAPPY BECAUSE IT HAS BEEN FREE, RULED BY THE LAST OF HIS LINE, THE KINDLY AND FATHERLY OLD EMPEROR, WU MING. BUT TODAY, IN *THE TEAHOUSE OF THE LOTUS BUD*, THERE IS MUCH SADNESS, FOR THE EMPEROR WU MING IS DEAD AND THE POETS SING IN MOURNING OF HIS PASSING...

THE LOTUS BLOSSOM ON THE TREE HAS BLOOMED FOR MANY GOLDEN YEARS. BUT NOW ITS PETALS, DRY, HAVE FALLEN AND WITH IT, WET, OUR SALTED TEARS.

YOUR SONG IS SWEET, CHOU PO, FOR ITS WORDS ARE THE WORDS THAT ARE IN ALL OF OUR HEARTS!

LET ME NOW READ MY SONG, MY FRIENDS...

B. Krigstein

THERE IS NO REASON FOR THE POETS THAT SIT NOW IN *THE TEAHOUSE OF THE LOTUS BUD* TO EXPECT CHINA TO CHANGE. THIS IS THE WAY IT HAS BEEN FOR CENTURIES...POETS GATHERING IN TEAHOUSES AND SINGING THEIR SONGS TO EACH OTHER...

BUT CHINA *HAS* CHANGED...*OVERNIGHT*...

UNDER *ARREST?* FOR *WHAT?* WE DID NO *WRONG!*

WE ARE POETS...

YOU HAVE VIOLATED THE *NEW EDICT* OF THE EMPEROR, *SHU WANG*, AND YOU MUST *DIE!*

THE RIVER OF TIME FLOWS ONWARD, UNENDING, AND A GRASSY BANK THAT LINES ITS SHORE IS CARRIED AWAY BY TIME'S CURRENT, UNBENDING, ONE LIFE, WORN AWAY, 'TIL IT IS NO MORE!

IN THE NAME OF THE EMPEROR, YOU ARE ALL UNDER ARREST!

1

Valor   6¼ x 9

SUDDENLY, ALL IS QUIET IN *THE TEAHOUSE OF THE LOTUS BUD*...

NEW EDICT? WE KNOW OF NO NEW EDICT!

THE EMPEROR HAS DECLARED THAT IT IS A *CRIME* FOR ANY MAN TO SIT ABOUT IDLY... TO WASTE HIS TIME READING VERSE. OUR EMPEROR MADE THAT LAW ONLY THIS MORNING...

THE POETS ARE STUNNED...

THIS MORNING! BUT THAT IS **UNREASONABLE!** WE HAVE HAD NO CHANCE TO *LEARN* OF THE NEW LAW!

SUCH A THING IS *UNHEARD OF!* OUR FATHERS HAVE SPOKEN POETRY FOR *CENTURIES!*

NEVERTHELESS, THAT IS THE LAW, AND YOU WILL ALL BE *PUNISHED*...

THE POETS ARE OUTRAGED, AND BECAUSE THEY ARE MANY AND THE GUARDS ARE FEW, THEY FLING THEMSELVES UPON THEIR OPPRESSORS...

DEATH FOR SO UNJUST A REASON!? NEVER! WE WOULD RATHER DIE *FIGHTING!*

IN THE NAME OF THE EMPEROR...

BUT THE YOUNG POET NAMED CHOU PO... A SMALL, SLENDER, SENSITIVE YOUTH...DOES NOT JOIN HIS FELLOWS IN THEIR STRUGGLE. HE REMAINS BACK AS THEY OVERWHELM THEIR WOULD-BE EXECUTORS...

WHEN THE EMPEROR'S GUARDS ARE FALLEN, THE POETS RUN FROM *THE TEAHOUSE OF THE LOTUS BUD*. THEY RUN FAR, UNTIL THERE IS NO BREATH LEFT FOR RUNNING...

AND WHEN THEY STOP, THEY TURN ANGRILY TO THE ONE CALLED CHOU PO...

WELL, CHOU! YOU ARE THE *ONLY* ONE AMONG US WHO *BEARS NO MARK!*

I DID NOT *FIGHT,* SU LING! WHAT DID YOU *GAIN* BY FIGHTING?

2

GAIN? DID YOU NOT *HEAR* CHOU?! THEY WOULD HAVE *BURIED US ALIVE!* WE HAVE GAINED OUR *FREEDOM!* OUR VERY *LIVES!*

YOUR *LIVES*, *YES*, BUT YOUR *FREEDOM*, *NO!* YOU ARE *FUGITIVES* NOW AND THE NEW EMPEROR'S LAW *STILL* HANGS ABOUT OUR NECKS!

BUT UNLESS WE *FIGHT*, IT WILL HANG ABOUT THE NECKS OF OUR *CHILDREN...* AND OUR *CHILDREN'S CHILDREN*... IF INDEED, WE *LIVE* TO HAVE WIVES AND FAMILIES!

WE *ARE* GOING TO FIGHT, CHOU...TO OUR *DEATHS*, IF WE MUST... TO *FREE* CHINA OF THIS *TYRANT!* ARE YOU *WITH* US?

IT IS WRITTEN: "DO NOT TRY TO MOVE THE MOUNTAIN. THE WAY AROUND IS FAR LESS PAINFUL." THERE ARE *HUNDREDS* OF PALACE GUARDS. YOU WILL BE *FOOLS* TO FIGHT THEM. THEY ARE BUT THE *PEBBLES*. YOU WILL *DIE IN VAIN* AND THE *MOUNTAIN* WILL *REMAIN!* NO, I WILL NOT DIE IN *VAIN!*

THE POETS ARE FURIOUS AT CHOU PO'S WORDS. THEY ORDER HIM AWAY AND INSULT HIM AND THROW STONES AT HIM...

NEVER LET US *SEE* YOU AGAIN!

YOUR NAME WILL BE AS *POISON* TO OUR LIPS!

A MAN WHO WILL NOT *FIGHT* IS *NO MAN AT ALL!*

YOU ARE A *COWARD*, CHOU PO!

SADLY, CHOU PO HURRIES AWAY...BRUISED AND HURT...

GO FIGHT, THEN! *GO DIE!* BUT WHO WILL BE LEFT TO REMIND TOMORROW'S CHILDREN THAT CHINA ONCE KNEW *FREEDOM?* WHO WILL TEACH THEM WHAT FREEDOM *MEANS?*

FOR DAYS AFTER THAT, THE POETS MEET IN SECRET. FINALLY, ARMED WITH SCYTHES AND STONES AND CLUBS, THEY MARCH ON THE PALACE OF THE DESPOTIC SHU WANG...

WHEN THE EMPEROR *SEES* US, HE WILL *KNOW* ALL CHINA IS ANGRY!

AND HE WILL BE *AFRAID!*

A LOOKOUT ON THE PALACE WALL SEES THE ARMED BAND APPROACHING, AND HE RUNS TO TELL THE EMPEROR. BUT THE EMPEROR IS *NOT* AFRAID...

AH... *VISITORS* ... AND *ARMED*, EH? LET THEM *ENTER* THE COURTYARD! FIND OUT WHAT THEY *WANT!*

3

Valor

THE GREAT GATES ARE THROWN OPEN, AND THE POET HORDE STRIDES ONTO THE PALACE GROUNDS. THE LONE GUARD FACES THEM...

WHY DO YOU *COME* HERE?

WE HAVE COME TO PROTEST THE EMPEROR'S NEW LAW...TO HAVE IT NULLIFIED *PEACE-FULLY*, IF WE *CAN*... OR BY *FORCE*, IF WE *MUST!*

SUDDENLY, A VOICE ECHOES FROM A BALCONY OVER-HEAD. THE POETS LOOK UP, AND THERE IS THE EM-PEROR IN HIS ROBES OF GOLD CLOTH... THE TYRANT, ROARING HIS WRATH...

YOU HAVE COME FOR BUT *ONE* THING...*TO DIE!* LET ALL CHINA KNOW THAT THE GODS HAVE GIVEN ME THE RIGHT TO MAKE *ANY* LAW! *CLOSE THE GATES! SEIZE THEM!*

THE GATES ARE SWUNG CLOSED. PALACE GUARDS POUR FROM THEIR HIDING PLACES. THE EMPEROR SMILES AS THE OVERPOWERED POETS ARE CUT DOWN LIKE FLIES...

AND WHEN THE CARNAGE IS COMPLETE AND EACH AND EVERY ONE OF THE HEROIC POETS LIES IN HIS OWN POOL OF BLOOD, THE EMPEROR SNARLS...

TAKE THEIR BODIES TO THE CITY, ERECT POLES AND TIE EACH TO A POLE, AND WHEN YOU ARE ASKED WHY THEY DIED, TELL THE PEOPLE IT WAS BECAUSE THEY QUESTIONED THE LAW OF THEIR EMPEROR...

SO BRAVE MEN FOUGHT TO RIGHT A WRONG AND NOW THEY ARE DEAD AND THERE IS STILL WRONG. THE YOUNG POET, CHOU PO WAS *RIGHT!* THEY *DID* DIE IN VAIN! SEE HIM NOW AS HE LOOKS UPON THEIR CORPSES WITH HEAVY HEART...

YOU CALLED ME A *COWARD* BECAUSE I *WOULD NOT WASTE MY LIFE IN VAIN!* IT IS WRITTEN: "HE IS CALLED A FOOL WHO FAILS A HERO'S MISSION. HE IS CALLED A COWARD WHO WILL NOT BE A FOOL." I AM *NO COWARD*...AND I WILL *BE NO FOOL!*

SOME WEEKS LATER, THERE IS MUCH EXCITEMENT IN THE CITY OF THE TYRANT SHU WANG...

A *PROCESSION* COMES! A *GREAT PROCESSION!*

THERE ARE *GUARDS* AND *NOBLEMEN!* IT MUST BE THE *EMPEROR!*

CLEAR THE WAY!

4

Valor

AND INDEED IT IS THE EMPEROR, COME TO SHOW HIMSELF TO HIS PEOPLE THAT THEY MIGHT KNOW AND FEAR HIM. BUT AS HE IS CARRIED PAST THE CRINGING THRONG, THERE IS ONE WHO DOES NOT SEEM TO FEAR HIM. A YOUNG WOMAN RUNS TO HIS GILDED CHAIR...

STOP HER! SHE IS TRYING TO ASSASSINATE OUR EMPEROR!

NO! SHE DARES TO APPROACH OUR ALMIGHTY RULER WITH A FLOWER! SEIZE HER!

THE PRETTY GIRL'S AUDACITY BRINGS A QUICK END TO THE PROCESSION. THE INFURATED EMPEROR ORDERS HER ARREST, AND LATER, IN HIS THRONE ROOM, SHE IS BROUGHT BEFORE HIM...

HOW DARE YOU! MY SUBJECTS WERE WARNED TO KEEP THEIR DISTANCE! I WANT THEM TO BE AFRAID OF ME... AFRAID TO BREAK MY LAWS!

BUT THE YOUNG WOMAN DOES NOT FLINCH. SHE SMILES SWEETLY AND HER WORDS ARE SOFT, LIKE GENTLE FLUTE NOTES...

MY FEAR OF YOU, OH, MIGHTY EMPEROR, WAS QUICKLY BANISHED WHEN I BEHELD YOUR BEAUTY! I COULD NOT CONTROL MY FEELINGS!

YOU...YOU ...RISE UP, LITTLE ONE!

THE DESPOT'S ANGER VANISHES AT THE LOVELY GIRL'S SWEET WORDS AND HE SMILES IN SPITE OF HIMSELF AS HE DRAWS THE TERRIFIED CREATURE TO HIM...

YOU FIND YOUR EMPEROR BEAUTIFUL TO BEHOLD?

MORE BEAUTIFUL THAN THE FLOWER WHICH I TRIED TO GIVE YOU, OH, EMPEROR!

THE EMPEROR LOOKS UPON THE GIRL AND FIND HER MOST PLEASING TO THE EYE. AND WHEN HE SEES THAT HIS COUNSELLORS, TOO, ARE FEASTING THEIR EYES UPON HER, HE BEAMS...THEN SPEAKS...

FOR AN OFFENSE SUCH AS YOURS, I COULD HAVE YOU TORN APART BY WILD HORSES. BUT I SHALL NEED... AH...TIME TO CONSIDER! GO TO MY CHAMBERS! WAIT THERE FOR ME! WE WILL SEE!

IN A WHILE, THE EMPEROR ENTERS HIS CHAMBERS AND FINDS THE GIRL WAITING FOR HIM. SHE BOWS LOW, BUT HER SOFT EYES ARE ARE EVER UPON HIM AND HE SEES IN THEM AN INVITATION...

I SOUGHT FEAR FROM ALL OF MY SUBJECTS, AND YET...YET I DELIGHT THAT I HAVE STIRRED LOVE INSTEAD...IN YOU!

COME CLOSER, SO THAT YOU MAY KNOW THE FULL EXTENT OF MY LOVE FOR YOU, OH, EMPEROR...

5

SILVER PRINTED   P-6   SILVER PRINTED   14

IT IS FULLY AN HOUR LATER THAT THE DOOR TO THE EMPEROR'S CHAMBERS OPENS, SURPRISING THE COUNSELLORS WHO WERE CLUSTERED ABOUT IT, LISTENING...

SH-H-H-H! THE EMPEROR IS *ASLEEP!*

COUGH...

AHEM...

THE EMBARRASSED YOUNG WOMAN BOWS LOW AND HURRIES DOWN THE LONG PALACE HALL...

SHOULD WE LET HER *GO?*

WOULD YOU DARE *WAKE* THE EMPEROR AND *ASK...?*

HE WILL *FIND HER* IF HE WANTS HER AGAIN!

AND SO, THE FRAIL CREATURE PASSES, UNCHALLENGED, THROUGH THE PALACE GATES...

...DOWN THE LONG WINDING ROAD...

...TO *THE TEAHOUSE OF THE LOTUS BUD...*

...WHERE, ONCE SAFELY INSIDE, THE BLACK WIG IS QUICKLY REMOVED...

...AND THE GLEAMING DAGGER IS WASHED CLEAN...

...THE TYRANT'S BLOOD THAT EVEN NOW, BACK IN THE PALACE, OOZES FROM A DOZEN WOUNDS THAT HAD SILENTLY BEEN ADMINISTERED BY A *SMALL, SLENDER, SENSITIVE POET DISGUISED AS A WOMAN...*

...A POET KNOWN AS CHOU PO WHO WOULD NOT BE A *FOOL,* AND WOULD NOT DIE IN *VAIN!*

THE END 6

Valor